Bioterrorism and
Biological Warfare

By the same author

Gunners from the Sky: 1st Air Landing Light Regiment in Italy and at Arnhem, 1942–44* (2023)
Factory Girls: The Working Lives of Women & Children* (2022)
A Historical Guide to Roman York* (2022)
A History of Britain in 100 Objects (2022)
The History of the World in 100 Pandemics, Plagues and Epidemics* (2021)
Rowntree's: The Early History* (2021)
The History of Sweets* (2021)
War in Roman Myth and Legend* (2020)
War in Greek Mythology* (2020)
Rome – Republic into Empire: The Civil Wars of the First Century BCE* (2019)
Emperors of Rome – The Monsters: From Tiberius to Theodora, AD 14–548* (2018)
British Army of the Rhine: The BAOR, 1945–1993* (2018)
Women at War in the Classical World* (2017)
Roman Military Disasters: Dark Days and Lost Legions* (2015)

* Denotes titles in print with Pen & Sword Books

Bioterrorism and Biological Warfare

Disease as a Weapon of War

Paul Chrystal

Pen & Sword
MILITARY

First published in Great Britain in 2023 by
Pen & Sword Military
An imprint of Pen & Sword Books Limited
Yorkshire – Philadelphia

Copyright © Paul Chrystal 2023

ISBN 978 1 39909 080 3

The right of Paul Chrystal to be identified as
Author of this Work has been asserted by him in accordance
with the Copyright, Designs and Patents Act 1988.

A CIP catalogue record for this book is
available from the British Library

All rights reserved. No part of this book may be reproduced or
transmitted in any form or by any means, electronic or mechanical,
including photocopying, recording or by any information storage and
retrieval system, without permission from the Publisher in writing.

Typeset by Mac Style
Printed in the UK by CPI Group (UK) Ltd, Croydon, CR0 4YY.

Pen & Sword Books Limited incorporates the imprints of After
the Battle, Atlas, Archaeology, Aviation, Discovery, Family History,
Fiction, History, Maritime, Military, Military Classics, Politics,
Select, Transport, True Crime, Air World, Frontline Publishing, Leo
Cooper, Remember When, Seaforth Publishing, The Praetorian Press,
Wharncliffe Local History, Wharncliffe Transport, Wharncliffe True
Crime and White Owl.

For a complete list of Pen & Sword titles please contact

PEN & SWORD BOOKS LIMITED
47 Church Street, Barnsley, South Yorkshire, S70 2AS, England
E-mail: enquiries@pen-and-sword.co.uk
Website: www.pen-and-sword.co.uk
or
PEN AND SWORD BOOKS
1950 Lawrence Road, Havertown, PA 19083, USA
E-mail: Uspen-and-sword@casematepublishers.com
Website: www.penandswordbooks.com

'*The supreme art of war is to subdue the enemy without fighting.*'
Sun Tzu, *Art of War* (孫子兵法), *c.*5th century BC

'*The object of war is not to die for your country but to make the other bastard die for his.*'
General George S. Patton to troops of the US Third Army in 1944, prior to the Allied invasion of France

'*War does not determine who is right – only who is left.*'
Wrongly attributed to Bertrand Russell

'*The moral compromise involved in using medical science to kill enemies, which had raised a ripple of concern during World War II, was casually dismissed … in the atmosphere of the early Cold War.*'
Stephen Endicott, *The United States and Biolgical Warfare* (1998)

'*We must do all we can to uphold international law and leave no stone unturned in our efforts to prevent the deliberate use of disease as a weapon against people.*'
Desmond Mpilo Tutu, Archbishop Emeritus, October 2002

Table of Contents

List of Plates   x
Preface   xiv
About the Author   xv
Introduction   xvi
Abbreviations   xxv

Chapter 1   Sumerians, Hittites, Assyrians and Scythians   1

Chapter 2   Ancient Greeks: Myth and History   8

Chapter 3   Biological Warfare in the Bible   27

Chapter 4   Rome and her Enemies   49

Chapter 5   The Middle Ages   59

Chapter 6   The Seventeenth to Nineteenth Centuries   67

Chapter 7   The First World War and After   88

Chapter 8   The Second World War   108

Chapter 9   The Biological Warfare Labs   151

Chapter 10   The Soviet Biological Weapons Programme   168

Chapter 11   The Cold War Years   183

Chapter 12   The Later Twentieth and Early Twenty-First Centuries   206

Chapter 13   Biological Weapons in the Arab World   214

Chapter 14   China   225

Chapter 15   Bioterrorism in the Modern World   228

Chapter 16	The Biowarfare and Bioterror Future	247
Epilogue	The Illegal 2022 Russian Invasion of Ukraine	254
Appendix	Arms Treaties	256

Sources and Bibliography — 260
Index — 271

'I found this a very interesting – if disconcerting – book. If I wasn't worried enough about the state of humanity by watching the daily news, I certainly am now.'

Linne Matthews, Editor

List of Plates

FRONT COVER: Russian pioneers in gas masks 1937: 'Defense of the Pioneers', Leningrad. (*https://russiainphoto.ru/search/photo/?year_from=1918&year_to=1941 &page=2&author_ids=763&index=3, MAMM/MDF, Rybchinsky and Gladkov Foundation, Photographer: Viktor Karlovich Bulla (1883–1938)*)
 The project 'History of Russia in Photographs' is a collection of photographs taken in Russian territory from 1840 to 1999. It includes photographs on various topics from museum archives and personal collections. The project was developed with the support of Yandex and the Ministry of Culture of the Russian Federation.

Scythian archer. Black-figure tondo from an Attic bilingual kylix, *c.*530 BC. (*Louvre Museum Department of Greek, Etruscan and Roman Antiquities, Sully, first floor, room 43, case 2*)

*Massacre of the Firstborn and Egyptian Darkness, c.*1490. (*National Gallery of Art, Washinton, DC, Rosenwald Collection. This file was donated to Wikimedia Commons as part of a project by the National Gallery of Art*)

Miniature from the Toggenburg Bible (Switzerland) of 1411. MS 78 E1. The image depicts Moses in the background with two people suffering from the biblical plague of boils described in Exodus 9:8-9.

The Hittite king Mursili II (also Muršili II, Mursilis II) prays to the gods to end the epidemic of plague. Clay tablet, thirteenth century BC (original tablet written in the fourteenth century BC) from Hattusa, Turkey. (*Istanbul Archaeological Museum, Osama Shukir Muhammed Amin FRCP(Glasg) via Wikimedia Commons*).

Victims of ergotism. Julius Caesar lost legions of soldiers to ergot poisoning during his campaigns in Gaul. Severe ergot epidemics in France between AD 900 and AD 1300 killed 20,000 to 50,000 people, leaving the nation susceptible to invasions that eventually toppled this Holy Roman kingdom into what became two nations, France and Germany. (*Pieter Bruegel, Louvre*)

A reconstruction of Myrtis gazes back at us from over 2,400 years ago. Myrtis was an 11-year-old girl who died during the plague of Athens and whose skeleton was found in the Kerameikos mass grave. (*National Archaeological Museum of Athens*)

In 401 BC in Colchis, Xenophon, historian and general, a hoplite commander, halted his troops at what looked to be the perfect place to camp. Xenophon says that there were numerous beehives in the region, and that his men ate many honeycombs during the evening they passed through the town. Soon after consumption, the men were reportedly violently sick with vomiting and diarrhoea, and had 'lost their senses', unable to stand or even walk upright. The men lay in a heap that evening, fully exhausted from the illness. The next day, the men had regained their faculties and were no longer sick; no one died. Four centuries later, the very same thing happened to a Roman army in the same region.

The Death of Hercules (1634) – through his poisoned shirt, the dreaded Shirt of Nessus – by Francisco de Zurbarán, in the Prado, Madrid.

Hunting with the deadly blow gun. From *The Andes and the Amazon* (1876).

Poisoned Well, by Jacek Malchevsky, 1905. (*National Museum, Poznan*)

A depiction of a confrontation between Pontiac, an Ottawa chief, and Colonel Henry Bouquet, a British soldier, who suggested using blankets to spread smallpox to indigenous Americans.

Russian soldiers of the Dukhovshchinsky Regiment wearing Zelinsky-Kummant gas masks, 1916. (*www.vokrugsveta.ru/telegraph/technics/629/*)

Dead Indian soldiers of the British force on the beach at Tanga, November 1914. A humiliating British defeat. (*Bundesarchiv Bild 146-1971-057-05*)

First World War British gas hood, c.1915. (*Photographer: Stephen C. Dickson*)

East German Young Pioneers during the war against the potato beetle. The boy on the left, Bodo, set a record for most beetles collected in one day, 2,000. The girl on the right, Magdalena, managed 800 specimens. (*German Federal Archives. Current location: Allgemeiner Deutscher Nachrichtendienst – Zentralbild (Bild 183)*)

US Army horse wears a gas mask to fend against German gas attacks. (*Courtesy of US National Archives*)

Belgian military dogs hauling a machine gun in the First World War.

Russian pioneers in gas masks, Leningrad 1937. (*Viktor Bulla*)

A mother and baby both in gas masks in 1941. The mother cradles her newborn baby in bed, shortly after giving birth. The mother is wearing her civilian respirator, whilst the baby is encased in a baby gas helmet, which buckles up around its bottom. The mother is demonstrating how the bellows on her baby's gas mask are pumped to supply the baby with air.

A prisoner in a special chamber in Dachau concentration camp loses consciousness in response to changing air pressure during high-altitude experiments. For the benefit of the Luftwaffe, conditions comparable to those found at 15,000 metres in altitude were created in an effort to determine if German pilots might survive at that height. March 1942–August 1942. (*https://collections.ushmm.org/search/catalog/pa1058429*, Photographer: Sigmund Rascher (d. 1945))

The island of Gruinard was officially out of bounds from 1942 to 1990 because of secret anthrax testing during the Second World War.

One of the many victims of Unit 731.

Unit 731, Museum Human Dissection Experiment Room.

In April 1943, Detrick Air Field near Frederick, Maryland, was requisitioned and badged Camp Detrick. Four biological agent production plants were developed here: Pilot Plant No. 1, activated in October 1943 for the production of botulinum toxin; Pilot Plant No. 2, completed in March 1944, produced the anthrax simulant *Bacillus globigii* and actual anthrax spores; Pilot Plant No. 3, completed in February 1945, produced plant pathogens. Pilot Plant No. 4 was opened in January 1945 and produced, in embryonated eggs, the bacteria that cause brucellosis and psittacosis.

The Scientific Experimental and Production Base (SNOPB), Stepnogorsk, Kazakhstan. SNOPB was under the authority of the Biopreparat organisation. Known only by its post office box, No. 2076, this facility tested and certified methods of producing BW agents developed in the laboratories of Biopreparat and the MOD, and issued technical documentation and recommendations. From 1984 to 1987, specialists and equipment from Sverdlovsk were transferred to SNOPB. As well as anthrax, the Stepnogorsk facility produced staphylococcus toxin SNOPB.

A chaplain wears an M-17 nuclear, biological and chemical warfare mask and hood during an exercise at Kadena Air Base, Okinawa, Japan. Scene Camera Operator: Senior Airman Walker. (*Released to Public; Combined Military Service Digital Photographic Files*)

A pre-1991 photo of a scientist working in a lab at VECTOR. The State Research Center of Virology and Biotechnology VECTOR, also known as the Vector Institute, is a biological research centre in Koltsovo, Novosibirsk Oblast. It has research facilities and capabilities for all levels of Biological Hazard,

List of Plates   xiii

CDC Levels 1–4. It is one of two official repositories for smallpox virus, the other being the CDC in Atlanta, Georgia. (*Unknown Soviet photographer*)

An Iranian soldier wearing a gas mask during the Iran-Iraq War. (*Released under GFDL licence*)

Subway passengers stricken by sarin nerve gas are treated near Tsukiji station in Tokyo in this 1995 file photo. (*Photo: Kyodo News via AP*)

The second anthrax note. One New York City day in the autumn of 2001 was no one's red letter day – for that was when a salvo of letters containing anthrax spores were sent by mail to two US senators' offices on Capitol Hill and news media agencies along the east coast.

The reward notice.

Members of the Alabama National Guard's 46th Civil Support Team work a threat scenario created by Dugway Proving Ground's Special Program Division mobile training teams, 18 June 2014. (*Photo courtesy of the US Army*)

Biological weapons research was conducted at PBA from 1953 to 1969 but operations ceased when President Nixon banned biological weapons after the furore over Agent Orange. Between 1954 and 1967, at least seven different biological agents were produced at the facility. All biological agents were destroyed between 1971 and 1973. The image shows 1,600-pound steel containers stored at Pine Bluff Arsenal, which once held hazardous materials and required decontamination. Operators decontaminated the last 4,307 ton containers in July 2011.

Firefighters triage victims of a simulated bioterrorism attack at the Armed Forces Reserve Center during the Portland Area Capabilities Exercise (PACE) Setter at Camp Withycombe in Clackamas, Oregon, May 2013. The purpose of the PACE Setter exercise is to test regional and interagency response to public health incidents affecting multiple agencies. (*Photo by Staff Sgt April Davis, Oregon Military Department Public Affairs*)

Medical Regiment 250 Squadron RAMC (Detachment), training in blood-taking during the Ebola pandemic in 2014–16, Queen Elizabeth Barracks, Strensall near York. (*Courtesty* York Press)

Animal Justice Project campaigners staged protests at Porton Down and in Salisbury, October 2020.

Preface

This important, disturbing and timely book focuses on the use of disease and germs as weapons of mass destruction (WMD) as well as on the threat that bioterrorism poses in an increasingly unpredictable and volatile world.

For context, it starts with the earliest days of primitive warfare, using effective methods such as infectious rams, poison-tipped arrows and rotting plague-infected corpses acting as toxic, disease-spreading projectiles, and continues through to the twenty-first-century industrial-scale weaponisation of biomedicine.

The book shows how biological weapons and acts of bioterrorism are especially adept at instilling terror, panic, death, famine and economic ruin on a large scale, shredding the public's confidence in their governments and in society itself. For the disaffected, lethal biological agents are comparatively easy to manufacture and obtain, and they have the advantage of being almost invisible as well as easy and quick to administer in lethal quantities through a variety of discreet delivery systems. Just what the terrorist wants.

We explore the sinister connection between the extensive proliferation of biological weaponry by state actors and the greater opportunities these developments and the growing bio-arsenals offer the increasingly scientific-minded and determined terrorist to manufacture his or her weapon of choice, taking advantage of state-of-the-art, sophisticated delivery systems.

The epilogue analyses the concerted but groundless 2022–3 disinformation campaign conducted by Russia, with support from China, relating to the claim that public health facilities in Ukraine are 'secret US-funded biolabs' purportedly developing biological weapons.

> Certainly the use of disinformation around chemical and biological weapons appears to be part of a wider information strategy to discredit Ukraine and justify the Russian invasion by alleging a perceived existential threat, particularly for a domestic Russian audience.
> Chatham House (https://www.chathamhouse.org/2022/03/ukraine-chemical-or-biological-attack-likely), 30 March 2022

Chatham House, March 2022

About the Author

Paul Chrystal was educated at the universities of Hull and Southampton, where he took degrees in Classics. For the past thirty-five years, he has worked in medical publishing, much of the time as an international sales director for one market or another and creating medical education programmes for global pharmaceutical companies.

More recently, he has been history advisor to Yorkshire visitor attractions, writing features for national newspapers, and broadcasting on talkRADIO, History Hack, BBC local radio, Radio 4's PM programme and on the BBC World Service.

He is contributor to a number of history and archaeology magazines and the author of over 150 books published since 2010 on a wide range of subjects, including classical and social history, the BAOR (British Army of the Rhine), the 'Troubles', pandemics (including COVID-19) and epidemics, and many local histories.

He is a regular reviewer for and contributor to 'Classics for All'. He has contributed to a six-part series for BBC2, 'celebrating the history of some of Britain's most iconic craft industries'. He is an editorial advisor for the Yale University Press classics list and a contributor to the classics section of 'Bibliographies on Line', published by Oxford University Press.

He is past editor of *York History*, journal of the York Archaeological and Architectural Society; and in 2019, he took over the history editorship of *Yorkshire Archaeological Journal*, the publication of the Yorkshire Archaeological and Historical Society. He is also contributor to the Routledge Companion to the Reception of Ancient Greek and Roman Sexuality and Gender. Also in 2019, he was guest speaker for Vassar College New York's London Programme in association with Goldsmiths University. In 2021, he assisted in the research for an episode of *Who Do You Think You Are?* He also assisted in the research for the new series of the Channel 4 award-winning *The Secret World of…* – secret world of sweets, in this case. In 2022, he was commissioned to produce a piece celebrating ninety years of Mars in the UK. He also goes into schools to talk on a wide range of subjects.

Paul is married with three children and lives near York.

Introduction

One of the more optimistic legacies of the COVID-19 pandemic will surely be a heightened awareness of just how destructive and disruptive an infectious disease can be to a society, culture or civilisation – not just in terms of public health, morbidity and mortality, but also economically, educationally, socially and psychologically. It is hoped, then, that this recent global experience of ours, particularly amongst biomedical scientists, disaster planners, public health officials, military strategists, politicians, educationalists and economists, will result in an equally newfound level of preparedness for what seems an increasingly likely eventuality: the deployment of biological agents in a war somewhere or other, or a medium or large-scale bioterrorist attack using a toxic and infectious biological agent on one population or another. Or both. Why is it 'increasingly likely' and why is this statement not just mere tabloid alarmism? Because the very same awareness relating to pandemic management and epidemiology that COVID-19 is gradually inculcating in societies and governments around the world today will, at the same time, be informing and insinuating itself in the minds and aspirations of hostile governments and deracinated political and religious extremists, alerting them to the very real terrorist opportunities offered by a well-placed, timely and precision biological attack. That's why it is 'increasingly likely'.

The book provides an up-to-date and alarming examination of biological (germ) warfare and bioterrorism – as noted, from the earliest days of infectious rams, poison-tipped arrows and rotting plague-infected corpses used as toxic projectiles to the twenty-first-century industrialised and progressive weaponisation of biomedicine. It is hoped that the book will assist in some small way in the global war against biowarfare and bioterrorism, and in its mitigation or avoidance, by encouraging judicious planning, prevention policies, adequately funded research and decisive preparation in the light of our growing collective knowledge of what has gone before, what is going on now and what might realistically go on in the future.

The deployment of biological agents in warfare and terrorism at whatever level is as old as warfare itself. This nasty, highly versatile and insidious weapon of devastation and disruption is particularly destructive because it is just as likely to target civilian populations, livestock, water supplies or crops as enemy combat forces. As noted, biological weapons and bioterrorism are especially suited to instilling terror, panic, death, famine and economic ruin on a large scale, wrecking public confidence in governments and law and order itself. Lethal biological agents are often comparatively easy to manufacture and obtain, and although they can be tricky to deliver effectively, they have the benefit of being almost invisible, and easy and quick to administer in lethal quantities through a variety of discreet delivery systems.

As an indicator of the power and potential economic fallout of an untrammelled disease outbreak we need only look at the cost of the 2001 foot-and-mouth episode in the UK (Bourn 2002): it came in at €800 billion. The 2003 avian influenza outbreak in the Netherlands cost the public and private sectors there some €800 million in lost trade and direct costs (Meuwissen 2006). The 2001 'anthrax letters' attack in New York City produced a bill for $320 million just to deep clean the buildings involved (Schmitt 2012).

The techniques of delivery of biological warfare agents have evolved over the centuries from the crude catapulting of plague corpses and excreta to the insidious use of infected, disease-harbouring clothing, insect vectors, and sophisticated, specialised weapon systems. This book describes the relentless progress the world has made in the offensive and defensive weaponisation of nature, reviewing as it does the often controversial history of biological war and bioterrorism, from Scythian archers through countless wars to anthrax and salad bar poisonings in the United States and germ-based ethnic cleansing warfare in Afghanistan and Syria.

We also explode the enduring myth that biological warfare and bioterrorism are relatively new features of our increasingly scientific, biomedical world. Not so: man has been slyly and dispassionately poisoning fellow men, women and children, their crops, water and animals for millennia through a cocktail of toxins, poisons, insect vectors, viruses and pollutants. Biological warfare and bioterrorism, then, are demonstrably nothing new – we have been at it ever since the time that prehistoric man picked up a rock and hit his fellow man with it. Bringing us right up to date, we cover episodes of biological warfare and bioterrorism that have proliferated since the Second World War to the present day. The National Consortium for the Study of Terrorism and Responses to Terrorism (Pinson 2013) lists seventy-four separate episodes from 1990 to 2011, while Carus (2001) identifies 153 from 1990 to 1999. Reassuringly, most failed and caused no deaths.[1]

To underscore the relentless importance and significance of disease as a factor in war – be it caused by gangrenous battlefield wound infection or naturally occurring pandemics such as influenza in 1918 – history tells us that until the Second World War, the number of soldiers dying from disease far exceeded those killed in combat. The numbers of troops dying in combat and through disease has of course diminished by significant strides in infectious disease management, military medicine and casualty extraction. Disease is a major factor in modern wars, accounting for 95 per cent of US hospital admissions in the Second World War and 82 per cent of those in the Korean War. For example, malaria alone contributed to 56–75 per cent of all hospital admissions of US Forces in the Vietnam War.

Our story begins many thousands of years ago – reaching back as it does far into prehistory, taking in along the way a blend of myth, legend, religion, ideology and ancient and recent history.

There are a number of ways in which the origins of a disease and its manifestation as a pandemic or an epidemic have been explained down the years. One is the infliction of pestilence by a judgemental pantheon or by a jealous, angry god, whose wrath will culminate in a final retribution on a hesitant, reluctant or downright disobedient population. This has been, and still is, an integral part of the human condition. Recovery from illness was, likewise, a god-given gift for these errant peoples. Greek and Roman gods, the Christian God and the deities of many other faiths were, are, perpetually dispensing pestilential judgements and punishments on their hubristic subjects, making these divine agencies – mythic and real alike – just as much bioterrorists or biological warmongers as the Scythian archer loosing his poison-tipped arrows at his enemy. A similar supernatural explanation is the prescription of a plague (in its broadest sense) on a population by a demon, devil, or, paradoxically perhaps, a malicious angel.

Later in time, we have the more rational explanation: the determination of a disease's origin based on empirical evidence from medical science, particularly since the advent of modern microbiology in the nineteenth century and the pioneering work by Louis Pasteur (1822–95) and Robert Koch (1843–1910). Long before that, the origin of disease was predicated on humoral theory as championed by, among others, Hippocrates and his acolytes in the fifth century BC, then Celsus, Soranus and Galen in the second century AD. These rational Greek scientists and physicians commonly believed that disease and plagues were caused by the inhalation of 'impurities' (*miasmata*) in the air and had nothing whatsoever to do with what they dismissed as ridiculous divine agencies or superstition. Indeed, one of the major planks of the *Hippocratic Corpus* is *On the Sacred Disease* (*c.*400 BC), which begins with a polemic against the many who believed that the gods were the cause of disease. The Hippocratics rubbished the religious and supernatural origin of illness in favour of causes that could be rigorously evaluated by rational thought, testing, experimentation and evidence.

Humoral theory posited that *the body is composed of four basic humors – black bile, yellow bile, phlegm and blood*. It became and remained the foundation for the development and practice of medical science until the late eighteenth century AD and as such has a crucial role to play in episodes of biological warfare and terrorism as perpetrated by successive cultures, countries and societies from the times of the ancient Greeks to the Napoleonic Wars (1803–15). Humoral theory prevailed until it was superseded by modern microbiology, bacteriology, toxicology, epidemiology and virology, which also have their role to play in germ warfare.

As well as relating what could seem at times to be a litany of death, misery, cunning and depredation, our book also offers an insight into the various institutions at work researching (and, hopefully, defending us against) the numerous lethal pathogens, the international conventions that are intended to safeguard the world, and the lessons we can learn to mitigate, even avoid, the very real likelihood of a large-scale act of bioterrorism or an outbreak of biology-assisted warfare. As stated, if anything, the COVID-19 pandemic has surely brought to the attention of and heightened awareness amongst planners, military people, economists, politicians and decision-makers as well as scientists and medical researchers a welcome, albeit worrisome, awareness of the potential health and economic carnage possible with targeted dissemination of a lethal virus into largely defenceless populations.

Biological Warfare and Bioterrorism: Disease as a Weapon of War covers biological warfare in its broadest sense, so includes the use of viruses, bacteria, fungi, or other toxins. It examines entomological warfare: the unleashing of bees, beetles and other stinging insects as disease vectors; exposure to malarial environments; the use of infected corpses – human and animal – and faeces as disease-bringing projectiles; well and other water supply contamination; gifting infected blankets and clothing; and despatching infected men and women into populations to spread disease. What it does not include is *chemical* warfare except where it is used in conjunction with biological warfare: so no Greek fire incendiary bombs, flamethrowers, choking smoke and asphyxiating gases, sarin, tabun, naphtha, Agent Orange, biocrime and the like.

Some definitions

Biological weapons
These are microorganisms like viruses, bacteria, fungi, or other toxins that are produced and released deliberately to cause disease and death in humans,

animals or crops and damage to water supplies and materiel. They consist of the agent and some delivery mechanism. Biological weapons can be extremely complex technically, such as a bomblet carrying a ballistic missile warhead or a cruise missile fitted with spray devices.

Biological agents
Agents like anthrax, botulinum toxin and plague can pose a refractory public health challenge, causing large numbers of deaths in a short amount of time while being difficult to contain. A biological agent might also be a microorganism that can damage materiel, such as bacteria that might attack the silicon on computer chips or tyre rubber or metal on tanks or artillery. The insidious use of entomology is a subtype of biological warfare; although insects are not biological agents they can act as vectors for biological agents and have been used to deliver pathogens. Biological weapons themselves are a subset of a larger class of weapons referred to as weapons of mass destruction (WMD): chemical, biological and nuclear weaponry.

(Adapted from World Health Organization (WHO) https://www.who.int/health-topics/biological-weapons#tab=tab_1)

According to Carus (2017):

> Potential biological warfare agents are not limited to some shortlist of pathogens but rather include all microorganisms pathogenic to humans, plants and animals, as well as those that could be used to attack materials. According to a 2007 survey (Woolhouse 2007), there were more than 1,400 human pathogens, including 541 bacteria, 189 viruses and 57 protozoa (the rest were parasites, such as ringworm and fungi). A more recent study (Woolhouse 2012) identified 219 pathogenic viruses and estimated that three to four more are identified every year. While many of the diseases are rare and may cause only mild illness, nearly 350 are considered clinically significant. (Hay 2013)

Biological warfare
This also goes by the name germ warfare and can be administered by states, terrorists, disaffected groups or individuals or criminals. Some probable biological warfare that occurred before the eighteenth century included the global spread of epidemic diseases such as tularaemia, plague, malaria, smallpox, yellow fever and Hansen's disease (leprosy).

Bioterrorism

Bioterrorism, according to the Centers for Disease Control and Prevention (CDC), is the malicious and intentional release or threat of release of biologic agents (i.e. viruses, bacteria, fungi, or their toxins) in order to cause disease or death among human population or food crops and livestock in order to terrorise a civilian population or manipulate its government. Bioterrorist attacks could also result in an epidemic, for example, if Ebola or Lassa viruses were used as the biological agents. Bioterrorism had already made its mark fourteen centuries before Christ, when the Hittites despatched infected rams to their enemies. One important characteristic of bio*terrorism* lies in the word itself: a bioterrorist attack can kill relatively small numbers of targets but its psychological and economic impact and effects can be disproportionately immense, causing widespread social anxiety, desperate panic and economic, social, educational and healthcare disruption. These collateral effects define the success of a bioterrorist attack, not just the casualty role.

Biocrime

Biocrime covers the actual or attempted murder of an individual or discrete group of individuals usually for financial gain, revenge, or, in the case of Georgi Markov in 1978, as a bleak warning from the KGB to other Russian dissidents. To date, biocrime has featured chemical rather than biological agents: for example, assaults on Alexander Litvinenko, Sergei and Yulia Skripal, and Kim Jong-nam.

Before the twentieth century, the military use of biological agents largely took three major forms: deliberate contamination of food and water with poisonous or contagious material; weaponisation of microbes, biological toxins, animals or plants (living or dead); and the use of infected fabrics and persons. The twentieth century saw the introduction of more sophisticated bacteriological and virological techniques facilitating the production of significant stockpiles of weaponised bio-agents, including:

- Bacterial agents: anthrax, brucella, tularaemia, etc.
- Viral agents: smallpox, viral haemorrhagic fevers, etc.
- Toxins: botulinum, ricin, etc.

The bad news is that virtually any biological agent from a vast range of human infection-causing pathogens might qualify as a potential biological weapon. The not so bad news is that only a small number of these agents fulfil the desirable criteria that enable manufacture in sufficient quantities and are deliverable in an effective and viable form. Anthrax spores pose the biggest bioterrorism threat because it is relatively easy to produce and conserve them; this bacterium delivers high case fatality rates, rapid transmission by aerosol and is stable in the environment, surviving in soil for many decades. It is these characteristics – the inherent stealth and virtual untraceability enjoyed by perpetrators – that account for anthrax bacilli being rated the most lethal.

A Royal Society report has identified the four main classes of agents that could be used in biological warfare (source: https://www.parliament.uk/globalassets/documents/post/pn166.pdf):

Table 1

Bacteria – any bacterium that causes human disease is a potential biological weapon (BW). These include *Bacillus anthracis*, the cause of anthrax, as well as the causative agents of plague (*Yersinia pestis*), tularaemia (a plague-like illness caused by *F. tularensis*), cholera (*V. cholerae*) and typhoid (*S. typhi*).

Viruses – commonly cited examples of possible viral BW include the Ebola and Marburg viruses and those causing yellow fever, smallpox, flu, haemorrhagic fever and various forms of encephalitis.

Toxins – naturally occurring poisons isolated from bacteria, fungi and plants. Examples include the bacterial *botulinum perfringens* and Staphylococcus enterotoxin B toxins, as well as fungal mycotoxins and ricin (which is isolated from castor beans).

Rickettsia/Coxiella – are classes of bacteria that are harboured by lice and other parasites. Of most concern are the causative agents of epidemic typhoid and Q fever.

Given its lethal nature, Ebola is classified as a biosafety level 4 agent, as well as a category A bioterrorism agent by the Centers for Disease Control and Prevention. It has the very real potential to be weaponised for use in biological warfare.

The CDC gives these agents as the most concerning in relation to Emergency Preparedness and Response:

Table 2

Category A
High-priority agents include organisms that pose a risk to national security because they can be easily disseminated or transmitted from person to person; result in high mortality rates and have the potential for major public health impact; might cause public panic and social disruption; and require special action for public health preparedness.

Agents/Diseases
Anthrax (*Bacillus anthracis*)
Botulism *(Clostridium botulinum toxin)*
Plague *(Yersinia pestis)*
Smallpox *(variola major)*
Tularaemia *(Francisella tularensis)*
Viral haemorrhagic fevers, including
   Filoviruses (Ebola, Marburg)
   Arenaviruses (Lassa, Machupo)

Category B
Second highest priority agents include those that are moderately easy to disseminate; result in moderate morbidity rates and low mortality rates; and require specific enhancements of CDC's diagnostic capacity and enhanced disease surveillance.

Agents/Diseases
Brucellosis (*Brucella* species)
Epsilon toxin of *Clostridium perfringens*
Food safety threats (Salmonella species, *Escherichia coli* O157:H7, *Shigella*)
Glanders *(Burkholderia mallei)*
Melioidosis (*Burkholderia pseudomallei*)
Psittacosis (*Chlamydia psittaci*)
Q fever (*Coxiella burnetii*)
Ricin toxin from *Ricinus communis* (castor beans)
Staphylococcal enterotoxin B
Typhus fever (*Rickettsia prowazekii*)
Viral encephalitis (alphaviruses, such as Eastern equine encephalitis,
   Venezuelan equine encephalitis and Western equine encephalitis)
Water safety threats (*Vibrio cholerae, Cryptosporidium parvum*)

> **Category C**
> Third highest priority agents include emerging pathogens that could be engineered for mass dissemination in the future because of availability; ease of production and dissemination; and potential for high morbidity and mortality rates and major health impact.
>
> **Agents**
> Emerging infectious diseases such as Nipah virus and hantavirus.

Source: https://emergency.cdc.gov/agent/agentlist-category.asp

Who were or are these malicious perpetrators? Roughly, they fall into three broad categories: state-sponsored agencies (governments), non-state-sponsored terrorists (non-state actors), and aggrieved, solo-operating individuals.

Governments can be motivated to inaugurate biological weapons programmes to attack other governments who may or may not have such programmes of their own and may be tempted to use them if they have. They may decide to develop programmes to defend against enemies in conflicts involving conventional weapons and/or biological weapons.

Terrorists graduate from a broad school equipped with multiple reasons and agenda to rationalise why they feel a need to terrorise and threaten governments, individuals, ethnic and religious groups, armies and societies generally. To make matters even more complicated, the terrorist may be motivated by religious, gender or racial hatred, or by extreme ideology. When terrorists turn away from the bomb and the bullet and resort to bioterrorism, they introduce numerous security, public safety and surveillance challenges related to detection, monitoring and apprehension.

The third category are disgruntled, often lone individuals who may be nursing a need to exact revenge on someone or a group of people for one reason or another. They may pose an even greater challenge, not only in terms of their unpredictability, identification and surveillance by security agencies, but also in how first responders and casualty staff can safely and effectively administer help at the scene of an attack and in a hospital setting.

Note

1. The National Consortium for the Study of Terrorism and Responses to Terrorism (START) offers a number of datasets related to terrorism. The most important of these is the Global Terrorism Database, a database of over 200,000 terrorist attacks from 1970 till 2019. The GTD is the most comprehensive unclassified database on terrorist attacks in the world, containing information on over 200,000 terrorist attacks, including 95,000 bombings, 20,000 assassinations, and 15,000 kidnappings and hostage events. Over 4 million news articles were reviewed to collect the data to build the GTD.

Abbreviations

BW: Biological warfare/biological weapons.
CBW: Chemical and biological warfare/weapons.
CDC: Centers for Disease Control and Prevention.
KGB: The Committee for State Security (Комитет государственной безопасности (КГБ), was the main security agency for the Soviet Union from 13 March 1954 until 3 December 1991.
MVD: Ministry of Internal Affairs (Russia) or its predecessor Ministry of Internal Affairs (Soviet Union), from (Ministerstvo Vnutrennikh Del), responsible for law enforcement in Russia.
NKVD: The People's Commissariat for Internal Affairs (Наро́дный комиссариа́т вну́тренних дел, abbreviated NKVD (НКВД) was the interior ministry of the Soviet Union.
SHAD: Shipboard Hazard and Defense Project.
USAMRIID: The United States Army Medical Research Institute of Infectious Diseases, Frederick, MD.
WMDs: Weapons of Mass Destruction.

Chapter 1

Sumerians, Hittites, Assyrians and Scythians

The first biological warfare: a gift from the gods

Possibly the first instance of biowarfare came in prehistoric times with Melanesian tribesmen (modern Vanuatu) who fired off arrowheads poisoned with *Clostridium tetani* (tetanus). To obtain this primitive warhead they smeared their arrowheads with the contents of crab burrows. The first recorded epidemic in human history was 'a great pestilence' that occurred in Egypt in the reign of Pharaoh Mempses in the First Dynasty, 3180 BC. Manetho, the Egyptian priest and historian (*fl.* early third century BC), noted in his list of pharaohs in *Aegyptiaca*, 'Mempses, for eighteen years. In his reign many portents and a great pestilence occurred.' This is our first example of public health surveillance, a discipline that dates back to this first recorded epidemic. In the absence of any evidence to the contrary, we can assume that the 'great pestilence' was a naturally occurring epidemic, and not the reaction of an angry god or a hostile enemy.

Rabies is first described in a Babylonian legal document, the *Eshnunna Code* (2300 BC), advising that the bite of a dog could be fatal and that the guilty animal's owner would be subject to a fine. Interestingly, the fine for biting a 'man' and causing his death was forty shekels of silver, and that for infecting and killing a slave was the cut rate of fifteen shekels. Presumably, this shows us that the understanding of diseases was increasing, as were efforts to control them and highlight the social consequences of not controlling them.

Contagion was no stranger to the early inhabitants of Central Asia, Mesopotamia and southern Asia. Indeed, outbreaks there are some of our earliest instances of angry gods appearing to blight and punish us mortals with various epidemics of contagious disease. The gods, it seems, were at the forefront of biological warfare. Strains of influenza, whether delivered by hostile gods in early bioconflict or through natural modes of transmission, repeatedly ravaged the centres of dense population in the reigns of Tiglath Pileser I (1114–1076 BC) and Nebuchadnezzar II (605–562 BC). The influenza virus also afflicted ancient Babylon in 1103 BC. There was an epidemic in Nineveh during the reign of Sargon II, king of Assyria (r. 722–705 BC).

The Mari tablets

Over 25,000 tablets – the Mari tablets, written in the Akkadian language over a period of fifty years from *c.*1800 to 1750 BC – were unearthed from the burnt-out library of the Mari king, Zimri-Lim. Among many other things, they give us information about disease contagion, social distancing and quarantine. One of the tablets, dating from 1770 BC, gives us our first record of precautions taken to avoid or mitigate infectious disease. It details how King Zimri-Lim had occasion to tell his scribe to send a note to Queen Shiptu regarding measures she should take to avoid infection from a servant called Nanname, who was exhibiting symptoms (lesions) of some disease or other. The king, with remarkable good sense and a heightened awareness of surface infection and infection control, advised his queen not to share cups with Nanname, and not to sit on or use chairs or beds used by him. 'She should not gather [these] many women about herself' (*Archives royales de Mari*, 10, No. 129, lines 10–19).

Despite its fame as the earliest written evidence so far recorded from Mesopotamia confirming a familiarity with contagious diseases and methods of arresting their spread, there is nothing new here – the tablet recommends practices that long predate it. Contagion, the isolation of patient carriers, as well as fomite transmission, already had a long tradition. Fomite transmission involves objects or materials that may carry infection, such as clothes, utensils, door handles and furniture.

Excavations on the Mari site have ground to a halt as a result of the Syrian civil war that began in 2011 and continues to the present day. Mari was an ancient Semitic-Sumerian city-state, which is now in modern-day Syria.

In a letter from *c.*1800 BC, the Assyrian king Shamshi-Adad ordered his son Yasmah-Addu to isolate and confine a group of ill soldiers and burn their battledress in a temple in Ekallatum in northern Iraq. Again, we have no way of knowing whether these prudent lockdown measures were caused by what were deemed heaven-sent biological attacks or acts of biological warfare from an enemy, or reaction to a naturally spreading epidemic. What we do know is that barracks were, and always have been, virulent reservoirs of infectious disease transmission.

The Hittites and rabbit fever (tularaemia)

We are on more certain ground with the Hittites: their empire stretched from modern-day Turkey to northern Syria. An enduring epidemic plagued the Eastern Mediterranean in the fourteenth century BC and can be traced back to the Arwad–Euphrates trading route.

F. tularensis is a hardy organism that can survive for weeks at low temperatures in water, moist soil, hay, straw or rotting animal carcasses.

Tularaemia is found as far back as 2500 BC in the same region, suggesting that it was endemic for the bacterium *tularensis*. The epidemic lasted thirty-five to forty years, infecting humans and animals, causing fever, disabilities and death, spreading via ship-borne rodents. The symptoms, mode of infection and geographical area confirmed it as tularaemia, which was also responsible for outbreaks around 1715 BC and 1075 BC. At first, the fourteenth-century epidemic contaminated an area stretching from Cyprus to Iraq and from Israel to Syria, sparing Egypt and Anatolia due to quarantine measures employed there.

Soon after, from 1320 to 1318 BC, the Arzawans from western Anatolia saw an opportunity to deal a blow to the weakened Hittites to their east and decided to strike in a bid to strengthen their borders, but they failed to take into account the Hittites' obvious knowledge of zoonotic infection. At the same time, records indicate that rams started wandering along roads in Arzawa. Tablets dating from the fourteenth to thirteenth centuries BC describe how a ram and a woman tending the animal were deliberately sent down the road, spreading the disease along the way. 'The country that finds them shall take over this evil pestilence,' is the tablet's doom-laden message. The Arzawans took the wandering animals back to their villages and used them for breeding; it did not take them long to draw a connection between the rams and the terrible disease that was now ravaging their communities. What they were witnessing was probably one of the earliest instances of biological warfare. The Hittites had gifted to the Arzawans a flock of tularaemia-infected (rabbit fever) rams. Being a zoonotic disease, tularaemia can pass from animals such as rabbits and sheep to humans through a number of vectors, most commonly through insects such as ticks that hop from one species to another. The bacterium causes a number of symptoms ranging from skin ulcers to respiratory failure. Without antibiotic treatment, about 15 per cent of infected individuals die; it remains a problem in some countries.

Zoonotic diseases are simply infectious diseases that can pass from animal or insect to man: up to thirty types of flea and over 200 species of mammal in seventy-three genera are potential vectors.

Around 1335 BC, letters to the Egyptian pharoah Akhenaten (r. *c*.1353–36 BC) reveal a pestilence in Simyra, a Phoenician city near what is today the border between Lebanon and Syria. The letters describe a horrible disease causing severe illness and death. Significantly, they also mention that, because of this contagion, donkeys were banned from caravans in an attempt to halt the spread of tularaemia. Ten years later, Hittites attacked the vulnerable area around

Simyra, stealing booty, including livestock. What they failed to realise was that they were also bringing home the tularaemia incubating in the livestock. Soon after, the Hittites were fighting an epidemic of tularaemia as well as the Simyrans.

When the Hittites attacked the Egyptian borderlands in Syria around the Litani River (now in Lebanon), infected prisoners and animals taken as plunder spread contagion along the length of the march back to the Anatolian heartland of the Hittite Empire. At the wealthy and bustling trading city-state of Ugarit in northern Syria, a number of merchants fell prey to the illness, struck down, the sources say, 'by the hand of god'. Tularaemia, like all deadly infectious diseases, was indiscriminate. In the Hittite capital of Hattusa, royalty status offered no protection: the powerful King Suppiluliuma (r. c.1344–22 BC) and his son and successor Arnuwanda II both succumbed, while the epidemic reached its peak during the reign of King Mursili II. The hand of god had a long reach and an indiscriminate clutch.

Hittite trade expeditions throughout the Mediterranean, especially in Egypt, continued to fuel the contagion: the Hittites rashly took prisoners, inadvertently ensuring that epidemic diseases spread from Egyptian captives to the Hittite army. In turn, soldiers in the army infected their families when they returned home. Thus, serious epidemics consumed Anatolia, converting many city-states into graveyards. Mursili desperately addressed his gods on one tablet, imploring, 'If I die too, who will make a vow to you?' No doubt, the gods were unimpressed. Another tablet from the Hittite period prescribes various rituals to eradicate fourteen epidemic diseases.

Apart from the destructive effect on trade and attempts by royalty to escape the 'plague' by removing to disease-free regions, the epidemic continued its destructive course. The Anatolians took increasingly desperate spiritual measures against the disease. Believing that they must, at some point in the past, have neglected the gods and omitted to make the required ritual vows, they set about redressing their careless negligence by celebrating festive days more enthusiastically and praying more in the hope that the gods would be reconciled and eradicate the disease. But the god who wages biological war on his subjects can be an implacable foe.

Assyrian well poisoning with rye ergot?

Assyrian soldiers, like those in other armies, were notorious for ransacking and torching enemy lands once they had replenished their supplies and had their fill of local grain, oil, wine and dates. Sargon II and Sennacherib, his son, were seasoned devastators, with enemy irrigation systems, granaries and fruit orchards all falling victim. When Sennacherib laid siege to Jerusalem in 701 BC as part of his campaign to subdue the Levant, he anticipated nothing less than a victory over Jerusalem's King Hezekiah. But not everything went as planned. The *Annals of Sennacherib* reveal that Hezekiah diverted an attack on his city by simply paying a lavish tribute, after which the Assyrians packed up and went home. An Old Testament account, however, describes how an angel of the Lord went through the Assyrian camp one night and killed countless soldiers (2 Kings 19:31 ff.):

> on a certain night that the angel of the Lord went out, and killed in the camp of the Assyrians one hundred and eighty-five thousand; and when people arose early in the morning, there were the bodies – all dead.

Making the drinkers sick and opening their ranks to Assyrian attack in the sixth century BC was the strategy when the Assyrians allegedly poisoned the water supplies with rye ergot, although evidence for this is decidedly thin on the ground. Ingesting grain products, particularly rye (the main vector), contaminated with the fungus *Claviceps purpurea* caused ergotism; convulsive symptoms include painful seizures and spasms, diarrhoea, paresthesias (a burning or prickling sensation that is usually felt in the hands, arms, legs or feet), itching, mania or psychosis, headaches, and vomiting (usually the gastrointestinal symptoms precede central nervous system effects). Dry gangrene results from vasoconstriction induced by the ergotamine-ergocristine alkaloids of the fungus; it affects the fingers and toes. Symptoms include desquamation or peeling, weak peripheral pulses, loss of peripheral sensation, oedema and, ultimately, the death and loss of affected tissues.

When C.H. Fuchs separated references to ergotism from erysipelas and other afflictions in 1834 – *Das Heilige Feuer des Mittelalters* (*The Holy Fire of the Middle Ages*) in Hecker's *Wissensehaftliche Annalen der Gesammten Heilkunde*, 1834; 28: 1–81) – he found the earliest reference to ergotism in the *Annales Xantenses* for the year 857: '[A] great plague of swollen blisters consumed the people by a loathsome rot, so that their limbs were loosened and fell off before death.' In the later Middle Ages, this gangrenous poisoning was known as 'holy fire' or 'Saint Anthony's fire', named after monks of the Order of St Anthony, who were particularly successful at treating this repellent ailment.

Early references to ergotism stretch back as far as 2500 BC, with a probable allusion to ergot on a Babylonian tablet. In 600 BC, an Assyrian tablet refers to it as a 'noxious pustule in the ear of grain'. The Parsees described 'noxious grasses that cause pregnant women to drop the womb and die in childbed'. In ancient Syria, ergot was called 'Daughter of Blood'. Around 300 BC, we have a probable allusion to ergot in the Hindu *Vasna* (encyclopaedia). The Roman Epicurean philosopher Lucretius (98–55 BC) called erysipelas *'Ignis Sacer'*, Holy Fire, which, as we have seen, was the name given in the Middle Ages to ergotism. It has been suggested (by Albert Hofmann) that *kykeon*, the beverage of choice for participants in the ancient Greek Eleusinian Mysteries cult, might have been based on hallucinogens from ergotamine, a forerunner of LSD, and ergonovine. AD 857 gives us our first recorded epidemic of ergotism and in 944, there was the epidemic of ergotism in Aquitaine, Limousin, Angoumois and Périgord. In AD 950, Abū Manṣūr Muwaffaq Harawī alludes to the poisonous properties of ergot, and seven years later, in 957, the devastating epidemic of ergotism hit Paris.

Knowledge of biology and its role in pharmaceuticals was growing all the time, as was, presumably, the role it could play in biological warfare. Abū Manṣūr Muwaffaq Harawī was a tenth-century Persian physician who was active in Herat (in modern-day Afghanistan), under the Samanid prince Mansur I, who ruled from 961 to 976. He compiled his treatise on *materia medica* between 968 and 977, the *Book of the Remedies* (*Kitab al-Abnyia 'an Haqa'iq al-Adwiya*, كتاب الابنيه عن حقائق الادويه). It deals with 585 remedies, of which 466 are derived from plants, 75 from minerals and 44 from animals, classified into four groups according to their action.

The Assyrian association with ergot poisoning was an act of biological warfare, early bioterrorism. Given the serious physical and psychological symptoms of ergotism, it is not difficult to comprehend the damage and mayhem a mass outbreak would cause in the ranks of an enemy.

Well poisoning

Well poisoning is defined as the act of malicious interference with drinkable water resources in order to cause illness or death, or to deny an enemy access to fresh water. Since times of antiquity, well poisoning has been recorded as a strategy during wartime, and was used both offensively as a terror tactic to disrupt and depopulate a target area and defensively as a scorched-earth tactic to seriously weaken an invading army by denying them potable water. Putrefying animal and human corpses thrown down wells were the pollutants of choice; in another of the earliest examples of biological warfare, corpses known to be infected with transmissible diseases such as bubonic plague or tuberculosis were often used for well poisoning. The besieged were especially vulnerable, with vitiated water supplies resulting in dehydration and death in man and domestic animals.

The conflict between the cities of Lagash and Umma, in modern-day southern Iraq, around 2450 BC saw some of the earliest water-related violence; in this case, it was over water rights and control of a prime patch of agricultural land, with Lagash ultimately triumphing. Eannatum, the king of Lagash, severed access to some canals and dried out others, inflicting on an increasingly arid Umma an unforgiving thirst. One of the surviving fragments of the Stele of the Vultures, a limestone slab on which Lagash documented its victory in cuneiform script, reveals how this was done.

Much later, the Assyrians followed suit when King Ashurbanipal (r. 668 BC–627 BC) dried out the wells of besieged Tyre, having posted guards to keep his defeated foes away from wells in a previous conflict. 'By sea and dry land, I took control of (all of) his routes,' Ashurbanipal's scribes wrote of the king of Tyre. 'I constricted (and) cut short their lives.'

Scythian archers dip their arrows into rotting corpses

And it was not just decomposing cadavers: snake venom and blood mixed with faecal matter were also used, thus contaminating the enemy with *Clostridium perfringens* and *Clostridium tetani* in the fourth century BC. Here is how it is done:

> They say that they make the Scythian poison with which they smear arrows, out of the snake. Apparently, the Scythians watch for those [snakes] that have just borne young, and taking them let them rot for some days. When they think that they are completely decomposed, they pour a man's blood into a small vessel, and dig it into a dunghill, and cover it up. When this has also decomposed, they mix the part which stands on the blood, which is watery, with the juice of the snake, and so make a deadly poison.
>
> Pseudo Aristotle, *De Mirabilibus Auscultationibus*: 141 (845a)

Apparently, the archers had a range of 1,600 feet and could launch twenty arrows every minute. Herodotus tells us how effective and elusive they were in his *Histories* (Book 4): 'None who attacks them can escape, and none can catch them if they desire not to be found.'

Ovid, in the early Roman Empire, corroborates the biocrime in his *Tristia*: 'To make wounds twice as deadly, these men [Scythians] dip in viper's venom every arrow-tip.'

Chapter 2

Ancient Greeks: Myth and History

Mythology and legend, and history are, for some, at polar extremes, and controversy has rumbled on since the days soon after Homer and Hesiod regarding what, in ancient Greek and Roman literature, is mythical and what is historical. Given that one of the functions of myths is to explain the origins of and reasons for the everyday in, for example, foundational tales or origin myths, we can say that myths are obviously not always complete fiction. They are inspired by real-world evidence, and while they may not describe a precise historical fact in time, they originate from real-world experiences that fashioned and defined those myths. So, if a myth, for example, described an episode of biological warfare initiated by a god, then it is reasonable to suppose that that myth, somewhere down the line, reflects something that actually did happen, obviously not through a god but through a mortal agency. Apollo's plague at Troy was not made up; it reflects something that happened probably in the early Iron Age.

The Iliad and Apollo's poison-tipped arrows

As we will see from the next chapter, on biological terrorism and biological warfare in the Bible, it all began in the beginning. In the case of the ancient Greeks, biological terrorism and biological warfare began in the beginning, too: they each appear in the opening lines of the first book of *The Iliad*, one of our first extant examples of Western literature, written down about 800 BC and telling of events that took place around the twelfth century BC.

It is Homer's *Iliad* that provides us with our most detailed account of a very short episode in the tenth year of the Trojan War. This is extended by the Greek tragedians, the Greek scholar Apollodorus, fragments of the epic cycle of poems, and the Roman poets Ovid and Virgil, who tell us about the aftermath and the experiences of some of the protagonists of the war and their relatives. The question is, how much of this is mythology and how much is based on real historical events?

Despite accepting some poetic licence and hyperbole on the part of Homer, many classical authors, including Herodotus, Thucydides and Dio Chrysostom, believed the Trojan War to be historical and a crucial conflict in the region, and that it took place around the Dardanelles in the twelfth century BC. Scepticism had set in by the mid-nineteenth century AD when the war and the city of Troy itself were relegated to mythology. However, in 1868, German archaeologist Heinrich Schliemann was persuaded by English amateur archaeologist Frank Calvert that Troy was a real city located near modern-day Hissarlik in Turkey. This is now widely accepted based on excavations conducted by Schliemann, among others. Schliemann's famous 1873 haul apparently included thirteen spearheads and fourteen battleaxes as well as daggers and a sword.

Somewhere between 1194 and 1184 BC is the favoured date for the legendary fall of Troy at the hands of the Mycenaean Greek armies, under the command of Agamemnon and with the tragic deployment of the duplicitous Trojan horse.

Apollo was the god of prophecy and oracles, music, song and poetry, archery and healing; most significantly, for us, he also included plague and disease in his portfolio. *The Iliad*'s slave girl and captured war booty characters Briseis and Chryseis are driving forces behind the Trojan War; they form a basis for Homer's description of the military action at the gates of Troy and the eventual raising of the siege there. Briseis first encountered Achilles at the wrong end of his sword when he ruthlessly slaughtered her father, mother, three brothers and husband during a Greek assault on Troy. A bereft Briseis was awarded to Achilles as war booty with a life of concubinage to look forward to; as such, she is our first real individual female victim of war.

Initially, all went well: the relationship between Briseis and Achilles blossomed into mutual love with the promise of marriage after the war assured by comrade Patroclus. However, Apollo and Agamemnon spoilt the party when the king was required to give up his own concubine, Chryseis. A petulant and selfish Agamemnon then insisted that Achilles hand over Briseis in recompense. Achilles did not react well: he withdrew his troops from the Greek force with dramatic strategic consequences and retired to sulk in his tent, mortified and wounded by his loss. From Achilles' point of view, if the cuckolding of Menelaus could start a war – this, the Trojan War – then what would constitute a proportionate response to Agamemnon taking Briseis from him? Answer: by withdrawing and thereby compromising any successful outcome to the war for the Greeks. It took the death of Patroclus and the return of Briseis – both of whom he loved in different ways – to spur Achilles back into action and save the Greek cause. Predictably, Agamemnon swore that he never laid a hand on Briseis. Well, he would, wouldn't he?

Chryseis, like Briseis, was war booty, given up to Agamemnon. He, with breathtaking insensitivity, tactlessly described her as better than his own wife,

Clytemnestra, with, as we know, fatal consequences when he finally got home from Troy. In Troy, Agamemnon stubbornly held onto Chryseis when her father, Chryses, a priest of Apollo at Chryse, attempted to ransom her:

> I would not accept that marvellous ransom for the girl, the daughter of Chryses, since I much prefer to keep her in my home. For sure, I prefer her to Clytemnestra, my wedded wife, since she is just as good as her, in terms of beauty or in stature, or in mind, or in any handiwork.

The priest's failure here, and Agamemnon's oafish, hubristic disrespect towards him angered the gods to such an extent that Apollo, on appeal from Chryses, unleashed a 'foul plague' (νουσον κακην) on the Greek armies. A few lines later, Achilles refers to the λοιμὸς (plague). If he wanted to have an army to command, Agamemnon had no choice but to renounce 'bright-eyed' Chryseis and return her to her father. As stated, Agamemnon then follows one miscalculation with another when he, with supreme military myopia, selfishly compensated himself by appropriating Briseis from Achilles – with menaces, should he refuse to relinquish her.

It is the spat between Achilles and Agamemnon over whose bed Briseis warmed that stalls the conflict and compromises the Greek war effort. Only when Briseis is returned does Achilles marshal his armies again with renewed vigour to avenge the death of Patroclus and win the war for the Greek alliance.

Apollo's nine-day biological assault on the Greek armies was destructive enough as salvo after salvo of arrows rained down on them. However, the funeral pyres were kept particularly busy because the arrows were tipped with a plague-spreading poison. Apollo's capability for biological warfare is one of its first European manifestations and, by its almost matter-of-fact deployment at this, the opening scene of the epic, suggests that perhaps loosing off poison-tipped arrows was not particularly unusual around the time of the Trojan War.

The contagion Apollo delivered was a zoonotic disease, which started with mules and dogs spreading it to the Greek warriors after they had been inoculated with the disease by Apollo's well-aimed arrows.

As an illustration of the intimate association of poison with arrows, it is significant that our word 'toxin' (and 'toxic' and 'intoxicate') is derived from the Greek word for 'arrow': *toxon* from Old Persian *taxa-*, 'an arrow'; *toxon* can also mean 'a bow and arrow'; an archer in Greek is '*toxotes*'. The noun ιός also means 'an arrow', as well as 'a serpent's poison'.

Crafty Odysseus

No indisputable evidence exists to prove that Odysseus routinely used poison-tipped arrows in combat. It is possible that the 'bitter' poison with which Menelaos was shot was a form of poison (*The Iliad* 4, 217–18) that Machaon sucked out and skilfully treated with efficacious medicines. We know that he went to Ephra in search of lethal poison so that he might have it to smear on his bronze-headed arrows (*Odyssey* 1, 259–62), but he was refused by the virtuous Ilus, who was concerned that gods may judge him impious if he was implicated in this ignoble and dishonourable form of warfare. Nevertheless, Odysseus got his deadly drug in the end, and presumably used it. His success here demonstrates if nothing else the ambivalence and controversy relating to the moral questions attached to the use of biological warfare that have raged through to the twenty-first century.

> He [Odysseus] ... had been to beg poison for his arrows from Ilos, son of Mermerus. Ilos feared the ever-living gods and would not give him any, but my father let him have some, for he liked him a lot.
>
> Homer, *The Odyssey* 1, 259

Odysseus' son, Telemachus, was rumoured to have been in favour of the use of poison, if the insistent suitors hanging around Penelope are to be believed. They mocked the young warrior, suggesting that he was plotting against them, with one of his options being to visit Ephyre to collect deadly drugs to mix in a wine bowl and kill them all. Appropriately, Ephyre was local to the infernal rivers Styx and Acheron near the entrance to the underworld (*Odyssey* 2, 323–30).

When Odysseus finally reached home and slaughtered the suitors, it was with his special bow and arrows. However, there is nothing to suggest that these were poisoned in any way: the adjective πικρὸν can be variously translated as 'sharp', 'pointed' or 'cruel': ἦ καὶ ἐπ' Ἀντινόῳ ἰθύνετο πικρὸν ὀϊστόν.

Ironically, it was a poison-tipped spear that killed Odysseus. Telegonus, his other son by witchy Circe, travelled to Ithaca to meet his birth father after learning his identity from his mother – as described in the epitome of the *Bibliotheca* of Pseudo-Apollodorus (7, 36). She gives him a magical spear, which is laced with the venomous sting of a stingray spine and was made by the god Hephaestus. On reaching shore, he steals some of Odysseus' cattle – a crime that displeased Odysseus and led to a confrontation between father and son. In the ensuing fight, Odysseus was fatally wounded by Telegonus' toxic spear.

Orion

Orion was a handsome giant granted the ability to walk on water by his father, Poseidon. Orion first appears as a great hunter in the *Odyssey*, where Odysseus meets his shade during the *nekuia* in the underworld. (The *nekuia* is a journey through the underworld in Greek epic poetry.) Accounts of his death are various: in one, he wanted to marry Artemis but her brother Apollo tricked the goddess into shooting him with an arrow as he was swimming far out at sea. In another version, Artemis slew him after he raped her handmaiden Oupis, a Hyperborean maiden in her band of huntresses. The most common, however, was that Orion boasted he would hunt down and kill all the beasts of the earth, so Gaia despatched a giant scorpion to sting him to death (Scholia on Homer, *Iliad* 18.486 citing Pherecydes; Ovid *Fasti* 5, 539; Horace *Odes* 2, 4. 72; Apollodorus 1, 4, 5). Orion and the Scorpion were afterwards placed amongst the stars as opposing constellations – one rises as the other sets.

Chiron

Chiron was a centaur, the eldest and the wisest and the immortal son of the Titan Cronus and a half-brother of Zeus. He was a celebrated teacher who mentored many of the greatest heroes of myth including the Argonauts Jason and Peleus, the physician Asclepius, the demi-god Aristaeus, and Achilles. As with Orion there are a number of versions of how Chiron died, including Pseudo-Apollodorus, *Bibliotheca* 2. 83–87; Diodorus Siculus, *Library of History* 4. 12. 8; and Pseudo-Hyginus, *Astronomica* 2. 38, for example. But it is those by Ovid (43 BC–AD 18) and Pausanias (*c.* AD 110–AD 180) which interest us most as both attribute a biological cause to his death through the poison arrows they describe. First Ovid:

> [Chiron], you, immortal just now and destined by your birthright to live on forever will long to die when you are tortured by the serpent's blood [i.e. poisoned by an arrow coated with Hydra's blood], that agonizing poison in your wounds; and, saved from immortality, the gods will put you under death's power, and the three Fates will unloose your threads of fate.
>
> Ovid, *Metamorphoses* 2. 649 ff. (trans. Melville)

And when the fatal spear drops onto Chiron's foot in an unfortunate needlestick injury:

Chiron blends picked herbs from the Pagasean hills, and soothes the wound with different treatments. The corrupting poison overwhelmed the therapies; disease penetrated bones and body. The blood of Lerna's Hydra and the Centaur's blood mingled, and gave no time for rescue.

Ovid, Fasti 5. 379 ff. (adapted trans. Boyle)

Now Pausanias:

> The Anigros [river Elis] descends from the mountain Lapithos in Arcadia, and right from its source its water does not smell sweet but actually stinks horribly … Some Greeks say that Chiron … when shot by Heracles fled wounded to this river and washed his injury in it, and that it was the Hydra's poison which gave the Anigros its foul smell.
>
> Pausanias, Description of Greece 5. 5. 9–10 (trans. Jones);
see also Strabo, 8.3.19.

In between Ovid and Pausanias, Pliny the Elder had noted *(HN* 21.177–179) that the Greek name for deadly nightshade (belladonna) was δορύκνιον, *dorycnion*, which comes from the Greek words 'dory' meaning 'spear' and 'knaein' meaning 'to smear', referring to the application of the poisonous sap of that plant on spears used in battle.

Heracles would later use arrows dipped in the Hydra's poisonous blood to kill other foes during his remaining labours, such as the Stymphalian birds and the giant Geryon. As we shall see, he later used one to kill the centaur Nessus; and Nessus' tainted blood was applied to the Tunic of Nessus, by which the centaur had his posthumous revenge. Roman military physicians carried iron rust and plant antidotes in their field kits.

Chrysame of Thessally and the mad bull

Polyaenus tells us how in about 1000 BC during the Greek colonisation of Ionia (western Turkey), Cnopus, son of Codrus, the king of Athens, was at war with the Ionians who held Erythrae, a wealthy city on the Aegean coast. Cnopus resorted to an oracle about how to achieve victory. The oracle advised him to send for Chrysame, a priestess of the goddess Hecate in Thessaly, to be his 'general'. Thessally was notorious for its witches and their *pharmaka* and its spells and potions – and all the famous witches lived there, not least Medea and Lucan's repellent Erichtho. Cnopus sent an ambassador to Thessaly and Chrysame agreed to sail to Ionia to direct his campaign against Erythrae. She soon got to work and selected a large and beautiful bull; she gilded his horns and adorned him with garlands and purple ribbons embroidered with gold. She then mixed into his feed a hallucinogenic cocktail that would induce madness and ordered that he be kept in the stall and fed the potion.

Anyone who ingested the concoction would be seized with madness. Moreover, anyone who ate the beef of the bull when it was in a state of mania would suffer the same affliction. When the Erythraians set up camp, Chrysame ordered an altar to be raised which they could see from afar. A grand (mock) sacrifice was prepared and the magnificently decorated bull was led out having fed on the herbal concoction. 'Crazy from the drug's influence and in a frenzy,' wrote Polyaenus, 'the bull leaped away and escaped,' running amok, crazily attacking everything in its path. Polyaenus described how Chrysame's stratagem worked: 'When the enemy saw the garlanded bull with golden horns charging from Cnopus's camp into their own camp, they welcomed it as a lucky sign and an auspicious omen.' They managed to seize the bull and offered him to their gods. All of the Erythraians ate some of the beef so the whole army was soon afflicted by the hallucinogen, and exhibited the same signs of abandon and frenzy as the bull: 'Everyone began to jump up and down, to run in different directions, to skip with joy.' Chrysame's drug was possibly strychnine extracted from deadly nightshade, known in antiquity for causing 'playful insanity'.

When Chrysame saw how the intoxicated guards had abandoned their posts and that the whole camp was in chaos, she ordered Cnopus and his army to take up their weapons and 'speedily attack the defenceless enemy. Cnopus destroyed them all and became master of the great and prosperous city of Erythrae.'

Nessus and Heracles

Nessus is known for his leading role in the story of the 'Tunic of Nessus', the poisoned shirt (chiton) that killed Heracles. It was Nessus' allegedly divinely appointed job to carry people over the river Eunos in Anatolia for a fee; he was a kind of upper world Charon. Heracles had been married to Deianeira for nearly three years, when, at a feast in the house of Oeneus, he accidentally killed Eunomus, the son of Architeles. Heracles, in accordance with the law, was ostracised with Deianeira, arriving at the river during their wanderings.

Nessus boasted to Heracles of his upstanding character and was given permission to carry Deianeira over the river. After doing this, Nessus, charlatan that he was, tried to rape her. Heracles heard his wife's screams and saw what was going on from the other bank. He shot a Hydra-poisoned arrow into Nessus' heart. While the centaur lay dying, as a final act of malice, knowing that his blood was now infected with the hydra's venom, Nessus told Deianeira that his blood would make a fail-safe love potion if mixed with some of the semen he had spilt during the attempted rape. It would always ensure that Heracles was true to her.

Ovid can always be relied upon to provide a vivid account:

> And now on the far bank and stooping for the bow he'd thrown, he heard a voice, his wife's, calling and sure that Nessus had in mind some villainy, 'You raping ravisher!' Hercules cried, 'Where are you going? So confident in your four feet! Nessus Two-Formed (*biformis*), listen! Hold off from me and mine. Maybe you feel no dread of me – at least your father's [Ixion's] wheel should hold you back from lust and lechery. Trust horse-strength if you will, you'll not escape. With wounds not feet I'll follow!' His last words were proved at once: an arrow flew and pierced the fleeing centaur's back: out from his breast the barbed point exited. Nessus wrenched the shaft away, and blood from both wounds spurted, blood that bore the Lernaean's [Hydra's] poison. Nessus scooped it up. 'I'll not die unavenged,' he thought and gave his shirt soaked in warm gore to Deianeira, a talisman, he claimed, to kindle love.
>
> Ovid, *Metamorphoses* 9, 101 ff. (adapted trans. Melville)

Deianeira believed him. Later, when she began to have doubts about Heracles' fidelity on account of Iole, she spread the centaur's blood on a robe and gave it to her husband. Iole was the beautiful young daughter of King Eurytus of Oechalia and was ripe for marriage. According to Apollodorus, Iole was claimed by Heracles for a bride, but Eurytus refused her hand. Iole was, in effect, indirectly the cause of Heracles' death because of Deianeira's jealousy of her. Heracles went to a gathering of heroes, where his passion got the better of him. Meanwhile, Deianeira accidentally spilled a portion of the centaur's blood onto the floor. To her horror, it began to smoke by the light of the rising sun. She realised it was poison and sent her messenger to warn Heracles but it was too late. Heracles lay dying a slow and painful death as the robe corroded his skin. Heracles was then taken to Mount Olympus by Zeus and was welcomed among the gods for his heroic exploits. Sophocles' play *The Trachiniae* is largely based on this myth.

The Tunic of Nessus story, or imitations thereof, has enjoyed an interesting, if tragic, history since the days of ancient Greece. During the Anabaptist Münster Rebellion of 1534, a 15-year-old girl named Hille Feyken tried to deceive Münster's Prince-Bishop Franz von Waldeck, who had been leading a protracted siege of the city. Her plan was to pretend to defect and tempt von

Waldeck with details of the city's defences while giving him a fine shirt soaked in poison. Before her plan could be carried out, she was betrayed by another defector, who warned the bishop; Feyken was tortured and killed.

In Act 4.12 of Shakespeare's *Antony and Cleopatra*, Mark Antony is incensed after losing the Battle of Actium and exclaims, 'The shirt of Nessus is upon me.' Milton refers to the 'envenomed robe' in *Paradise Lost* (II, 541–544):

> Hell scarce holds the wild uproar.
> As when Alcides, from Œchalia crowned
> With conquest, felt the envenomed robe, and tore
> Through pain up by the roots Thessalian pines

Thomas Carlyle (1795–1881) avoided hypocrisy as he would 'poisonous Nessus shirts': 'It is now almost my sole rule of life to clear myself of cants and formulas, as of poisonous Nessus shirts.' (*Letters to his Wife* 108; 1835.)

Major General Henning von Tresckow was one of the conspirators in the 20 July 1944 plot to assassinate Adolf Hitler; he famously referred to the 'Robe of Nessus' when he realised that the assassination plot had failed and that he and others involved in the conspiracy were now doomed: 'None of us can complain about our own deaths. Everyone who joined our circle put on the "Robe of Nessus".' (H. Mommsen, *Alternatives to Hitler: German Resistance Under the Third Reich*, p. 7).

Philoctetes

Hercules' biological weapons – the arrows coated with the poison of the Hydra – ended up being deposited in a temple in Italy by the famous archer Philoctetes, who offered them to Apollo, the god who spread the plague with his arrows at the start of *The Iliad*. He had been bequeathed the bow and arrows of Heracles in return for lighting his funeral pyre.

Philoctetes was abandoned on the island of Lemnos by the Greeks on the way to Troy. Again, there are various explanations for this but they all indicate that he received a wound on his foot which putrified and gave off a terrible smell. One version says that Philoctetes was bitten by a snake that Hera sent to bite him as punishment for his or his father's service to Heracles. Another has it that when the Achaeans, en route to Troy at the beginning of the war, came to the island of Tenedos, Achilles angered Apollo by killing King Tenes, allegedly the god's son. When, in expiation, the Achaeans offered a sacrifice to Apollo, a snake emerged from the altar and bit Philoctetes.

Artemis

More revenge for naked hubris than actual biological warfare, perhaps the cruellest fate of all was reserved for Niobe, the Queen of Thebes and wife of Amphion. Niobe bore seven boys and seven girls. In her pride, Niobe claimed that she was more fertile than Leto, who had only one boy and one girl, Artemis and Apollo.

Artemis and Apollo loved their mother so it is not surprising that they were angered by this hubristic boast. Using poison arrows, Artemis killed Niobe's seven daughters while Apollo claimed her sons. In some versions, the twin deities spared one of each sex while Artemis turned Niobe to stone. Devastated, Amphion committed suicide.

Dogs of war in ancient Greece

Aelian tells how in his *Varia Historia* (14.46) in the mid-seventh century BC during the war waged by the Ephesians against Magnesia on the river Maeander, their horsemen were each accompanied by a war dog and a spear-bearing attendant. Dogs were released first and broke the enemy ranks, followed by an assault of spears, then a cavalry charge. An epitaph records the burial of a Magnesian horseman named Hippaemon with his dog Lethargos, his horse, and his spearman. Strabo, 4.5.2, says that the Celts too used dogs in warfare, though he doesn't specify how.

The Siege of Kirrha

Kirrha was a coastal town in Phocis that served as the harbour of Delphi and its famous oracle. Over time, Kirrha grew in importance, which excited the jealousy of the Delphians, not least because the Kirrhaeans levied crippling tolls on the supplicants who disembarked at the town on their way to Delphi, and were rumoured to have assaulted Phocian women on their return from the temple. As a result, the Amphyctyonic League of Delphi declared war, the First Sacred War, on the Kirrhaeans in about 595 BC, and at the end of a ten years' siege, finally managed to take the city, which was razed to the ground. The medical writer Thessalus (*fl.* fifth and fourth centuries BC) reports that the attackers discovered a secret water pipe leading into the city after it was shattered by a horse's hoof: the result was that when the thirsty Kirrhaeans drank the poisoned water, they were debilitated with acute gastrointestinal distress to such a degree that they could no longer defend their walls. To this day, there is a salt spring near the ruins of Kirrha with water that has a purgative effect similar to the hellebore of the ancients. The entire population of the city was slaughtered.

Alternative versions exist: Frontinus (c. AD 40–AD 103) was a prominent Roman civil engineer, soldier, senator, and author of *Strategemata* – examples of military stratagems from Greek and Roman history, for the use of generals. He says that after discovering the pipe, the Amphyctyonic League cut it, causing great thirst within the city. They then restored the pipe and the desperate Kirrhans immediately began drinking the water, unaware that Kleisthenes had poisoned it with hellebore. According to Polyaenus, a writer of the second century and author of *Stratagems in War*, the attackers added the hellebore to the spring from which the water came. Polyaenus also gave credit for the strategy not to Kleisthenes but to Eurylochus, who he claimed advised his allies to gather a large amount of hellebore from Anticyra. According to Pausanias, active in the second century, Solon diverted the course of the river Pleistos to avoid Kirrha but the enemy was able to get enough water from their wells and rainwater collection. Solon then added a great quantity of black hellebore root (skunk cabbage) to the waters of the Pleistos and let it flow into Kirrha.

All helleborus plant varieties are toxic, and all parts of the helleborus plant are toxic. Hellebore plants are usually avoided by animals such as deer and rabbits because the leaves produce poisonous alkaloids, making them distasteful to animals. Black hellebore was used by the Greeks and Romans to treat paralysis, gout and other diseases, and, more particularly, insanity. Black hellebore causes tinnitus, vertigo, stupor, thirst, anaphylaxis, vomiting, catharsis, bradycardia (slowing of the heart rate) and, finally, collapse and death from cardiac arrest.

In Greek mythology, Melampus of Pylos used hellebore to save the daughters of the king of Argos from a madness, induced by Dionysus, that caused them to run naked through the city, crying, wailing and screaming. In a fit of madness induced by Hera, Heracles killed his children by Megara. His madness was cured using hellebore.

Pheretima

The story of Pheretima (d. 515 BC), wife of the Greek Cyrenaean King Battus III and the last queen of the Battiad dynasty, provides a cautionary lesson for Herodotus' audience. When Arcesilaus, Battus' son, left Cyrene for Barca, Pheretima ruled the city as regent, but Arcesilaus was murdered by exiled Cyrenaeans intent on revenge. Pheretima sped to Arysandes, the Persian governor of Egypt, seeking help in avenging the death of her son; Arysandes loaned her Egypt's army and navy, at the head of which she marched to Barca and demanded the surrender of those Barcaeans responsible for the murder of Arcesilaus. When the Barcaeans refused to own up, Pheretima laid siege to their city for nine months and finally took it when Amasis, her Persian commander, tricked the Barcaeans. Pheretima, still crazed by vengeance, ordered the Barcaean wives' breasts to be cut off, and enslaved the rest of the Barcaeans to the Persians.

Such an atrocity was appalling enough, but for it to be committed by a woman – however strong her maternal love for a lost son – would have shocked many Greeks. Herodotus is at pains to show that such war crimes committed by a foreigner, and a woman foreigner at that, would not go unpunished. Pheretima went back to Egypt and returned the army and navy to the governor. However, while there, she contracted a contagious parasitic disease and died in late 515 BC. Herodotus tells us that she was eaten alive by the worms spawned by her disease as punishment by the gods for her butchery of the women of Barca: 'For while still alive she teemed with maggots: thus does over-brutal human revenge invite retribution from the gods' (Herodotus 4, 205 ff.). Pheretima lives on in the name of the worm that infested her: *Pheretima* is a genus of earthworm found in New Guinea and other parts of Southeast Asia; the worms are still used as a medicine in China and carry biological agents efficacious in the treatment of epilepsy. The *Pheretima aspergillum* worm contains hypoxanthine – a herb used as an antipyretic, sedative, and anticonvulsant. It lowers blood pressure and contains a platelet-activating factor.

The Plague of Athens 430 BC

> I shall simply set down its nature, and explain the symptoms by which perhaps it may be recognised by the student, should it ever break out again. This I am qualified do, as I had the disease myself, and have watched its course in others.
>
> Thucydides, *History of the Peloponnesian War*, 2, 48

Athenian historian, political philosopher and military general (*strategos*), Thucydides is famous for his *History of the Peloponnesian War*, a defining work that has led to him being called the father of 'scientific history' because of his rigorous research, reliance on eyewitness accounts, lucid evidence gathering, and analysis of cause and effect. Unlike the work of Herodotus before him, Thucydides' history is devoid of interventions by the gods. He omits the arts, literature and the social circumstances in which the events take place, focusing instead on actual events, on hard facts, excluding what he may have seen as frivolous or irrelevant. Thucydides thereby initiated a historiographical tradition that would become the model for future historians.

Thucydides' description of the plague in Athens (Λοιμὸς τῶν Ἀθηνῶν) is a shocking and vivid account of a public health disaster, the like of which the city, or any Greek city, had never suffered before. Its appearance so soon after the stirring and patriotic Funeral Oration lends it a sharper focus and imbues it with even more realism and horror in its depiction of the fragility of human life. Pericles' Funeral Oration (Περικλέους Επιτάφιος) is a landmark speech delivered by Pericles, the pre-eminent Athenian politician and general, at the end of the first year of the Peloponnesian War (431–404 BC) as a part of the annual public funeral for the war dead. The remains of the dead were left lying in state in a tent for three days so that offerings could be made. Then a funeral procession was held, with ten cypress coffins carrying the remains, one for each of the Athenian tribes, and another left symbolically empty for the missing or those whose remains could not be recovered. Finally, they were buried at a public grave at Kerameikos. The culmination of the ceremony was a speech delivered by a prominent Athenian citizen chosen by the state.

This Funeral Oration is significant because it differs from the usual form of Athenian funeral speeches. David Cartwright, in his 1997 *A Historical Commentary on Thucydides*, describes it as 'a eulogy of Athens itself'. The speech glorifies Athens's achievements, designed to stir the spirits of a state still at war.

The Plague of Athens was an epidemic that devastated the city-state during the second year of the Peloponnesian War against the Spartans; this was at a time when Athens was under siege by Sparta, although an Athenian victory was still a real possibility. Over the next three years, most of the population was infected, and perhaps as many as 75,000 to 100,000 people, 25 per cent of the city's population, died. The epidemic broke in early May 430 BC, with subsequent waves in the summer of 428 and in the winter of 427/426 (Thucydides 3, 87). It lasted almost five years. Before Thucydides, it was commonly believed that it was the gods who visited plagues on mankind in punishment for disrespect, hubris or ungodly behaviour. We see this in Herodotus, and we will see it in the *Book of Exodus*. There is no reason to believe that the besieged Athenians did not assume that their plight – siege compounded by plague – was not a punishment handed down by their gods.

This plague was a major contributory factor in Athens' defeat: it exterminated highly trained sailors and first-line soldiers as well as generals, including Pericles and his sons Paralus and Xanthippus. It weakened Athens' military power and left her morale in tatters.

Innate Greek superstition played its part: the Athenians saw the plague as evidence that the gods favoured Sparta, and this was supported by an oracle that Apollo himself (the god of disease and medicine) would fight for Sparta:

but when Apollo was asked by the Athenians 'whether they should go to war, he answered that if they put their might into it, victory would be theirs, and that he would himself be with them'. Alarmingly, an earlier oracle had warned that 'A Spartan war will come and bring a pestilence with it'.

> Supplications in the temples, divinations, and so forth were found equally pointless, till the all consuming nature of the disaster at last put a stop to them altogether. (2.47)
>
> [The plague] was a disaster of epic proportions that altered not only the Peloponnesian War, but the whole of Greek, and consequently world, history. While the war would not end for nearly 26 years after the first wave of sickness, there is little doubt that the Great Plague changed the course of the war (being at least in part responsible for Athens' defeat) and significantly shaped the peace that came afterward, planting the seeds that would weaken and then destroy Athenian democracy.
>
> Katherine Kelaidis, Resident scholar at the National Hellenic Museum: 'What the Great Plague of Athens Can Teach Us Now', *The Atlantic*, 23 March 2020

There has been endless discussion and argument about the infectious agent or agents responsible for the plague. What concerns us, though, is the possibility that bioterrorism was deployed by the Spartan forces by poisoning the Athenian wells. Papagrigorakis (2013) tells us that recent data implicate *Salmonella enterica serovar Typhi* as a causative pathogen: 'According to Thucydides, the sudden outbreak of the disease may link to poisoning of the water reservoirs by the Spartans.' The purpose of besieging a city was to exhaust the supplies of a population's food and water, which often led to epidemics. 'Poisoning of the water reservoirs of a besieged city as an act of bioterrorism would probably shorten the necessary time for such conditions to appear.'

This is how Thucydides reveals to his readers the conjecture that bioterrorism and biological warfare may have been a factor (2.48.2):

> Suddenly descending on Athens, it [the plague] first attacked the population in Piraeus – which is why they say that the Peloponnesians [Spartans] had poisoned the reservoirs, there being as yet no wells there – and afterwards appeared in the upper city, when the deaths became much more frequent.

Sanitation in ancient Athens comprised facilities and utilities such as wells, cisterns and aqueducts to supply water, with cesspools for waste disposal

(Wycherley 1977: 240). In normal times, these were adequate but they would have come under enormous pressure with the huge influx of refugees into the city at the beginning of the Peloponnesian War. Any poisonous agent introduced into the sanitation system would have enjoyed a wide take-up from so many victims crowding in. The intense febrility suffered by the infected and the associated thirst did not help when:

> What they would have really liked to do would have been to throw themselves into cold water; as indeed some of the neglected sick did, who plunged into the rain tanks in their torment of unquenchable thirst; though it made no difference whether they drank little or much. (2.49.5; 2.52.3)

So, the plague was initially blamed on the poisoning of water sources in Piraeus by the Spartans (Alford 1998). However, this theory was later doubted when the pestilence encroached on the city, because water sources in the port were not connected to the city wells, which were also on higher ground.

Thucydides also described the horrific outcome of the rout of the Athenians after they invaded Sicily in 413 BC, their worst defeat in the Peloponnesian War. In their failed siege of Syracuse (415–413 BC), during the ill-fated Sicilian Expedition, the Athenians had destroyed the pipes conveying drinking water to the city. But the tide shifted and the Syracusans retaliated in kind. They pursued the demoralised Athenian forces overland, constantly denying them access to water. When the parched army, already sickened by swamp fevers, finally reached a river, chaos erupted as the mass of delirious soldiers trampled each other trying to reach the water. The Syracusans stood on the cliffs above and slaughtered the Athenians, who kept on drinking the muddy water, now fouled with blood and gore, until the river was dammed up with heaps of bodies.

Similar scenes were witnessed in the next century, in India, when Alexander the Great's army was so laid low by extreme thirst that the frantic soldiers would leap into wells still wearing armour. Strabo wrote that the crazed troops drowned while trying to drink, weighed down and under water. Their bloated corpses floated to the surface, polluting their only available source of water.

Clearchus of Heraclea

Successful army commanders have to know much more about their enemies than just military strength, equipment and tactics. As Clearchus (*c.*401 BC–353 BC) would have told us, a familiarity with the local environment in which conflict is to take place is also strategically very useful. Polyaenus (*Strategemata* 2, 30) tells how, in around 360 BC, Clearchus, the tyrant of Heraclea, desperately needed a fortified citadel in his city so he duplicitously despatched mercenaries by night to plunder, rob, assault and do as much damage locally as possible, thus unnerving the citizens and persuading them of the need for a fortified citadel. The citizens obviously were unaware of how this was happening and complained to Clearchus, begging for his protection.

> He told them it would be impossible to stop the depredations of the troops unless they were confined within walls, which is what he wanted to recommend to them. The citizens agreed, and assigned part of the city, where he could raise a wall and build a citadel. In fact, this citadel offered no protection to the citizens, but it enabled Clearchus to maltreat them in any way he chose.

Clearchus then announced his intention to dismiss his guards, and restore the republic to the council of Three Hundred, who convened to express their gratitude to him for the restitution of the republic. Clearchus then went to the house of the council, and placed an armed guard at the door, ordering the Three Hundred to be called out one by one; the soldiers seized them as they came out, and took them away to the citadel.

Clearchus was of the belief that there were too many citizens to ensure the safety of his government, but had no way of removing them, so he organised an expedition against the city of Astacus in the hot, sultry days of summer. He recruited a citizen army and when he got near to Astacus, established a camp on a flat marsh, which was full of stagnant water. He ordered them to watch the Thracians, while he himself advanced with the mercenaries and took up position on a hill, which was shaded by trees and refreshed by streams. He protracted the siege, until all the citizens were dead from the infectious diseases (malaria, presumably) emanating from the stagnant waters. Mission accomplished, he raised the siege.

Aeneas Tacticus

Aeneas Tacticus (*fl.* fourth century BC) was one of the earliest Greek writers on the art of war and is credited as the first author to provide a complete guide to securing military communications. Polybius described his design for a hydraulic semaphore system. Tacticus was also author of a number of manuals (Ὑπομνήματα) on the subject. The only extant one, *How to Survive under Siege*, deals with the best methods of defending a fortified city. He recommended the besieged to poison the water supply of their city to deter the attackers.

It was Aelian (AD 175–235), in his *On Animals*, who first told us, in a variation of the axiom that an army marches on its stomach, that the simplest medico-biological ruse, other than denying an enemy drinking water, was to capitalise on their hunger and encourage overindulgence in eating and drinking: 'men by their unbridled appetite are the victims of plots against their food and drink.'

As Pliny the Elder had told us a century or so earlier, 'Most of man's trouble is caused by the belly … it is chiefly through his food that a man dies.' Aeneas the Tactician advised commanders to wait until the enemy grows reckless and begins 'looting to satisfy their greed'. They will 'stuff themselves with food and drink and, once inebriated [will] become careless … and impaired in performance'.

Xenophon's honey trap

In 401 BC in Colchis, Xenophon, historian and military general, a hoplite commander, halted troops at what looked to be the perfect place to camp. The village was well stocked with food, not least copious supplies of wild honey, which the soldiers found and helped themselves to. Soon after gorging themselves they became a delirious and intoxicated horde of madmen, collapsing by the thousands; most were totally incapacitated and some even died. This toxic honey was produced by bees that collected nectar from poisonous rhododendron flowers. Four centuries later, the very same thing happened to a Roman army in the same region.

Scaphism

The ancient Persians were one of the earliest civilisations to use insects as devices of torture, one manifestation of which was the repellent practice of subjecting a condemned man to 'the boats' and known as scaphism (from the ancient Greek *skaphe*, from which we get the word 'skiff', a small, flat-bottomed boat). The victim was initially force-fed milk and honey to bring on severe diarrhoea. Then the victim was stripped, lashed to a skiff (or a hollowed-out tree trunk) so that the head, hands and feet protruded over the sides, smeared with honey and set adrift on a stagnant pond or simply left to fry in the sun. Wasps swarmed to the honey and delivered excruciating stings, but the worst bit was when all manner of insects were inexorably drawn to the diarrhoea faeces swilling around in the boat. Flies would breed in the filth and then begin laying eggs in the victim's anus and increasingly gangrenous flesh. Although the misery could be prolonged by providing the victim with continuing doses of milk and honey, the condemned would eventually succumb to sepsis from being infested with maggots.

The Harmatelian-envenomated arrows

In 326 BC, Alexander the Great and his army arrived at the fortified city of Harmatelia (probably Mansura in modern-day Pakistan), where, according to Diodorus Siculus, they faced a 'new and grave danger'. Strangely, morale seemed to be running high in the 3,000-strong Harmatelian camp; little did Alexander know that, in the words of Quintus Curtius, the Harmatelians 'had smeared their weapons with a drug of mortal effect', of which the slightest scratch would kill a man. This toxin was harvested from a type of viper: the snakes were killed and left to rot in the sun; heat decomposed the flesh and the venom suffused with the liquefying tissue. Recent herpetological research reveals that not only the rotting flesh of whatever prey had been digested in the snake's stomach would contain toxic bacteria, but also that vipers retain large amounts of faeces in their bodies over many months. In a dead viper, rotting excrement would add yet more decomposing bacteria to the mix. A wounded man immediately went numb, suffering stabbing pains and convulsions. Then, their skin became cold and they vomited bile. Black froth spewed from the wound and green gangrene spread rapidly – a truly horrible death. Even a 'mere scratch' brought the same gruesome death. It seems likely that the snakes used were the deadly Russell's viper, *Vipera russelli russelli*.

The plague of Thebes

Sophocles' *Oedipus Rex* was first performed around 429 BC. Thebes is beset by plague as a result of corruption and the murder of Laius, the former king of the city. The attempts of Oedipus, the incumbent ruler, to allay the plague bring him only to the realisation that he himself is the cause of the plague. His murder of his own father and incest with his mother, he finally realises, is what brought the curse to Thebes.

Antonis Kousoulis tells how 'the plague in Thebes is a serious matter', as in line 23, where it is referred to as 'weltering surge of blood' (φοινίου σάλου). In line 28, the word plague (λοιμός) appears with the Greek word for disease (νόσος) being used in lines 150, 217, and 303.

> Sophocles describes the main characteristics of the epidemic through sporadic sentences. Early in the play it is clarified that the disease is a

cattle zoonosis of high mortality rate ('a blight upon the grazing flocks and herds', line 26, with the herds being cattle). The lethality of this epidemic is particularly terrifying for the protagonists of the play, and the disease's severity is evinced by the first sentences of the tragedy ('reek of incense everywhere', line 4). Oedipus fears mass destruction of the city of Thebes ('with the god's good help success is sure; 'tis ruin if we fail', line 146), while the words 'weltering surge of blood' (line 24), 'fiery plague' (line 166), 'the land is sore distressed' (line 685), and 'wailing on the altar stair, wives and grandams rend the air, long-drawn moans and piercing cries blent with prayers and litanies' (lines 184–6) all illustrate vividly the severity of the situation.

Kousoulis adds that it is clear that the causative pathogen leads to miscarriages or stillbirths ('a blight on wives in travail', lines 26–7, meaning women give birth to dead babies). The plague's effects are also pointed out by the Chorus: 'earth her gracious fruits denies' and 'women wail in barren throats' (lines 151, 215).

the pathogens that include most (5 of 7) of the features described by Sophocles in *Oedipus Rex* are *Leishmania* spp., *Leptospira* spp., *Brucella abortus*, *Orthopoxviridae*, and *Francisella tularensis*. Among the diseases caused by these pathogens that can affect humans are the following: 1) tularemia, which is a disease mainly transmitted through rabbits; 2) smallpox, which is not a cattle zoonosis; 3) leishmaniasis, which is not a highly contagious disease; and 4) leptospirosis, which has been associated with epidemics after rainfall and flooding in relation to rodent infestation. Thus, the most probable cause of the plague in Thebes is *B. abortus*. Brucellosis is a highly contagious zoonosis caused by ingestion of unsterilized milk or meat from infected cows or close contact with their secretions. The mortality rate for untreated brucellosis is difficult to determine from the literature of the preantibiotic era; nevertheless, an 80% rate has been reported in situations of comorbidity with endocarditis. Epidemics, stillbirths, and miscarriages caused by *B. abortus* have been reported since the time of Hippocrates, which is when this disease was initially described.

Chapter 3

Biological Warfare in the Bible

It all began in the beginning.

In the halcyon days of the Garden of Eden, there was no disease, no suffering and no need to work. All was well with the world and God must have been a very happy god, more than pleased with his fabulous creation. Then along slithered the serpent, intent on spoiling it all, and spoil it he did: that serpent has been spoiling it all ever since because the blandishments with which he seduced Adam and Eve, their original sin, has had, in the ideologies of believers, repercussions to this day. One of those repercussions was the introduction of disease, pain and suffering and the need to go out to work. God was now less than pleased; he became an angry, vengeful and jealous god, implacably set on a never-ending programme of punishments for humankind, one of the manifestations of which was the regular dispensation of plagues – most of which were biological, involving debilitating and deadly disease, rapacious insects or festering sores on an epidemic scale. War, famine and climate change were, indeed are, disease's sinister bedfellows. This new, vindictive and punitive god, like the Greek and Roman gods contemporary with or after him, was now something of a bioterrorist, handing down terror, disease and death to engender unstinting compliance, respect and obedience amongst a frequently wayward and capricious populace. God declared: 'Vengeance is Mine, I will repay'; 'the Lord will judge His people.' Diseases were the 'wages of sin' in much the same way as death was (Romans 6:23): the two were never always mutually exclusive.

With the Bible we come back to that question of historicity we grappled with when describing biological warfare and bioterrorism in Greek mythology: how much of it is based, however loosely, on actual fact? How much of it actually happened? No modern attempt to identify a historical Egyptian prototype for Moses, for example, has been widely accepted, and no period in Egyptian history matches the biblical accounts of the Exodus. Some elements of the story defy rational explanation, such as the Plagues of Egypt and the Crossing of the Red Sea. Despite the absence of any archaeological evidence, though, many scholars agree that the Book of Exodus probably has some historical basis. Kenton Sparks calls it 'mythologised history' (Sparks 2010).

Greek myth and the stories in the Old Testament reflect the origins of and reasons for various events, institutions or customs that were prevalent in the days of Homer onwards or, in the case of the Bible, what the authors of the various books wanted to convey about God and their religion.

The Bible is not that old in terms of the available records of disease: the Old Testament was written down between the sixth and first centuries BC, well after the eighth-century BC Homer and Hesiod; as we have seen, records of infectious diseases and possible biological warfare survive on ancient Egyptian stele, in tomb paintings, and on papyri and Akkadian tablets, reaching far beyond the Near East to India and China. Scholars generally agree that the *Torah* was published in the fifth century BC. The Book of Deuteronomy, composed between the seventh and sixth centuries BC, mentions the 'diseases of Egypt' (Deuteronomy 7:15 and 28:60) but as an affliction of the Israelites, not the Egyptians, and never specifies the plagues.

The traditional number of ten plagues visited on Egypt is not actually mentioned in Exodus, while other sources differ; Psalms 78 and 105 list only seven or eight plagues and order them differently.

Biblical plague

> It is not easy to be rational when faced with a plague and mythical accounts, often focusing on divine retribution and the supernatural, are common.
>
> Professor Roger S. Wotton, *The Ten Plagues of Egypt*

The hand of God, obviously, is everywhere throughout the Bible. God was, as noted, a jealous god; during his affliction of the Egyptians with the ten plagues he was at pains to demonstrate that 'there is none like me in all the earth' (Exodus 9:14). It may surprise, indeed anger, some to know that God, as with the gods of neighbouring cultures, can be identified as an inveterate wager of biological warfare, a bioterrorist, no less. Plagues, as we have noted, are one of the constituents of that unholy trinity that is made up of disease, famine and war. The Hebrew people living in Egypt had been suffering terribly for 400 years under the tyrannical rule of the Pharaoh (as in *The Haggadah* – Hebrew: הַגָּדָה,). Moses asked the Pharaoh to let them return to their homelands in Canaan, but he refused.

So, ten devastating plagues were inflicted on the Egyptians over a ten-month period as an unrelenting expression of God's displeasure towards the Egyptians. They are 'signs and marvels' given by God to answer Pharaoh's taunt that he does not know or recognise Yahweh: 'Who is the Lord, that I should obey his voice to let Israel go? I know not the Lord, neither will I let Israel go.' To which God retorts: 'The Egyptians shall know that I am the Lord.' These 'marvels' are usually referred to as 'plagues' sent from the God of Israel, as undeniable proof that the 'one true God' was far greater than all of the multiple gods of the Egyptian pantheon. The plagues were intended to dissuade Pharaoh from his intractable policy of detaining the Israelites and are, at the same time, precisely targeted at the contemporary Egyptian deity that corresponds most closely with the plague in question.

Herodotus puts the plague dates around 1570–50 BC, when Egypt was under the rule of the Hyksos (an Asiatic tribe), but there was no pharaoh until Ahmose I (1550–25 BC) rebelled and overthrew the invaders. About this time, apocalyptic rainstorms devastated much of Egypt, and were described on the Tempest Stele of Ahmose I. These have been attributed to short-term climatic changes caused by the Thera volcanic eruption on Santorini around 1630 BC. Trevisanato (2005) suggests this eruption was also the trigger event for the plagues.

The plagues incubating in God's biological warfare arsenal were as follows:

- **Turning river waters to blood** [*Dam*]: Ex. 7:14–24; *target deity*: Hapi – Egyptian God of the Nile, a water bearer. First, the waters of the land of Egypt were turned into blood. Moses walked with Aaron to the river bank where Aaron raised his staff, struck the waters, and changed them into streams of blood. All the people of Egypt even Pharaoh himself observed this miracle; they saw the fish die as the blood flowed over the land, and they turned with disgust from the noisome smell of the sacred river. It was impossible for them now to drink the waters of the Nile, famous as it was for its delicious taste; and they tried to dig deep into the ground for water. Unfortunately for the Egyptians, not only the floods of the Nile but all the waters of Egypt, wherever they were, had turned to blood. The fish died in the rivers and lakes, and for a whole week man and beast suffered terrible thirst. Unfortunately for God the Pharaoh's court magicians were partially able to duplicate this miracle of turning water to blood, leaving Pharaoh unimpressed with this great wonder from God.
- **Clogging up the Nile with frogs** [*Tzefardeia*]; Ex. 7:25–8:15: *target deity*: Heket – Egyptian Goddess of Fertility, Water, Renewal. Heket had the head of a frog. Aaron reached out over the waters of Egypt, and frogs swarmed out. God threatened, 'I will plague your whole country with frogs. The Nile will teem with frogs. They will come up into your palace and your bedroom and onto your bed, into the houses of your officials and on your people, and

into your ovens and kneading troughs.' Pharaoh was frightened by this, so he asked Moses and Aaron to pray to God to eliminate the plague, promising that he would immediately liberate the Jewish people. But as soon as the frogs disappeared, he broke his promise and refused to let the children of Israel go.

- **Despatching swarms of lice or gnats to plague man and beast**: [*Kirim*]; Ex. 8:16–19: *target deity*: Geb – Egyptian God of the Earth who ruled over the dust of the earth. Next God ordered Aaron to strike the dusty earth with his staff, and as soon as he did so all over Egypt insects crawled out from the dust to cover the land. Man and beast suffered untold misery from this terrible plague. The magicians of Pharaoh were at last humiliated, unable to compete with this power; they professed 'this is the finger of God'. But Pharaoh remained implacable and relentless in his determination to keep the children of Israel in bondage.

- **Wild animals roaming around**: [*Arov*] Ex. 8:16–28/ 8:20–32: the fourth plague involved hordes of wild animals roving all over the country, and destroying everything in their path. Only the province of Goshen where the children of Israel had settled was unaffected by this as well as from the other plagues. Again Pharaoh promised to let the Hebrews go out into the desert on condition that they did not wander too far. Moses prayed to God, and the wild animals disappeared. But as soon as they had gone, Pharaoh again withdrew his promise. Differing sources use either 'wild animals' or 'flies'. If flies, then the target deity is Khepri – God of creation, movement of the Sun, rebirth who had the head of a fly.

- God said: 'Let my people, the Israelites, go, so that they may worship me. If you refuse to release them and continue to hold them back, the hand of the Lord will bring a terrible plague on the livestock in your fields – on your horses and donkeys and camels and on your cattle and sheep and goats.' [*Dever*] Exodus 9, 1–7. *Target deity:* Hathor – Egyptian goddess of love and protection. Usually this goddess was depicted with the head of a cow. Her particular plague promised famine, travel disruption and military and civil transportation issues for the Egyptians. When they saw their majestic horses, the pride of Egypt, perish they were devastated; when all the cattle were stricken at the word of Moses; and when the animals died from plague – the ones which they considered as gods. The situation was made worse when they saw that the Israelites' animals remained unscathed. Yet Pharaoh stood firm, and would not let the Israelites go.

- Perhaps one of the more painful plagues for the Egyptians involved boils: [*Shechin*] Ex. 9:8–12: target deity: Isis – goddess of Medicine and Peace. The Lord said to Moses and Aaron, 'Take handfuls of soot from a furnace and have Moses toss it into the air in the presence of Pharaoh. It will turn into a fine dust over the whole land of Egypt, and festering boils will erupt on men and animals throughout the land.' This plague renders the people 'unclean'.

- A mighty destructive thunderstorm of hail and fire: Ex. 9:13–35: [*Barad*]; target deity: Nut – goddess of the sky. Now Moses told Pharaoh that a violent hailstorm the like of which had never been seen, would devastate the land; no living thing, no tree, no greenery was to escape its fury undamaged; they will fill your houses and those of all your officials and all the Egyptians – something neither your fathers nor your forefathers have ever seen from the day they settled in this land till now. Some Egyptians took this on board but the reckless and the stubborn left their cattle with their slaves in the fields. When Moses stretched out his staff, the hail poured down with unprecedented violence; deafening thunder rumbled over the earth, and lightning split the heavens asunder, running like fire along the ground. The hail did its destructive worst: man and beast in its raging path died instantly; vegetation was scattered to the wind, and trees lay shattered on the ground. But the Israelites' land of Goshen, untouched by the ravages of the storm, bloomed like a garden amidst the general devastation. However, the crops that were destroyed by the hail were flax and barley – not the staples of the Egyptian diet, but used more specifically for their clothing and libations. This would make their life uncomfortable, but as far as affecting their food supply, the wheat still survived and gave the Egyptians still another chance to turn to 'the One True God', and renounce their own Egyptian gods and goddesses. Pharaoh sent for Moses and finally (pretended to) acknowledge his sins (Exodus 9:27). 'I have sinned this time. The Lord is the righteous One, and I and my people are the guilty ones. Beg the Lord, and let this be enough of God's thunder and hail, and I will let you go.' Moses replied: 'When I leave the city, I will spread my hands to the Lord. The thunder will stop, and there will be no more hail so that you know that the land is the Lord's.' And it happened just as Moses had said: the storm abated – but Pharaoh remained adamant.

- **Locusts** [*Arbeh*]: Ex. 10:1–20; target deity: Seth – god of storms and chaos. When Moses and Aaron next came before Pharaoh, he seemed somewhat conciliatory and asked them who was involved in the worship the Israelites wanted to hold in the desert. When they told him that everyone without exception, young and old, men and women, and animals, were to attend, Pharaoh suggested that only the men should go, and that the women and children, as well as all their possessions, should remain in Egypt. Moses and Aaron declined the offer at which Pharaoh got angry and ordered them to leave his palace. This they did but not before Moses warned him to expect new and unprecedented suffering. But Pharaoh remained unrelenting even though his advisers advised compliance. As soon as Moses left the palace, he raised his arms towards heaven and an east wind brought swarms of locusts into Egypt, blotting out the sun, and devouring everything green that had escaped the hail and previous plagues. Never in the history of the world had there been such a devastating plague of locusts as this one. It brought complete ruin upon Egypt, already thoroughly ravaged by the previous catastrophes. Again Pharaoh sent for Moses and Aaron, and implored them to pray to God to stop the plague. Moses complied, and God sent a strong west wind that drove the locusts into the sea. With normality came a return of Pharaoh's obstinacy, and he refused to liberate the people of Israel.

- **Three days of complete darkness**: [*Choshech*]; *target deity:* Ra – the Sun god; Ex. 10:21–29: The ninth plague saw Egypt enveloped in an inky and impenetrable blanket of darkness which blotted out all light. The Egyptians were terrified and stayed glued to the spot wherever they stood or sat. Only in Goshen was there light. But not all of the Jews survived this plague: some wanted to be seen as Egyptians rather than as members of the Hebrew race, and who tried to assimilate themselves; they did not want to leave Egypt. These people died during the time of darkness. The sun, the most revered god in Egypt other than Pharaoh himself, was emasculated, he gave no light. The Lord thus showed that he had control over the sun and had ultimate power over life and death. The psychological and religious impact would have had a profound influence on the Egyptians at this point. Darkness was a representation of death, judgment and hopelessness.

- **Death of the firstborn children**: [*Makkat Bechorot*]; *target deity:* Pharaoh – The Ultimate Power of Egypt. Ex. 11:1–12:36. Again Pharaoh tried to strike a deal with Moses and Aaron, bidding them depart with all their people, but leaving their flocks and herds behind as a pledge and to replace the innumerable domestic animals lost in the previous plagues. This was totally unacceptable as the animals were to be used as the actual sacrifice to the Lord. In any event Moses and Aaron would accept nothing less than complete freedom for the men, women, and children, and declared that they were taking all their belongings with them. Pharaoh became angry again and ordered Moses and Aaron to leave and never come back: if they did they would die: 'Get thee from me, take heed to thyself, see my face no more; for in that day thou seest my face thou shalt die.' Moses replied that it would not be necessary for them to see Pharaoh, for God would send one more plague over Egypt, after which Pharaoh would give his unconditional permission for the children of Israel to leave Egypt. Every firstborn son in Egypt will die, from the firstborn son of Pharaoh, who sits on the throne, to the firstborn of the slave girl, who is at her hand mill, and all the firstborn of the cattle as well. There will be loud wailing throughout Egypt – worse than there has ever been or ever will be again. A bitter cry would sweep Egypt, and all the Egyptians would be gripped with terror, lest they all die. Then Pharaoh himself would meet the leaders of the Hebrews, and beg them to leave Egypt immediately. Moses and Aaron left a Pharaoh who was seething with rage. The children of Israel and their livestock were, of course, exempted by virtue of the Passover Sacrifice named after the time when the Lord 'passed over the houses of the Israelites in Egypt'. Midnight of the fourteenth to the fifteenth of Nissan came, and God, as predicted, struck all firstborn in the land of Egypt, from the firstborn of King Pharaoh, down to the firstborn of a captive languishing in a dungeon somewhere, and all the firstborn of the cattle, exactly as Moses had warned. There was a loud and bitter wail in each house where a loved one lay fatally stricken. Then Pharaoh called for Moses and Aaron and said to them: 'Arise, go out from among my people, both you and the children of Israel; and go, serve the Lord as you have said; and take your flocks and your herds, as you have said, and go, and bless me also.' Finally then, the pride and resolve of the refractory Pharaoh was broken.

'Plague', of course, is used in a generic sense in the Plagues of Egypt but clearly, they are plagues of a biological, medical, entomological, agricultural or veterinary nature. Although the plagues were not precise historical events, they do at one level illustrate quite vividly early religious beliefs relating to sin and punishment, judgement, heaven and hell. On another level, some scholars believe the plagues to be explained away by climatological and geological events and as metaphors for natural disaster caused by climate change over a period of time and focused on the city of Pi-Ramesses in the Nile delta. As an example, the reign of Ramesses II (1279 BC–1213 BC) was witness to an unusually warm and wet period followed by a marked drop in temperature, which led the Nile to dry up and become a semi-stagnant area of infertile mud flats around its delta; such conditions are ideal for the formation of algae called Burgundy Blood (*Oscillatoria rubescens*), which, when they die, stain the water red, taking on the appearance of blood. Another theory names *chromatiaceae* bacteria as the culprit. Whatever, the algae would have attracted lice and flies while causing the frogs to flee the river in search of new habitats; their absence would have allowed mosquitos to thrive while the three days of darkness could have been the consequence of volcanic activity in the region.

The messaging behind the Plagues of Egypt can also be found in Psalm 91, which reinforces the axiom that pestilence surely awaits the sinful or disobedient; indeed, this was the text that formed the basis of many a sermon during times of plague, epidemics and pandemics in the Christian world over centuries, giving an explanation and hope:

> Thou shalt not be afraid for the terror by night; nor for the arrow that flieth by day;
> Nor for the pestilence that walketh in darkness; nor for the destruction that wasteth at noonday.
> A thousand shall fall at thy side, and ten thousand at thy right hand; but it shall not come nigh thee.
> Only with thine eyes shalt thou behold and see the reward of the wicked.
>
> [King James Version (KJV)]

Renounce sin and follow the Lord and you will escape plague: only those who don't won't.

The Ark of the Covenant as plague vector

There are of course many other instances of biological warfare and bioterrorism in the pages of the Bible. 1 Samuel 4 tells that in 1141 BC the Israelites lost 40,000 men in a battle with the Philistines; not to be outdone, they orchestrated another battle, this time parading their precious Ark of the Covenant as a saviour. The Ark was the large sacred chest containing the tablets of the Mosaic Law – the Ten Commandments – and signifying to the people of Israel that God was with them. It was kept in the most sacred part of the temple in Jerusalem, which was completed in 957 BC.

The Philistines were crestfallen and morale sank to an all-time low, remembering as they did what befell the Egyptians when the 'Mighty Gods smote the Egyptians with all the plagues in the wilderness'. This, however, had the opposite effect and the Israelites promptly lost a further 30,000 men at the hands of the Philistines. Worse still, the Philistines captured the Ark from the Israelites and set it up in the temple of Dagon, a major Philistine deity, in front of his statue, in the city of Ashdod. The following morning, the Philistines found Dagon facedown in front of the Ark. Restoring the idol to its rightful position, the priests left, only to return to find Dagon on the ground again with his head and hands cut off. For their troubles, the Philistines endured an outbreak of 'tumours' (Hebrew *ophal*) or haemorrhoids (*emerods*), an affliction of their 'secret parts', which followed them relentlessly as they moved with the Ark from city to city (1 Samuel 5 and 6): Ashron, Gath and Ekron over seven months. Stirrup points out that the 'severity of the punishments increases through the passage': tumours in Ashdod (vv. 6–8), extensive tumours and panic in Gath, which had volunteered to take on the Ark (vv. 9,10a), and tumours on those who did not die and deathly panic in Ekron, which was 'volunteered' to take the Ark (vv. 10b-12). The text explicitly ascribes the plague to 'God's hand' (1 Samuel 5:6) although some add that 'mice sprang up in the midst of their country'. Nevertheless, it did not take long for the Philistines to convince themselves that the Ark was the vector for this ongoing disease disaster, so, seven months after its capture, the leaders generously decided to return it to the Israelites along with a 'trespass offering' of five golden tumours and five golden mice (*akbar*), representing the five Philistine rulers. But, soon after in Beth-shemesh, seventy Israelites died 'because they had looked into the Ark of the Lord', while a further 50,000 later succumbed throughout Israel. Some scholars have concluded that the outbreak was bubonic plague, evidenced by its associated *emerods* or buboes.

Now, it is quite plausible that the Philistines delivering the Ark transmitted the epidemic quite naturally. But there is a tradition of stories about diseases that emerge when a sealed container is opened, and, given our knowledge relating to surface transmission, it may be that the Ark contained fomites, such as clothing or insects, that carried the infectious agent, or perhaps some type of insect that acted as a vector and went on to infect rodents in Philistine territory? Interestingly, when the Ark was finally returned to the great temple in Jerusalem, the Israelites avoided direct contact and carried it suspended by poles that were passed through two rings. The Israelite, Uzzah, was driving the cart that carried the Ark when the oxen stumbled, causing the Ark to tilt; he naturally steadied the Ark with his hand but this was in direct violation of the divine law relating to touching holy things, and he was immediately killed by the Lord for his transgression (2 Samuel 6:3–8; Numbers 4:15 and 1 Chronicles 13:7–11): a biblical explanation for surface transmission?

Some scholars argue that the plague or plagues were secreted by Solomon in a secure location in anticipation of an eventual military invasion. The ancient legend about the sealing of the 'demons of the plague' and its deposit in the temple of Jerusalem appears in Solomon's will and in Hebrew, Gnostic and Greek texts between the first and fourth centuries AD. Solomon apparently convened a motley group of spirits from disease and disaster and forced them to collaborate in the construction of his temple. He then deposited them in copper containers and sealed them with silver, stored them in large jars and buried them among the foundations of the temple.

This, like the Plagues of Egypt and the infections caused by the Ark, raised the idea of contagion as a weapon; in Solomon's will he predicted that when his temple was destroyed by the king of the Chaldeans, the spirits of the plague would be released. Indeed, in 586 BC, Nebuchadnezzar plundered and burned the temple in Jerusalem. 'During the looting', the invaders found the copper vessels and, believing them to be full of treasures, broke their seals. At that moment, the pestilential demons were unleashed and 'harassed the men again'.

But that was nothing compared to what was to come. Many good things awaited the Israelites ('You will be blessed in the city and blessed in the country. ... Your basket and your kneading trough will be blessed') so long as they 'fully obey the Lord your God and carefully follow all his commands I give you today'. However, Deuteronomy 28 has a chilling warning for non-compliance, with God threatening yet more plague in a resumption of his role as bioterrorist:

> If thou wilt not observe to do all the words of this law that are written in this book, that thou mayest fear this glorious and fearful name, the Lord Thy God, then the Lord will make thy plagues 'wonderful', and the plagues of thy seed, even great plagues, and of long continuance, and sore sicknesses. Moreover he will bring upon thee all the diseases of Egypt, which thou wast afraid of; and they shall cleave unto thee. Also every sickness, and every plague, which is not written in the book of this law, them will the Lord bring upon thee, until thou be destroyed.

In short, God had fifty-four or so plagues, curses and other misfortunes lined up for delivery to recalcitrant, disobedient Israelites. They include:

- You will be cursed in the city and cursed in the country.
- Your basket and your kneading trough will be cursed.
- The fruit of your womb will be cursed, and the crops of your land, and the calves of your herds and the lambs of your flocks.
- You will be cursed when you come in and cursed when you go out.
- The LORD will turn the rain of your country into dust and powder; it will come down from the skies until you are destroyed.
- The LORD will cause you to be defeated before your enemies. You will come at them from one direction but flee from them in seven, and you will become a thing of horror to all the kingdoms on earth.
- Your carcasses will be food for all the birds of the air and the beasts of the earth, and there will be no one to frighten them away.
- The LORD will afflict you with the boils of Egypt and with tumours, festering sores and the itch, from which you cannot be cured.
- The LORD will afflict you with madness, blindness and confusion of mind.

- At midday you will grope about like a blind man in the dark. You will be unsuccessful in everything you do; day after day you will be oppressed and robbed, with no one to rescue you.
- You will be pledged to be married to a woman, but another will take her and ravish her. You will build a house, but you will not live in it. You will plant a vineyard, but you will not even begin to enjoy its fruit.
- Your ox will be slaughtered before your eyes, but you will eat none of it. Your donkey will be forcibly taken from you and will not be returned. Your sheep will be given to your enemies, and no one will rescue them.
- Your sons and daughters will be given to another nation, and you will wear out your eyes watching for them day after day, powerless to lift a hand.
- The LORD will afflict your knees and legs with painful boils that cannot be cured, spreading from the soles of your feet to the top of your head.
- You will become a thing of horror and an object of scorn and ridicule to all the nations where the LORD will drive you.
- You will sow much seed in the field but you will harvest little, because locusts will devour it.
- You will plant vineyards and cultivate them but you will not drink the wine or gather the grapes, because worms will eat them.
- In hunger and thirst, in nakedness and dire poverty, you will serve the enemies the LORD sends against you. He will put an iron yoke on your neck until he has destroyed you.
- Because of the suffering that your enemy will inflict on you during the siege, you will eat the fruit of the womb, the flesh of the sons and daughters the LORD your God has given you.
- The most gentle and sensitive woman among you – so sensitive and gentle that she would not venture to touch the ground with the sole of her foot – will begrudge the husband she loves and her own son or daughter the afterbirth from her womb and the children she bears. For she intends to eat them secretly during the siege and in the distress that your enemy will inflict on you in your cities.
- You will live in constant suspense, filled with dread both night and day, never sure of your life.
- In the morning you will say, 'If only it were evening!' and in the evening, 'If only it were morning!' – because of the terror that will fill your hearts and the sights that your eyes will see.
- The LORD will send you back in ships to Egypt on a journey I said you should never make again. There you will offer yourselves for sale to your enemies as male and female slaves, but no one will buy you.

Not much hope there then for anyone contemplating disobedience or disrespect towards God; the penalties run the whole gamut of punishment – social, psychological, political and military – but a good number constitute biological terrorism in one form or another.

To these we can add a number of other instances of God's biological warfare – terrorism against man:

- God threatens the people of Israel if they turn against the Lord. Part of God's judgment included plague (Leviticus 26:25):

    And I will bring the sword on you to avenge the breaking of the covenant. When you withdraw into your cities, I will send a plague among you, and you will be given into enemy hands.

- Numbers 21: 6,8 and Deuteronomy 8:15 both refer to a fiery serpent, possibly Guinea worm, which causes dracunculiasis, a parasitic infection contracted by drinking infected water, as detected in mummies from the period.

    Numbers: Then the LORD sent venomous snakes among them; they bit the people and many Israelites died. The people came to Moses and said, 'We sinned when we spoke against the LORD and against you. Pray that the LORD will take the snakes away from us.' So Moses prayed for the people. The LORD said to Moses, 'Make a snake and put it up on a pole; anyone who is bitten can look at it and live.'

The Deuteronomy piece describes the wilderness of Paran with its fiery serpents and scorpions, which bit the Israelites.

- God despatched a three-day plague to exterminate 70,000 men after King David sinned by holding a census of the people of Israel (2 Samuel 24:10–17) against the advice of Joab and his own senior officers. Ten months later, David had his numbers but God was not pleased and gave him three choices, reported to him by the prophet Gad, David's seer:

    'Thus says the LORD: I offer you three things; choose one of them for yourself, that I may do it to you.' So Gad came to David and told him; and he said to him, 'Shall seven years of famine come to you in your land? Or shall you flee three months before your enemies, while they pursue you? Or shall there be three days' plague in your land? Now consider and see what answer I should take back to Him who sent me.'

David chose the three days of plague. In any event, he had to succumb to God's anger: If he had chosen war, he was in no danger, because there was already an ordinance preventing him from going to battle. Had he chosen famine, his own wealth would have ensured his and his own family's support. But he chose the pestilence, which would have exposed him and his household to its ravages equally with the lowliest of his subjects.

- Amos prophesied that God would send judgments against Israel, including plagues similar to those endured in Egypt (Amos 3:1,7, 4:10, 5:64:10):

  'I sent plagues among you as I did to Egypt. I killed your young men with the sword, along with the horses I captured. I filled your nostrils with the stench of your camps, yet you have not returned to me,' declares the Lord.

- God sent several judgments against the nation of Judah, including a plague, when he sent King Nebuchadnezzar to sack Jerusalem (Jeremiah 21:7, 24:10, 29:17):

  After that, declares the LORD, I will give Zedekiah king of Judah, his officials and the people in this city who survive the plague, sword and famine, into the hands of Nebuchadnezzar king of Babylon and to their enemies who want to kill them. He will put them to the sword; he will show them no mercy or pity or compassion ... I will send the sword, the famine and the pestilence upon them until they are destroyed from the land which I gave to them and their forefathers.

In I Kings 6. (35-40), Solomon, on the occasion of the dedication of the temple in Jerusalem when the Ark of the Covenant is brought there, lists the various plagues that God inflicts on man:

When there is famine in the land, pestilence or blight or mildew, locusts or grasshoppers; when their enemy besieges them in the land of their cities; whatever plague or whatever sickness there is; whatever prayer, whatever supplication is made by anyone, or by all Your people Israel, when each one knows the plague of his own heart, and spreads out his hands towards this temple: then hear in heaven Your dwelling place, and forgive, and act, and give to everyone according to all his ways, whose heart You know (for You alone know the hearts of all the sons of men), that they may fear You all the days that they live in the land which You gave to our fathers.

Overall, there are almost 100 references to plague in the Bible, mainly in the Old Testament; the Bible writers use ancient Hebrew and Greek words for pestilence and plagues at least 127 times.

Deuteronomy 20 – the Rules of War

Deuteronomy 20 gives us some explicit rules on how war should be conducted.

- Genocide and ethnic cleansing:
    But when you take cities in the land that the Lord your God is giving you, you must kill everyone. You must completely destroy all the people – the Hittites, Amorites, Canaanites, Perizzites, Hivites, and Jebusites.
- The seizing of women (rape and enslavement), children and cattle:
    If the city refuses to make peace with you and fights against you, you should surround the city. And when the Lord your God lets you take the city, you must kill all the men in it. But you may take for yourselves the women, the children, the cattle, and everything else in the city. You may use all these things. The Lord your God has given these things to you.

Heinous as they are, each of these atrocities is deemed acceptable, endorsed by the writers and, presumably, their readers. However, there is one aspect of biological warfare that is strictly forbidden – the chopping down of fruit trees:

> When you are making war against a city, you might surround that city for a long time. You must not cut down the fruit trees around that city. You may eat the fruit from these trees, but you must not cut them down. These trees are not the enemy, so don't make war against them. But you may cut down the trees that you know are not fruit trees. You may use these trees to build weapons for making siege works against that city. You may use them until the city falls.
>
> (Trans. Bible League International)

This contrasts with the custom of other armies. For example, the Assyrians: when a city held out against them, they would usually withdraw and burn and destroy the harvest, the trees and the houses of the surrounding areas.

Pestilence and the Book of Revelation

> The horseman on the white horse was clad in a showy and barbarous attire. ... While his horse continued galloping, he was bending his bow in order to spread pestilence abroad. At his back swung the brass quiver filled with poisoned arrows, containing the germs of all diseases.
>
> Vicente Blasco Ibáñez (1916),
> *The Four Horsemen of the Apocalypse* (ch V)

It is impossible not to be struck by the ubiquity of references in the Bible to pestilence, specifically in its close association with war and famine. Cartwright and Biddiss describe this catastrophic coalition as follows according to Frederick Cartwright in his 1994 *Disease and History*:

> Pestilence, famine and war interact and produce a sequence. War drives the farmer from his fields and destroys his crops, destruction of the crops spells famine; the starved and weakened people fall easy victims to the onslaught of pestilence. All three are diseases. Pestilence is a disorder of the human. Famine results from disorders of plants and cattle, whether caused by inclement weather or more directly by insect or bacterial invasion. Even war may be regarded, though more arguably, as a form of mass psychotic disorder.

Famine had the added disadvantage of encouraging the stockpiling of food reserves in towns and villages, which, in turn, attracted plague-infected rodents.

The association of the three, of course, is given lurid and everlasting publicity by the Four Horsemen of the Apocalypse. The horsemen ride into our lives in the New Testament's final book, Revelation, as well as in the Old Testament's prophetic Book of Zechariah, and in the Book of Ezekiel, where they are named as agents of punishment from God. They have been firmly lodged in the recesses of our collective memory by believers and non-believers ever since.

For centuries, god-fearing people all around the globe, and in numerous religions, cultures and civilisations, have believed, and have been encouraged to believe, that their wars and everything that comes with them were holy (and justifiable) wars and, on the minus side, that famine and disease were just rewards for living a life of sin and defying their gods.

In the three septets that symbolically depict the course of history in the Book of Revelation, the seals (6.1–8.5), the trumpets (8.6–11.19) and the bowls (15.1–25), the main protagonists are angels who are agents of God, enablers of God's wrath, usually dispensing death and carnage. Therefore, we can see how plagues and afflictions are seen as godsent punishments for humankind. As Peerbolte remarks (2021):

> They are usually described as elements from the divinely ordained sequences of seven phenomena that strike the earth. As will become clear, the apocalyptic tradition of Western Christianity is thus firmly rooted in the idea that plagues and disasters are part of the cosmic scheme and thus do not contribute to but confirm God's rule.

The first four seals introduce the four riders on horses, who cause perdition and slaughter, the fourth of whom is Death itself. Devastation and perdition continue right through the sixth seal.

Revelation 8: the Seven Trumpets

Seven trumpets are sounded, one at a time, to herald apocalyptic events seen by John of Patmos (Revelation 1:9) in his vision (Revelation 1:1). The seven trumpets are sounded by seven angels and the events that follow are described in detail from Revelation Chapters 8–11:

- The first angel of the seven sounded his trumpet: 'And hail and fire followed, mingled with blood, and they were thrown to the earth' burning a third of the Earth's vegetation, scorching all green grass. (Revelation 8. 7)
- The second angel sounded his trumpet: 'And something like a great mountain burning with fire was thrown in the sea, and a third of the sea became blood' killing a third of everything in the ocean, sinking ships. (Revelation 8. 8–9)
- The third angel sounded: And a great star, named 'Wormwood', fell from heaven poisoning fresh water from rivers and water springs. Many died. (Revelation 8, 10–11)
- The fourth angel sounded: The sun, the moon and stars are struck, so that a third of their light diminished to the point of complete darkness for a third of a day, even during the night. (Revelation 8. 12)
- The fifth trumpet prompts a personified star to fall from heaven. The star is given the key to the bottomless pit. After opening it, the smoke that rises out of the pit darkens the air and blocks the sunlight. Then, from out of the smoke, locusts are unleashed: scorpion-tailed warhorses that have a man's face with lion's teeth. Their hair is long and they fly with locust-like wings. They wear golden crowns and are protected with iron breastplates. They are commanded by their king, Abaddon, to torment anyone who does not have the seal of God on their forehead, by using their scorpion-like tails. It is also made clear to them that they must not kill anyone during the five months of torment. (Revelation 8, 12; 9, 1–12)

Robert Witham, a Catholic commentator, in his *Annotations on the New Testament*, in 1733 suggested that the locusts may have represented the invasion of the Goths and 'those barbarous People' who threatened the Roman Empire during the reign of Decius (r. AD 249 to 251). Alternatively, the locusts may have represented the Jewish heretics who denied Christ: Theodotus, Praxeas, Noetus, Paul of Samosata, Sabellius, and Arius.

- The sixth, the 'second woe', is where four angels are released from the 'great river Euphrates'. They command a force of two hundred million mounted troops whose horses expel plagues of fire, smoke, and brimstone from their mouths. The mounted horsemen wore breastplates with the colour of fire, hyacinth, and brimstone. The horses have a lion's head and their tails look like a serpent with a head. The plagues emanating from the horses will kill a third of all mankind. (Revelation 9. 13–21)
- The sound of the seventh trumpet signals the 'third woe'. This is the final trumpet and the final woe. Loud voices in Heaven will say: 'The kingdom of the world has become the kingdom of our Lord and of His Messiah, and He will reign forever and ever.'

The first six trumpet blasts are a timely wake-up call to the sinners on Earth and a siren for their repentance. Each blast escalates the disaster visited on humankind while the trumpet is used to build anticipation and tells the reader that an alert, announcement, or warning is about to be made.

A Preterist interpretation sees these blasts as war trumpets against an apostate Israel and that they correspond to events in the Jewish Wars against Rome. For example, the second trumpet is Rome depicted as a mountain, symbolic for great nations in the Old Testament, and its destruction of Galilee, and the Sea of Galilee becoming full of blood and dead bodies.

Revelation 11:6 reads:

These witnesses have power to shut the sky so that no rain will fall during the days of their prophecy, and power to turn the waters into blood and to strike the earth with every kind of plague as often as they wish.

In Revelation 15, John of Patmos writes of seven angels with seven plagues that deliver the wrath of god, the last plagues ever to occur. He states that until the plagues are complete no one can enter the Temple of God. The seven plagues are described in Revelation 16.

Here we learn of a set of plagues in bowls representing apocalyptic events that were seen in the vision of the Revelation of Jesus Christ, by John of Patmos. Seven angels are given seven bowls brimming with God's anger, each consisting of judgements replete with the wrath of God. These seven bowls of God's wrath are poured out on the wicked and the followers of the Antichrist after the sounding of the seven trumpets. To some degree, they correspond with the ten Plagues of Egypt. Peerbolte (2021) again:

> The underlying assumption of this description seems to be that God is rightly vengeful with regard to his creation and that divine action consists of executing revenge by the plagues brought by the angels. Seen in this perspective, Revelation contains an intensely dark view of human history, and seems to push the reader into embracing this dark view and thus accepting the fact that suffering and plagues are part and parcel of the human condition. Still … it seems that the plagues brought by the angels are expected to usher in the eschatological era in which all this misery is overturned. It is not by accident that the climax of the book describes a New Jerusalem in which God will live directly among humankind and will even wipe off the tears of humans' eyes.

- First Bowl
  The first angel poured out his bowl on the earth: injurious and painful sores (possibly boils or carbuncles) were inflicted on the people who bore the mark of the beast and worshipped its image.

- Second Bowl
  The sea turns to blood when the second angel poured out his bowl on the sea, and it turned into the blood of a corpse; and every living creature in the sea died.

- Third Bowl
  Then the third angel poured out his bowl on the rivers and springs of water, and they too became blood. And I heard the angel of the waters say:
  'You are righteous, oh Lord, the one who is and who was and who is to be', because you have judged these things. For they have shed the blood of saints and prophets, and you have given them blood to drink. For 'it is their just reward'.
  And I heard another from the altar saying, 'Even so, Lord God Almighty, true and righteous are your judgements.'

- Fourth Bowl
  The fourth angel pours out the contents of his bowl and the sun unleashes a catastrophic heatwave to scorch the people with fire. The incorrigibly wicked refuse to repent while they blaspheme the name of God.

- Fifth Bowl
  When the fifth bowl is emptied a pitch darkness overwhelms the kingdom of the beast. People gnawed their tongues in anguish and cursed the God of heaven for their pain and sores. The wicked continue to stubbornly defame the name of God while refusing to repent and glorify God.

- Sixth Bowl
  When the sixth bowl is poured out, the great river Euphrates dries up so that the kings of the east might cross over in preparation for battle. And I saw, coming out of the mouth of the dragon and out of the mouth of the beast and out of the mouth of the false prophet, three unclean spirits like frogs. For they are demonic spirits, performing signs, who go abroad to the kings of the whole world, to assemble them for battle on the great day of God the Almighty. ('Behold, I am coming like a thief! Blessed is the one who stays awake, keeping his garments on, that he may not go about naked and be seen exposed!') And they assembled them at the place that in Hebrew is called Armageddon.

- Seventh Bowl
  The seventh angel poured out his bowl into the air, and a loud voice boomed out of the temple, from the throne, saying, 'It is done!' And there were flashes of lightning, rumblings, peals of thunder, and a great earthquake such as there had never been since man walked the earth, so great was that earthquake. The magnificent city was split into three parts, and the cities of the nations fell, and God remembered Babylon the great, to make her drain the cup of the wine of the fury of his wrath. And every island fled away, and no mountains could be found. And great hailstones, about one hundred pounds each, fell from heaven on people; and they cursed God for the plague of the hail, because the plague was so severe.

Revelation 18:8 : 'Therefore her [the city of Babylon] plagues will come in one day – death and grief and famine – and she will be consumed by fire, for mighty is the Lord God who judges her. Babylon is "the great prostitute", the great city who rules over the kings of the earth' (Revelation 17:18).

Plague is also mentioned in the Book of Hosea 13 in the Hebrew Bible: 'I will ransom them from the power of Sheol; I will redeem them from Death. Where O Death, are your plagues? Where, O Sheol, is your sting?'

Jesus warned in Matthew 24:

> Take heed that no man deceive you. For many shall come in my name, saying, I am Christ; and shall deceive many. And you shall hear of wars and rumours of wars: see that you be not troubled: for all these things must come to pass, but the end is not yet. For nation shall rise against nation, and kingdom against kingdom: and there shall be famines, and pestilences, and earthquakes, in various places. All these are the beginnings of sorrows.

Compare Luke 21:10–12:

> Then He said to them, 'Nation will rise against nation, and kingdom against kingdom. And there will be great earthquakes in various places, and famines and pestilences; and there will be fearful sights and great signs from heaven. But before all these things, they will lay their hands on you and persecute you, delivering you up to the synagogues and prisons. You will be brought before kings and rulers for My name's sake.

On one occasion, God uses Satan to deliver his biological attack: Job was afflicted with a terrible disease – an attack by Satan that was sanctioned by God which the Scriptures also make clear was not a judgment for Job's unrepented sins, as he was 'blameless, upright, fearing God and turning away from evil' (Job 1:1). Satan uses this and other attacks on Job and his family to divert Job away from God. Yet God uses these traumas to bring Job closer to Himself.

On the other hand, the Book of Numbers reveals that Miriam – the sister of Moses – was inflicted with a terrible, infectious disease as a judgment because of her unrepentant sins against God. The text tells us that 'the anger of the Lord burned' against the disobedience of many Israelites, including Miriam, and that Moses had to intercede in prayer for their healing (Numbers 12:1–15).

Similar stories occur at 2 Kings 5:15 (Naaman, the commander of the Syrian army) and with cases of Hansen's Disease (leprosy): Matthew 8:1–4 and Luke 17: 11–19.

On a larger, national scale, Leviticus and Deuteronomy have much to say about how to cope with pestilence and plagues when they come. Not surprisingly, repentance, atonement and turning back to God are the key directives. Yet the Lord also instructs the nation of Israel on personal hygiene and social distancing in combating infectious diseases such as Hansen's disease, as found in Leviticus chapters 13-15.

Numbers 16:41-50 tells how:

The Lord spoke to Moses, saying, 'Get away from among this congregation, that I may consume them instantly.' Moses said to Aaron ... 'Make atonement for them, for wrath has gone forth from the Lord, the plague has begun.' Then Aaron took it as Moses had spoken, and ran into the midst of the assembly, for behold, the plague had begun among the people. So, he put on the incense and made atonement for the people. He took his stand between the dead and the living, so that the plague was checked. But those who died by the plague were 14,700.

Numbers 25:1-9 tells how:

While Israel remained at Shittim, the people began to play the harlot with the daughters of Moab. For they invited the people to the sacrifices of their gods, and the people ate and bowed down to their gods. So Israel joined themselves to Baal of Peor, and the Lord was angry against Israel. Those who died by the plague were 24,000.

In the Book of Samuel 1: 5–6, God sent a plague against the Philistines living in and around Gaza due to their constant and unrepentant sin. 'He smote the men of the city, both young and old, so that tumours broke out on them.' In 2 Samuel, we read how David sinned and 'the anger of the Lord burned against Israel' (24:1). 'So the Lord sent a pestilence upon Israel from the morning until the appointed time, and 70,000 men of the people from Dan to Beersheba died.' Jeremiah 28:7–8 has a similar threat, while Ezekiel 5: 5–12 is nothing short of apocalyptic in its warning to other cities and nations not to follow a recalcitrant Jerusalem:

This is Jerusalem; I have set her at the centre of the nations, with lands around her. But she has rebelled against My ordinances more wickedly than the nations and against My statutes more than the lands which surround her; for they have rejected My ordinances and have not walked in My statutes. ... One third of you will die by plague or be consumed by famine among you, one third will fall by the sword around you, and one third I will scatter to every wind, and I will unsheathe a sword behind them. ... So, it will be a reproach, a reviling, a warning and an object of horror to the nations who surround you when I execute judgments against you in anger, wrath and raging rebuke. ... Moreover, I will send on you famine and wild beasts, and they will bereave you of children; plague and bloodshed also will pass through you, and I will bring the sword on you.

The Hebrew prophet Ezekiel warned the nation of Judah time and time again that judgments of plagues and pestilences were coming (see Ezekiel 6:11–12, 7:15, 12:16, 14:19, 14:21). Ezekiel 28:20–24 describes the same fate for a disobedient Sidon.

Israel gets more dire warnings of plague and pestilence in Habakkuk 1:5, 2:1–2, 3:1–2, 5, 13.

Clearly, biblical plague frequently forms part of God's judgment against sin. Sometimes, God sent plagues or pestilences against unbelievers as, for example, when Egypt enslaved and oppressed the people of Israel. At other times, God delivered a plague against his own people to judge their sin. God sent many prophets to the people of Judah, but they still did not reject sin. So Jeremiah reports God's word when he said, 'Though they fast, I will not hear their cry, and though they offer burnt offering and grain offering, I will not accept them. But I will consume them by the sword, by famine, and by pestilence' (Jeremiah 14:12).

Two further examples of biological warfare from the Bible which are somewhat marginal feature Samson, he of the long hair and Delilah. Samson did not always use orthodox weapons: when he once encountered a frenzied roaring lion, he had no weapons at all, so, resorting to bare hands and brute strength, he tore the lion apart as if it was a young goat (Judges 14:6). On another occasion, he picked up the jawbone of a donkey and, using it as a club, slew 1,000 Philistines with it (Judges 15:15).

Chapter 4

Rome and her Enemies

Some Romans were implacably opposed to the prosecution of biological warfare, believing it to be contrary to Rome's noble rules of war and the revered practices of the ancestors, the *mos maiorum*. For example, in the *De Officiis* (1, 34-36), Cicero (106 BC–43 BC) asserts, regarding war generally, that:

> The only excuse, therefore, for going to war is that we may live in peace unharmed; and when the victory is won, we should spare those who have not been blood-thirsty and barbarous in their warfare. For instance, our forefathers actually admitted to full rights of citizenship the Tusculans, Acquians, Volscians, Sabines, and Hernicians, but they razed Carthage and Numantia to the ground ... the rights of war must be strictly observed. For since there are two ways of settling a dispute: first, by discussion; second, by physical force (*unum per disceptationem alterum per vim*), and since the former is characteristic of man, the latter of the brute, we must resort to force only in case we may not avail ourselves of discussion ... (*illud proprium sit hominis, hoc beluarum*). We should always strive to secure a peace that shall not admit of guile. ... Not only must we show consideration for those whom we have conquered by force of arms but we must also ensure protection to those who lay down their arms and throw themselves upon the mercy of our generals, even though the battering-ram has hammered at their walls.

Cicero could point to the magnanimity of the Romans when they defeated the Tuscans and other Italian cities. He deplored the sacking of Corinth, but saw this as necessary to avoid a future threat to Roman hegemony in the Mediterranean. Cicero's noble sentiments are echoed by Virgil a few decades later, when the ghost of Anchises prescribes to Aeneas in Book 6 of *The Aeneid* the Roman way of civilising; a cornerstone of this was sparing the conquered and crushing the proud (*parcere subiectis et debellare superbos*). Cicero was at pains to separate the men from the brutes. Plunder and booty were legitimate reasons for going to war, but fair play was important too.

Plague of one sort or another was present right at the very start of Roman civilisation when mythical Aeneas and his men, defeated in the Trojan War, were sailing around the Mediterranean looking for the place where they were to found Rome. Centuries later, in the very early days of Rome, Tullus Hostilius (r. 673–642 BC), the legendary third king of Rome, negligent in his duty to respect the gods, died in 642 BC of the plague. Towards the end of his reign, Rome was beset by bad omens: a shower of stones fell on the Alban Mount; a supernatural voice boomed out complaining that the Albans had failed to show due devotion, the consequence of which was that a plague struck Rome. Tullus was so intent on proceeding with war that he initially refused to stand down the army during the pestilence, thus causing much death, distress and enmity. Tullus himself, as noted, fell ill and died of the plague. Hubris got you nowhere in early Rome.

Livy mentions plague and pestilence a number of times, including: 437 BC at 4, 20, 9 (*pestilentia, inopia frugum*); 437 BC at 4, 21, 2 *(quia pestilentia populum invasit)*; 436 BC at 4, 21, 6 (*pestilentior inde annus*). In fact, between books 2 and 5, Livy records sixteen occasions when one disease or another infected Rome. For Livy, disease is comparable with war and famine as the worst evils that a state could suffer, and he writes that people attributed these calamities to *ira deum*, the wrath of the gods. There is, however, no evidence to suggest that these outbreaks did not develop through natural modes of transmission rather than through biological warfare.

Roughly three years before the plague at Athens, Livy tells us that Rome was similarly affected with a two-year long contagion (4, 25, 3–7). Was this possibly the same plague that later raged in Athens, brought to Greece on Carthaginian and other trade routes?

Poisoning the wine

Two different Carthaginian commanders, Himlico and Maharbal, defeated their enemies with poisoned wine. According to Polyaenus, Himilco had lost several battles when plague swept through his armies in 406 and 400 BC. With his army severely depleted, he devised a biological strategy to vanquish the Libyans in 396 BC. Himilco won the day by taking advantage of the Libyan fondness for wine. He poisoned jugs of the stuff in his own camp with mandragora (mandrake) and feigned retreat, leaving said jugs for the Libyans. The Carthaginians returned and killed the paralytic Libyans who had 'drunk greedily of the wine'.

In a repeat episode, Hannibal's cavalry officer, Maharbal, mixed up a large quantity of wine with pulverised mandrake root and left it in his camp.

Frontinus (2, 5) tells how the barbarians 'captured the camp and in a frenzy of delight greedily drank the drugged wine'. Maharbal came back and 'slaughtered them as they lay stretched out as if dead'.

The Autariatae, cannibals and Apollo's plague

The Autariatae were a highland Illyrian people who lived between the valleys of the Lim and the Tara, beyond the Accursed Mountains. When the Celts and Autariatae were at war the fourth-century BC historian Theopompus reported that the Celts 'drugged their own food and wine with debilitating herbs and left it all behind in their tents', then abandoned camp at night. The Autariatae, thinking the Celts had fled, 'seized the tents and freely enjoyed the wine and food'. The effect was immediate: they 'lay about powerless, undone by violent diarrhoea. The Celts returned and murdered them as they lay helpless.'

The Autariatae routinely murdered their weak and wounded to prevent frail individuals from falling into the hands of their enemies. This may have been motivated by the superstitious belief that their enemies, by drinking the blood of prisoners and by eating parts of their bodies containing their good attributes, would become even stronger and acquire a special power over the Autariatae.

Appian (95 BC–165 BC) records (1, 4) that the Autariatae were punished by Apollo for raiding the Pythian Oracle together with the Celtic Cimbri. This could explain why the Autariatae vanish from history after 310 BC:

> The Autarienses were overtaken with destruction by the vengeance of Apollo. Having joined Molostimus and the Celtic people called Cimbri in an expedition against the temple of Delphi, the greater part of them were destroyed by storm, hurricane, and lightning just before the sacrilege was committed. ... At last they fled from their homes, and as the plague still clung to them (and for fear of it nobody would receive them), they came, after a journey of twenty-three days, to a marshy and uninhabited district of the Getæ, where they settled near the Bastarnæ.

In 412 BC, it seems there was a flu pandemic. We hear of it from Hippocrates when it scourged northern Greece, and from Livy as it ravaged the city of Rome. Livy's account is interesting because it highlights two of the impacts that a pandemic can have on a population: people start to think more about the life-work balance and of their families; and how a pestilence can trigger famine:

After this year [412 BC–411 BC] … a pestilence broke out, which, though it threatened more than it killed, made men think less of the Forum and politics than of their homes and the care of the sick. … The state had escaped with very few deaths, considering the great number of those who had fallen ill, when the year of pestilence was succeeded … by a scarcity of corn, owing to diminished harvesting in such times.

Livy 4, 52, 3–5

Livy (5, 42) tells of a pestilence, probably malaria, in 390 BC during the Gallic sack of Rome. The Gauls were camped in a cauldron of a valley where conditions fell well short of salubrious: it was dry, very hot and dusty – the complete opposite to the climate and environment they were used to back in Gaul. They were soon plagued by an epidemic, exacerbated, no doubt, by the putrefying corpses of the unburied dead.

The Greek historian Diodorus Siculus records (14, 41, c.90 BC–c.30 BC) a raging pestilence in 592 BC with Carthaginians in Libya suffering headache, coma and death. At the Siege of Syracuse in 396 BC (Diodorus 14, 70–71; Livy 25, 26) we learn more about the impact of disease when plague struck, again helped by questionable hygiene on marshy grounds and malaria. Numerous soldiers and sailors succumbed to the disease, burial parties were overwhelmed, bodies were hastily buried, new burials were almost impossible and the stench of decaying bodies filled the air. Fear of infection may have prevented proper care being given to the sick. The cause of the contagion was attributed to the Carthaginians and their desecration of Greek temples and tombs. If the Carthaginian general, Himilco, took any measures to combat the plague they were ineffective; Carthaginian morale plummeted because of the disease, along with combat effectiveness.

Aquillius and the poisoned wells

Manius Aquillius (cos. 129 BC) would not have been in Cicero's mind when he was expatiating on the noble conduct of war. Aquillius brought the war waged against Aristonicus, the son of Eumenes II of Pergamum, to an end by poisoning the water sources. An outraged Florus, the historian, tells us how (3.1):

Aquilius settled the last remnants of the Asian war and was criminal enough to poison the fountains, in order to obtain the surrender of certain cities. He hastened thus, but at the same time dishonoured his victory. In defiance of the divine laws and the customs of our ancestors, he defiled by these infamous poisons the hitherto unblemished honour of Roman arms.

Mithridates and mad honey

We have already seen the effects of mad honey in our description of Xenophon's encounter. Grayanotoxins are produced by rhododendron species and other plants in the family *Ericaceae*. Honey made from the nectar and so containing pollen of these plants also contains grayanotoxins and is commonly referred to as mad honey. Consumption of the plant or any of its secondary products, including mad honey, can cause a rare poisonous reaction called grayanotoxin poisoning, mad honey disease, honey intoxication, or rhododendron poisoning.

Physical symptoms from grayanotoxin poisoning include various cardiovascular effects, nausea and vomiting, and a change in consciousness. The cardiovascular effects may include hypotension (low blood pressure) and various cardiac rhythm disorders such as sinus bradycardia (slow, regular heart rhythm), bradyarrhythmia (slow, irregular heart rhythm) and partial or complete atrioventricular block. Other early-onset symptoms may include diplopia and blurred vision, dizziness, hypersalivation, perspiration, weakness and paresthesia in the extremities and around the mouth.

As noted, Xenophon in 401 BC in his *Anabasis* 4, 8, describes the 'Retreat of the 10,000' following Cyrus the Younger's failed attempt to conquer the Persian Empire; an invading Greek army was accidentally poisoned by harvesting and eating the local honey, but most made a quick recovery, with few fatalities. Having heard of this incident, and realising that foreign invaders would be ignorant of the dangers of the local honey, Mithridates, king, commander, multilinguist and toxicologist, later used the honey as a deliberate poison when Pompey's army attacked the Heptakometes in Asia Minor in 69 BC. As the army of 1,000 soldiers advanced through a narrow pass in Trebizond, they found jars of honey lining the roads as 'tribute' to the would-be conquerors. Tempted, the soldiers indulged and soon found themselves delirious, at which point the Heptakometes attacked.

Mithridates was no stranger to poisoning: it was his murder weapon of choice; this is how he despatched his mother, brother and four sons. 'Obsessed with poison' would be an understatement when describing Mithridates: he was constantly attended by the shaman Scythian Agari, who were famous for their snake venom-based poisons; he routinely ingested a soupçon of one toxin or other every day – just enough to confer immunity should his body encounter the toxin again through an assassination attempt, for example. So effective was this regime that when he came to commit suicide in 63 BC, poisons were of no use to him whatsoever and he had to resort to having his Gaulish bodyguard run him through with a sword.

Pliny the Elder, writing a century later, consulted Mithridates' personal toxicology library while researching his *Natural History* and was able to cite several antidotes written out in Greek in the king's own hand. Antidotes he discovered in Mithridates' biotoxins research laboratory included the blood of Pontic ducks, who maintained a natural toxicity by living on poisonous plants; a pink flower he called *mithridatia*; and *polemonia*, 'the plant of a thousand powers' (Pliny *NH* 25.5–7, 37, and 62–65; 29.24–26. Dio Cassius 36–37; Appian *Mithridatic Wars* 12; Strabo 12.3.30–31).

Mithridates also cruelly tested various *pharmaka* on prisoners and slaves who were forcibly poisoned or bitten by venomous snakes and scorpions. Ultimately, he conjured up a sophisticated concoction of the fifty-four best antidotes mixed with honey – possibly the toxic honey of his native land – into a single drug for his own protection. This became known as his *mithridatium* – a word we still use today. Over time, this was elaborated on by many a toxicolgist, including Thessalus of Tralles (*fl. c.* AD 70–95), the personal physician to Nero, who added ten more ingredients, including chopped viper flesh and opium. Galen too prepared daily doses of his new, improved *mithridatium* for three emperors paranoid about being poisoned: Marcus Aurelius, Commodus and Septimius Severus. Indeed, Marcus Aurelius' paranoia over assassination by poison and plague convinced him to ingest a dose of Galen's opium-fortified *mithridatium* every day. In a classic example of an antidote backfiring, not only did Marcus Aurelius become an opium addict, but he died of the plague that was brought back to Rome from Babylon by his own army, commanded by Verus.

Mithridatium

In 2002, the *New York Times* reported that Indonesian army military training included drinking the blood of venomous snakes to boost immunity against poison and venom – in that eternal, desperate search for the perfect *mithridatium*; Mithridates would have been impressed. The age old dream of such a *mithridatium* that would protect civilians against modern biowarfare is one of the aspirations of a New Age organisation called Tetrahedron. In 2001, the company began selling 'Essential Oils for Biological Warfare Preparedness' on the Internet. They maintain that one of their oils was originally mixed by Moses to protect the Israelites from the plagues that God inflicted on the Egyptians – an early example of anticipated blue on blue. Other oils are claimed to protect against bioterrorist attacks with anthrax and bubonic plague.

Julius Caesar and mandrake poisoning

Around 75 BC, Julius Caesar was kidnapped by Cilician pirates on a voyage from Rome to Bithynia in what is now north-western Turkey near Cape Malea. The pirates sailed on to Miletus and demanded a large ransom for Caesar's release. Caesar sent a secret message to the Milesians requesting that they bring double the ransom money, along with provisions for a 'great feast' – actually jars of wine well spiked with mandrake, and another huge pot with swords hidden inside. 'Overjoyed at the large amount of money', the unsuspecting pirates celebrated their bonus with the wine and collapsed en masse on the deck of the ship. The Milesians returned and stabbed them all to death; Caesar returned the ransom money.

Lucullus and the tunnel bears and bees

Lucius Licinius Lucullus (118–57 BC) gave Rome over twenty years of almost continuous distinguished military and government service. He became the conqueror of the eastern kingdoms in the course of the Third Mithridatic War, exhibiting extraordinary generalship in diverse situations, most famously during the Siege of Cyzicus, 73–72 BC, and at the Battle of Tigranocerta in Armenian Arzanene, 69 BC. His style received favourable attention from ancient military experts, and his campaigns appear to have been studied as examples of skilful generalship. Compared with what was to follow in the inexorable decline of the Republic into corruption and internecine warfare, Lucullus' career was a model of probity and military skill. However, he had to deal with multiple instances of bioterrorism.

In 76 BC, Nicodemus IV of Bythinia died, having bequeathed his kingdom to Rome. This served to rekindle the wrath of Mithridates, who invaded Bythinia in 73, thus sparking the Third Mithridatic War with Rome. Before the start of the war, Mithridates allied himself with King Tigranes II of Armenia and Ptolemaic Egypt, as well as with the Roman rebel Sertorius, who was in Hispania. He later allied with Spartacus. The war (73–63 BC) saw victory for the Romans, the demise of Pontus as a power, the death of Mithridates, and Armenia absorbed as a client state into the Roman Empire.

According to Appian, when Lucullus laid siege to:

> Themiscyra, which is named after one of the Amazons and is situated on the river Thermodon, the besiegers of this place brought up towers, built mounds, and dug tunnels so large that great subterranean battles could be fought in them. The inhabitants cut openings into these tunnels from

above and thrust bears and other wild animals and swarms of bees into them against the Romans.

Appian, *History of Rome: The Mithridatic Wars* 11.78

As if savage bears and stinging bees were not enough for the armies of Lucullus to contend with, they later had to endure burning bitumen poured down on them at the Siege of Tigranocerta and poison arrow tips as they made their way through Armenia. Not just any poisonous arrow tips, though: these were fashioned in such a way that, according to Dio Cassius, they inflicted 'dangerous and incurable wounds' because the arrows were designed with an extra point that would break off at the tip when they were removed. This left the poison and painful metal deep inside the wounds. The poison was usually fatal and caused days of agony before death.

Pestilentia manu facta

We have Seneca the Younger (c. 4 BC–AD 65) to thank for coining this disturbing phrase, meaning 'man-made pestilence', but it is Dio Cassius (b. AD 161) who gives us details about two specific instances of the deliberate and malicious use of 'plague' to cause death and terror in equal measure. The first was in AD 90–91 during the reign of the tyrannical Domitian, when conspirators dipped needles into toxic substances and went about needlesticking people. It is mentioned by Dio in his description of a recurrence of this sinister bioterrorism during the reign of Commodus (r. AD 176–AD 192) and the ravages of a Antonine Plague resurgence.

> A sickness occurred greater than any I have known – in fact, two thousand often died on a single day in Rome. Many people were also killed in another way, not only in the city, but throughout practically the whole Empire, by evil men: for they would smear little needles with some deadly drugs and for a fee would inject the poison into others, a thing which also happened during the time of Domitian. And while these people died without even a word, Commodus ended up more troublesome to the Romans than all the diseases and criminals together, because among other reasons the people were forced to assign to him out of fear and by command those things which had been bestowed out of respect upon his father [Marcus Aurelius] at the ballot box.
>
> Dio Cassius, *Roman History*, 72.14

Roman insect wars

Bees were not the only insects weaponised in combat: we also hear of the use of scorpions, assassin bugs, and various beetles. In AD 198, during the reign of Septimius Severus, the fortified caravan city of Hatra in Upper Mesopotamia – a buffer state between the Roman and Parthian/Persian empires in present-day northern Iraq – the citizens made ready against the Romans utilising clay pot 'bombs' filled with scorpions. These earthenware pots were then sealed and dropped onto the attackers, where they would break open, emitting their lethal passengers. Bites from these insects were said to be incredibly painful, inflicting a lingering death that would last three days; this was accompanied by anxiety, sweating, convulsions and swollen genitals.

The scorpion attack followed an equally devastating encounter when the defenders poured burning naphtha on the soldiers and their siege engines. Here is how Herodian (39. 3–8) described it all:

> The Atrenians fought back bravely; pouring down a steady stream of stones and arrows, they did considerable damage to the army of Severus. Making clay pots, they filled them with winged insects, little poisonous flying creatures. When these were hurled down on the besiegers, the insects fell into the Romans' eyes and on all the unprotected parts of their bodies; digging in before they were noticed, they bit and stung the soldiers. The Romans found the air at Hatra intolerable, stifling from the hot sun; they fell sick and died, and more casualties resulted from disease than from enemy action.

The Antonine Plague, AD 165–AD 180

> The Antonine Plague was the first of three highly destructive pandemics, the others being the Plague of Cyprian (AD 249–AD 262) and the Justinian Plague (AD 541–AD 542), which rocked the Roman Empire to the core due to their high mortality rates.
>
> Kyle Harper, 2017, *The Fate of Rome: Climate, Disease, and the End of an Empire*

A blend of legend and historical fact give two different explanations as to how the plague developed to infect the human population. In one, Emperor Lucius Verus is said to have opened a closed tomb in Seleucia during the sacking of the city and in so doing released, Pandora-like, the disease. This suggests that the epidemic was a supernatural punishment because the Romans violated an oath to the gods not to pillage the city. In the second story, a Roman soldier opened a golden casket in the temple of Apollo in Babylon, allowing the plague to escape. Two different fourth-century sources, *Res Gestae* by Ammianus Marcellinus (*c.* AD 330–AD 400) and the biographies of Lucius Verus and Marcus Aurelius in the famously unreliable *Historia Augusta*, ascribe the outbreak to a sacrilege by the Romans when violating the sanctuary of a god. Other Romans preferred to blame Christians for angering the pagan gods by refusing to worship them, believing that angry gods sent the plague as a punishment.

Interestingly, the Romans used the same word, *veneficium*, for both 'poisoning' and 'magic' or 'sorcery' – so close was the connection between the two.

The elephant and the pig at the Siege of Edessa

The Siege of Edessa (Justinopolis) took place in AD 544 during an invasion of the Byzantine Empire under Justinian I by the Sasanian Empire under Chosroes I during the ongoing Lazic War. The city withstood the fierce siege; some Christians have put the result down to divine intervention. In *History of the Wars*, Procopius recounts how the defenders of the city dangled a squealing pig from the walls to scare away the single siege elephant in Chosroes' army and deny the attackers access over the city walls.

Chapter 5

The Middle Ages

With the Middle Ages (*c.* AD 500–*c.* AD 1500) we begin to benefit from improved methods of recording events and better historiography generally.

Soldier bees in Guatemala

A bee does not have to have a sting to cause mayhem on the battlefield. The *Popul Vuh*, sacred book of the ancient Quiché Maya of the mountains of Guatemala, tells how when a town was besieged by another tribe, the defenders gathered hornets, wasps and stingless bees and posted mannequins along the parapets of their city. The fake warriors were kitted out with cloaks, spears and shields, even war bonnets to cover the gourds that served as heads – heads that were teeming with pernicious insects. When an attacking army got close to the battlements, the gourds were smashed open and the assailants were overcome by swarms of stinging insects:

> And the insects flew out like smoke, flew in the eyes, noses and mouths of the enemy, hung on their legs and arms which they stung and forced the enemy to throw down their weapons, at which point they were attacked and killed by the defenders of the town.

Saint Gobnait and her attacking bees

The Celts held bees in high esteem, believing that the soul left the body as a bee or a butterfly. Saint Gobnait (*fl.* sixth century and patron saint of bees and beekeepers) was a keeper of bees and is said to have developed a lifelong affinity with them. She may well have used honey in her work as a healer and is credited with saving the people at Ballyvourney in County Cork from the plague. One story tells of how she drove off a bandit by sending a swarm of bees after him and forcing him to return the cattle he had stolen. It is this legend that inspired the Harry Clarke stained glass window in the Honan Chapel at University College Cork. The beautiful window shows Gobnait dressed in royal blue robes; her face is surrounded by bees, at her feet she is shown carrying a honeycomb, while bees are depicted chasing away the thieves who threaten to rob her church. Another version has the beehive turning into a bronze helmet and the bees themselves transmogrifying into soldiers.

More bee attacks

In the eleventh century, Emperor Henry I's troops, commanded by General Immo, defended their fortifications by launching a barrage of beehives from the cliff tops at the siege forces of Duke Giselbert of Lorraine. The horses were stung by the bees and panicked; the siege was over.

King Richard I (Richard the Lionheart) used beehives as bombs against Saladin and the Saracens during the Siege of Acre (Accra) in the Third Crusade (1189–92). One hundred ships carrying 8,000 men had left England for France to reinforce Richard whence they sailed with additional ships to Acre; significantly, some of these vessels carried beehives and their keepers. Food in Acre remained limited, the water supply became contaminated with human and animal corpses, and epidemics soon began to spread. On arrival of the reinforcements, Richard deployed his own siege engines, including two enormous mangonels named 'God's Own Catapult' and 'Bad Neighbour'. He used trebuchets to hurl the hives into the city, causing panic and mayhem.

Next day, Acre offered new terms of surrender, which Richard accepted. His men entered the city and captured the Muslims. Saladin delivered the first of three payments for his captured citizens. The Christian nobles who had been part of the deal were excluded from the prisoner exchange so Richard waited nine days, and when they still did not turn up, he had 2,700 of the Muslim prisoners from the garrison of Acre decapitated. Saladin responded in kind and executed his Christian prisoners.

In the early fourteenth century, Albert II the Lame (1298–1358) of Austria led an invasion in Gussing, Hungary; he was repulsed with a fusillade of hot water, fire and bees thrown from the battlements of the city.

At the Siege of Thun-l'Évêque in northern France in 1340, during the Hundred Years' War, the Duke of Normandy catapulted rotting animals into the besieged castle. This putrescent bombardment continued for days on end until the besieged garrison was decimated by pestilential diseases and was forced to surrender.

During the Middle Ages, English longbowmen generally did not draw their arrows from a quiver; rather, they stuck their arrows into the ground in front of them. This allowed them to loose their arrows faster and had the added advantage that the dirt and soil stuck on the arrow tips would make the wounds much more likely to become infected.

The Siege of Caffa, 1346

> A principal source on the origin of the Black Death is a memoir by the Italian Gabriele de' Mussi. ... This narrative contains some startling assertions: that the Mongol army hurled plague-infected cadavers into the besieged Crimean city of Caffa, thereby transmitting the disease to the inhabitants; and that fleeing survivors of the siege spread plague from Caffa to the Mediterranean Basin. If this account is correct, Caffa should be recognised as the site of the most spectacular incident of biological warfare ever, with the Black Death as its disastrous consequence. After analysing these claims, I have concluded that it is plausible that the biological attack took place as described and was responsible for infecting the inhabitants of Caffa; however, the event was unimportant in the spread of the plague pandemic.
>
> M. Wheelis, *Biological Warfare at the 1346 Siege of Caffa*

Feodosia is a port in Crimea on the Black Sea coast. In the fourteenth century, it was called Caffa and was the site of one of the earliest examples of biological warfare in the post-classical age when victims of infectious diseases became weapons themselves. During the protracted Siege of Caffa, then a well-fortified Genoese-controlled seaport, the Mongol army's Golden Horde under Jani Beg was reportedly suffering badly from the disease. Not to be outdone, though, these Tatars converted their misfortune into an opportunity by hurling the cadavers of their dead comrades into the city, thus igniting a plague epidemic, which forced the Genoese to retreat.

Caffa was described in 1348 by Gabriel de' Mussis, who made two important claims: first, plague was transmitted to the citizens of Caffa by hurling those diseased cadavers – de' Mussi's 'mountains of dead' – into the besieged city, and Italians fleeing from Caffa spread the plague into the wider Mediterranean when ships carrying plague-infected refugees (and maybe rats, too) sailed to Constantinople, Genoa, Venice and other seaports. This second assertion is doubtful, as there were overland caravan routes from the East that would have been carrying the disease into Europe as well. Whatever, the Siege of Caffa reminds us of the horrific consequences when diseases are used as weapons.

Well poisoning – Barbarossa, Saladin and Vlad the Impaler

We have already witnessed episodes of well poisoning in the chapter on ancient civilisations. It was used offensively by attackers and antagonists as a terror tactic to disrupt or depopulate an area, and defensively as a scorched-earth tactic to prevent an invading army having access to clean water. The practice reached greater heights, or depths, in the Middle Ages, when rotting human and animal corpses were thrown down wells – corpses that were preferably infected with transmissible diseases such as bubonic plague or tuberculosis.

One of the more repellent acts of biological warfare involved the twelfth-century Emperor Frederick Barbarossa (1122–90), also known as Frederick I, who was Holy Roman Emperor from 1155 until his death. Frederick is reputed to have dumped putrefying human corpses down wells during his First Italian Campaign, of 1154–5; his aim was probably just to vitiate the water supply rather than actively spread disease.

During the Third Crusade in 1187, before the Battle of Hattin, Saladin interfered with the availability of fresh water to severely disadvantage his enemies, the Franks. The Frankish army set off towards Tiberias, harassed constantly by Muslim archers passing the Springs of Turan, which were insufficient to provide the army with water. They changed course and headed for the Springs of Kafr Hattin, 6 miles away, whence they could march down to Tiberias the following day. The Muslims positioned themselves between the Frankish army and the water so that the Franks were forced to pitch camp overnight on the arid plateau near the village of Meskenah. The Muslims surrounded the camp so closely that 'a cat could not have escaped'. According to Ibn al-Athir, the Franks were 'despondent, tormented by thirst', whilst Saladin's men were jubilant in anticipation of their victory. He supposedly later blocked up local Christians' wells with sand as punishment for aiding his enemies. Throughout the night, the Muslims applied psychological pressure on the Crusaders – keeping them up all night by praying, singing, beating drums and chanting. They set fire to the dry grass to parch the Crusaders' throats even more. The Crusaders were increasingly thirsty, demoralised and exhausted. The Muslim army, by contrast, had a caravan of camels relaying goatskins of water up from Lake Tiberias (the Sea of Galilee).

In 1462, Prince Vlad III the Impaler of Wallachia spoiled water sources to delay his Ottoman Turk adversaries who were pursuing him. He deliberately polluted the water supplies of his fellow Romanians even at the cost of their lives; for Vlad, the main thing was that it slowed down his Muslim foes.

In 1489, Russian troops pursued by a horde of Tatars abandoned their camp, leaving copious supplies of mead for the Tatars to find. They drank themselves into a stupor, whereupon the Russians returned and ruthlessly slaughtered them.

Fantasy biological warfare and scapegoating

Scapegoating was rife through the Middle Ages just as it was and is in any age where blame might be apportioned. Jews, homosexuals and lepers predictably took the brunt for well poisoning and for the Black Death itself: after all, how else was the jealous and angry Christian god to be seen to deliver his vengeance? Well poisoning was one of the three gravest antisemitic accusations made against Jews during this period, the other two being host desecration and blood libel. If Jews, for example, were seen to be the purveyors of infectious diseases then it is but a short step to branding them with the blame for various forms of biological warfare and bioterrorism.

During the Plague of Justinian of AD 541 to 542, the eponymous emperor blamed the epidemic on 'Jews, Samaritans, pagans, heretics, Arians, Montanists and homosexuals' – on anyone, really, other than on Justinian.

'During the Black Death, the bubonic plague killed many, and some people interpreted this as a sign of mass poisoning,' says Tzafrir Barzilay, a historian of medieval European society at the Hebrew University of Jerusalem. It seems that people, without the benefit of even the most basic knowledge of virology, infectious diseases or bacteriology, were happy to blame Jews and lepers for what they saw as a clandestine biological war on the rest of the population. The Black Death in all its horror not only slew millions, it also was the trigger for mass hysteria, masochistic flagellent processions and persecution of the Jews. Jews were blamed and accused of a raft of crimes including contaminating food supplies through their concoctions 'of frogs and spiders mixed into oil and cheese to destroy Christendom'. The usual pogroms followed. The *Germania Judaica* reports the annihilation of at least 235 Jewish communities around the time of the Black Death.

France and Belgium saw lepers, when accused of poisoning springs and streams in the early fourteenth century, burnt alive – after 'they [the wells] were corrupted by the Jews'. A number of cities such as Vienna introduced regulations banning Jews from consuming food and drink meant for Christians, for fear of poisoning.

Indeed, such prejudice and ugly scapegoating has pursued minorities and marginal populations throughout the history of disease. The central thesis of Rana Hogarth's 'Medicalising Blackness' (2020) is that 'Marginal groups such as immigrants, Jews, gypsies, Chinese and black people often took the blame, as usual and were persecuted accordingly.' Some blamed immigrants in general for introducing the plague to London. Miranda Kaufmann (2020) takes up the unfortunate story:

The 'filthy keeping' of foreigners' houses was identified by the city authorities as 'one of the greatest occasions of the plague'. This might have helped to trigger the anti-immigrant feeling expressed by London apprentices in the spring of 1593. The trouble began in April when they set up 'a lewd and vile ticket or placard' on a post in London threatening violence against 'the strangers'. A series of 'divers lewd and malicious libels ... published by some disordered and factious persons' appeared in the following weeks. One castigated the 'beastly brutes, the Belgians, or rather drunken drones, and fainthearted Flemings: and you, fraudulent father, Frenchmen' and threatened that if they did not 'depart out of the realm' by 9 July, over 2,000 apprentices would rise up against them. The verse set upon the wall of the Dutch church at Austin Friars in the City of London in early May did 'exceed the rest in lewdness': 'Strangers that inhabit in this land! ... Egypt's plagues, vexed not the Egyptians more/ Than you do us; then death shall be your lot'. The threatened violence never actually erupted. Some of the culprits were rounded up and 'put into the stocks, carted and whipped, for a terror to other apprentices and servants'. The Privy Council encouraged the Lord Mayor to use torture if necessary to prevent these 'lewd persons' from their 'wicked purpose to attempt anything against strangers'. For 'out of such lewd beginnings, further mischief doth ensue'.

The blame game, xenophobia and racism reached their respective ugly zeniths. Why? Because, apparently, immigrants and travellers often carried cholera from infected areas, and infectious disease became associated with the marginalised in each society. Historically, the Italians blamed the Jews and gypsies, the British accused the 'dirty natives', and the Americans put cholera down to the Filipinos.

Poisoning and syphilis in the Naples campaign

Poisoning wine and similar commodities – turning what the Indian Kautilya had termed the 'enemy's physical enjoyments' into a weapon – recurred with considerable regularity in the Middle Ages. Andrea Cesalpino (1524–1603), the Italian physician, philosopher and botanist, records that during the Naples campaign of 1494–5 in the Italian War, the Spanish abandoned a village to the French, slyly leaving behind caskets of wine that had been mixed with tainted blood drawn from leprosy and syphilis patients at Saint-Lazare Hospital. When Naples fell to Charles VIII in 1495, the plague took hold among the French leader's troops so that when the army dispersed after the campaign, the troops returned to their homes and disseminated the disease across Europe.

There were two mighty consequences of this. First, the League of Venice, which led to the political marriage arranged by Maximilian I, Holy Roman Emperor; Philip the Handsome married Joanna the Mad (daughter of Ferdinand II of Aragon and Isabella of Castile) to reinforce the anti-French alliance between Austria and Spain. The son of Philip and Joanna would become Charles V, Holy Roman Emperor, in 1519, succeeding Maximilian and controlling a Habsburg empire that included Castile, Aragon, Austria and the Burgundian Netherlands, thus encircling France. Secondly, this outbreak was the first widely documented outbreak of syphilis in human history, and eventually led to the Columbian theory of the origin of syphilis for which there are two primary hypotheses: one proposes that syphilis was carried to Europe from the Americas by the crew(s) of Christopher Columbus as an unintentional by-product of the Columbian Exchange, while the other proposes that syphilis previously existed in Europe but went undetected. Because it was spread by French troops, the disease was known as the 'French disease', but it was not until 1530 that the term 'syphilis' was first applied by the Italian physician and poet Girolamo Fracastoro.

The Hussite Wars and Karlštejn Castle

The Hussites, as the Bohemian reformists have come to be called, became one of the most vocal and influential reform movements of the late Middle Ages; they were a religious sect from Bohemia who predated the Protestant Reformation begun by Martin Luther but nonetheless opposed the political and societal domination of the Roman Catholic Church.

The Hussites, acolytes of Jan Hus (*c.*1372–1415), theologian and philosopher, were engaged in ongoing warfare from 1420–34, a period that also led to the rise of Czech nationalism.

As with many armies of the time, disease claimed more casualties than did the actual conflict, often due to the atrocious levels of hygiene and sanitation. The Hussites exaggerated and expedited this by weaponising the large quantities of raw excreta they had accumulated from animals and humans. Not only dead bodies, but 2,000 cartloads of faeces were repeatedly catapulted over the walls of the castle by Prince Sigismund Korybut to induce severe illness and death among the Catholic defenders in Karlštejn Castle. The Hussites severely weakened the Catholic forces in what was a highly effective use of a particularly repellent biological weapon.

Siberian insect torture

Early Siberian tribes tied prisoners to a tree and waited for the flies and mosquitoes that swarmed around the forests in their millions: and so mosquitoes (*Culicidae*), black flies (*Simuliidae*), biting midges, deer flies, and others ensured an eye-wateringly excruciating ordeal until sepsis or dehydration delivered a merciful ending. Recent studies from the Canadian arctic suggest that an unprotected person can receive as many as 9,000 bites per minute – a rate sufficient to drain half of the blood from a large man in about two hours.

In 1513, during the reign of Emmanuel the Fortunate, king of Portugal, General Baruiga was repelled from Tauris in Xantiane by the Moors, who threw hives down on his troops from the citadel walls.

Chapter 6

The Seventeenth to Nineteenth Centuries

The inhumane brutality conferred on humankind in the Middle Ages continued apace throughout the seventeenth to nineteenth centuries.

In 1642, in the Thirty Years' War the Swedes besieged Bad Kissingen, Bavaria. After shelling the city wall for about twelve days, the Swedes decided to bring down the badly damaged wall with an attack the following day. Peter Heil, a beekeeper in the city, proposed the distribution of bee baskets on the city walls to hurl at the Swedes. The baskets broke on the ground and the bees, en masse, stung the Swedes and forced them to end the siege.

Around the same time in the same war, bees saved the town of Beyenburg in Prussia. When soldiers passed through the defenceless town, they found a convent. Anxious to preserve their virginity, the nuns overturned the skeps surrounding their nunnery and hid inside them. The marauding soldiers left, none the wiser, and the town was renamed Beyenburg ('Beyen' = bees) in honour of the holy defenders of their town.

The Siege of Candia 1648–69

During the Venetian-Ottoman War, the city of Candia (Heraklion, Greece) was under siege by the Ottomans from 1648–69. Lasting a seemingly endless twenty-one years, this is the world's longest siege. Candia was the capital of the Kingdom of Candia (Crete), which had been a Venetian possession since the fall of Constantinople during the Fourth Crusade in 1204. The island was the key to the hegemony of the Eastern Mediterranean, constantly fought over by Venice and the Ottoman Empire: in 1463–79, 1499–1502, 1537, and 1571 in the naval Battle of Lepanto.

Information relating to the siege was obtained from the Archives of the Venetian State detailing an operation undertaken by the Venetian Intelligence Services: the Inquisitori di Stato di Venezia (Inquisitors of the State of Venice), which had been established in 1539. This intelligence service was one of the most effective and deadly in the history of espionage: Venice could boast an astonishing network of spies, which excelled in political plots, torture, and countless assassination attempts, successful and unsuccessful.

This was the plan: in February 1649, the heads of the Inquisitori, Piero Morosini, Piero Querini and Geronimo Giustiniani, received a highly secret letter from Zara (now Zadar, Croatia), a Venetian possession on the Dalmatian Coast. In it, the Provveditore Generale di Dalmazia et Albania, Lunardo Foscolo, proposed a plan to end the siege by infecting the Ottoman forces with a poisonous liquid that he described as 'the quintessence of the plague'. The noxious solution was made from the spleen, the buboes, and carbuncles of plague victims in Dalmatia; it was ready for use and distilled by a doctor expert in pharmacology, Michiel Angelo Salamon, 'and this, when mixed with other ingredients, will have the power wherever it is scattered to slay any number of persons'. The plan was unlikely to be detected because plague outbreaks occurred frequently on Crete: indeed, since the Black Death, twenty outbreaks had occurred on the island from 1348 to 1645. The objective now was to lift the siege by infecting the Ottoman soldiers with plague.

To make sure of its success, and because an outbreak seen to be focused only in the Ottoman camp surrounding Candia would be suspicious, Foscolo proposed a diversionary 'perfect plan': an extensive plague attack was to be launched against all the Ottoman camps around the island (Retimo, Cannea, and San Todero), which would appear to be a large-scale epidemic. The plan is detailed at length by Foscolo in a letter to the Venetians as follows:

> I believe, however, that some ruse must be adopted to entice the Turks into the trap, and would suggest that we should make use of the Albanian fez, or some other cloth goods, which the Turks are accustomed to buy, so that the poison may pass through as many hands in as short a time as possible. The cloth should be made up in parcels as if for sale, after having been painted over with the quintessence, and then placed in separate boxes destined for the various places where we desire to sow the poison. The quintessence, well secured in several cases for the greater safety of those who have to handle and transport it, should be sent to the commander-in-chief that he may take the necessary steps for causing it to pass into the enemies' hands.

Although the plan was 'managed with all circumspection', and the lethal concoction was ready to use, the attack was never actually carried out. Sensible quarantine precautions against cross-infection, face coverings and the like, and widespread contagion were, nevertheless, to be taken by the agent who was to produce and deliver the 'plague':

when the operation is over he [the agent] must go through a rigorous quarantine. While handling the quintessence, it will be of use to the operator to stuff his nose and mouth with sponges soaked in vinegar; and while poisoning the cloth, he may fasten the brush to an iron rod, and when finished, he must put brush and rod into the fire. Having given the Turk the plague, every care must be taken to prevent our people coming in contact with them.

State archives of Venice. Inquisitors of the State, b. 274, 5 Feb, 18 Mar, 10, 29 Apr, 14, 18 Oct, 1 Dec 1650, 3 Aug 1651

Foscolo appreciated that the plan was 'a violent course, unusual, and perhaps not admitted by public morality' but justified it because 'desperate cases call for violent remedies, and in the case of the Turks, enemies by faith, treacherous by nature, who have always betrayed your Excellencies, in my humble opinion, the ordinary considerations have no weight'. Foscolo justified the potential atrocity in the name of religious faith, fuelled by a deep fanaticism on the part of Christians and Muslims. Sadly, throughout history, those driven by religious fervour have caused and continue to cause numerous crimes against innocent populations – crimes against humanity.

The story ends abruptly. No further information exists, and probably no further details will ever emerge.

Casimir Siemienowicz and the 'dogs' slobber'

Kazimirz Siemienowicz (*c.*1600–51), Lithuanian-born Lieutenant General of Ordnance in Service to the King of Poland, knew everything there is to know about guns, artillery, and canine saliva. He was the celebrated author of *Artis magnae artilleriae pars prima* (*Great Art of Artillery, the First Part*) (Amsterdam: Jan Jansson). Siemienowicz released the book in 1650 and it was translated into French in 1651, German in 1676, English and Dutch in 1729, and Polish in 1963. For over 200 years, this work was used throughout Europe as the cutting-edge artillery manual and was the first book to systematically present knowledge about the development of multistage rockets and rocket artillery. Death prevented Siemienowicz from completing what was originally intended to be a two-part *Compleat Art of Artillery*; the five sections of the Latin first edition deal with calibre, pyrotechnics, rockets, fire-balls and the building of firework set-pieces.

Siemienowicz served in the armies of the Polish-Lithuanian Commonwealth and of Frederick Henry, Prince of Orange, ruler of the Netherlands. He was of the view that the use of poison gases in war was dishonourable. In his work, he wrote:

> and most of all, they shall not construct any poisoned globes, nor other sorts of pyrobolic inventions, in which he shall introduce no poison whatsoever, besides which, they shall never employ them for the ruin and destruction of men, because the first inventors of our art thought such actions as unjust among themselves as unworthy of a man of heart and a real soldier.

Although this clearly relates to chemical warfare, it is a reasonable assumption that he was equally opposed to aspects of biological warfare. Nevertheless, Siemienowicz sponsored the firing of artillery containing the saliva of rabid dogs ('slobber') during a 1650 battle. It demonstrated that he had made an educated guess about the communicability of rabies that was not actually confirmed until the eighteenth century.

More weaponised bees and fomite transmission

At the Siege of Alba Graexa, the Turks breached a wall of the city only to find that the inhabitants had piled swarming beehives there as a barricade and were thus prevented from penetrating the city. The navy weaponised bees too: in the Mediterranean, the crew of a small corsair vessel, a mere fifty men, boarded and captured a much larger galley manned by a small army of 500 soldiers – but only after the pirates cast beehives from the masts of their ship down onto the crew of the galley, whose plan it was to capture the pirates.

During the 1785 Siege of La Calle, Tunisian forces flung diseased clothing into the city (Hobbes 2003).

In parts of sub-Saharan Africa, when a swarm of bees attacks people, it is generally assumed that the bees have been sent by an enemy, often with the intent to kill. Bees have been used in warfare, for example, in Cameroon and the Democratic Republic of Congo, and in Chad during the war between the Moundang and the Foulbé, or in Kenya when there was a conflict between the Kamba and the Maasai. The Tiiv of Nigeria kept bees in special horns containing powdered poisons. This dusting increased the efficacy of the bees' venom before they were released in battle to attack the Tiiv's enemies, although it is not recorded how the bees distinguished between the Tiiv and their foes.

The Great Northern War 1700–21

This was a conflict in which a coalition led by the tsardom of Russia successfully contested the supremacy of the Swedish Empire in Northern, Central and Eastern Europe. The early leaders of the anti-Swedish alliance were Peter I of Russia, Frederick IV of Denmark-Norway, and Augustus II the Strong of Saxony-Poland-Lithuania.

Russia and Sweden found themselves infested with bubonic plague and at war with each other. The Swedish city of Reval was overcrowded with refugees who had fled behind its walls to escape the approaching Russian Army, which had destroyed all the villages and farms as it advanced.

By the time the Russians reached Reval's gates, the city was giving refuge to nearly 20,000 people, with limited sanitation, overcrowding and no disease protection. To exacerbate this dreadful situation the Russians catapulted the corpses of Swedes over the city walls; many were plague victims. The lice and fleas inhabiting the clothing and hair of the dead soon found new hosts in Reval, spreading the contagion within the bustling city.

Reval surrendered to the Russians, who wisely remained outside of the city; within ten weeks, the city population was reduced to fewer than 2,000, with more than 15,000 having succumbed to the plague. To make matters even worse, those who had been allowed by the Russians to leave fled to other cities in Europe, often exporting the plague with them to their new destinations. Many arrived in Finland, which was soon being ravaged by the disease, with over 60 per cent of the population of Helsinki dying of the disease before the end of the year.

Fascinating and plausible as this is, there is no hard evidence to support its veracity, as elucidated by Carus (2016). Despite this, however, the 'incident' continues to feature in the literature. Thalassinou (2015), for example, alludes to it in the context of similar biological atrocities at Caffa and Candia.

British atrocities at Fort Pitt in Pontiac's War

> I will try to inoculate the bastards with some blankets that may fall into their hands, and take care not to get the disease myself.
> Colonel Henry Bouquet, July 1763

Smallpox is particularly suited to deployment in biological warfare: in the eighteenth century, the British tried to infect Native American populations with the agent at the Siege of Fort Pitt, Philadelphia, in 1763. Barbara Alice Mann's book *The Tainted Gift: The Disease Method of Frontier Expansion* gives disturbing accounts of four other incidents: the 1763 smallpox epidemic among Native peoples in Ohio during the French and Indian War; the cholera epidemic during the 1832 Choctaw removal; the 1837 outbreak of smallpox among the High Plains peoples; and the alleged 1847 poisonings of the Cayuses in Oregon. Before all that, we have the testimony of a colonist's letter in 1752: 'Twere desirable that [smallpox] should break out and spread ... among the Indians. It would be fully as good as an army' (Stearn 1945). By then it was well established that smallpox was spreadable through contaminated clothing, bedding and laundry (fomite transmission); the Indians soon got suspicious when it became apparent that infections amongst their peoples followed close on the heels of colonial newcomers.

The Spanish blamed the French, the French the English, leaving the Natives to try to seek revenge. The French tried to avert this in 1768 with the survivors of an epidemic donating a million livres' worth of blankets 'to cover the dead' and protesting that the English had sent the contagion.

As far as the Americas go, the very first evidence of deliberate infection was the devastation by smallpox of the Inca in 1493. A 1613 account tells how Spaniards had sent 'a messenger in a black cloak' who presented 'the Inca [king] with a small, locked case'. The messenger withdrew on the pretext that his orders were that 'only the Inca [king] should open it'. The contents of the box flew out 'like scraps of paper' bringing 'the smallpox plague'. Within days, scores had died, 'covered in burning scabs'. The 1887 publication of an Ottawa Indian tradition is eerily reminiscent of this: when they had helped the French fight the English they were sold a tin box which was to remain closed until 'after they had reached home'. The box contained a Russian doll sequence of other boxes until the last was opened and revealed 'nothing but mouldy particles': soon 'there burst out a terrible sickness among them'. Furthermore, Jesuit records reveal that a Canadian tribe was ravaged by smallpox after the king of France sent them a present of 'clothes in the French fashion'. An attempt at reciprocating the gift failed when the child's clothes the Indians sent for the king's son were refused by the Jesuits lest 'it may carry the slightest contagion'. No one can say that the French did not know what they were doing with their initial 'gift'.

In 1770, a fur trader invited Indians to a peace parley at which he gave the Indians a keg of rum wrapped in a smallpox-infected American flag with specific instructions not to unfurl it until they got home. This was an act of revenge: the Chippewa had earlier robbed the trader. Similar stories are legion.

It was General Jeffrey Amherst, the British commander-in-chief in North America, who determined policy towards American Indians, which involved military matters and regulation of the fur trade. Amherst arrogantly believed that with France out of the picture the Indians would have no choice but to accept British rule.

A confederation of Natives which included western Lenape, Odawa and Shawnee Indians, unhappy with British rule in the Great Lakes region following the French and Indian War (1754–63), initiated a Native uprising, Pontiac's War, in a bid to drive settlers from Native American territory. When colonists in western Pennsylvania fled to the refuge of Fort Pitt after the outbreak of the war, nearly 550 people were crowded inside, including more than 200 women and children. Simeon Ecuyer, the Swiss-born British officer in command, wrote, 'We are so crowded in the fort that I fear disease … the smallpox is among us.' Delawares and others attacked the fort on 22 June 1763, and maintained the siege throughout July. Meanwhile, Delaware and Shawnee war parties raided into Pennsylvania, taking captives and killing unknown numbers of settlers.

In June 1763, Amherst wrote to Colonel Henry Bouquet, who was preparing to lead an expedition to relieve Fort Pitt: 'Could it not be contrived to send the small pox among the disaffected tribes of Indians? We must on this occasion use every stratagem in our power to reduce them.' Bouquet replied that he would try to spread smallpox to the Indians by giving them blankets that had been exposed to the disease. Amherst replied to Bouquet on 16 July, endorsing the plan. As noted above, Bouquet to Amherst, 13 July: 'I will try to inoculate the bastards with some blankets that may fall into their hands, and take care not to get the disease myself.' Amherst to Bouquet, 16 July: 'You will do well to inoculate the Indians by means of blankets, as well as every other method that can serve to extirpate this execrable race.'

It did not take long after replacing Amherst for Gage to continue the desire for ethnic cleansing; he approved a 1763 bill for 'Sundries got to Replace in kind those, which were taken from people in the Hospital to Convey the Smallpox to the Indians'. The British officers obviously justified their atrocities by an imperative need to subdue what they perceived as their uncivilised, 'execrable' enemies. Amherst wrote in 1763: 'I cannot but wish, that Whenever we have any of the Savages in our Power, who have in so Treacherous a way Committed any Barbarities on our People, a Quick Retaliation may be made, without the least Exception or hesitation.'

For the British, then, anything goes in the quest to destroy the Native Americans.

Fort Pitt was too well fortified for the Indians to take it by force. In a parley during the siege, Ecuyer tells how items exposed to smallpox from a smallpox infirmary were given as spurious gifts to the Native American envoys (gifting to the Natives had become an established practice). William Trent wrote, 'We gave them two blankets and a handkerchief out of the smallpox hospital. I hope it will have the desired effect.' The British were all too aware of the very real potential of this to cause an epidemic among the American Indians; Trent submitted an invoice to the British Army, writing that the items had been 'taken from people in the Hospital to Convey the Smallpox to the Indians'. The expense was approved by Ecuyer, and ultimately by General Thomas Gage, Amherst's successor. The fact that the invoice was signed off confirms that the British high command endorsed Trent's actions.

A reported outbreak that began the spring before left as many as 100 Native Americans dead in Ohio Country from 1763 to 1764. It is not clear, however, whether the smallpox was a result of the Fort Pitt incident or the virus was already present among the Delaware people as outbreaks happened independently every dozen or so years. Controversy continues to rage over whether the British attempt was effective, indeed, some scholars argue, implausibly, that it was never the intention of the British to spread smallpox (e.g. Gill 2004; Ranlet 2000; *cf.* Mayor 1995).

The Battle of Bunker Hill

Bunker Hill was fought on 17 June 1775, during the Siege of Boston in the early stages of the American War of Independence. Boston was itself being steadily reduced by meagre rations and smallpox, 'this most dangerous Enemy', and British troops were denied passage in and out of the city, with few exceptions. When smallpox erupted in the town, the British were largely immune: by the 1770s, the British Army having learnt from experience, unlike colonial forces, would routinely inoculate its troops against smallpox, notwithstanding strict New England laws and military sanctions against the practice. So, for the New England troops outside of the town it was a very different story until Washington initiated an inoculation programme. Nevertheless, British officers attempted to take advantage of the Americans' susceptibility to the disease by releasing some Bostonians infected with smallpox to the Americans outside of the city, thus debilitating and reducing Washington's army.

The *London Evening Post* published a letter (25–28 March 1775) from a Boston correspondent who claimed that British 'soldiers try all they can to spread the smallpox, but I hope they will be disappointed. One of their officers inoculated his whole family without letting any person know it.' Although the officer was probably doing nothing perfidious and was simply protecting himself and his family, the correspondent's suggestions that they 'try all they can' to spread smallpox, and engage in clandestine inoculation, implies biological warfare. Whether this officer had a nefarious motive we will never know, yet the belief that the British were capable of such sinister action was widely believed by American colonists.

In a report to the provincial Council of Massachusetts on 3 December 1775, Washington's aide-de-camp, Robert H. Harrison, reveals what he considered to be an 'unheard-of and diabolical scheme', when 'Four [British] deserters have just arrived at headquarters giving an account that several persons are to be sent out of Boston ... that have lately been inoculated with the smallpox, with the design, probably, to spread infection to distress us as much as possible' ('Robert H. Harrison to the president of the Council of Massachusetts Bay', 3 December 1775, Force, American Archives, vol. 4, no. 4, 168). A Boston physician admitted 'that he had effectually given the distemper among those people' who were leaving the city.

When Washington received the intelligence that the British were releasing victims of the disease – slaves – into the American lines he redoubled his efforts. American commanders questioned why the British would release refugees and clearly believed that the plan was to spread smallpox. Washington reported that month that the British were sending Bostonians out of the city, and that 'a Sailor says that a Number of these coming out have been inoculated with the design of Spreading the Small pox through this Country and Camp.' Soon after, resident Thomas Crafts alerted the Massachusetts Council and Washington that 'The smallpox has broken out in two families that came out of Boston on the first vessels.' Although reluctant to believe the British capable of such perfidy, Washington wrote to the Continental Congress a few days later that he had no option but to give credence to the notion of germ warfare:

> The information I received that the Enemy intended spreading the smallpox amongst us, I could not suppose them capable of; I now must give some credit to it, as it has made its appearance on several of those who last came out of Boston.

Seth Pomeroy, British military commander-in-chief at Boston in 1775 and a former colleague of Gage during the Seven Years' War, wrote: 'If it is in General Gage's power I expect he will Send ye Small pox Into ye Army.' In 1777, Robert Donkin, a British officer, published a pamphlet in which he suggested a strategy to defeat the Americans: 'Dip arrows in matter of smallpox, and twang them at the American rebels. ... This would ... disband these stubborn, ignorant, enthusiastic savages. ... Such is their dread and fear of that disorder.' More talk of 'savages' lends weight to the idea that biological warfare would have been seen as justified against the Americans according to military thinking of the time.

Bunker Hill and Fort Pitt were not the only occasions when the British maliciously tried to spread smallpox within Native North American, American and French forces. For example, in 1781, the *Pennsylvania Gazette* accused the British general Lord Cornwallis of spreading smallpox to infect American and French soldiers at Yorktown. When the British sent an expedition to Virginia that same year, General Alexander Leslie revealed to Cornwallis his plan to spread disease among the Americans. He said that 'above 700 Negroes are come down the River with the Small Pox', whom he proposed to distribute 'about the Rebell Plantations'. We do not know for sure if he carried out his plan. These slaves had attached themselves to Cornwallis's army as he traversed Virginia, with thousands retained behind the redoubts and barriers of the British Army. Under cover of darkness, the infected former slaves were forced through the British lines and left where rebel and French forces would find them, with the intention of spreading the disease throughout the camps surrounding the English forces.

Manipulated smallpox contagion reared its head in the failure of American forces to capture Quebec on 31 December 1775. Rumour has it that General Guy Carleton (1724–1808), British commander in Quebec, took advantage of the festering presence of diseases in the camp outside Quebec, not least smallpox, which was exerting a significant toll on the besiegers, as did the general lack of provisions. Smallpox ravaged the 1,200 American troops of Major General Richard Montgomery and Benedict Arnold's forces, largely due to exposure to infected civilians tactically released from Quebec. Carleton clearly condoned this practice, realising it would severely weaken the American siege effort. Moreover, Carleton is reported to have sent out several prostitutes infected with smallpox who in turn passed it on to the Continental Army. Thomas Jefferson was convinced the British were responsible for illness in the lines. He later wrote, 'I have been informed by officers who were on the spot, and whom I believe myself, that this disorder was sent into our army designedly by the commanding officer in Quebec.' After the defeat at Quebec the American troops gathered at Crown Point, where John Adams found their condition deplorable:

> Our Army at Crown Point is an object of wretchedness to fill a humane mind with horrour [*sic*]; disgraced, defeated, discontented, diseased, naked, undisciplined, eaten up with vermin; no clothes, beds, blankets, no medicines; no victuals, but salt pork and flour.

Just before Virginia's last royal governor, John Murray, 4th Earl of Dunmore PC (1730–1809), known as Lord Dunmore, left his base at Norfolk in 1776,

Purdie's *Virginia Gazette* reported that Dunmore had infected two slaves who had joined his forces and sent them ashore in order to spread smallpox, 'but it was happily prevented'.

Poisoning too ... Dr John Potts (or Pott) was a physician and Colonial Governor of Virginia at the Jamestown settlement in the Virginia Colony. Potts and his wife Elizabeth had sailed from London aboard the *George* in March 1619. After a two-month passage, the vessel docked in Jamestown, Virginia. In 1623, Dr Potts gained notoriety as the physician who prepared the poison given to the Native Americans during a 'peace ceremony' at Jamestown, killing 200 of them in retaliation for the Indian Massacre of 1622, in which 350 – nearly a third – of the colonists were slaughtered by the Powhatan.

On 22 May that same year, Captain William Tucker with twelve men went to the Potomac River to secure the release of English prisoners held by Indians. When the party arrived, it invited the Indians' leader and his men to conclude a peace treaty with a drink of sack that Potts had prepared for the occasion. The Indians demanded that the English interpreter take the first drink, which he did, but out of a different container. Afterwards a group of Indians, including two chiefs, were walking with the English interpreter. At a preordained signal, the interpreter fell to the ground and the English discharged a volley of shot into the Indians. The English reported that about 200 'savages' died of poison and fifty from wounds. The colonists had invited the Indian leader Opechancanough, the mastermind behind the uprising, to attend the party and were disappointed by not finding him among the dead. Potts was cleared of the charge and restored to his council seat. The mystery remains unsolved.

Indians, of course, had little or no exposure to Old World diseases so they suffered appallingly and disproportionately from smallpox, experiencing mortality rates as high as 40 per cent. During the French and Indian War from 1754 to 1763, Potawatomi Indians (of the Great Plains, upper Mississippi River, and western Great Lakes region) who fought at Lake George believed the British had deliberately infected them with smallpox. The Indians charged British traders with selling them 'a showy tin box' filled with 'mouldy particles' that carried the disease, according to the nineteenth-century linguist and historian Andrew Blackbird.

New South Wales, Australia

Similar controversy surrounds the allegations by Australian aborigines (Kooris) and various scholars that the British deliberately spread smallpox in 1789 among native peoples (Foley 2001; Davis 1980). The arguments only received impetus in the 1980s when Noel Butlin suggested, 'there are some possibilities that ... disease could have been used deliberately as an exterminating agent' (Butlin 1983). In 1997, David Day claimed there 'remains considerable circumstantial evidence to suggest that officers ... or perhaps convicts or soldiers ... deliberately spread smallpox among aborigines', and in 2000, John Lambert argued that 'strong circumstantial evidence suggests the smallpox epidemic which ravaged Aborigines in 1789, may have resulted from deliberate infection'. Judy Campbell concluded in 2002 that it is highly improbable that the First Fleet was the source of the epidemic on the grounds that 'smallpox had not occurred in any members of the First Fleet'. The only possible source of infection from the Fleet was exposure to variolous matter imported for the purposes of inoculation against smallpox, but Aboriginal people were never actually exposed to it. She contends that regular contact between fishing fleets from the Indonesia archipelago, where smallpox was endemic and Aboriginal people in Australia's North as a more likely source for the introduction of smallpox.

In 2007, Christopher Warren demonstrated that the British smallpox may have been still viable, leading later scholars to argue that the British committed biological warfare in 1789 near their new convict settlement at Port Jackson (Finzsch 2008 and Mear 2008). John Carmody has since argued that the epidemic was an outbreak of chickenpox, which struck the Aboriginal population without immunological resistance.

Napoleon and the spread of malaria

During the Siege of Mantua (July 1796 to February 1797), French armies under Napoleon Bonaparte besieged and blockaded a large Austrian garrison until it surrendered. This, together with the heavy losses incurred during four unsuccessful relief attempts, led indirectly to the Austrians suing for peace in 1797. The siege occurred during the War of the First Coalition, part of the French Revolutionary Wars.

Mantua is bounded on its north and east sides by a large and swampy lake formed by the Mincio River. The Mantua urban area was plagued by malaria from 1190, when a complex artificial lake system was created for defence, inadvertently creating a habitat for the Anopheles mosquito, vector of the disease. In the eighteenth century, the city was still notoriously unhealthy in the summer months because the nearby marshes and lakes formed the perfect breeding ground for malarial mosquitoes. Napoleon took advantage of this and worked closely to ensure his new ally, the mosquito, exacted as big a toll as possible on the Austrians.

Biological warfare and just war theory

We saw in our discussion of biological warfare in the Roman period how influential men like Cicero and Florus deplored the use of biological agents. By the seventeenth century, European military leaders were again becoming receptive to ethics in warfare, and rules to follow in so-called 'civilised war' were slowly being developed. Dutch lawyer Hugo Grotius (1583–1645) published his rules of war in 1625 in *De Jure Belli ac Pacis*; he did not regard the entire population of an antagonist state as the enemy and thereby they should not be subject to enslavement or extermination. Other writers also believed a distinction should be made between combatants and non-combatants.

Emmerich de Vattel's *Le droit des gens* or *Law of Nations* was published in 1758, in which he argued for just war 'without reference to the theological base that informed Augustine and Aquinas'. De Vattel (1714–1767) believed:

> the enemy may be deprived of his property and of whatever may add to his strength and put him in a position to make war … a belligerent lays waste to a country and destroys food and provender in order that the enemy may not be able to subsist there. … Such measures are taken in order to attain the object of the war, but they should be used with moderation and only when necessary.

Between them, Grotius and de Vattel excluded clergy, teachers, women and children, as well as the elderly and infirm, from the 'enemy'. Interestingly for us, they also considered it wrong to use bombs and poison weapons and to contaminate drinking water. However, neither actually condemned the intentional spread of disease among the enemy.

The 1837 Great Plains smallpox epidemic

We have seen documented cases of smallpox allegedly spread intentionally among the indigenous people of the Americas by white fur traders and settlers. This ineffably atrocious behaviour lies somewhere between bioterrorism on a prodigious scale and ethnic cleansing. According to Esther Wagner Stearn (1945):

> this disease [smallpox] was the most dreaded of scourges, the most frequent disastrous dictator of destiny and action among the Indians. This fact the white man soon learned, for history records numerous instances of the French, the Spanish, the English, and later on the Americans, using

smallpox as an ignoble means to an end. For smallpox was more feared by the Indian than the bullet: he could be exterminated and subjugated more easily and quickly by the death-bringing virus than by the weapons of the white man.

A further example of this despicable behaviour comes from fur trader James McDougall, quoted as saying to a gathering of local chiefs:

> You know the smallpox. Listen: I am the smallpox chief. In this bottle I have it confined. All I have to do is to pull the cork, send it forth among you, and you are dead men. But this is for my enemies and not my friends.

Likewise, another fur trader threatened Pawnee Indians that if they failed to agree to certain conditions, 'he would let the smallpox out of a bottle and destroy them'.

Not unreasonably, all this made Native Americans suspicious and nervous of vaccination, as observed by artist and writer George Catlin: 'They see white men urging the operation so earnestly they decide that it must be some new mode or trick of the pale face by which they hope to gain some new advantage over them.' So deep was the distrust of the settlers that the Mandan chief Four Bears denounced the white man, whom he had previously treated as a brother, for deliberately imposing the disease on his people. After losing his wife and children to smallpox, and acquiring the disease himself, his final speech to the Arikara and Mandan tribes before dying on 30 July 1837 ended, according to Frances Chardon, the American trader at Fort Clark, with:

> I have Never Called a White Man a Dog, but to day, I do Pronounce them to be a set of Black harted Dogs ... all that you hold dear, are all Dead, or Dying, with their faces all rotten, caused by those dogs the whites, think of all that My friends, and rise all together and not leave one of them alive.

Four Bears died later that same day. The Mandans, who had numbered between 1,600 and 2,000 in June 1837, were reduced to about 138 by October of the same year. A handful of Mandan survivors joined other tribes, most of them moving eventually to the Fort Berthold reservation in North Dakota.

Ward Churchill claimed in 1837 that at Fort Clark the United States Army deliberately infected Mandan Indians by distributing blankets that had been exposed to smallpox, adding that the blankets were taken from a military infirmary in St Louis, that smallpox vaccine was withheld from the Indians, and that an army doctor had ordered the infected Indians to disperse, further spreading the disease and causing over 100,000 deaths.

Meanwhile, the response to the epidemic was pathetically inadequate: Chardon was dispensing Epsom salts while, 'The Rees are Makeing Medicine for their sickness. Some of them have made dreams, that they talked to the Sun, others to the Moon, several articles has been sacrificed to them both.' He tells of a complete breakdown in local society.

The Confederacy yellow fever plot

Yellow fever is a short-lasting viral disease with symptoms that typically include fever, chills, loss of appetite, nausea, muscle pains particularly in the back, and headache. These usually get better within five days but in about 15 per cent of patients, within a day of improving, the fever returns with a vengeance and victims enter a second, toxic phase of the disease. They then suffer recurring fever, accompanied by jaundice due to liver damage, as well as abdominal pain, bleeding in the mouth, nose and eyes as well as the gastrointestinal tract, triggering vomit containing blood – hence the Spanish name for yellow fever, *vómito negro*, 'black vomit'. There may also be kidney failure, hiccups and delirium. The mortality rate is 20 to 50 per cent. Severe cases may have a mortality greater than 50 per cent.

Survivors enjoy lifelong immunity, and normally no permanent organ damage results. In 1927, yellow fever virus became the first human virus to be isolated.

Yellow fever is caused by yellow fever virus and is spread by the bite of an infected female mosquito, *Aedes aegypti*, a type found throughout the tropics and subtropics. But other *Aedes* mosquitoes such as the tiger mosquito (*Aedes albopictus*) can also be a vector. The virus is an RNA virus of the genus Flavivirus. There is now a safe and effective vaccine.

Yellow fever spread to South and Central America with the slave trade in the seventeenth century with mosquito larvae flourishing in water kegs on board the slave ships: rapid transmission in the crowded confines came when some of the slaves, infected with yellow fever, were bitten by mosquitoes, which then bit uninfected people, spreading the disease. In the eighteenth and nineteenth centuries, yellow fever was regarded as one of the most dangerous infectious diseases.

Barbados had been systematically ecologically transformed with the introduction of sugar cultivation by the Dutch. Those rain forests so plentiful in the 1640s were completely levelled by the 1660s. By the early eighteenth century, Jamaica, Hispaniola and Cuba were subjected to the same sugar plantation depredation. Sugar plantations and the environmental and ecological disruption they caused to natural habitats have a lot to answer for: they created the perfect conditions for mosquito and viral reproduction, leading to subsequent outbreaks of yellow fever. Deforestation reduced populations of insectivorous birds and other creatures that fed on the pernicious mosquitoes and their eggs.

It did not take long for the epidemic to spread north so that between 1668 and 1699, there were reported outbreaks in New York, Boston and Charleston. Bermuda went on to endure four yellow fever epidemics in the 1800s, which in total claimed the lives of 13,356 people, military and civilian. During the 1864 epidemic, a Dr Luke Pryor Blackburn, from Halifax, Nova Scotia, and an expert on the disease, visited the island several times to assist the local medical community. When he departed in October 1864, he left behind some trunks of soiled clothing that were to have been sent on to him in Canada.

It transpired that Blackburn's visits had been bankrolled by the Confederacy, and that a certain Union informer had been offered $60,000 to distribute Dr Blackburn's trunks of soiled clothing to Union cities including Boston, Philadelphia, Washington and Norfolk. One trunk also went to New Bern and was identified as having introduced yellow fever to that city, claiming the lives of 2,000 people.

Blackburn was arrested and tried, but acquitted owing to lack of evidence, which still left the toxic trunks unaccounted for. In 1878, he went on to fight yellow fever in Kentucky, where he had set up a practice in Louisville and was eventually elected governor.

Smallpox in British Columbia – more cases of genocide

When European settlers first descended on Canada's Pacific shelf, they liked to think of themselves as harbingers of light, ushering in as they did the glow of the European enlightenment. Natives saw it very differently; what they experienced was an envelope of darkness, which began with settlers intentionally spreading smallpox in a systematic programme to displace the indigenous peoples in what is now British Columbia. Their aim: to 'cleanse' the region of the indigenous population.

It started with a gold rush. On 12 March 1862, the San Francisco steamer *Brother Jonathan* docked at the busy colony of Vancouver Island, a former Hudson Bay Company fur trading post that had witnessed an explosion in population after a mainland gold rush. 'The town was taken completely by surprise,' according to the *British Colonist*, reporting that along with merchandise and mules, the ship carried 350 passengers to Victoria – home to 4,000–5,000 colonists, with slightly more indigenous people from various nations in camps nearby hoping for trade and work.

According to Joshua Ostroff (2017):

> Most of the passengers were heading to a new gold strike on the Salmon River. But along with his pickaxe and gold pan, one of these miners brought another cargo: smallpox. The man was quarantined. But the *Colonist* noted that 'the measures the colonial government chose – limited vaccination efforts, and declining to try a general quarantine, which would have kept the crisis localized – wound up leading to an epidemic when police emptied the camps at gunpoint, burned them down, and towed canoes filled with smallpox-infected Indigenous people up the coast. Over the next year, at least 30,000 indigenous people died, representing about 60 per cent of the population – a crisis that left mass graves, deserted villages, traumatized survivors and societal collapse.'

When, on 4 July 1862, Francis Poole and eight men from what had begun as a party of forty arrived at Fort Alexandria in the Nuxalk Ancestral Territory, smallpox carriers knowingly left the disease at Nanaimo, Fort Rupert (North Vancouver Island), and at a Heiltsuk community on the approach to Bella Coola. Rumour has it that the disease arrived in blankets that had been infected with smallpox and then repackaged as new for trade. As in other documented cases, such as that of John McLain, who admitted taking smallpox-infected blankets to Tatla, those traders were also carriers of the disease. Within thirty days, an eyewitness estimated 75 per cent of the Nuxalk at Bella Coola were dead or dying from the disease.

One Indigenous nation, though, fought back to defend its land. In 1864, the Tsilhqot'in declared war after being threatened with smallpox by the foreman of a road being built through their territory. This battle, the Chilcotin War, ended with the hanging of five chiefs – known as the martyrdom of the 'Chilcotin Chiefs'. Over 75 per cent of all the Tsilhqot'in people would be dead before the year's end – a sign of systematic disease introduction? Events in Nuxalk territory during this 'smallpox war' connects the violence in Tsilhqot'in territory with similar smallpox epidemics elsewhere in the British Pacific Colonies. Shawn Swankey (2015) tells how:

> In the sudden catastrophe flowing from these artificial epidemics, 70 per cent or more of all the Tsilhqot'in died in a year or less. Some other indigenous peoples in BC [British Columbia] suffered similar death tolls. In the face of this carnage, the Tsilhqot'in held a war council, killed up to

20 settlers implicated in smallpox distribution schemes and closed their territory. BC then invaded Tsilhqot'in territory with two settler militias. Unable to find the war party, agents for the Crown invited Tsilhqot'in representatives to a peace conference. The Colony violated the conditions of the conference to ambush the Tsilhqot'in and five, including the 'Head War Chief', were put through show trials and executed.

'The smallpox epidemic ... it changes everything in British Columbia,' says John Lutz, the head of the University of Victoria's History department and an indigenous-settler relations specialist. 'The citizens of Victoria, one could say, panicked. Or, one could say, with a less charitable view, that they deliberately drove the Indigenous people out of town, and that spread the disease back to their home communities up and down the coast.' If they had contained those people who contracted smallpox within the Victoria area, the indigenous population would be much higher today. The government clearly wanted to be able to claim those lands without having to compensate or recognise indigenous title.

Colonist numbers duly surged as indigenous populations fell by as much as 90 per cent in some areas. Cole Harris reports in *The Resettlement of British Columbia* that by 1863 in south-eastern British Columbia, large areas were 'almost completely depopulated' and that census takers on the north coast found the Haida people had fallen from a pre-epidemic count of 6,607 to only 829 in 1881.

On the 150th anniversary of the hanging in 2014, British Columbia exonerated six Tsilhqot'in leaders hanged in 1864–65; the Premier, Christy Clark, expressed British Columbia's 'profound sorrow' for this execution of officials who had done no more than seek to protect their people from genocide through the continued intentional introduction of smallpox.

Apache ant torture

The Apache Indians are said to have used ants to deliver a long, lingering, excruciating death to invaders on their lands. There are several credible reports from the late 1800s of Apaches staking captives on anthills. The victims either had honey smeared on their eyes and lips or had their mouths held open with sharpened skewers. However, in at least one case, an Apache reported, 'Old Eskimi[n]zin says he buried an American alive in the ground once and let the ants eat his head off.' Indian tactics probably became increasingly vicious in response to continuing abuse at the hands of the Spanish and Mexicans who themselves practised torture.

An eminent anthropologist working for the US Bureau of Ethnology has provided a compelling account of how another tribe used ants as instruments of torture. While embedding himself with the Zuni Indians of New Mexico, Frank Hamilton Cushing (1857–1900) earned his acceptance into an order of Zuni priests through a series of decidedly challenging trials, including the following:

> Still fasting, bareheaded, and stripped nearly to the skin, I was set at sunrise on a large ant-hill of the red fire ants of the Southwest, so named because of their bites, and there all day long I had to sit, motionless, speechless, save to priests in reply to instructions.

He 'went native', living with the Zuni from 1879 to 1884, and becoming anthropology's first participant observer. After some initial difficulties – the Zuni considered killing him as they believed he had come for their sacred secrets – Cushing was accepted by the community. He was adopted by the Governor of the Pueblo, Patrico Pino (Balawahdiwa), and permitted to participate in Zuni activities. In 1881, Cushing was initiated into the warrior society, the Priesthood of the Bow. For this, he was given a Zuni name – Tenatsali, meaning 'medicine flower'.

The Bug Pit of Bukhara

Nasrullah Bahadur-Khan (r. 1827–60), Emir of Bukhara (present-day Uzbekistan), was one of history's pre-eminent sadists, up there with Mengele and Shirō Ishii – and perhaps best remembered by history as the emir who in 1842 imprisoned and eventually executed the British soldiers Lieutenant Colonel Charles Stoddart and Arthur Conolly, and imprisoned but eventually released Joseph Wolff, an Anglican priest who came looking for them in 1843 and who had the sense and courtesy to do his research on the emir. But then there was what the locals called 'Si(y)ah Cha', which meant 'Black Well' or 'Black Hole' – a hole 21 feet deep, covered with an iron grate and accessible only by a rope. The emir regularly replenished the 'Bug Pit' with fresh insects, rodents and reptiles to assure a relentless, torturous experience for his victims. The notorious hole was in Zindon prison in the Ark Fortress in Bukhara. The public beheadings were a grim, ironically merciful, finale to months of daily torture in Zindon.

Stoddart and Conolly were embroiled in a regional power game between Russia and the British; they were mere pawns and victims of what was an instance of typical British (un)diplomatic arrogance, riding roughshod over local customs and etiquette. Stoddart had been tasked with delivering a letter of reassurance to the emir, stating that the British had no intention of extending their invasion of Afghanistan into his kingdom. However, Stoddart made a costly gaffe riding into the Ark on horseback rather than walking, which was the custom, and arrived without a gift for Nasrullah Khan. Nasrullah Khan was outraged at these insults, and anyway viewed the British Empire as a weakened and insignificant power after their defeat in Afghanistan. Therefore, he had the two British jailed, tortured by insect, and executed. The British Empire did not respond. This is how one of Stoddart's fellow officers described the diplomatic fiasco: 'To attack or defend a fortress, no better man than Stoddart could be found; but for a diplomatic mission, requiring coolness and self-command, a man less adapted to the purpose could not readily have been met with.' Nor did the British bother to fully comprehend the nature and defining characteristics of the emir; his official title – the Shadow of God Upon Earth – should have rung alarm bells. Secretly, the citizens of Bukhara referred to their ruler as 'the Butcher'.

The most repellent of the emir's six-legged conscripts were the assassin bugs and the eight-legged sheep ticks (*Dermacentor marginatus*).

> Assassin bugs belong to the *Reduviidae*, a family of carnivorous insects. The proclivity of some species for cannibalism accounts for the common name of the group. These creatures range in size from 1/10 [of an inch] to nearly 2 inches and are endowed with a stout, curved beak for piercing their prey. Assassin bugs inject toxic saliva that paralyses and kills other insects, along with enzymes that liquefy the innards of the prey, allowing the predator to suck it dry. A few assassin bugs feed on mammals, but the bite of these insects – also known as kissing bugs – is not usually painful. Stealth makes sense when securing a meal from a creature thousands of times larger than you. Most likely, the emir used species that do not normally bite humans, but when starved will feed on any animal tissue. The bite of these insects has been compared to being pierced with a hot needle, and the digestive enzymes that they inject cause suppurating sores.
> https://www.insectomania.org/biological-weapons/insects-as-tools-of-torture.html

The jailer described how the two British prisoners were slowly eaten alive as 'masses of their flesh had been gnawed off their bones'.

Microbiology, bacteriology, virology and disease

> Antony van Leeuwenhoek (1632–1723) is universally acknowledged as the father of microbiology. He discovered both protists and bacteria. More than being the first to see this unimagined world of 'animalcules', he was the first even to think of looking – certainly, the first with the power to see. Using his own deceptively simple, single-lensed microscopes, he did not merely observe, but conducted ingenious experiments, exploring and manipulating his microscopic universe with a curiosity that belied his lack of a map or bearings.
>
> Nick Lane, Philosophical Transactions of the Royal Society B, 2015

The revelation that there was a connection of microorganisms to disease goes back to the nineteenth century, when German physician Robert Koch introduced the science of microorganisms to the medical field. He identified bacteria as the cause of infectious diseases and the process of fermentation in diseases. Louis Pasteur developed techniques to produce vaccines; both Koch and Pasteur helped improve antisepsis in medical treatment. This had a huge beneficial effect on public health and gave a better understanding of the body and diseases. The importance of bacteria was recognised as it led to a study of disease prevention and treatment of diseases by vaccines and antibiotics.

Unfortunately, it also led to the facilitation of new, more sophisticated methods of biological warfare, including the isolation and production of stocks of specific pathogens, as we shall see in the following chapters.

Chapter 7

The First World War and After

Much of the work in and around the First World War years focused on chemical warfare and mainly involved toxic, asphyxiating and blistering gases. The associated images, artworks, memoirs, novels, films and poetry are all etched on our minds. Who, once they have read it once, can forget

> Drunk with fatigue; deaf even to the hoots
> Of gas-shells dropping softly behind.
>
> Gas! GAS! Quick, boys! – An ecstasy of fumbling,
> Fitting the clumsy helmets just in time;
> But someone still was yelling out and stumbling,
> And flound'ring like a man in fire or lime…
> Dim, through the misty panes and thick green light,
> As under a green sea, I saw him drowning.
>
> In all my dreams, before my helpless sight,
> He plunges at me, guttering, choking, drowning.
>
> Excerpt from Wilfred Owen, *Dulce et Decorum Est*,
> published posthumously in 1920

Anthrax and glanders and 'Tony's Lab'

There is substantial evidence that the Germans launched an ambitious and audacious biological warfare programme during the First World War. This featured covert operations that included attempts by Germans to ship horses and cattle inoculated with disease-producing bacteria, such as *Bacillus anthracis* (anthrax) and *Pseudomonas pseudomallei* (glanders), to the USA and other neutral countries. An example is the infection of Argentinian livestock intended for export to the Allied forces, resulting in the death of 200 mules in 1917 and 1918. The same agents were used to infect Romanian sheep earmarked for export to Russia. Other allegations of attempts by Germany to spread cholera in Italy and plague in St Petersburg followed, as well as attempts to infect Norwegian reindeer. Germany denied all these allegations, including the accusation that biological bombs were dropped over British positions.

> The microbes were suspended in liquid in test-tubes, and a crew of longshoremen recruited by the Germans wandered among the stockades where animals were collected for trans-shipment, jabbing them with needles dipped into the microbial cultures. This went on for about a year, until a few months after Dilger returned to Germany early in 1916.
>
> Mark Wheelis, 'First shots fired in biological warfare', *Nature* 395, 213 1998

These diseases are so virulent that if Dilger could infect them just before they were loaded onto the ships, by the end of their journey most if not all of the animals would be dead or dying.

Anton Casimir Dilger (1884–1918) was an American-educated surgeon who specialised in wound surgery at Johns Hopkins University, Baltimore. After signing up with the German Army in 1914, he suffered a nervous breakdown and was sent to his parents' home in Virginia to recuperate. The United States was at this time neutral in the war. He also became a protagonist in the above German biological warfare sabotage programme during the First World War. Germany wanted to prevent neutral countries from supplying Allied forces with livestock, and the fact that Dilger had a US passport from 1908 onwards facilitated his travel to and from America. Along with his brother Carl, Dilger established a laboratory in a private house in Chevy Chase district of Washington, DC, 'Tony's Lab', in which cultures of the causative agents of anthrax and glanders were produced. A 1941 report revealed that the bacteria were to be smeared onto the nostrils of horses.

In the US, Baltimore stevedores, who were at first recruited by German officers to plant incendiary devices among ships and wharves, were eventually given bottles of liquid culture with orders to infect horses near Van Cortland Park. The stevedores claimed to have done the deed using rubber gloves and needles. The bacteria from 'Tony's Lab' were delivered to Captain Frederick Hinsch, who was using a house at the corner of Charles and Redwood Streets in Baltimore. Hinsch inoculated horses in Baltimore that were awaiting shipment to Europe. Dilger also attempted to establish a second biological warfare laboratory in St Louis, Missouri, but gave up after a cold winter killed the cultures.

The methods of infecting livestock became more advanced as the war progressed and went from crude needles to capillary tubes of bacterial culture hidden inside sugar cubes. The effects of the German effort to sabotage neutral support of Allied countries is unknown.

Under suspicion of being a German agent by the Federal Bureau of Investigation, Dilger eventually fled to Madrid where, ironically, he died during the 1918 flu pandemic.

Wheelis adds that in mid-1915, Captain Rudolf Nadolny of the general staff's Berlin headquarters targeted the Romanian animal trade with Russia when he shipped anthrax and glanders cultures to the German embassy in Bucharest for use by Bulgarian agents collaborating with the Germans. The programme obviously came to a halt in August 1916, when Romania broke its neutrality and declared war on Austria-Hungary. After the German diplomats were expelled, the Romanian police searched the embassy grounds, discovering anthrax and glanders cultures. No one at the time suspected that it was evidence not merely of intent to commit a single act of biological warfare, but rather of an ongoing operation.

The Germans tried a similar covert operation in Spain too when Spanish horses to be shipped to France were the main targets, although other targets in the French Pyrenees and Portugal were probably also involved. The Spanish programme used ampoules of bacteria concealed in sugar cubes to be fed to intended victims. Spain was the staging point for shipment of cultures and agents to neutral Argentina, a major supplier of cattle, horses and mules to the Allies. Wheelis tells how German agent Herman Wuppermann travelled by U-boat probably carrying cultures from Croatia to neutral Spain, then by commercial steamship to Argentina and was dependent on replenishment of infected sugar cubes from Berlin.

Bad as this was, it was nothing compared to what the British journalist Henry Wickham Steed reported: he told the world in 1934 ('Aerial Warfare: Secret German Warfare', pp. 1–15) that German agents were investigating the possible impact of biological and chemical aerial attacks on London and Paris.

Clandestine activities of German agents operating in the United States in 1915 were revealed after the war. Erich von Steinmetz, a captain in the German Navy, entered the United States disguised as a woman, bringing with him cultures of glanders with which to inoculate horses intended for the Western Front. After failing in this, he posed as a research scientist and took the cultures to a laboratory, where they were found to be dead.

In 1916, a German agent intent on spreading a biological agent was arrested in Russia. In 1917, Germany was accused of poisoning wells in the Somme area with human corpses, and dropping fruit, chocolate and children's toys infected with lethal bacteria into Romanian cities. German agents tried to infect horses with glanders and cattle with anthrax in France. A more successful attack was the infection of some 4,500 mules with glanders by a German agent in Mesopotamia. Another reported attack was with cholera in Italy. As noted, a 1929 report also accused the Germans of dropping bombs containing 'plague' over British positions during the war. Some of these reports were of questionable authenticity and were vehemently denied by the Germans.

Ricin

Ricin, *Ricinus communis*, is a lectin (a carbohydrate-binding protein) and a powerful toxin when inhaled, injected or ingested; it is produced in the seeds of the castor oil plant. Ricin can be made from the waste material left over from processing castor beans. It can be in the form of a powder, a mist or a pellet, or it can be dissolved in water or weak acid. An estimated lethal oral dose in humans is approximately 1 milligram per kilogram of body weight.

Ricin could be spread in two ways. The first involved sticking ricin to shrapnel bullets in artillery shells. As detailed in a technical report in 1918, these experiments illustrate two crucial things: clearly, preparations of ricin can be made to adhere to shrapnel bullets, and there is no loss in toxicity when fired, even with the crudest method of coating the bullets. It is reasonable to suppose that every wound inflicted by a ricin-coated shrapnel bullet would result in a serious casualty, so many wounds that may otherwise have been trivial would have escalated to become a fatality.

The second method of delivery involved the production of a ricin dust cloud. However, due to limited amounts of ricin being produced and the inefficient delivery via the respiratory tract, little progress seems to have been made. The First World War ended before the United States weaponised ricin. During the Second World War, the United States and Canada studied ricin for use in cluster bombs. Plans for mass production and field trials with different bomblet concepts came to nothing when it was found that ricin was no more economical than using phosgene. Interest continued for a short period after the Second World War, but soon subsided when the US Army Chemical Corps began a programme to weaponise sarin.

Glanders

Glanders is a disease that mainly affects horses, mules and donkeys. As we have seen, in the First World War, German forces reportedly spread glanders to debilitate Allied cavalries and pack horses. The bacteria that causes glanders, *Burkholderia mallei*, also infects humans. Due to the high mortality rate in humans and the small number of organisms required to establish infection, glanders is a good candidate for biological warfare and bioterrorism; the same applies to the closely related organism *B. pseudomallei*, the causative agent of melioidosis. Glanders also is known to have been developed by various bioweapons programmes: in a single year between 1982 and 1984, the Soviet Union produced more than 2,000 tons of dry agent for glanders for use in the Afghan War (Van Zandt 2013).

The bacteria can enter the body through cuts in the skin or the membranes of the eyes and nose. The bacteria can also be inhaled, and as an aerosol, glanders would be an effective deadly weapon.

Baron Otto Karl von Rosen and the anthrax sugar lumps

Recent detective work, as reported in *Nature*, by the British Germ Defence unit and the Norwegian military began when the curator of the police museum in Trondheim, Norway, found a bottle with two sugar lumps in an archive. On inspection, the curator found that each lump was pierced by a small hole; one hole contained a tiny sealed glass tube. An attached note described the exhibit: 'A piece of sugar containing *anthrax bacilli*, found in the luggage of Baron Otto Karl von Rosen, when he was apprehended in Karasjok in January 1917, suspected of espionage and sabotage.' The sugar lumps lay unnoticed until 1997. 'The spores were still alive,' museum registrar Lars Koen said. 'They have now been sterilised and sent back to the museum for display.' Their identification as *Bacillus anthracis* was confirmed by two separate methods, including one that amplifies and examines the molecular structure of an organism's genetic material, or DNA.

What intrigued the scientists was what the baron – 'a Swedish-German-Finnish aristocrat' – and his colleagues intended to do with the anthrax. After the baron had been expelled to Sweden, a later inspection of his baggage produced bottles of deadly curare, microbial cultures and nineteen sugar lumps.

The scientists say that Berlin had approved a microbial attack on army horses and reindeer used for sledging British armaments to Russia from the port of Skibotn in northern Norway. Local newspapers of the day speculated that the toxic sugar cubes were also used to poison horses involved in war transport. 'The grinding of the sugar and its glass insert between the molar teeth of horses would probably result in a lethal infection,' the scientists wrote.

Bacillus anthracis, the etiologic agent of anthrax, is one of the most potent biological warfare agents because its spores are extremely resistant to natural conditions and can survive for several decades in the environment. *B. anthracis* spores enter the body through skin lesions (cutaneous anthrax), lungs (pulmonary anthrax), or gastrointestinal route (gastrointestinal anthrax) and germinate, giving rise to the vegetative form. Anthrax is a zoonotic disease that is mainly associated with herbivores and domestic animals. The disease occurs regularly in countries where widespread vaccination of animals is not practised. Human anthrax is less common and usually spreads to populations through close proximity to infected livestock, by handling infected domestic animals including cattle and goats or their products like skin, meat, hides and bones.

Ajay Kumar Goel explains why anthrax has such potential as a biological warfare agent:

> The surprisingly resistant spores have earned the status of potential bioterror weapon for anthrax. The possibility to create aerosol from spores makes B. anthracis a lethal biological weapon. All the attributes of spores: high resistance to temperature, pressure, pH, ionizing radiations and half-life of 100 years make them a suitable bioterror agent. After production and purification, anthrax spores can be stored in a dry form which remains viable for decades. Spores may survive in the water, soil and on surface for several years. Inhalation of spores causes inhalational anthrax, which is the most dangerous form of disease. Inhalational anthrax is dangerous for obvious reasons as initial symptoms resemble that of flu, making its early diagnosis difficult; by the time disease is correctly recognised it's too late.
>
> Ajay Kumar Goel,
> *Anthrax: A disease of biowarfare and public health importance*

Operation Alberich

In early 1917, the German Army made a strategic withdrawal 25 miles to a shorter, more defensible line in northern France, the Hindenburg Line (*Siegfriedstellung*); this critical manoeuvre is known as Operation Alberich. With fighting on the Eastern Front detaining much of his army, the Kaiser sought to reduce the impact on his outnumbered divisions in the west. At the same time, he wanted to make sure that this surrendered land, a greater gain than the Allies had managed in two-and-a-half years of war, could be of no value or material advantage to his opponents. The intention was to destroy anything the Allies might find useful, from electric cables and water pipes to roads, bridges and entire villages. The town of Bapaume was destroyed in forty-five minutes, one of more than 200 places that were completely razed to the ground. Alberich began on 9 February 1917 under Erich Ludendorff (1865–1937): railways and roads were dug up, trees were felled, water wells were polluted, towns and villages were demolished and numerous land mines and other booby traps were planted – in short, the systematic destruction of 938 square miles of French territory by the German Army.

The Battle of Tanga, or the Battle of the Bees, 1914

Bees sent flying at the enemy or booby-trapped to topple over with tripwires were used to the advantage of both sides during skirmishes in the First World War. German soldiers rigged a number of beehives in Tanga, East Africa, with tripwired explosives. Advancing British troops triggered the hives, causing many injuries.

On 4 November 1914, in a bid to overrun German East Africa (the mainland portion of present-day Tanzania), a British force largely made up of 8,000 poorly equipped and trained soldiers from the Indian Expeditionary Force 'B' (27th (Bangalore) Brigade) attacked the important port and railway terminus of Tanga. Although the German defenders were heavily outnumbered eight to one, they were well prepared under the command of Colonel Paul von Lettow-Vorbeck. The British attack was soon in trouble.

The Indians made no progress against von Lettow-Vorbeck's reinforced defences; the Germans even went on the offensive. Matters were made worse when the fighting disturbed swarms of aggressive bees whose hives were in trees on the battlefield. The angry bees launched their own (neutral) attack, stinging the troops of both sides and causing some of the British force to fall back in panic. The combination of machine-gun and bee attacks proved devastating and on the following day, the British retreated to their ships. This is considered one of the greatest victories of the Schutztruppe in Africa, not least because of all the abandoned modern military equipment the Germans inherited. British propaganda transformed the bee interlude, a simple instance of happenstance, into a cunning German plot, inventing the presence of hidden tripwires to agitate the hives.

The battle was a total disaster, and was recorded in the *British Official History of the War* as 'one of the most notable failures in British military history'. Casualties included 360 killed and 487 wounded on the British side; the Schutztruppe lost 16 Germans and 55 Askaris killed, and 76 wounded. History does not record any fatalities amongst the bees.

Badger hair shaving brushes

Wars tend to throw up all sorts of curiosities. One that implicated soldiers and anthrax infection but was *not* an instance of biological warfare although originally thought to be is a good example. In 1915, the British military detected that an unusually large number of newly recruited British and American soldiers were developing anthrax infections on their heads and necks – classic symptoms of cutaneous anthrax infection. At first, the outbreak, the Centers for Disease Control and Prevention (CDC) tells us, was attributed to 'diabolical tactics of the enemy'. But crafty German biological warfare was not to blame; rather, the cause of the skin problems were the shaving brushes the soldiers were issued on enlistment, *de riguer* because a clean-shaven face made a gas mask more effective.

Before the war, shaving brushes were usually made with badger hair, the bristles of choice for lathering up. With the onset of the war, the supply of high-quality badger bristles from Russia was interrupted so suppliers switched to horsehair from Russia, China and Japan – but they sent the tufts directly to brush manufacturers in the United States without any disinfection. Anthrax is a zoonotic disease, which means that livestock and other animals can spread the anthrax to humans, though it is not otherwise contagious. Inhaling or ingesting anthrax spores can cause a dangerous infection, but anthrax infections on the skin are rarely lethal if properly treated. Between 1915 and 1924, 149 American soldiers, 28 British servicemen and 67 civilians in both countries contracted the disease. Between 1915 and 1924, the New York City Board of Health found that brushes were the culprit, and quickly published new guidelines on brush cleaning; after 1930, brushes were safe to use again.

Postwar

In 1970, the World Health Organization (WHO) estimated that a city with a 5 million population attacked with 50 kg of anthrax would be looking at a death toll of 100,000 with 250,000 incapacitated in a projected affected downwind area of 20 km. For plague, they estimated 50 kg in a 5 million-population city would cause 150,000 initial infections and 36,000 deaths, translating into 500,000 hospitalisations and up to 100,000 deaths over a number of weeks.

A later (1993) report by the US Congressional Office of Technology Assessment looked at a scenario involving release of 100 kg of anthrax aerosol upwind of the Washington, DC area. It estimated that this would cause at least 130,000 deaths, and possibly as many as 3 million. An economic model developed by the Centers for Disease Control and Prevention estimated a cost of $26.2 billion per 100,000 people exposed to a bioterrorist attack.

Table 3

AGENT	Downwind reach (KM) (KM)	Fatalities	Incapacitated
Anthrax	>20	100,000	250,000
Tularaemia	>20	30,000	125,000
Brucellosis	10	500	100,000
Q fever	>20	150	125,000

Souce: Yuen, *Biological Warfare, the facts/https://researchbriefings.files. parliament.uk/documents/POST-PN-166/POST-PN-166.pdf*

Sir Frederick Grant Banting and Suffield Experimental Station, Alberta

Sir Frederick Grant Banting (1891–1941) was a Canadian medical scientist, physician and Nobel laureate, awarded to him as the co-discoverer of insulin and its therapeutic potential. By 1938, Banting had developed an interest in aviation medicine, which led to him working with the Royal Canadian Air Force (RCAF) in research on the physiological problems encountered by pilots operating high-altitude combat aircraft. Banting headed the RCAF's Number 1 Clinical Investigation Unit (CIU), which was housed in a secret facility on the grounds of the former Eglinton Hunt Club in Toronto. It was at the CIU that Banting worked with Wilbur Franks on the invention of the anti-gravity g-suit to stop pilots from blacking out when they were subjected to g-forces while turning or diving. Another of Banting's projects during the Second World War involved treating mustard gas burns; Banting even tested the gas and antidotes on himself to see if they were effective. During the war, the Canadian Forces Base, Suffield Experimental Station, Alberta, was Canada's cutting-edge secret facility for the development of lethal and non-lethal aerosols designed to be dropped from aircraft. In 1941, British and Canadian forces began testing chemical warheads on the vast weapons range at the Canadian Forces Base Suffield.

Canada, the United Kingdom and the United States also began collaborating on weaponising anthrax, ricin, plague and other biological agents, as well as developing defences against them. This effort took place both at Suffield and at Connaught Laboratories at Grosse Île in the St Lawrence River. Banting worked there as director of chemical research until he was killed when his aircraft crashed returning to base.

During a 1927 Arctic trip with A.Y. Jackson, Banting observed that either the crew or passengers on board the Hudson's Bay Company (HBC) paddle wheeler SS *Distributor* were inadvertently responsible for spreading the influenza virus down the Slave and Mackenzie rivers, a virus that had over the summer and autumn spread extensively, devastating the aboriginal population of the north. When he got back from the trip, Banting gave an interview with a *Toronto Star* reporter on the understanding that his statements about HBC would remain off the record. The conversation was nonetheless published in the *Toronto Star* and soon reached a wide audience across Europe and Australia. Banting was angry at the leak, having promised the Department of the Interior not to make any statements to the press prior to them granting clearance.

The article said that Banting had given the journalist C.R. Greenaway repeated instances of how the fox fur trade always favoured the company: 'For over $100,000 of fox skins, he estimated that the Eskimos had not received $5,000 worth of goods.' He connected this situation to native health, consistent with reports made in previous years by Royal Canadian Mounted Police officers, suggesting that 'the result was a diet of "flour, biscuits, tea and tobacco", with the skins that once were used for clothing traded merely for "cheap whiteman's goods".'

The fur trade commissioner for the Hudson's Bay Company called Banting's remarks 'false and slanderous', and a month later, the governor and general manager of HBC met Banting to demand a retraction. Banting stated that the reporter had betrayed his confidence, but did not retract his statement and reaffirmed that HBC was responsible for the death of indigenous residents by supplying inappropriate and insufficient food and introducing diseases into the Arctic.

According to Frank Tester:

He noted that 'infant mortality was high because of the undernourishment of the mother before birth'; that 'white man's food leads to decay of native teeth'; that 'tuberculosis has commenced. Saw several cases at Godhavn, Etah, Port Burwell, Arctic Bay'; that 'an epidemic resembling influenza killed a considerable proportion of population at Port Burwell'; and that 'the gravest danger faces the Eskimo in his transfer from a race-long hunter to a dependent trapper. White flour, sea-biscuits, tea and tobacco do not provide sufficient fuel to warm and nourish him.'

Frank Tester (2008), 'A Voice of Presence: Inuit Contributions toward the Public Provision of Health Care in Canada, 1900-1930', *Social History/Histoire Sociale* 41 (82): 535–61

Chemical warfare usually enjoyed more attention during the 1930s, while biological warfare received very little. In 1933, Major Leon A. Fox of the US Army Medical Corps wrote a highly sceptical if not pragmatic article on bacterial warfare for the *Military Surgeon*. It began: 'Bacterial warfare is one of the recent scare-heads that we are being served by the pseudo-scientists who contribute to the flaming pages of the Sunday annexes syndicated over the Nation's press.' He then pointed out the difficulties involved in weaponising biological agents. For example, bubonic plague would create significant problems for friendly troops as well as the enemy:

> The use of bubonic plague today against a field force, when the forces are actually in contact, is unthinkable for the simple reason that the epidemic could not be controlled. Infected personnel captured would provide the spark to set off possible outbreaks of pneumonic plague in the ranks of the captors. Infected rats would also visit and spread the condition. An advance over terrain infected with plague-bearing rats would be dangerous. Therefore, except as a last desperate, despairing hope of a rapidly retreating army, the use of plague by forces in the field is not to be considered.

After dismissing the causative organisms of malaria, yellow fever, anthrax, and other such agents, Fox concluded:

> I consider that it is highly questionable if biologic agents are suited for warfare. Certainly at the present time practically insurmountable technical difficulties prevent the use of biologic agents as effective weapons of warfare.
>
> L.A. Fox, 'Bacterial warfare: The use of biologic agents in warfare',
> *Military Surgeon* 1933; 72(3): 189–207

At roughly the same time, Germany stepped up its military training in offensive biological warfare and reportedly covertly tested *Serratia marcescens*, a biological simulant, in the Paris Metro ventilation shafts and near several French forts. In 1936, they carried out experiments with foot-and-mouth disease on animals on Lüneburg Heath in northern Germany. The next year, the German Military Bacteriological Institute in Berlin began developing anthrax as a biological weapon, while the Agricultural Hochschule in Bonn researched the spraying of crops with bacteria.

In 1936, the UK formed a committee to examine offensive and defensive biological warfare issues. By 1940, the British chemical laboratory at Porton Down was extended to include a biological warfare laboratory.

France

One of the leading French scientists working on biological warfare was André Trillat (1853–1932) – a world expert on airborne dissemination of disease and director of the Naval Chemical Research Laboratory. The programme was active from 1921 to 1927, and was resumed in 1935 in the light of Nazi expansionism policies. Trillat overturned the belief that microbes were too fragile to survive explosive impact followed by exposure outside their animal host bodies to dry air; he thus proved the viability of biological weapons. Trillat favoured liquid cultures of bacterial agents detonated to form bacterial clouds and dropped as bombs from aeroplanes.

The French focused on tularaemia, brucellosis, melioidosis (similar to glanders), plague, anthrax, and botulinum toxin. Smallpox was rejected due to the availability of a vaccine, while tuberculosis, diphtheria and polio were considered to be too slow acting. Trillat remained at the helm until the German occupation of France in 1940. The French could also draw on the unrivalled expertise residing in the Pasteur Institute in Paris, giving access to some of the world's leading biological scientists.

When Trillat and his colleagues began researching dissemination technologies and techniques, they left no stone unturned, even to the extent of releasing microorganisms in the Paris subway to determine how much they would disperse. They studied botulinum toxin and discovered that it could survive the destructive forces of an exploding artillery shell. Similarly, they researched dissemination of animal diseases and tried to implement some defensive measures, including the production of anti-anthrax sera.

In the months before the start of the Second World War, the French explored several different types of biological weapons, including an aircraft bomb, an artillery shell and a hand grenade. The French tested some of these devices in early 1940 with positive results. Interestingly, it appears that the devices disseminated 'bovine plague virus', probably a reference to 'cattle plague' or rinderpest – an animal disease that does not affect people, so the objective must have been to attack the thousands of horses used by German Army units.

When the programme ended in 1940, the French destroyed most of their records and work, and hid others. When the Germans discovered some of their research, it could hardly fail to influence German thinking about biowarfare and biodefence, despite their earlier arrogance.

The Pasteur Institute, Paris

The Pasteur Institute is a French non-profit private centre of excellence dedicated to the study of biology, microorganisms, diseases and vaccines. The institute was founded in 1887 and for 150 or so years has been at the leading edge of infectious diseases research. It was the first institution to isolate HIV, the virus that causes AIDS, in 1983. Over the years, it has been responsible for discoveries that have enabled a better management of diseases through the development of vaccines for tuberculosis, diphtheria, tetanus, yellow fever and poliomyelitis.

During the First World War, the priority was to vaccinate troops against typhoid fever, which typically ran riot through soldiers in close proximity in trenches and barracks. By September 1914, the institute was able to deliver 670,000 doses of the vaccine and continued to produce it throughout the conflict.

Gabriel Bertrand invented a grenade based on chloropicrin and Fourneau discovered the chemical reaction that led to the formation of methylarsine chloride. Bertand's endeavours were to counter the German use of concentrated chloropicrin against Allied forces as a tear gas; it caused vomiting and forced Allied soldiers to remove their masks to vomit, exposing them to other, more toxic chemical gases used as weapons during the war.

In the Second World War, such was the arrogance of the German scientists that after the occupation of France, the Germans never bothered to garner information from the institute's research or allow it to dictate research programmes; they believed that their own work was far superior so their only interest was in the serums and vaccines that they could give their troops and allies. This enabled the institute to become a virtual pharmacy for the Resistance thanks to the initiative of Louis Pasteur Vallery-Radot (1886–1970), Louis Pasteur's grandson. The Germans became suspicious of the institute's staff only after an outbreak of typhoid in a Wehrmacht division that was stationed near Paris waiting to be sent to the Russian front. The cause of the epidemic was later found to be a member of the institute stealing a culture of the germ responsible for the disease and adulterating a large quantity of butter used in German meals for their troops. Afterwards, the German authorities put in place safety measures; they ordered that the institute's stores containing microbial cultures could be opened only by specified personnel. Two biologists, a Dr Wolmann and his wife, as well as three lab assistants, were sent to a concentration camp.

The respect the institute attracted saved it from the ravages of war even during the battles for Paris's liberation; the fear that involving it in any type of conflict might 'free the ghosts of long defeated diseases' was also a factor.

The First World War and After

Hungary

The small Hungarian biowarfare programme became operational in August 1938 at what was known as the Health Control Station of the Hungarian Royal Defence Forces based in a converted artillery warehouse in Budapest. Despite only having six scientists, it made considerable progress before being destroyed during a bombing raid in April 1944. The Hungarians researched *Bacillus anthracis*, *Clostridium perfringens*, *Salmonella paratyphi*, and *Shigella dysenteriae*. They also explored various dissemination techniques, including glass bombs capable of carrying 1–50 kilograms of a biological agent, either wet or dry.

Italy

The Italians initiated a small BW programme in 1934 based in a military hospital in Rome. In 1936, Mussolini was keen to employ biological weapons against hostile forces during the invasion of Abyssinia. However, senior commanders opposed the proposal, fearing that such attacks would undermine support from Ethiopians sympathetic towards the Italians. It seems likely that the programme folded in 1940 when its director and chief advocate were posted to the front.

Poland

It is hardly surprising to find that the Polish BW programme was catalysed by concerns over the biological warfare work that their Soviet Union neighbours were doing. The Polish programme was underway by 1928, and was under the authority of the intelligence services operating in rigorous security and independently from a dedicated military laboratory. The primary military objective was the development of a capacity for conducting biological sabotage operations against military forces (Russian) invading Polish territory. By 1938, sixty-seven researchers were busy in their research institute although some key BW scientists fled Poland ahead of the invading Germans in September 1939 after destroying the military laboratory.

Zhongma Fortress – Zhong Ma Prison Camp or Unit Tōgō, Japan

Zhongma was a prison camp in which the Japanese Kwantung Army performed covert biological warfare research. Built in Beiyinhe, near Harbin, Manchukuo, during the Second Sino-Japanese War (1937–45), the camp was effectively a centre for human subject experimentation and could hold up to 1,000 prisoners. In 1937, the prison camp was erased and testing operations transferred to Pingfang under Unit 731.

Surgeon General Shirō Ishii (1892–1959), a Japanese microbiologist, army medical officer, and war criminal, was the director of Unit 731. He is probably in the same league as Nazi Josef Mengele in terms of bestial inhumanity against his fellow man but is considerably less well known. Like Mengele, he got away with his crimes aginst humanity. At Ishii's funeral, his daughter, Harumi Ishii, in her eulogy revealed, 'My father had much respect for the German people and their culture.' Ishii and his fellow monsters were later granted immunity in the International Military Tribunal for the Far East by the United States government in exchange for information and research for the US biological warfare programme. What price industrial-scale atrocity?

The Ishii family was the largest local landholder and exercised a feudal dominance over the local villages. Ishii studied medicine at Kyoto Imperial University. In 1921, he was commissioned into the Imperial Japanese Army as a military surgeon with the rank of army surgeon. In 1922, Ishii was posted to the 1st Army Hospital and Army Medical School in Tokyo, from where he returned to Kyoto to take a post-graduate biomedical degree in microbiology in 1924.

In 1928, Shirō Ishii embarked on a two-year fact-finding tour of foreign biomedical research establishments in the West. On returning, he reported that all the major powers were covertly researching biological warfare and so urged the Japanese War Ministry to set up a biological weapons programme; with the backing of Army Minister Sadao Araki and the dean of the Tokyo Army Medical College, Koizumi Chikahiko, a biological weapons programme was indeed established under a newly formed department of immunology. Ishii began his research in biological warfare as the head of the Epidemic Prevention Research Laboratory in Tokyo. Former colleagues say that he exhibited eccentric work habits such as working late at night in the lab after carousing with friends on the town. He was also well known for his heavy drinking, womanising and embezzling. His reputation as a vehement nationalist helped him access the people who could provide him with the funds for his malicious plans. He and other officers were impressed by the successful German use of chlorine gas at the Second Battle of Ypres, in which the Allies suffered 5,000 deaths and 15,000 wounded.

Although part of the Japanese programme involved protecting Japanese troops from disease, his laboratory's principal objective was to develop an efficient and effective means to spread epidemics among enemy populations. Preliminary results with laboratory animals were promising, so Ishii moved seamlessly on to human trials.

Scythian archer. Black-figure tondo from an Attic bilingual kylix, *c*.530 BC. (*Louvre Museum Department of Greek, Etruscan and Roman Antiquities, Sully, first floor, room 43, case 2*)

Massacre of the Firstborn and Egyptian Darkness, *c*.1490. (*National Gallery of Art, Washinton, DC, Rosenwald Collection. This file was donated to Wikimedia Commons as part of a project by the National Gallery of Art*)

Miniature from the Toggenburg Bible (Switzerland) of 1411. MS 78 E1. The image depicts Moses in the background with two people suffering from the biblical plague of boils described in Exodus 9:8-9.

The Hittite king Mursili II (also Muršili II, Mursilis II) prays to the gods to end the epidemic of plague. Clay tablet, thirteenth century BC (original tablet written in the fourteenth century BC) from Hattusa, Turkey. (*Istanbul Archaeological Museum, Osama Shukir Muhammed Amin FRCP(Glasg) via Wikimedia Commons*).

Victims of ergotism. Julius Caesar lost legions of soldiers to ergot poisoning during his campaigns in Gaul. Severe ergot epidemics in France between AD 900 and AD 1300 killed 20,000 to 50,000 people, leaving the nation susceptible to invasions that eventually toppled this Holy Roman kingdom into what became two nations, France and Germany. (*Pieter Bruegel, Louvre*)

A reconstruction of Myrtis gazes back at us from over 2,400 years ago. Myrtis was an 11-year-old girl who died during the plague of Athens and whose skeleton was found in the Kerameikos mass grave. (*National Archaeological Museum of Athens*)

In 401 BC in Colchis, Xenophon, historian and general, a hoplite commander, halted his troops at what looked to be the perfect place to camp. Xenophon says that there were numerous beehives in the region, and that his men ate many honeycombs during the evening they passed through the town. Soon after consumption, the men were reportedly violently sick with vomiting and diarrhoea, and had 'lost their senses', unable to stand or even walk upright. The men lay in a heap that evening, fully exhausted from the illness. The next day, the men had regained their faculties and were no longer sick; no one died. Four centuries later, the very same thing happened to a Roman army in the same region.

The Death of Hercules (1634) – through his poisoned shirt, the dreaded Shirt of Nessus – by Francisco de Zurbarán, in the Prado, Madrid.

Hunting with the deadly blow gun. From *The Andes and the Amazon* (1876).

Poisoned Well, by Jacek Malchevsky, 1905. (*National Museum, Poznan*)

A depiction of a confrontation between Pontiac, an Ottawa chief, and Colonel Henry Bouquet, a British soldier, who suggested using blankets to spread smallpox to indigenous Americans.

Russian soldiers of the Dukhovshchinsky Regiment wearing Zelinsky-Kummant gas masks, 1916. (*www.vokrugsveta.ru/telegraph/technics/629/*)

Dead Indian soldiers of the British force on the beach at Tanga, November 1914. A humiliating British defeat. (*Bundesarchiv Bild 146-1971-057-05*)

First World War British gas hood, *c.*1915.
(*Photographer: Stephen C. Dickson*)

East German Young Pioneers during the war against the potato beetle. The boy on the left, Bodo, set a record for most beetles collected in one day, 2,000. The girl on the right, Magdalena, managed 800 specimens. (*German Federal Archives. Current location: Allgemeiner Deutscher Nachrichtendienst – Zentralbild* (*Bild 183*))

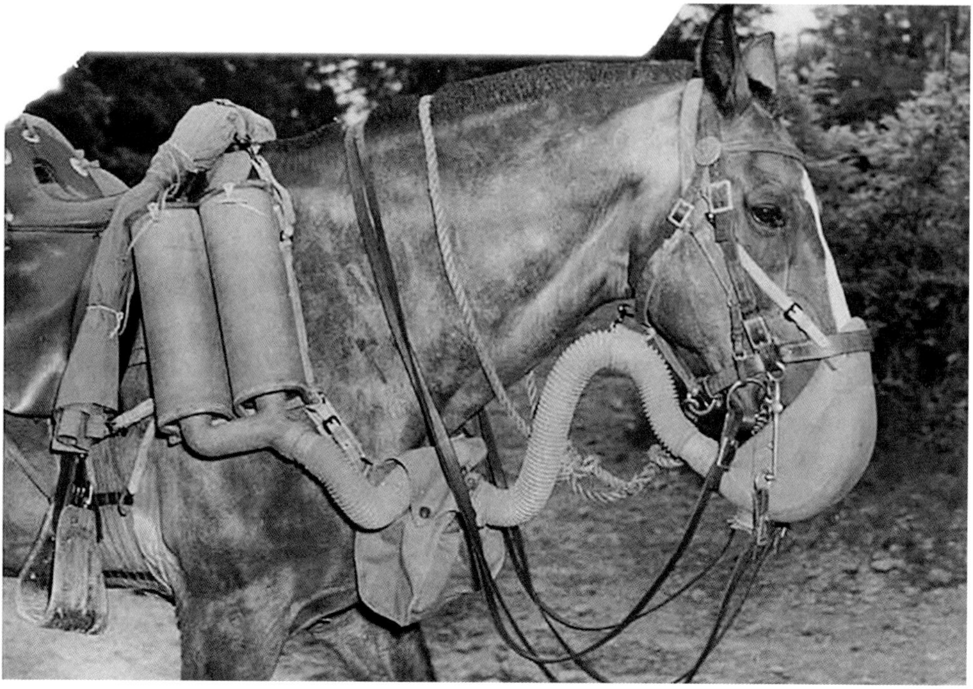

US Army horse wears a gas mask to fend against German gas attacks. (*Courtesy of US National Archives*)

Belgian military dogs hauling a machine gun in the First World War.

The Scientific Experimental and Production Base (SNOPB), Stepnogorsk, Kazakhstan. SNOPB was under the authority of the Biopreparat organisation. Known only by its post office box, No. 2076, this facility tested and certified methods of producing BW agents developed in the laboratories of Biopreparat and the MOD, and issued technical documentation and recommendations. From 1984 to 1987, specialists and equipment from Sverdlovsk were transferred to SNOPB. As well as anthrax, the Stepnogorsk facility produced staphylococcus toxin SNOPB.

A chaplain wears an M-17 nuclear, biological and chemical warfare mask and hood during an exercise at Kadena Air Base, Okinawa, Japan. Scene Camera Operator: Senior Airman Walker. (*Released to Public; Combined Military Service Digital Photographic Files*)

A pre-1991 photo of a scientist working in a lab at VECTOR. The State Research Center of Virology and Biotechnology VECTOR, also known as the Vector Institute, is a biological research centre in Koltsovo, Novosibirsk Oblast. It has research facilities and capabilities for all levels of Biological Hazard, CDC Levels 1–4. It is one of two official repositories for smallpox virus, the other being the CDC in Atlanta, Georgia. (*Unknown Soviet photographer*)

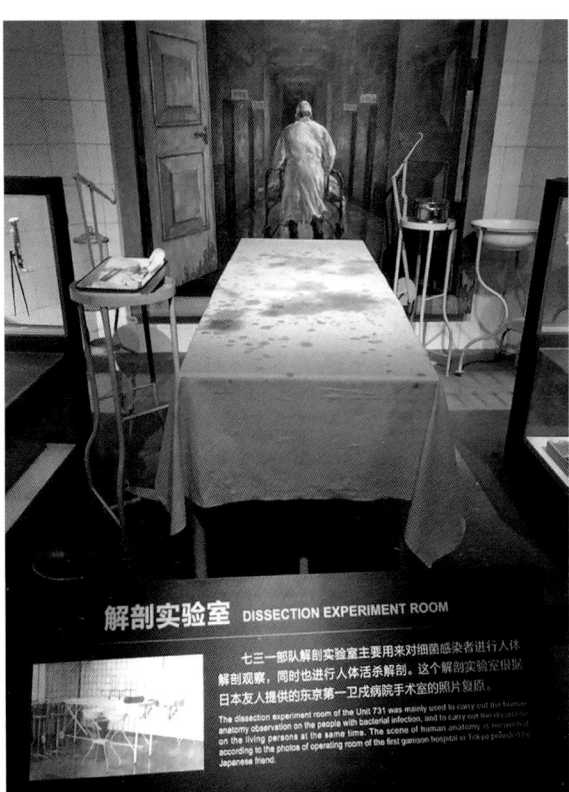

Unit 731, Museum Human Dissection Experiment Room.

In April 1943, Detrick Air Field near Frederick, Maryland, was requisitioned and badged Camp Detrick. Four biological agent production plants were developed here: Pilot Plant No. 1, activated in October 1943 for the production of botulinum toxin; Pilot Plant No. 2, completed in March 1944, produced the anthrax simulant *Bacillus globigii* and actual anthrax spores; Pilot Plant No. 3, completed in February 1945, produced plant pathogens. Pilot Plant No. 4 was opened in January 1945 and produced, in embryonated eggs, the bacteria that cause brucellosis and psittacosis.

The island of Gruinard was officially out of bounds from 1942 to 1990 because of secret anthrax testing during the Second World War.

One of the many victims of Unit 731.

Russian pioneers in gas masks, Leningrad 1937. (*Viktor Bulla*)

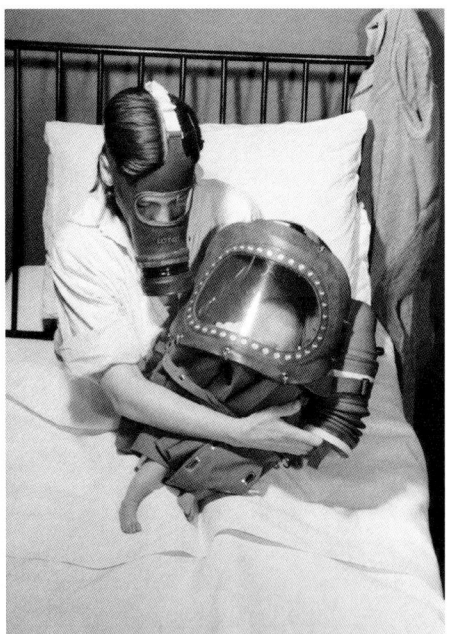

A mother and baby both in gas masks in 1941. The mother cradles her newborn baby in bed, shortly after giving birth. The mother is wearing her civilian respirator, whilst the baby is encased in a baby gas helmet, which buckles up around its bottom. The mother is demonstrating how the bellows on her baby's gas mask are pumped to supply the baby with air.

A prisoner in a special chamber in Dachau concentration camp loses consciousness in response to changing air pressure during high-altitude experiments. For the benefit of the Luftwaffe, conditions comparable to those found at 15,000 metres in altitude were created in an effort to determine if German pilots might survive at that height. March 1942–August 1942. (*https://collections.ushmm.org/search/catalog/pa1058429, Photographer: Sigmund Rascher (d. 1945)*)

An Iranian soldier wearing a gas mask during the Iran-Iraq War. (*Released under GFDL licence*)

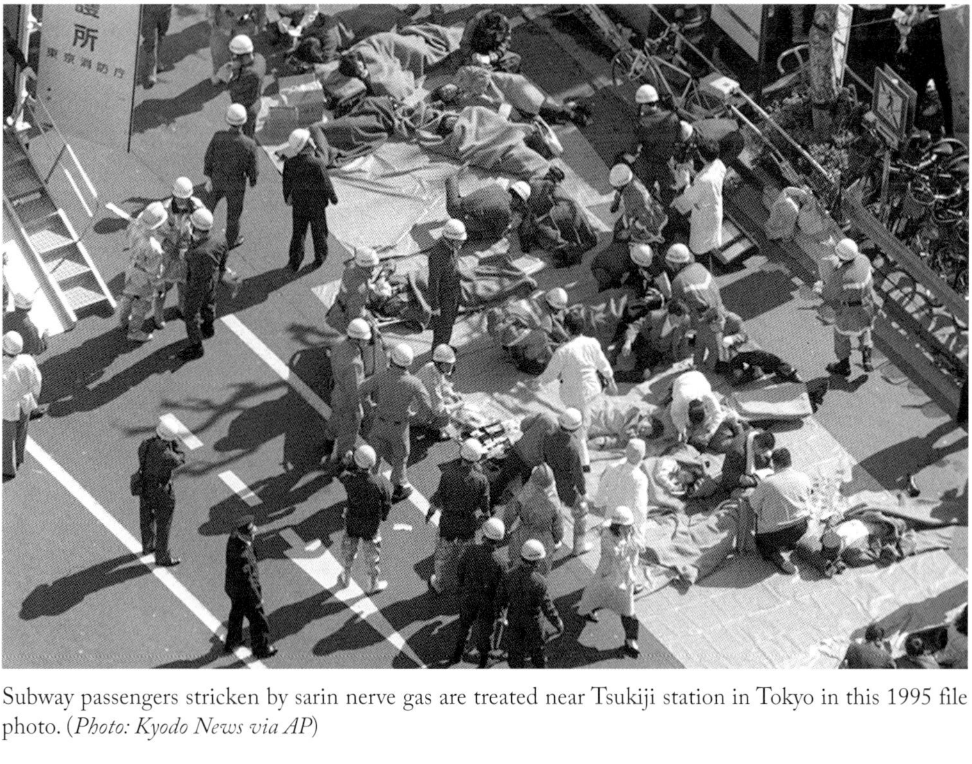

Subway passengers stricken by sarin nerve gas are treated near Tsukiji station in Tokyo in this 1995 file photo. (*Photo: Kyodo News via AP*)

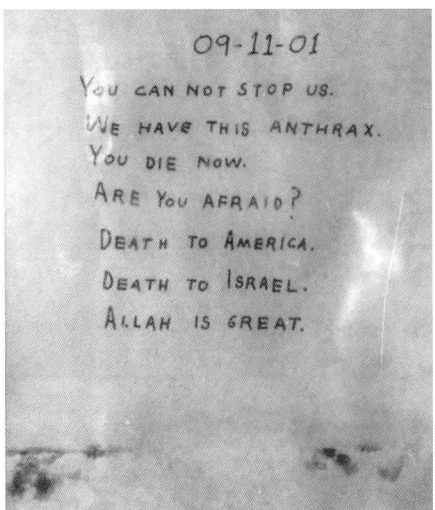

The second anthrax note. One New York City day in the autumn of 2001 was no one's red letter day – for that was when a salvo of letters containing anthrax spores were sent by mail to two US senators' offices on Capitol Hill and news media agencies along the east coast.

The reward notice.

Members of the Alabama National Guard's 46th Civil Support Team work a threat scenario created by Dugway Proving Ground's Special Program Division mobile training teams, 18 June 2014. (*Photo courtesy of the US Army*)

Biological weapons research was conducted at PBA from 1953 to 1969 but operations ceased when President Nixon banned biological weapons after the furore over Agent Orange. Between 1954 and 1967, at least seven different biological agents were produced at the facility. All biological agents were destroyed between 1971 and 1973. The image shows 1,600-pound steel containers stored at Pine Bluff Arsenal, which once held hazardous materials and required decontamination. Operators decontaminated the last 4,307 ton containers in July 2011.

Firefighters triage victims of a simulated bioterrorism attack at the Armed Forces Reserve Center during the Portland Area Capabilities Exercise (PACE) Setter at Camp Withycombe in Clackamas, Oregon, May 2013. The purpose of the PACE Setter exercise is to test regional and interagency response to public health incidents affecting multiple agencies. (*Photo by Staff Sgt April Davis, Oregon Military Department Public Affairs*)

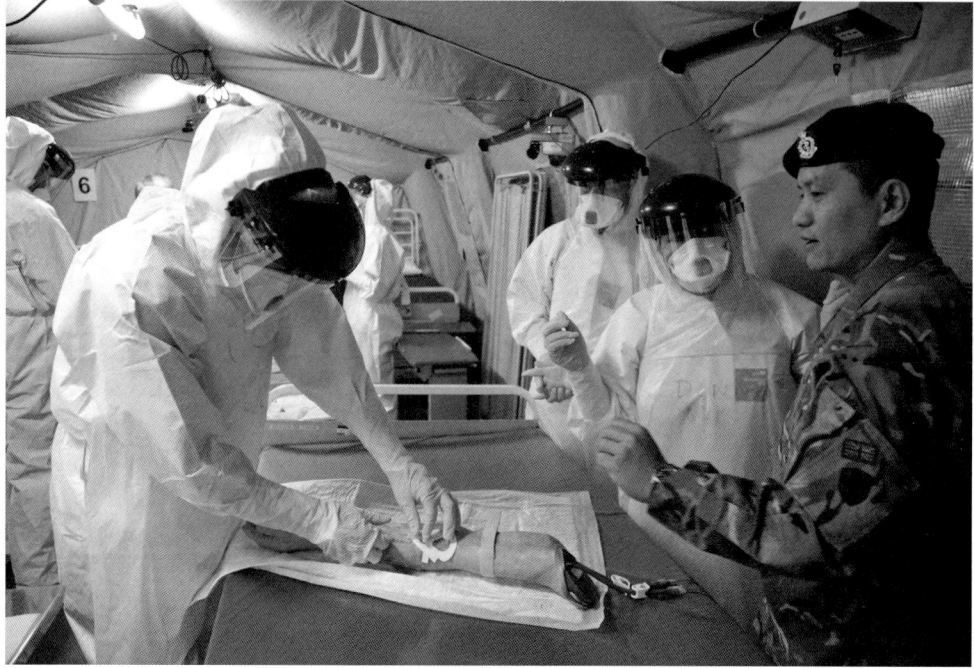

Medical Regiment 250 Squadron RAMC (Detachment), training in blood-taking during the Ebola pandemic in 2014–16, Queen Elizabeth Barracks, Strensall near York. (*Courtesy* York Press)

Animal Justice Project campaigners staged protests at Porton Down and in Salisbury, October 2020.

In September 1931, the Japanese Imperial Army invaded Manchuria following the Manchurian Incident. Newly occupied Manchuria was just the place for Ishii's research on human subjects that 'could be plucked from the streets like rats'. Ishii relocated his laboratory about 100 kilometres to the south of Harbin at Beiyinhe, a village of about 300 homes known locally as Zhong Ma City. The Japanese displaced the local inhabitants and burnt down the village, except for a large building suitable for use as a headquarters.

The prison camp was a veritable medieval-like fortress, boasting 9.8ft earthen walls topped with electrified barbed wire and a moat with drawbridge. Inside were hundreds of rooms and laboratories, offices, barracks and dining facilities, warehouses and munitions storage, crematoria, and the prison cells. The Japanese conscripted local Chinese labour for the construction. To guarantee security and secrecy, labourers were always escorted by armed guards and forced to wear blindfolds so they could have no idea what they were building or where. Those working on the more sensitive areas of the camp, such as the inner section of medical laboratories within the prisoners' quarters, were executed once construction was complete to ensure absolute secrecy.

The prisoners brought to Zhongma for trials were intended to give a broad cross-section of the population and included common criminals, captured bandits, anti-Japanese partisans, political prisoners, infants, the elderly, pregnant women, the homeless and mentally handicapped, as well as people rounded up by the Kempeitai military police for alleged 'suspicious activities'.

Prisoners were generally well fed on a wholesome diet of rice or wheat, meat, fish, and occasionally even the treat of alcohol, with the intention of maintaining prisoners in their normal state of health and mind. Then the inhumane experiments began: in many cases, prisoners were drained of blood over several days, with careful records kept on their deteriorating physical condition. Others were subject to experiments on nutrient or water deprivation. Prisoners were also injected with microbes and plague bacteria. Data sheets reveal that in at least one case, after prisoners developed a fever of 104°F, they were vivisected while unconscious – still alive, that is. Nakagawa Yonezo, a professor emeritus at Osaka University, was a student at Kyoto University during the war, and witnessed footage of human experiments and executions from Unit 731. He testified about the 'playfulness' of the experimenters:

> Some of the experiments had nothing to do with advancing the capability of germ warfare, or of medicine. There is such a thing as professional curiosity: 'What would happen if we did such and such?' What medical purpose was served by performing and studying beheadings? None at all. That was just playing around. Professional people, too, like to play.

Not surprisingly, average life expectancy of a prisoner at the camp was one month. Prisoners who survived the experiments, but who were considered too weak for further tests, were simply murdered. The facility was estimated to have held 500–600 prisoners at any one time, with a capacity for over 1,000. Prisoners were routinely raped by guards.

Prisoners had their limbs amputated in order to study blood loss. Those limbs were sometimes reattached to the opposite side of the body. Some prisoners had their stomachs surgically removed and the oesophagus reattached to the intestines. Parts of organs, such as the brain, lungs and liver, were removed from some prisoners. Imperial Japanese Army surgeon Ken Yuasa suggests that the practice of vivisection on human subjects was widespread even outside Unit 731, estimating that at least 1,000 Japanese personnel were involved in it in mainland China.

August 1934 was a surpringly good month; it was the time of the traditional summer festival when the prisoners were given a ration of special foods. However, insurrection was in the air: one prisoner, named Li, managed to overpower his guard and seize the keys, and freed about forty of his fellow prisoners. Although their legs were shackled, their arms were free and the prisoners were able to climb over the outside walls. A heavy downpour had fortuitously knocked out the facility's electricity, disabling the searchlights and electric fence. Ten or so of the escapees were shot by guards while others were recaptured and subjected to sadistic treatment in reprisal; sixteen did escape. Some soon died from exposure, hunger, cold, and the festering injuries from their experiments but several managed to survive, and spread word of the crimes against humanity being conducted by Shiro and his staff. Although the Kuomintang ignored these reports, the Zhongma Fortress was closed down due to the bad publicity and the breach in security, and its activities transferred to a new site closer to Harbin called Pingfang (Heibo), which came to be known as Unit 731. The testimony of one of the escapees, Ziyang Wang, was collected in the 1980s by Xiao Han, deputy director of the Pingfang museum.

In 1936, Ishii was awarded control over Unit 731 and its research facilities where he and his men performed those heinous experiments on live humans, including infecting living subjects with plague, forced pregnancies, vivisections often conducted without anaesthesia, and inducing severe frostbite. Army engineer Hisato Yoshimura conducted these experiments by taking captives outside, dipping various appendages into water of varying temperatures, and allowing the limb to freeze. Once frozen, Yoshimura would strike their affected limbs with a short stick, 'emitting a sound resembling that which a board gives when it is struck'. Ice was then chipped away, with the affected area being subjected to various treatments such as being doused in water or exposed to the heat of fire.

Naoji Uezono, a member of Unit 731, described in a 1980s' interview a gruesome scene where Yoshimura had 'two naked men put in an area 40–50 degrees below zero and researchers filmed the whole process until [the subjects] died. [The subjects] suffered such agony they were digging their nails into each other's flesh.' Yoshimura's lack of remorse was evident in an article he (incredibly) had published in the *Journal of Japanese Physiology* in 1950 in which he admitted to using twenty children and a three-day-old infant in experiments that exposed them to 0°C ice and salt water. Although this article inevitably drew criticism, Yoshimura denied any guilt when contacted by a reporter from the *Mainichi Shimbun* (a Japanese newspaper).

We also hear how prisoners were taken outside in freezing weather and left with exposed arms, periodically drenched with water until frozen solid. The arm was later amputated; the doctor would repeat the process on the victim's upper arm to the shoulder. After both arms were gone, the doctors moved on to the legs until only a head and torso remained. The victim was then used for plague and other disease experiments.

Emperor Hirohito authorised the expansion of Unit 731 and its integration into the Kwantung Army as the Epidemic Prevention Department. It was divided into the 'Ishii Unit' and 'Wakamatsu Unit' with a base in Hsinking. The decree also called for the establishment of an additional biological warfare development unit called the Kwantung Army Military Horse Epidemic Prevention Workshop (later referred to as Manchuria Unit 100) and a chemical warfare development unit called the Kwantung Army Technical Testing Department (later Manchuria Unit 516). After the Japanese invasion of China in 1937, sister chemical and biological warfare units were founded in major Chinese cities, and were referred to as Epidemic Prevention and Water Supply Units. Detachments included Unit 1855 in Beijing, Unit Ei 1644 in Nanjing, Unit 8604 in Guangzhou and later, Unit 9420 in Singapore. Together these units comprised Ishii's network; at its height in 1939, it gave work to more than 10,000 personnel.

Tularaemia

In 1911, when George McCoy was investigating bubonic plague in squirrels, he accidentally discovered a new infection; he transmitted the disease to experimental animals and isolated the causative organism. He called it *Bacterium tularense*, after Tulare County, California. In 1919, Edward Francis determined that an infection called 'deer-fly fever' was the same disease as

McCoy's, naming it 'tularaemia'. He showed that it occurred in wild rabbits and when he and all his laboratory staff contracted the illness, concluded that it was highly infectious, requiring inoculation with or inhalation of as few as ten organisms to cause disease. Naturally acquired human infection occurs through a variety of mechanisms such as: bites of infected arthropods; handling infectious animal tissues or fluids; direct contact or ingestion of contaminated water, food or soil; and inhalation of infective aerosols. *F. tularensis* is so infective that examining an open culture plate can transmit infection. Human-to-human transmission has not been documented.

Soon after, this astonishing infectivity prompted studies of its potential as a candidate as a biological weapon, including, as we have seen, non-consensual human experimentation by Japan among civilian, political and military prisoners, and its probable use in warfare during the Second World War. Later, as we shall see, in the United States, voluntary human experimentation took place in the 1950s and 1960s with convicts and non-combatant soldiers. Soviet Union scientists allegedly developed a vaccine-resistant strain, which they tested as a biological weapon in 1982 and 1983.

A 1970 World Health Organization expert committee reported that if 50 kg of virulent *F. tularensis* were dispersed as an aerosol over a metropolitan area with a population of 5 million, there would be an estimated 250,000 incapacitated casualties, including 19,000 deaths. Aerosol dissemination of *F. tularensis* in a populated area would be expected to cause the abrupt onset of large numbers of cases of acute, non-specific, febrile illness beginning three to five days later (incubation range, 1–14 days), with pleuropneumonitis developing in a significant proportion of cases over the ensuing days and weeks. Without antibiotic treatment, the clinical course could progress to respiratory failure, shock and death. The overall mortality rate for severe Type A strains has been 5–15 per cent.

The Soviet Union's smallpox programme

The 1930s saw the start of the Soviet Union's development of smallpox as a biological weapon. Research and development continued until the late 1980s – and maybe beyond? The Soviet Union first attempted to cultivate the smallpox virus by growing it on the chorioallantoic membrane of developing chicken embryos and used the chicken embryo technique almost exclusively for over five decades, during which time it was modified somewhat to accommodate mechanisation and automation, thereby making it more efficient and productive. The result was the Soviet production of smallpox virus in large quantities. By the end of the 1980s, most of the production issues were resolved and a new reactor-based smallpox biological weapon in liquid form was developed.

Because of the increased threat of terrorism, the risk posed by various microorganisms as biological weapons needs to be evaluated and the historical development and use of biological agents better understood. Biological warfare agents may be more potent than conventional and chemical weapons. During the past century, the progress made in biotechnology and biochemistry has simplified the development and production of such weapons. In addition, genetic engineering holds perhaps the most dangerous potential. Ease of production and the broad availability of biological agents and technical know-how have led to a further spread of biological weapons and an increased desire among developing countries to have them.

Stefan Riedel, 'Biological warfare and bioterrorism: a historical review'.

Chapter 8

The Second World War

The interwar years and the Second World War mark the beginning of what might be described as the scramble for weapons of mass destruction (WMD): nuclear, chemical and biological, in a bid to achieve strategic superiority over the other powers involved in that unseemly scramble. One of the unsavoury hallmarks of the Second World War was the atrocious enlistment of soldiers and civil populations for non-consensual or ill-informed medical experimentation. Weapons using infectious microbes had been produced and used on a limited scale scale during the First World War, but significant deployment reached its zenith, or should that be nadir, in the first half of the twentieth century despite its prohibition by the Geneva Convention in 1925. Human guinea pigs were callously and unscrupulously utilised for biological experimentation in order to refine the technology to produce some of the most destructive military bioweapons.

When we take into consideration the hellish impact Zyklon B had on occupied Europe, Germany's biological warfare programme was much less extensive than its chemical programme. Most of the Germans' work was on antipersonnel agents such as the causative organisms of plague, cholera, typhus and yellow fever. They also investigated the use of vectors to destroy animals and crops. Zyklon B was the trade name of a cyanide-based pesticide invented in Germany in the early 1920s. It comprised of hydrogen cyanide (prussic acid).

The US biological weapons programme

The apparent use of cholera, dysentery, typhoid, plague, anthrax, and paratyphoid by the Japanese against Chinese troops finally led to an American decision to conduct research and establish a retaliatory biological warfare capability. In response to the potential threat, in 1941 (before the attack on Pearl Harbor), Secretary of War Harry L. Stimson requested the National Academy of Sciences to appoint a committee to study biological warfare, the Biological Warfare Committee. However, the committee did not have time to prepare before war was declared, which left the army unprepared for the threat of biological warfare by Japan.

Immediately after the attack on Pearl Harbor, the army's Hawaiian Department took special precautions against biological attack by both external enemies and local residents. Guards were placed on the water supplies in Hawaii to defend against sabotage by biological warfare, and daily checks for chlorine content were made. Food production plants were also guarded, and drinking fresh, but not canned milk, in particular, was prohibited. A general order was issued banning the sale of poisons to the general public except with special dispensation.

In February 1942, the Biological Warfare Committee recommended that the United States should reduce its vulnerability to biological warfare. After President Roosevelt approved the plan, this led to the formation of the War Research Service (WRS) in August 1942 under the leadership of George W. Merck, president of Merck Company, a major global pharmaceutical company. The WRS was, however, only a coordinating committee attached to the Federal Security Agency; it relied on existing government and private institutions to do the actual work and drew its scientific data from a committee of scientists from the National Academy of Sciences and the National Research Council. In December 1943, US Intelligence reports predicted that Japan might use biological warfare.

In January 1944, the biological warfare programme was transferred from the WRS to the War Department, and the WRS was abolished. The War Department split the biological warfare programme between the CWS and the US Army Surgeon General. Merck became a special consultant to the programme. This arrangement was further modified in October 1944 when the secretary of war established the US Biological Warfare Committee with Merck as the chairman. The CWS assigned the biological warfare programme to its Special Projects Division.

At first, the army's biological warfare programme was headquartered at Edgewood Arsenal in Maryland. In April 1943, Detrick Airfield near Frederick, Maryland, was requisitioned and badged Camp Detrick. Four biological agent production plants were developed here: Pilot Plant No. 1, activated in October 1943 for the production of botulinum toxin; Pilot Plant No. 2, completed in March 1944, produced the anthrax simulant *Bacillus globigii* and actual anthrax spores; Pilot Plant No. 3, completed in February 1945, produced plant pathogens; and Pilot Plant No. 4, opened in January 1945, produced, in embryonated eggs, the bacteria that cause brucellosis and psittacosis. Smaller pilot plants were set up to explore the many other antipersonnel, antianimal and antiplant agents under scrutiny.

Building 470, referred to as 'Anthrax Tower', was a pilot plant for testing optimal fermentor and bacterial purification technologies. Research here shaped the fermentor technology that was later used by the pharmaceutical industry to revolutionise the production of antibiotics and other drugs. The facility acquired the nickname 'Fort Doom' while offensive biological warfare research was undertaken there. Five thousand bombs containing anthrax spores were produced at the base during the Second World War.

The existing Vigo Ordnance Plant near Terre Haute, Indiana, was also acquired by the CWS in 1944 for conversion into a biological agent weapon production plant divided into four subplants: agent production, munitions assembly, munition packaging and storage, and the animal farm. Although the plant was ready to produce biological agents by the summer of 1945, none was actually produced.

Edgewood is notorious for its classified human subject research, which took place from 1948 to 1975 under the US Army Chemical Corps. The objective was to evaluate the impact of low-dose chemical warfare agents on military personnel and to test protective clothing, pharmaceuticals, and vaccines. Some were aimed at psychochemical warfare research and euphemistically named the 'Medical Research Volunteer Programme' (1956–75). The MRVP was also driven by intelligence requirements and the need for new and more effective interrogation techniques.

Overall, about 7,000 soldiers took part in these experiments, which involved exposures to more than 250 different chemicals. Some volunteers exhibited symptoms at the time of exposure to these agents but long-term follow-up was not part of the plan.

Anthrax was the most important biological warfare agent. Although anthrax was never disseminated in a weapon in the United States during the war, anthrax simulant was tested in large 100 lb and 115 lb bombs, and small 10 lb bombs, shotgun shell (SS) bombs, and the 4 lb SPD Mk I bomb. The smaller bombs, suitable for use in larger cluster bombs, proved the most successful in static tests. Only the SPD Mk I bomb was considered ready for production and the first and, apparently, only large-scale munition order was placed at Vigo in June 1944 for production of 1 million bombs. The order was cancelled at the end of the war.

The US biological weapons programme also homed in on German and Japanese vegetable crops. Tests for anticrop bombs included using spores of brown spot of rice fungus and 2,4-dichlorophenoxyacetic acid (VKA, for vegetable killer acid) in the SPD Mk II bomb and a liquid (VKL, for vegetable killer liquid) in the M-10 spray tank. Scientists were also working on defoliants in the programme.

Eggs were important in US biological warfare. They were disinfected and drilled before being inoculated with *Brucella suis* or *Chlamydia psittaci*, the bacteria that cause brucellosis and psittacosis. Viral agents such as Venezuelan equine encephalitis virus were also produced in eggs. The facility at Fort Detrick had incubator capacity for approximately 2,000 chicken eggs.

Depending on the agent being produced, eggs were incubated for one to ten days between inoculation and harvest. The work was done by hand, in an assembly line, with little mechanical assistance.

Other national biological weapon programmes

During the Second World War, many countries other than the US strove to acquire a BW capability; they included Russia, the UK, Canada, France, Italy, Germany, Japan and Hungary. The UK and Canadian BW programmes had started in the 1930s, focusing on agents deleterious to crops and animals. In 1941, the UK had developed anthrax as an agent against cattle, while Canada undertook extensive work on rinderpest; rinderpest – cattle plague – was a disease caused by the rinderpest virus, which mainly infected cattle and buffalo. Infected animals endured symptoms such as fever, wounds in the mouth, diarrhoea, discharge from the nose and eyes, and eventually death. The abandoned USA-UK-Canadian BW programme focused on anthrax as an antipersonnel weapon. The UK BW programme, though, was retaliatory, deploying agents against cattle, in the form of cattle cakes containing anthrax organisms. The UK produced 5 million of these cattle cakes but they were never used. Bomb testing went ahead on the island of Gruinard off the Scottish coast during 1942. Plans between the UK, Canada and the USA for a joint BW cluster bomb never got to production stage during the war. Some studies were carried out on botulin, and on plague and Salmonella, while field tests were carried out on BW munitions. Generally, research focused on anthrax, botulin, and vectors to spread disease.

Gruinard Island

Gruinard is in Gruinard Bay, about halfway between Gairloch and Ullapool. In 1942, British military scientists from the Biology Department of Porton Down initiated a biological warfare test on Gruinard to establish the feasibility of a bioweapons attack using anthrax. Long-lasting contamination of the area by anthrax spores determined that a remote and uninhabited island was required. The anthrax strain chosen was a highly virulent type called 'Vollum 14578', named after R.L. Vollum, Professor of Bacteriology at the University of Oxford, who supplied it. Eighty sheep were taken to the island and bombs filled with anthrax spores were exploded close to where selected groups were tethered. The sheep became infected with anthrax and began to die within days of exposure.

Some of the experiments were recorded on 16 mm colour movie film, which was declassified in 1997. One sequence shows the detonation of an anthrax bomb fixed at the end of a tall pole supported with guy ropes. After the bomb exploded, a brownish aerosol cloud drifts away towards the target animals. A later sequence shows anthrax-infected sheep carcasses being burned in incinerators.

Later, a Wellington bomber, flying at 7,000 feet, dropped an anthrax bomb on the island, but it landed in a bog and failed to explode. The experiment was repeated, this time on a beach at Penclawdd, near Swansea. The bomb was dropped from 5,000 feet, exploded on target, and sheep as far away as 300 yards were infected. Tests continued until August 1943, when a heavy storm struck the Scottish coast and driving rains washed several contaminated sheep carcasses buried on Gruinard across to the mainland, which infected and killed a number of 'civilian' livestock. The outbreak was quickly contained and blame was (laughably) attributed to a passing Greek ship that the UK government said had discarded contaminated carcasses overboard. The local farmers were compensated and operations on Gruinard Island were halted. Did anyone ask why the Greeks would be transporting anthrax-infected sheep carcasses when they had no capacity to produce the bacillus? Nevertheless, it was concluded that a large release of anthrax spores would thoroughly pollute German cities, rendering them uninhabitable for decades to come.

Crucially, it was impossible to decontaminate Gruinard because the spores were hardy enough to survive efforts to do so. In 1945, the owner of the island wanted it back. Because of the contamination, the Ministry of Supply could not derequisition Gruinard until it was deemed safe. In 1946, the government agreed to acquire the island and to take responsibility for it. The owner or her heirs would be able to repurchase the island for £500 only when it was declared 'fit for habitation by man and beast'. Gruinard Island was quarantined indefinitely. Visits to the island were prohibited, except for periodic checks by Porton Down personnel to determine the level of contamination.

Everything went the Ministry of Defence's way until 1981, when newspapers began receiving messages with the heading 'Operation Dark Harvest', relating to a group calling themselves Dark Harvest Commando of the Scottish Citizen Army. They demanded that the government decontaminate the island and reported that a 'team of microbiologists from two universities' had landed on there with the aid of local people and collected 140 kilograms of Gruinard soil.

The group threatened to leave samples of the soil 'at appropriate points that will ensure the rapid loss of indifference of the government and the equally rapid education of the general public'. The same day, a sealed package of soil was left close to the London–Exeter railway line near Porton Down; tests revealed that it contained anthrax bacilli. A few days later, another sealed package of soil was left in Blackpool, where the ruling Conservative Party was holding its annual conference. The soil did not contain anthrax, but officials said that it was similar to that found on the island. The group claimed to be returning the 'seeds of death' to their source.

From 1986, serious efforts were eventually made to decontaminate Gruinard: 280 tonnes of formaldehyde solution diluted in seawater was sprayed over all 196 hectares of the island and the worst contaminated topsoil around the dispersal site was removed. A flock of sheep was then introduced to the island: they remained healthy. On 24 April 1990, after forty-eight years of quarantine and four years after the formaldehyde solution was applied, the island was declared safe and the warning signs were removed. On 1 May 1990, the island was repurchased by the heirs of the original owner for the original sale price of £500. Some confusion followed when strange people from around the world sent letters to the British government asking to purchase the island for £500.

Dead mules fouling wells

> In 1942, when valiant Greek resistance fighters increased their attacks from their mountain hideouts, German troops responded in kind with relentless anti-guerilla operations. Very soon, central and northern Greece was turned into a dead zone of ruined property and rotting harvests. Most peasants were afraid to approach their fields lest they be killed; in some cases, villagers were actually forbidden by the Germans to sow or reap their crops.
>
> Mark Mazower, *Inside Hitler's Greece: The Experience of Occupation, 1941–44*

During the last stages of the German withdrawal, many villages, including Agios Georgios near Karpenisi, were devastated, their wells fouled with the corpses of dead mules.

Entomological warfare

Insects played their part, too. As noted, entomological warfare comes in three distinct forms: the first involves deliberately infecting insects with a pathogen and then releasing them over or in enemy territory. These insects then infect humans and animals through stings and bites. The second type is when insects are used to destroy agricultural crops, depriving the enemy of food resources and causing famine. The third type involves the use of non-infected insects, such as wasps or bees, to assail opponents.

A biological attack by the Japanese was launched in 1941 at the Battle of Changde, China, against the Chinese Army and civilians; this was a response to a fiersome counteroffensive by the Chinese, which the Japanese could not repel. It not only led to 10,000 deaths from cholera in the Chinese population caused by ingestion of *Vibrio cholerae* – contaminated food and water – but also 1,700 deaths among Japanese troops who were unprepared for the blowback that occurred.

The Japanese planned to use plague fleas in 1944 on the strategically valuable Mariana Islands, which had been captured by the American forces.

In another incident, Belgian soldiers trapped in a bee house escaped by throwing frames of bees at attacking German soldiers.

Typhus

Typhus is caused by infection with one or more rickettsial bacteria. Fleas, mites (chiggers), lice or ticks (arthropods) transmit it when they bite you. Whenever and wherever large numbers of people are crowded together under less than sanitary conditions, then there is a potential for lethal typhus to rear its head. It is inextricably associated with the social and health-related upheavals caused by war, imprisonment and famine. When the Germans polluted a large reservoir with sewage, it caused outbreaks of highly contagious typhus. The Nazis themselves relied on taking blood tests of local people to avoid going into areas contaminated with typhus. In Poland, however, their defence strategy was turned against them when local doctors secretly injected the Poles with a vaccine that gave false-positive readings for typhus in the Nazis' blood tests, convincing the Germans to avoid the area.

Rudolf Stefan Jan Weigl

Rudolf Stefan Jan Weigl (1883–1957) was a Polish biologist and inventor of the first effective vaccine against epidemic typhus. In the First World War, Weigl was drafted into the medical service of the Austro-Hungarian army and began research on typhus and its causes. He founded the Weigl Institute in Lwów (now Lviv), where he conducted vaccine research. Weigl attracted the attention of the Nazi occupiers.

The Nazis ordered Weigl to produce a typhus vaccine: he created a technique that involved raising millions of infected lice in a laboratory and harvesting their guts to get the materials for a vaccine. Lice that had been infected with typhus bacteria would be encouraged to feed on human volunteers and then, after about five days, the lice would be painstakingly dissected one by one. Scientists would pull out the 'louse gut', where the typhus bacteria grow and multiply, put it in a pot and simply mash it up with a chemical solution to make the vaccine.

Weigl's lab in Lviv sheltered Polish intellectuals, Jews and resistance fighters by employing them as lice feeders; they allowed thousands of lice – some infected with typhus, some not – to suck their blood. All intellectual life migrated to Weigl's laboratory. The lice were put in tiny cages that were attached to people's legs. To avoid catching the illness themselves, these volunteers had to be clean, have healthy skin and, hardest of all, be able to resist scratching. At the same time, Weigl was sending weakened vaccines to the German Army. His robust vaccines were smuggled into ghettos in Lviv and Warsaw, saving countless lives, until the institute was shut down by the Soviet Union following their 1944 anti-German offensive.

Other entomological warfare

France pursued an entomological warfare programme during the Second World War. As with Germany, the French suggested that the highly destructive Colorado potato beetle be aimed at the enemy's crops. Germany had developed plans to drop the beetles on English crops and carried out testing of its Colorado potato beetle weaponisation programme south of Frankfurt, where they released 54,000 of the beetles; they had stockpiles of 30 million of the pestiferous insects. Canada led the way in vector-borne warfare. Working closely with the United States during the Second World War, G.B. Reed, chief of Kingston's Queen's University's Defense Research Laboratory, focused his research efforts on mosquito vectors, biting flies and plague-infected fleas. He pioneered the dispersion of infected insect bait over a targeted area, experimenting with a 500 lb bomb that could carry 200,000 flies using tinned salmon as infected bait.

The eminent British scientist J.B.S. Haldane concurred that Britain was vulnerable to entomological attack courtesy of the Colorado potato beetle. In 1942, the United States shipped 15,000 Colorado potato beetles to Britain for research into how to weaponise them.

Japan and Unit 731

> The fellow knew that it was over for him, and so he didn't struggle when they led him into the room and tied him down, but when I picked up the scalpel, that's when he began screaming. I cut him open from the chest to the stomach, and he screamed terribly, and his face was all twisted in agony. He made this unimaginable sound, he was screaming so horribly. But then finally he stopped. This was all in a day's work for the surgeons, but it really left an impression on me because it was my first time.
>
> Excerpt from an interview with an anonymous 72-year-old former medical assistant with the Japanese Army at Unit 731, published by the *New York Times*

Responsible for one of the most systematic and ambitious biological warfare programmes known to date, the notorious Unit 731 (also known as Manshu Detachment 731, the Kamo Detachment and Ishii Unit; the official name was the Army Epidemic Prevention Research Laboratory or Epidemic Prevention and Water Purification Department of the Kwantung Army) was set up in 1932 at Zhongma Fortress in Beiyinhe, near Harbin, Manchukuo during the Second Sino-Japanese War (1937–45). The camp was effectively a centre for human subject experimentation (who were internally referred to as *maruta*, 'logs' or '*Holzklotz*', which is a German word for log) and could hold up to 1,000 prisoners. Researchers in Unit 731 audaciously published some of their results in peer-reviewed journals, masquerading their research as if it had been conducted on non-human primates called 'Manchurian monkeys' or 'long-tailed monkeys'. In 1937, the prison camp was erased and testing operations transferred to Pingfang, Manchuria, 15 miles south of Harbin under Unit 731.

Unit 731 was housed in a huge complex covering nearly 4 square miles, with more than 150 buildings surrounded by a wall and high-voltage wires, with living quarters and amenities for up to 3,000 staff, 300–500 of whom were medical doctors and scientists.

The Japanese had 4,500 containers for raising fleas, six giant cauldrons to produce various chemicals, and around 1,800 containers to produce biological agents in the complex. Apart from this, bacterial diseases were studied to determine their warfare potential (including plague, anthrax, dysentery, typhoid, paratyphoid and cholera); insects, novel drugs, chemical toxins and frostbite were also subjects of research. By the beginning of the Second World War, General Shirō Ishii was focused on deploying vectors such as the common fly to carry the biological agents.

By 1940, the irrepressible Ishii had developed and tested nine different kinds of biological bombs in the field and had produced over 1,600 bombs: the 40 kg Ha bomb, filled with a mixture of shrapnel and anthrax spores; the 25 kg Type 50 UJI bomb, also filled with anthrax spores, came out as the most effective. Conventional bombs filled with biological agents failed to disseminate the agent efficiently. The Japanese were able to disseminate typhus rickettsia, cholera bacteria, and plague-infested fleas through Ning Bo in China, where 500 villagers died from plague epidemics.

It was later discovered that during this programme, the Japanese attacked at least eleven Chinese cities with anthrax and other biological agents by spraying them directly onto homes from aircraft. Plague was 'sown' in paddy fields and along roads previously untouched by the pestilence.

A 1941 expedition to Nanking involved spreading typhoid and paratyphoid germs into the wells, marshes, and houses of the city, as well as infusing them into street food to be distributed among the locals. Epidemics broke out shortly after, to the glee of many researchers, who concluded that paratyphoid fever was 'the most effective' of all the pathogens.

We have already noted some of the inhumane experiments visited on prisoners in the run up to the Second World War. They continued apace during the war. Prisoners were tied to stakes and used as targets to test pathogen-releasing bombs. In other tests, subjects were deprived of food and water to determine how long it took them to die; they were placed in low-pressure chambers until their eyes popped from the sockets; experimented upon to determine the relationship between temperature, burns and human survival; hung upside down until dead; crushed with heavy objects; electrocuted; dehydrated with hot fans; placed into centrifuges and spun until dead; injected with animal blood; exposed to lethal doses of x-rays; subjected to various chemical weapons inside gas chambers; injected with seawater; and burned or buried alive.

Prodigious amounts of blood were drained from some prisoners on the pretext of studying the effects of blood loss, according to former Unit 731 vivisectionist Okawa Fukumatsu; he highlights one case, where half a litre of blood was drawn at two to three-day intervals. Unit 731 also performed transfusion experiments with different blood types. Unit member Naeo Ikeda wrote:

> In my experience, when A type blood 100cc was transfused to an O type subject, whose pulse was 87 per minute and temperature was 35.4 degrees C, 30 minutes later the temperature rose to 38.6 degrees with slight trepidation. Sixty minutes later the pulse was 106 per minute and the temperature was 39.4 degrees. Two hours later the temperature was

37.7 degrees, and three hours later the subject recovered. When AB type blood 120cc was transfused to an O type subject, an hour later the subject described malaise and psychroesthesia in both legs [an abnormal condition in which part of the body, though warm, feels cold]. When AB type blood 100cc was transfused to a B type subject, there seemed to be no side effect.

This terrible litany does not include the many chemical agents that prisoners were subjected to. At least 10,000 Chinese died as a consequence of these foul experiments. In the war, the programme employed 5,000 workers, with 600 prisoners a year dying in the various treatment centres.

Unit 731 scientists subjected prisoners to other ineffably cruel experiments, including vivisection, and, as we have seen, weapons tests and germ warfare attacks. The prisoners were inoculated with organisms causing cholera, smallpox, botulism, bubonic plague, anthrax, tularaemia, and various sexually transmitted infections, and then callously left untreated in order to observe the various effects of the diseases over time. The Japanese used live patients but no anesthesia, thinking, absurdly, that otherwise, they would be unable to obtain accurate information on precisely what effect these diseases were wreaking on the human body.

They also carried out research on how to protect themselves against such diseases, so their biological weapons programme was strong both offensively and defensively. The research undertaken by Unit 731 encouraged the Japanese army to conduct large-scale trials of more sophisticated and ambitious biological weapons, such as the development of bombs used to spread pathogens, and the dropping of plague-infected fleas, and infected food and clothing by aircraft into areas of China that were not occupied by Japanese soldiers. It is estimated that several thousands of people perished, including 1,400 Japanese soldiers, illustrative of the difficulty of strictly controlling the dissemination of biological weapons. The Japanese Army was also accused of using biological warfare against the Soviet Union and Mongolia.

General Ishii focused also on the plague bacterium as a potential biological weapon because it delivered a higher casualty rate than other diseases. He constructed a clay bomb filled with oxygen and plague-infected fleas that could be dropped from aircraft at a height of 600–900 feet without leaving a trace. Each bomb contained 30,000 fleas.

The Japanese had begun using poison gas against the Chinese around 1937 as a military tactic as well as a bid to test world political sensitivities. When compelling evidence of chemical warfare was brought to the League of Nations in 1939, nothing was done. Japan had already resigned from the

League to protest against its condemnation of the Manchurian occupation and the international community's attention was set firmly on German aggression in Europe. While the rest of the world turned a blind eye, Japan turned to the development of more sophisticated entomological weapons.

In the summer of 1940, plague broke out in the city of Xingning on the Tibetan Plateau following what may have been the first attack using flea-charged Uji bombs. However, there is no categorical evidence for the complicity of the Japanese or the scale of suffering. Nevertheless, the role of Unit 731 in subsequent disease outbreaks became increasingly unambiguous, as Ishii reported that his new six-legged allies could be relied on to administer death with an even more efficient delivery system.

On 4 October 1940, the Japanese dropped plague and typhoid-infected fleas over Quzhou, a small town in western Zhejiang Province, as well as in Ningbo and Changde. It took just one year for more than 2,000 people in Quzhou to perish from this plague. The following year, a railway worker brought the plague from Quzhou to the city of Yiwu: and more than 1,000 people in Yiwu died within a year. Between 1940 and 1948, more than 300,000 Chinese civilians in the area contracted the plague and other diseases, and an estimated 50,000 died in Quzhou alone.

For over thirteen years, the atrocities continued at Unit 731. Their heinous activities only ended in 1945, when Russia invaded Manchuria. Unit 731 was razed and most evidence destroyed. General Shirō Ishii and the other workers were never punished for their war crimes.

By modifying their aerial spraying equipment, the scientists found that aircraft could directly release clouds of fleas over enemy targets. This method was used at Chuhsien, where plague erupted a month after the attack – twenty-one people died and many more were afflicted.

The attacks escalated: the stockpile at Hangzhou for an impending raid included 11 pounds of cholera bacilli, 150 pounds of 'typhus' lice and 15 million plague-infected fleas. Ishii delegated Colonel Ota Kiyoshi to the raid on Changteh. Kyoshi was not taking any chances of disappointing Ishii: he detailed more than 100 men to produce, load and release 100 million infected fleas. Within days, an 11-year-old girl had died of plague and an outbreak was up and running, racing through the city and into the surrounding villages. It left 7,500 dead. Over the next two years, Unit 731 would assail more than a dozen villages, towns and cities, causing more than 100,000 casualties.

Archie Crouch, an American missionary, was perhaps the only Western eyewitness of an entomological raid by the Japanese – in this case, a joint operation by Unit 731 and Unit 1644. Crouch was based in Ningbo, a port city with sultry weather, hordes of wharf rats and a crowded population of humans. This is a chilling extract from his diary:

> October 27, 1940. ... It was unusual to have an air-raid alarm that late in the day. ... I heard nothing until the plane was over the city. It was flying very low, and that, too, was unusual, since the bombers usually came in groups of three, six, or nine. As this lone plane circled over the heart of the city a plume of what appeared to be dense smoke billowed out behind the fuselage. I thought it must be on fire, but then the cloud dispersed downward quickly, like rain from a thunder head on a summer day, and the plane flew away ... the gossip around the city that morning was that the plane had dropped a lot of wheat, so much in some streets that the people were sweeping it up for chicken feed.

In fact, the payload was something very different: it had included millions of fleas along with sand, sorghum, wheat and rice. The grain was to attract rodents to the drop site, so that the fleas could feast on them. But these were not just any fleas. One week later, Crouch wrote:

> We would soon learn that fleas carrying bubonic plague can cause more civilian and economic destruction than squadrons of planes carrying bombs ... when the first bubonic plague symptoms appeared among people who lived in the center of the city. The first wave of sickness swept up 20 people, a modest start but sufficient to catalyze an epidemic. Along with the spread of disease came another outbreak, every bit as important to the Japanese goal of economic and industrial disruption – terror. Unless the authorities took decisive action, panicked people would flee the infected zones and spread plague throughout the city and into the countryside. Understanding the gravity of the situation, the Chinese organized a Herculean quarantine program. ... Armies of brick masons were organized to build a fourteen-foot-high wall around the six square blocks in the center of the city where plague was concentrated. The plan was to burn that section of the city as soon as the wall was completed and the people evacuated. ... No one who lived in the area enclosed within the wall was allowed to leave except through the decontamination sheds.

With the evacuation complete, the Chinese laid down trails of sulphur in the quarantined area, ignited the powder, and watched as 'fires from the burning sulfur raced through the maze like sparkling snakes'. Inevitably, some infected rats and fleas survived the conflagration, causing plague to return to the city in 1941, 1946 and 1947, with minor outbreaks until 1959. The death rate was unusually high because the Japanese had used a particularly virulent strain cultured from human subjects.

Back in Unit 731, handling millions of infected fleas was always going to throw up accidents; one such accident is described by Ishibashi Naokata, a civilian employee:

> Once, during a transfer, the fleas got loose and got all over the airport. There was a scare that everyone working in there would become infected, and a lot of commotion followed. We sprayed large quantities of insecticides over the airfield, and because of it extensive areas of grass died and turned a bright red.

The attack on the Zhejian region involved conventional troops with microbial and entomological weapons in a huge, coordinated campaign in which Unit 731 assigned more than 300 men to support the 14,000 Japanese infantry in a retaliatory offensive in savage response to Liuetenant Colonel Jimmy Doolittle's famous April 1942 bombing raid of Tokyo, Yokohama and other cities – the first air operation to strike the Japanese archipelago. Sixteen B-25B Mitchell medium bombers were launched from the US Navy aircraft carrier USS *Hornet* off Japan with no fighter escort. After the bombing, the B-25 crews were to continue westward to land in China; the Japanese knew that the American pilots had received sanctuary in the villages of Zhejian.

The only consolation was that the Japanese campaign was comparatively ineffectual with the assailants at greater risk than the defenders – the Japanese suffered 10,000 biological casualties and 1,700 fatalities, while relatively few Chinese contracted the disease.

At Unit 731, there were ninety-six cement pans to breed yellow rats and fleas. Pingfang kept around 3 million rats annually.

Unit 731 responded with a determination to enrol cholera as a contagion spreader: polluting the enemy's water had failed so they turned back to insects to convey the cholera. What followed has been called 'the greatest military success in the modern annals of biological warfare'. Humble house flies (*Musca domestica*), or 'filth flies', provided the answer. The city of Baoshan lay on the Allied supply line into China, delivering Chiang Kai-shek's Nationalist forces with the materiel and arms essential for them to resist the Japanese. On 4 May 1942, fifty-four Japanese bombers attacked Baoshan, unleashing tons of explosive and incendiary bombs. The city was devastated: 10,000 people died in the raid and more than 75 per cent of the buildings were destroyed. It was, however, no conventional bombing raid, for mixed in with the conventional ordnance were a number of unusual-looking ceramic-shelled bombs. At first, they were taken to be UXBs – Lin Yoyue, a retired elementary school teacher, described the bizarre contents as being a 'yellow waxy substance [with] many live flies struggling to fly away'. He had stumbled on Unit 731's secret weapon: the Yagi bomb, or 'maggot bomb'.

The Yagi was divided into a section packed with a gelatinous slurry of bacteria and a compartment loaded with flies. On impact, the casing burst and the insects were splattered with a slimy coating of cholera bacteria. The flies were then free to spread into the decimated city. The planes returned for three more bombing runs on 5, 6 and 8 May, causing the survivors, many of whom were infected with cholera, to evacuate their flattened city and seek refuge in the countryside: the Japanese thereby had the regional epidemic they had planned for.

By June, cholera had spread into more than half of Yunnan Province. Villages were ravaged as far as 125 miles from Baoshan, with 25 to 50 per cent mortality typical. Some 60,000 of the city refugees died of the disease, with more than twice this number succumbing throughout the region. The final tally reached 200,000 although an international symposium of historians declared in 2002 that Japanese entomological warfare in China was responsible for the deaths of 440,000 Chinese. The Allies' supply line was contaminated to the point that the Chinese Nationalist Army could no longer station troops in the region, enabling the Japanese to divert thousands of soldiers to other fronts.

During the Philippines campaign in March 1942, the Japanese considered releasing 200 lb of plague-carrying fleas (about 150 million insects) in each of ten separate attacks, but the Americans surrendered at Bataan before the plan was implemented. Around the same time, the Japanese made a series of anthrax and glanders attacks on numerous villages in the Jinhua area of Zhejiang Province, infecting 6,000 inhabitants. More than 3,000 people died.

In August 1943, the Japanese replicated their 'decimate-and-contaminate' ploy, bombing in the northern province of Shandong. There was one crucial difference, though: because Japanese troops were operating in the area, their soldiers were vaccinated against cholera to prevent casualties to 'friendly fire'. As expected, an epidemic tore through the region, afflicting towns and villages and spreading into parts of adjacent provinces.

Yunnan and Shandong became the Hiroshima and Nagasaki of China, with flies and microbes taking as many lives as atomic bombs took in Japan. General Chiang Kai-shek communicated these attacks to Churchill and Roosevelt: Roosevelt threatened to retaliate if the entomological raids did not stop; they did not.

Although rarely carried out as direct elements of the thriving offensive biological warfare programme, the experiments on humans did occasionally show the perpetrators how the body might act in given combat situations and with specific traumas. An associated objective of many of these sickening human experiments was to develop new treatments for medical problems that the Japanese Army faced in combat. Feeble as this justification is for what was simply naked sadism, some argue that Unit 731's work saved many Japanese lives. For example, the unit proved scientifically that the best treatment for frostbite was not rubbing the limb, which had been the traditional method, but rather immersion in water just warmer than 100 degrees – but never more than 122 degrees. How can you justify this in the pursuit of medical research? Takeo Wano, a 71-year-old former medical worker in Unit 731, said he once saw a 6-foot-high glass jar in which a Western man was pickled in formaldehyde. The man had been cut into two pieces, vertically. Likewise, experimentation on the effect of STIs, pregnancy and rape had no military relevance whatsoever. Female and male prisoners were raped by infected men to see how syphilis spreads in the body. Women were involuntarily impregnated and then experiments were performed on them to investigate how syphilis affected the mother as well as the foetus. Sometimes the mother would be vivisected in order to see how the foetus was developing.

Meanwhile, the biological war proper was relentless. When the United States prepared to attack the strategically important island of Saipan in the Northern Mariana Islands in the late spring of 1944, a submarine was sent from Japan to deliver flea-based biological weapons to the 30,000 defenders. The submarine was sunk by the American submarine *Swordfish*. The battle cost the Americans 3,426 killed and 10,364 wounded. Of the defenders, only 921 were taken prisoner. Some 20,000 Japanese civilians perished during the battle, including over 1,000 who jumped from 'Suicide Cliff' and 'Banzai Cliff' rather than be taken prisoner.

Around November 1944, Japan had broadened its horizons and made plans to use their weapons on targets on the United States mainland. They launched a total of 9,300 hydrogen-filled 'Fu-Go' (fire balloons), carrying biological agents, incendiaries to start forest fires and antipersonnel bombs carried by balloons that were designed to rise to 30,000 feet and then be swept eastward by the jet stream to the United States. At least 300 balloons actually reached the US: they killed six American civilians near Bly, Oregon; crashed into a farm in Medford, Oregon; and caused a short circuit in the power lines supplying electricity for the nuclear reactor cooling pumps in the Manhattan Project's production facility at the Hanford Site in Washington. A backup system restored power. These fire balloons were the first 'intercontinental weapons'.

During the Battle of Iwo Jima, another biological attack was considered against the invading Americans. Pilot Shoichi Matsumoto later recounted how two gliders carrying pathogens were to be towed over the battle and released, but the gliders that were supposed to take off from mainland Japan to Matsumoto's airfield in Pingfang District in preparation for the attack never reached their destination.

In the spring of 1945, the Japanese laid plans to deploy kamikaze pilots to bomb San Diego with ordnance carrying plague-infected fleas. This audacious operation was ludicrously called 'Operation Cherry Blossoms at Night'. The plan was finalised on 26 March 1945. Five of Japan's new I-400-class long-range submarines were to be despatched across the Pacific Ocean, each carrying three Aichi M6A Seiran aircraft loaded with plague-infected flea balloon bombs. The submarines were to surface and launch the aircraft towards the target, to drop the fleas via balloon bombs or crash in enemy territory. Either way, the hope was that plague would then infect and kill thousands of people in the area.

The plan was scheduled to be rolled out on 22 September 1945 but this did not happen due to the surrender of Japan on 15 August. Although the American government censored reports at the time, some 200 balloons landed in western states, and bombs carried by the balloons killed a woman in Montana and six people in Oregon. When China released two (alleged) weather balloons (one of which drifted into US airspace) in February 2023, the Pentagon must have been anxious to exclude the possibility that they carried biowarfare balloon bombs.

When it became clear that the Japanese were going to lose the war, Unit 731 workers did their best to destroy as much of the evidence of the experiments as possible. The Japanese government did not admit to the atrocities committed by Unit 731 until 1988. Because of this lack of acknowledgment, in 1982 they established a museum on the site of Unit 731's operations. According to the 2002 International Symposium on the Crimes of Bacteriological Warfare, the number of people killed by the Imperial Japanese Army germ warfare and human experiments was around 580,000.

Like many of the Nazi doctors who conducted cruel experiments on prisoners and concentration camp inmates, few of those complicit in the experiments at Unit 731 were ever brought to justice for their crimes. On the contrary, many were able to rejoin society and went on to have very successful careers in their fields, rising to positions that included governor of Tokyo, president of the Japan Medical Association and head of the Japan Olympic Committee. American forces, chiefly the military governor of Japan, General Douglas MacArthur, had decided not to put workers of Unit 731 on trial.

MacArthur granted those involved immunity in exchange for full disclosure of the scientific knowledge and data they had acquired from their experiments. Even General Shirō Ishii was allowed to live peacefully until his death from throat cancer in 1959.

Ishii was arrested by United States authorities and, along with other senior officers, was supposed to be thoroughly interrogated by Soviet authorities. Although the Soviet authorities wished the prosecutions to take place, the United States objected after the reports of the investigating US microbiologists. Dr Edwin Hill, the chief of Fort Detrick, stated that the Unit 731 information was 'absolutely invaluable'; it 'could never have been obtained in the United States because of scruples attached to experiments on humans' and 'the information was obtained fairly cheaply'. On 6 May 1947, Douglas MacArthur wrote to the president, saying 'additional data, possibly some statements from Ishii probably can be obtained by informing Japanese involved that information will be retained in intelligence channels and will not be employed as "War Crimes" evidence.'

Ishii's immunity cover-up was concluded in 1948 and, as noted, he was never prosecuted for any war crimes, while his exact whereabouts or occupation were unknown from 1947. Some say that Ishii later went to Maryland to advise on bioweapons; others that he remained in Japan, where he opened a clinic, performing treatments for free. Ishii kept a diary, but it did not mention any of his wartime activities with Unit 731.

On 11 March 1948, thirty people, including several doctors and one female nurse, were brought to trial by the Allied war crimes tribunal. Charges of cannibalism were dropped, but twenty-three people were found guilty of vivisection or wrongful removal of body parts. Five were sentenced to death, four to life imprisonment, and the rest to shorter terms. In 1950, MacArthur commuted all of the death sentences and significantly reduced most of the prison terms. All of those convicted in relation to vivisection were free after 1958.

The only good news is that in 2018, Japan disclosed the names of thousands of members of Unit 731. The country's national archives passed on the names of 3,607 people in response to a request by Katsuo Nishiyama, a professor at Shiga University of Medical Science. 'This is the first time that an official document showing the real names of almost all members of Unit 731 has been disclosed,' Nishiyama told the *Mainichi Shimbun* newspaper. 'The list is important evidence that supports testimony by those involved. Its discovery will be a major step toward unveiling concealed facts.'

The document lists members of Unit 731 and is dated 1 January 1945. It includes the names, ranks and contact details of more than 1,000 army medical staff, as well as dozens of doctors, surgeons, nurses and engineers.

The Soviet Union captured some Unit 731 personnel while in their flight from Manchukuo. Some of them stood trial in the Khabarovsk war crime trials held in December 1949: twelve Japanese medical army researchers were convicted of war crimes. Major General Yoshiyuki Kawashima testified that Unit 731 had dropped plague-contaminated fleas on Chinese cities that had caused epidemic plague outbreaks. However, these trials were dismissed as propaganda by the United States: the trials did not offer sufficient independent verification on the subject and certain crucial points.

As we have noted, many of the leaders in Japan's secret biological warfare programme went on to have successful careers in the USA. Many of the activities undertaken by the Japanese Army are omitted from Western textbooks and do not feature in Western culture generally.

Unit 731 did not work alone. In fact, it was part of a wide network supporting their research.

Unit 100

Unit 100 was an Imperial Japanese Army unit, otherwise called the Kwantung Army Warhorse Disease Prevention Shop, which focused on the development of biological weapons. It was operated by the Kempeitai, the Japanese military police, and focused on the military use of animals and animal diseases. It was headquartered in Mokotan, Manchukuo, a village just south of the city of Changchun. Between 600 and 800 people worked at Unit 100.

Unit 100 comprised six sections: Bacteriological section; Pathology section; Animal Experimentation; Organic chemistry; Botanical, and plant pathology; Poisoning, or infecting, plants with the help of bacteria; Preparations for bacteriological warfare.

The main purpose of Unit 100 was to conduct research about diseases originating from animals (zoonotic diseases). Most armies of the time relied on horses for haulage and transport so the Japanese Army sought ways to kill them and reduce an enemy's capabilities and logistics. Additionally, they hoped to use infected horses to spread disease to other, enemy, animals and to enemy populations. This involved experiments with human beings, which, as we have seen, were the remit of Unit 731. Although smaller than Unit 731, Unit 100 was still a sizeable organisation: its annual bacteria production capacity was projected to reach 1,000 kg of anthrax, 500 kg of glanders, and 100 kg of red rust (fungus). The goal was never reached.

Senior Sergeant Kazuo Mitomo coldly described some of Unit 100's inhuman human experiments:

I put as much as a gram of heroin into some porridge and gave this porridge to an arrested Chinese citizen who ate it; about 20 minutes later he lost consciousness and remained in that state until he died 15–16 hours later. We knew that such a dose of heroin is fatal, but it did not make any difference to us whether he died or lived. On some of the prisoners I experimented 5–6 times, testing the action of Korean bindweed, bactal and castor oil seeds. One of the prisoners of Russian nationality became so exhausted from the experiments that no more could be performed on him, and Matsui ordered me to kill that Russian by giving him an injection of potassium cyanide. After the injection, the man died at once. Bodies were buried in the unit's cattle graveyard.

Unit chief Yujiro Wakamatsu ordered the purchase of hundreds of cattle to be put out to pasture along the Siberian border north-east of Hailar, ready to be infected by airborne dispersion. It was the plan that in the event of a Soviet invasion, these infected livestock would mingle with local herds to cause epidemics and destroy food supplies.

Unit 100 staff routinely poisoned and drugged Russians, Chinese and Koreans with heroin, castor oil, tobacco and other substances for weeks at a time. Some died during the experimentation but when survivors were deemed no longer useful for experimentation staff told them they would receive a shot of medicine, but instead they executed them with potassium cyanide injections or by gunshot.

Unit 100 could produce 1,000 kilograms of anthrax germs, 500 kilograms of glanders germs, and 100 kilograms of redrust germs in a single year. Unit 100 focused on testing these potential agents: *Yersinia pestis*, which causes plague; *Burkholderia mallei*, for glanders in horses (testimony was given after the war that Unit 100 released horses infected with glanders); and *Bacillus anthracis*, which causes anthrax.

The atrocities committed by Units 100 and 731 form part of the war crimes committed under Emperor Hirohito which resulted in the deaths of millions of people and has become known as the 'Asian Holocaust'. Some estimates of the number of deaths that resulted from Japanese war crimes range from 3 to 14 million through massacre, human experimentation, starvation, and forced labour that was either directly perpetrated or condoned by the Japanese military and government. And that takes no account of the mass rapes of civilian women and the abduction of women to serve as *ianpu* ('comfort women') or *jongun-ianpu* ('women of military comfort') used in military brothels as sex slaves.

Unit Ei 1644

Unit Ei 1644 – also known as Unit 1644, Detachment Ei 1644, Detachment Ei, Detachment Tama, The Nanking Detachment, or simply Unit Ei – was a Japanese laboratory and biological warfare facility under the control of the Epidemic Prevention and Water Purification Department. It was established in 1939 in Japanese-occupied Nanking as a satellite of Unit 731.

During the Second Sino-Japanese War (1937–45), Unit Ei engaged in 'producing on a mass scale lethal bacteria to be used as weapons against the Chinese forces and civilian population' and 'took a direct part in employing bacteriological weapons against the Chinese forces and local inhabitants during the military operations of the Japanese troops', according to its chief, Shunji Satō.

Satō testified that while he was chief of the unit, it was:

> devising bacteriological weapons and producing them on a mass scale. For this purpose the Nanking Detachment Ei was supplied with high-capacity equipment and with bacteriological experts, and it produced lethal bacteria on a mass scale. Under my direction ... the Training Division every year trained about 300 bacteriologists with the object of employing them in bacteriological warfare.

The facility also bred fleas for the purposes of plague infection. Satō testified about the equipment of Unit Ei: 'The output capacity of the Nanking Detachment Ei 1644 for the production of lethal bacteria was up to 10 kilograms per production cycle. Captain Murata was in charge of breeding fleas.'

In late August 1942, Unit Ei participated in a biological attack against Chinese citizens and soldiers in Yushan County, Jinhua, and Fuqing. As Kawashima Kiyoshi testified, the 'bacteriological weapon was employed on the ground, the contaminating of the territory being done by sabotage action. ... The advancing Chinese troops entered the contaminated zone and came under the action of the bacteriological weapon.' Cholera and plague cultures used during the attack were made at Unit Ei. Satō testified he was told that 'plague, cholera and paratyphoid germs were employed against the Chinese by spraying. The plague germs were disseminated through fleas, the other germs in the pure form – by contaminating reservoirs, wells, rivers, etc.' The plague fleas were also from Unit Ei.

Unit 1855

Unit 1855 was a facility for human experimentation and was part of the central Epidemic Prevention and Water Purification Department of the North China Army of the Imperial Japanese Army, stationed in Beijing between 1938 and 1945. It was set up by the North China Army in 1938 in premises near to the Temple of Heaven in Beijing, and had a staff of about 2,000 men. The unit was commanded by the surgeon Colonel Nishimura Yeni, who reported directly to Shirō Ishii at Unit 731.

According to the testimony of the Korean Choi Hyung Shi, who worked as an interpreter with Unit 1855 between 1942 and 1943, the unit conducted experiments with plague, cholera and typhus on Chinese and Korean immigrants to China:

> When I first arrived there, some one hundred prisoners were already in the cells. ... The test subjects were infected with plague, cholera and typhus. Those not yet infected were kept in different rooms. There were large mirrors in the rooms with the subjects so that those undergoing the testing could be observed better. I spoke with the prisoners using a microphone and looking through the glass panel, interpreted the questions from the doctors: 'Do you have diarrhoea? Do you have a headache? Do you feel chilly?' The doctors made careful records of all answers. With the typhus test, ten people were forced to drink a mixture of the germs, and five were administered the vaccine. The two groups were separated from each other. The vaccine proved effective with all five to whom it was administered. The other five suffered horribly. In the plague tests, the prisoners suffered with chills and fever, and groaned in pain ... until they died. From what I saw, one person was killed every day.

It has been estimated that Unit 1855 killed about 1,000 people between 1938 and 1945.

Unit 8604

Unit 8604 was also known as Detachment Nami or Detachment Nami 8604; it was the Epidemic Prevention and Water Purification Department unit of the Japanese Southern China Area Army, secretly researching biological warfare and other topics through human experimentation. It was headquartered at Sun Yat-sen University of Medical Sciences.

The unit was commanded by Major General Satō Shunji, a physician, and staffed by 800 personnel: 100 commissioned officers, many with medical or scientific backgrounds, 200 medical and scientific researchers, and 500 soldiers and noncommissioned officers. Shigeru Maruyama, a former member of the unit, said that one experiment involved starving prisoners to death and talked of seeing victims being operated on almost every day.

Unit Oka 9420

Unit Oka 9420 was the central Epidemic Prevention and Water Purification Department of the Southern Expeditionary Army Group of the Imperial Japanese Army formed in 1942 to support the Japanese Southern Army. Unit 9420 consisted of two units: the Umeoka Unit, which specialised in the plague, and the Kono Unit, which focused on malaria, with most of its work containing the spread of disease in Singapore.

Unit commander was Major General Kitagawa Masataka, headquartered in the Permai Hospital in Tampoi, Johor, at the southern tip of the Malay Peninsula, 9 miles north-east of Singapore, with some evidence that it also had subunits operating in Thailand working on unknown diseases. As well as its work on the plague, the unit was also responsible for rat-catching.

According to the testimony of Othman Wok, a politician, Singapore was also an important biological weapons base; a laboratory was established within days of the Japanese victory there and it became one of the largest BW installations outside mainland China. It was staffed with approximately 150 physicians and scientists, and produced huge quantities of pathogens every year. Naito and his staff worked primarily with typhus, plague, and pesticides.

We have noted how Japan's extended reticence and the lack of documents regarding their biological warfare programmes in the 1930s and 1940s has bedevilled evidence-based research and has led to a reliance on anecdotal evidence. Many crucial records and files were destroyed, lost or covered up. Much of the information held by the United States had been kept classified until recently.

Historian Sheldon Harris later developed this groundbreaking work when he compiled research from people who had direct knowledge and experience of the events. Additionally, he shed light on the other units involved in the biological weapons programme.

Harris and other scholars found that US Intelligence authorities had seized the Japanese researchers' archive after the technical information was provided by Japan. The information was transferred in an arrangement that involved keeping the information a secret and not pursuing war crimes charges; this also allowed the Japanese government to deny knowledge of the use of BW weapons by Japan's military in China during the Second World War.

Here is Harris on Project 112:

> The tests, presumably, were conducted at what research officers designated, but did not name, 'satellite sites'. These sites were located both in the continental United States and in foreign countries. The tests conducted there were aimed at both human, animal and plant reaction to BW. It is known that tests were undertaken in Cairo, Egypt, Liberia, in South Korea, and in Japan's satellite province of Okinawa in 1961, or earlier. This was at least one year prior to the creation of Project 112. The Okinawa anti-crop research project may lend some insight to the larger projects 112 sponsored. BW experts in Okinawa and 'at several sites in the Midwest and south' conducted 'field tests' in 1961 for wheat rust and rice blast disease. These tests met with 'partial success' in the gathering of data, and led, therefore, to a significant increase in research dollars in fiscal year 1962 to conduct additional research in these areas. The money was devoted largely to developing 'technical advice on the conduct of defoliation and anti-crop activities in Southeast Asia'. By the end of fiscal year 1962, the Chemical Corps had let or were negotiating contracts for over one thousand chemical defoliants. The Okinawa tests evidently were fruitful.
>
> Sheldon H. Harris, *Factories of Death: Japanese Biological Warfare, 1932–45, and the American Cover-up* (2002)

The US refused to cooperate when the Soviet Union tried to pursue war crimes charges against the Japanese. Douglas MacArthur denied that the US military possessed any captured records on Japan's military biological programme. However, a top-secret report by the US War Department at the end of the Second World War clearly reveals that the United States exchanged Japan's military technical information on BW experimentation against humans, plants and animals for war crimes immunity. The War Department notes, 'The voluntary imparting of this BW information may serve as a forerunner for obtaining much additional information in other fields of research.' Being armed with Nazi and Imperial Japanese biowarfare know-how enabled the United States government and its intelligence agencies to begin conducting widespread field testing of potential BW capabilities on American cities, crops and livestock.

The Khabarovsk war crime trials were held between 25 and 31 December 1949, in the Soviet Union's industrial city of Khabarovsk, close to Japan. There, twelve members of the Japanese Kwantung Army were tried as war criminals for manufacturing and using biological weapons during the Second World War. In the course of the trials Major General Kiyoshi Kawashima testified that, as early as 1941, some forty members of Unit 731 air-dropped plague-contaminated fleas on Changde. These operations caused epidemic plague outbreaks. All twelve accused were found guilty, and sentenced to terms ranging between two and twenty-five years in a labour camp. In 1956, those who were still serving their sentences were released and repatriated to Japan.

Operation Vegetarian 1942

Operation Vegetarian was a British plan to liberally spread linseed cakes infected with anthrax spores over the fields of Germany. The cakes would then have been eaten by cattle, which would in turn be consumed by the civilian population, causing the deaths of millions of German civilians. Not only that, it would have exterminated most of Germany's cattle, exacerbating an already critical food shortage for the rest of the population that remained uninfected; even uninfected sources of beef would come under suspicion, with an effect on food supplies and morale. Preparations were not complete until early 1944. In the 1940s, gastrointestinal anthrax would quickly kill up to 60 per cent of all animals or people who ate its bacterial spores. Inhaled anthrax was deadlier still, with a fatality rate of up to 95 per cent.

The director of the Porton Down biology department, Paul Fildes, was briefed to find suitable suppliers for the chemicals needed for production of both the anthrax and the cakes themselves, along with the customised containers to carry them to prevent contamination during transport. Some RAF planes required modification so that they could drop the payloads without destroying them in the process. The linseed cake production was outsourced to the Olympia Oil and Cake Company, operators of the largest linseed oil crushing and refining plant in Europe, based in Blackburn Meadows at Tinsley, Sheffield, in order to produce large batches of full cakes. The slicing of the cakes into the appropriate sizes was given to a soap manufacturer J & E Atkinson. They were contracted to cut cakes into sizes of '2.5cm in diameter and 10 grammes in weight', with an order of 180,000 to 250,000 pieces per week, and a final target of 5,273,400 cakes by the end of April 1943.

An electronically triggered 4 lb anthrax bomb was designed. One hundred and six of these could be packaged cluster-bomb-style into a single 500 lb bomb. Estimates indicated that 1,000 of the bombs containing a total of 106,000 anthrax bomblets could extinguish life in a 25-square-mile area. Berlin, Wilhelmshafen, Frankfurt, Aachen and Hamburg were potential targets.

The anthrax bacteria were produced at a laboratory operated by the Ministry of Agriculture, Fisheries and Food along with research on the injection method required to introduce the anthrax into the linseed cake slices. The RAF arrived at a wooden tray system that could be attached to Avro Lancasters, Handley Page Halifaxes, and Short Stirlings.

Another account has it that in November 1942, Fildes and a colleague went to Washington, where they invited the United States to set up production facilities sufficient to produce large amounts of anthrax bacterial spores (called 'Agent N') and botulinum toxin ('Agent X'). Their initial order was for 7 lb of Agent X; an American team headed by Ira Baldwin at Camp Detrick started work on this in June 1943 and fulfilled the order within a few months.

As described above, the testing of anthrax as an animal elimination process was carried out on Gruinard Island. Operation Vegetarian was good to go by spring of 1944 and plans were made for the cakes to be dropped in the summer, when German cattle would be grazing openly in the fields. They had to be dropped after the spring grass had been consumed and the amount of food left to the cattle was limited, thus making the linseed cakes all the more attractive. However, the planned raid coincided with the Normandy invasion, which ultimately would, if all went to plan, eventually see Allied troops advancing across northern Europe. Operation Vegetarian was to be abandoned and the 5 million cakes were destroyed in an incinerator shortly after the end of the Second World War. Did they not see D-Day coming?

Paul Fildes

Sir Paul Gordon Fildes, OBE, FRS (1882–1971) was a pathologist and microbiologist who worked on the development of chemical-biological weaponisation at Porton Down during the Second World War.

Fildes insisted that he was involved with Operation Anthropoid – the assassination of Nazi Reinhard Heydrich in Prague in May 1942 – by providing the Czech agents of the Special Operations Executive with modified No. 73 grenades filled with botulinum toxin. There is some doubt about this given that Heydrich displayed none of the highly distinctive symptoms of botulism.

In 1940, Fildes was given responsibility for the newly created Biology Department at Porton Down to study the defensive implications of a bacterial attack; there he built up a team of microbiologists to study the use of biological weapons, including anthrax and botulinum toxin, and the stockpile of the million anthrax-impregnated cattle cakes referred to above. He also assisted with the anthrax strain tests on Gruinard Island, performing necropsies on the bodies of anthrax-exposed sheep, to determine if they had died as a direct result of anthrax poisoning.

The Canadian biological warfare programme

In Kingston, Ontario, a Queen's University laboratory was busy weaponising anthrax during the Second World War; a simulated attack released bacteria over Winnipeg, Manitoba. Canadian scientists tested American chemical and biological weapons in Suffield, Alberta, throughout the 1960s.

Canada's involvement with bioweapons begins in 1940 when Dr Frederick Banting warned of the likelihood of germ warfare; Canada is up there with United Kingdom, the United States, Russia and the former Soviet Union in the league table of bioweapon development. The UK and the US opposed Canada's plan to vaccinate soldiers against botulism before they used it on the enemy, the reason being that their own unprotected troops might suffer psychological stress if they learnt that their Canadian counterparts had been vaccinated and they had not.

Three test kits that may have contained live anthrax samples were sent to Canada by the US Army laboratory at Dugway Proving Ground in Utah; the three kits were supplied to two different labs. The National Microbiology Laboratory in Winnipeg received one of them; the Defence Research and Development Suffield Research Centre got the other two in 2007. 'Our records indicate that the 2006 samples in question have not been accessed in the last five years and there have been no safety issues associated with this sample at the Suffield Research Centre,' National Defence said. The shipment came in 2006 with testing kits sent from the US Department of Defense that were meant to help the lab validate its anthrax detection tests. The kits were supposed to contain 'dead' or inactive anthrax bacteria.

Nazi human experimentation: *Blitzableiter* (Lightning Rod) – the Nazi biological warfare programme

> These researches ... can be performed by us with particular efficiency because I personally assumed the responsibility for supplying asocial individuals and criminals who deserve only to die from concentration camps for these experiments.
>   Heinrich Himmler letter to Erhard Milch concerning the high altitude and freezing experiments, nuremberg.law.harvard.edu.

The Nazi human experimentation programme was an ongoing, extensive series of medical experiments on huge numbers of prisoners, including children, in its concentration camps in the early to mid-1940s. Victims included Jews from all Nazi-occupied countries, Romani, Sinti, ethnic Poles, Soviet PoWs, disabled Germans and Germans considered to be political enemies of the Nazi regime.

As with the atrocities going on simultaneously in Japan at Unit 731 and other facilities, there was no consensuality and the victims were coerced into participation. Worse still, there was no anesthesia and subjects who survived were left with life-changing and lifelong psychological and physical trauma and scars that resulted in disfigurement and permanent disability – medical torture at its most ineffable.

As with the repellent 'research' undertaken in Unit 731, the Germans had a feeble excuse for this abhorrent industrial-scale extermination and sadism: selected inmates were subjected to various experiments that were apparently designed and justified in order to help better prepare German military personnel in combat situations, to develop new weapons, to aid in the treatment of military personnel who had been injured, and to advance the Nazi racial ideology and eugenics. Only the last was not a form of indirect biological terrorism and/or warfare where a warped form of medical science and research was enlisted to help German military fight better and more successfully.

The Doctors' Trial after the war and revulsion at the abuses perpetrated led to the development of the Nuremberg Code of medical ethics. The Nazi defendants argued that their experiments were justified as a military necessity and compared their actions to the significant and substantial death and destruction caused by the Allied bombings of Germany.

Here are just some of the vile experiments conducted in the name of medical research to help the Germans militarily. There were many others, but these – for example, those on twins, mustard gas, seawater, sterilisation and fertility experiments – were conducted for non-military purposes or as part of chemical warfare programmes.

Bone, muscle, and nerve transplantation experiments
From around September 1942 to December 1943, Ravensbrück concentration camp was the location of experiments conducted for the benefit of the German Armed Forces to study bone, muscle and nerve regeneration, and bone transplantation from one person to another. Subjects had their bones, muscles and nerves removed without anesthesia. Naturally, many victims suffered excruciating agony, mutilation and permanent disability. Prisoners also had their bone marrow injected with bacteria to study the effectiveness of new drugs being developed purportedly for use on the battlefield.

Malaria experimentation
Between 1942 and about April 1945, there were numerous experiments conducted under Kurt Blome and Claus Schilling at Dachau to investigate

immunisation for treatment of malaria. Healthy inmates were infected by mosquitoes or by injections of extracts of the mucous glands of female mosquitoes. They were exposed to malaria mosquitoes in cages strapped to their hands or arms so as to guarantee infection with the parasite. After contracting the disease, the subjects were plied with various drugs to test their relative efficacy. Over 1,200 people were used in these experiments and more than half died as a result. Other victims were left with permanent disabilities. According to the testimony of August H. Vieweg, the patients used were Poles, Russians and Yugoslavs.

Eduard May, director of the Entomological Division of the SS Institute for Practical Research in Military Science, was commissioned to experiment on camp prisoners with 'humanly harmful insects' starting in October 1943, and this was closely connected with Blome's biological warfare programme. May collaborated with him in experiments on 'the artificial mass transmission of the malaria parasite to humans', with infected mosquitoes dropped from planes.

Similar experiments were also conducted in Buchenwald and in a psychiatric clinic in Thuringia, where Professor Gerhard Rose tested malaria drugs on mentally ill Russian prisoners of war. Claus was put to death for his criminal research in 1946; Rose was condemned to lifelong imprisonment in 1947, not for his malaria research but for his shocking experiments with epidemic typhus sera, which he also had performed in concentration camps and with prisoners of war in Russia. In addition, the Wehrmacht's Veterinary Section, which included research projects on animal diseases being conducted by Erich Traub at the Insel Riems (Riems Island) Institute, was developing methods to spread these by aircraft over Britain, the US and the Soviet Union.

Like Kurt Blome's cancer research institute in Posen, the State Research Institute at Insel Riems was a dual-use facility where some biological warfare experiments were conducted. It was founded in 1909 to study foot-and-mouth disease and by the Second World War employed about twenty scientists and ancillary staff of about 70–120. Hans-Christoph Nagel, a veterinarian and biological warfare expert for the German Army, was in charge of research into the use of animal and insect diseases as biological weapons. Like Blome, Traub was also employed after the war by the US government as a biological warfare expert. Riems is an island in the Bay of Greifswald, between the German mainland and the island of Rügen in the Baltic Sea.

The immersion hypothermia project
In 1942, the Luftwaffe conducted experiments to establish the most effective treatment for victims of immersion hypothermia, particularly Luftwaffe crews who had been shot down into the freezing waters of the North Sea. There were

360 to 400 experiments and 280 to 300 victims, indicating that some endured more than one experiment. Typically, the subjects were male civilian prisoners; their participation was usually forced, but occasionally it was 'voluntary' in response to promises, rarely fulfilled, of release from the camp or commutation of the death sentence. In August 1942, at Dachau, prisoners were immersed in a tank of ice water. Some were anesthetised, others conscious; many were naked, but others were clothed. Several different methods of rewarming the subjects were also tested. Responses of body temperatures, clinical manifestations, and selected biochemical and physiologic measurements were purportedly monitored, and autopsies were performed.

Sigmund Rascher, an SS doctor at Dachau, reported directly to Heinrich Himmler and released the results of his freezing experiments at the 1942 'Medical Problems Arising from Sea and Winter' medical conference. In a letter from 10 September 1942, Rascher describes an experiment on intense cooling performed in Dachau where people were dressed in fighter pilot uniforms and submerged in freezing water. Rascher had some of the victims completely underwater and others only submerged up to the head.

Epidemic jaundice
Experiments on epidemic jaundice from June 1943 until January 1945 were conducted at Sachsenhausen and Natzweiler. The test subjects were injected with the disease in order to discover new inoculations. These tests were, of course, conducted for the benefit of the German Armed Forces. Most subjects died in the experiments; those who survived experienced great pain and suffering.

Sulphonamide experiments
From July 1942 to September 1943, experiments to investigate the effectiveness of sulphonamide, a synthetic antimicrobial agent, were conducted at Ravensbrück. This involved wounding the victim, who was then infected with bacteria such as *Streptococcus*, *Clostridium perfringens* – a major causative agent in gas gangrene – and *Clostridium tetani*, the causative agent in tetanus. Blood circulation was interrupted by tying off blood vessels at both ends of the wound to create a condition similar to that of a battlefield wound. Researchers also aggravated the subjects' infection by forcing wood shavings and ground glass into their wounds. The infection was treated with sulphonamide and other drugs to establish their effectiveness.

Poison
Between December 1943 and October 1944, Buchenwald scientists, including Joachim Mrugowsky, investigated the effect of various poisons, which were

covertly administered to experimental subjects in their food. The victims invariably died as a result of the poison. In September 1944, subjects were shot with poisonous bullets and usually died.

Incendiary bomb experiments

From around November 1943 to January 1944, Buchenwald was also the camp where tests took place to examine the effect of various pharmaceuticals on phosphorus burns. These burns were inflicted on prisoners using phosphorus material extracted from incendiary bombs.

High altitude experiments

In early 1942, prisoners at Dachau were unfortunate enough to be used by Sigmund Rascher in experiments to help improve outcomes for German pilots who had to eject at high altitudes. A low-pressure chamber containing these prisoners was used to simulate conditions at altitudes of up to 68,000 feet. Apparently, Rascher performed vivisections on the brains of victims who survived the initial experiment. Of the 200 subjects, eighty died immediately while the others were murdered. In a letter from 5 April 1942 between Rascher and Heinrich Himmler, Rascher explains the results of a fatal low-pressure experiment that was performed on an otherwise healthy prisoner who was slowly suffocated while Rascher and another unnamed doctor detailed his reactions.

In a letter from Himmler to Rascher in April 1942, Himmler ordered Rascher to continue the high-altitude experiments and to 'determine whether these men could be recalled to life'. If a victim was successfully resuscitated, Himmler commanded that he be pardoned from 'concentration camp for life'.

Hubertus Strughold (1898–1986) was a German-born physiologist and eminent medical researcher. From 1935, he served as chief of aeromedical research for the Luftwaffe, a position he held throughout the Second World War. In 1947, he was brought to the United States as part of Operation Paperclip, and held a series of high-ranking medical positions with both the US Air Force and NASA. For his role in pioneering the study of the physical and psychological effects of manned spaceflight, he became known as 'The Father of Space Medicine'.

Following his death, Strughold's activities in Germany during the Second World War came under greater scrutiny and allegations surrounding his involvement in Nazi-era human experimentation irreparably damaged his reputation. In 2004, questions about Strughold's complicity in human experimentation emerged following an investigation conducted by the Historical Committee of the German Society of Air and Space Medicine. The inquiry uncovered evidence of oxygen deprivation experiments carried out by Strughold's Institute for Aviation Medicine in 1943. According to these findings, six epileptic children, between the ages of 11 and 13, were taken from the Nazis' Brandenburg Euthanasia Centre to Strughold's Berlin laboratory, where they were placed in vacuum chambers to induce epileptic seizures in an effort to simulate the effects of high-altitude sicknesses, such as hypoxia.

Blood coagulation experiments

Sigmund Rascher experimented with the effects of Polygal, a coagulant made from beet and apple pectin. He predicted that the prophylactic use of Polygal tablets would reduce bleeding from gunshot wounds sustained during combat, or from surgery. Subjects were given a Polygal tablet, shot through the neck or chest, or had their limbs amputated without anesthesia. Rascher published an article on his experience of using Polygal, without reference to the nature of the human trials, and set up a company staffed by prisoners to manufacture the substance.

Bruno Weber was in charge of the Hygienic Institution at Block 10 in Auschwitz and injected his subjects with blood types that differed from their own; this caused the blood cells to congeal. When the Nazis extracted blood from a victim, they usually did so by entering a major artery, causing the subject to die of catastrophic blood loss.

Here are brief details of some of the principal perpetrators in the Nazi programme of human experimentation carried out in the name of furthering medical research to assist the German military.

Kurt Blome (1894–1969)

Kurt Blome was tried at the Doctors' Trial in 1947 on charges of practising euthanasia and conducting experiments on humans. His only admission was that he had been ordered in 1943 to experiment with plague vaccines on concentration camp prisoners. In fact, he 'assumed responsibility for all research into biological warfare sponsored by the Wehrmacht' and the SS. Although he was acquitted of war crimes charges, it was generally accepted that he had indeed participated in chemical and biological warfare experiments on concentration camp inmates. As Plenipotentiary for Cancer Research in the Third Reich, Blome had a longstanding interest in the 'military use of carcinogenic substances' and cancer-causing viruses.

Blome claimed that his work there involved only 'defensive' measures against biological weapons; Himmler, Goering, and Erich Schumann, head of the Wehrmacht's Science Section, backed the offensive use of chemical and biological weapons against Britain, the Soviet Union and the United States. In 1943, Schumann wrote to Dr Heinrich Kliewe, one of the Wehrmacht's biological warfare experts that, 'in particular, America must be attacked simultaneously with various human and animal epidemic pathogens as well as plant pests'. According to Kliewe, plague, typhoid, cholera and anthrax were under development as weapons, as well as a new 'synthetic medium for the spread of these bacteria', which would maintain their virulence for eight to twelve weeks.

As part of the Nazi biological warfare programme – *Blitzableiter* (Lightning Rod), Blome's institute was, in reality, 'a camouflaged operation for the production of biological warfare agents'. Its construction was overseen by Karl I. Gross, an SS officer and specialist in tropical diseases, who had conducted lethal experiments on 1,700 prisoners at the Mauthausen concentration camp. Something of a fortress, it was surrounded by a 10-foot high wall and guarded by a special SS unit, designed to prevent the accidental release of the various biological agents in production there. By May 1944, the institute had departments devoted to physiology-biology, bacteriology and vaccines, radiology, pharmacology, cancer statistics and a tumour farm, and had received at least 2.7 million Reichsmarks in funding from the Wehrmacht and SS between 1943 and 1945.

Blome studied storage methods and dispersal of biological agents such as plague, cholera, anthrax and typhoid; he also infected prisoners with plague in order to test the efficacy of vaccines. The University of Strasbourg had a 'special unit' where researchers tested typhus, hepatitis, nephritis, and other chemical and biological weapons on concentration camp inmates. Kurt Gutzeit was in charge of hepatitis research for the German Army, and he and his colleagues carried out virus experiments on mental patients, Jews, Russian PoWs and gypsies in Sachsenhausen, Auschwitz, and other camps. In October 1944, Himmler ordered Blome to experiment with plague on concentration camp prisoners.

Blome also investigated the use of insect vectors in biological warfare. As we have seen, in 1943 he proposed spreading malaria 'artificially by means of mosquitoes'; he also experimented on prisoners at Dachau and Buchenwald with lice in order to cause typhus outbreaks.

Blome also worked on aerosol dispersants and methods of spraying nerve agents like tabun and sarin from aircraft, and tested the effects of these gases on prisoners at Auschwitz. I.G. Farben had developed nerve gas in 1936 from its research into insecticides, and Blome's duties included preparing defensive measures against possible Allied use of insect-borne biological weapons, either in a first strike or in retaliation for German use of such weapons. As early as

September 1940, Wolfram Sievers, director of the SS Ahnenerbe Institute, had warned Blome of the need to expand the production of insecticides to deal with such an eventuality. This led Blome to experiment with the dispersal of insecticides, fungicides and nerve gas from aircraft, boosted after Hitler had ordered a 'drastic increase' in the production of tabun and sarin at I.G. Farben's Dyhernfurth factory in eastern Germany. On orders from Himmler in 1944, Blome also tested these on inmates at Auschwitz.

In January 1945, Blome fled from his Posen laboratories to escape the advancing Red Army. He went to Geraburg in Thuringia, where the Wehrmacht and SS had already constructed another biological warfare facility disguised as a cancer research institute. Blome brought his biological cultures with him from Poland, and was still promising Hitler a *Wunderwaffe* or 'miracle weapon' that would turn the tide of war in Germany's favour, but the Geraburg facility was captured by the US Army in April 1945, along with its records and equipment.

Blome was arrested in Munich in May 1945 by the United States Counter Intelligence Corps. He was acquitted at Nuremberg in exchange for information about biological warfare and nerve gas, and providing advice to the American chemical and biological weapons programmes. In November 1947, two months after his acquittal, Blome was interviewed by four representatives from Camp Detrick, in which he 'identified biological warfare experts and their location and described different methods of conducting biological warfare'.

In 1951, he was hired by the US Army Chemical Corps under Project 63, one of the successors to Operation Paperclip, to work on chemical warfare. He was employed at European Command Intelligence Center at Oberursel, West Germany, working on a never-declassified top-secret project labelled as 'Army, 1952, Project 1975'. Amazingly, he also continued to practise medicine in West Germany, and was active in politics as a member of the national-conservative German Party. He died in Dortmund in 1969.

Erich Traub (1906–85)
Eric Traub was a German veterinary scientist and virologist who specialised in foot-and-mouth disease, Rinderpest, and Newcastle disease virus – a virus that causes a deadly infection in many kinds of birds. He reported directly to Heinrich Himmler, as the lab chief at the Reich Research Institute for Virus Diseases of Animals – the Nazis' premier bioweapons facility on Riems Island. Traub was assisted by Anna Bürger, who, like Traub, was later allowed to go to the United States after the war, to work on the Navy's biological warfare programme. Himmler detailed Traub to work on weaponising foot-and-mouth disease virus, which had reportedly been dispersed by aircraft onto

cattle and reindeer in Russia. In 1944, Blome sent Traub to acquire a strain of rinderpest virus in Turkey but this strain proved nonvirulent and therefore plans for a rinderpest agent were abandoned.

Claus Schilling (1871–1946)
Claus Karl Schilling was a German tropical medicine expert who was heavily involved in human experiments at Dachau, purportedly on clinical research relating to malaria. After retiring from the Robert Koch Institute in 1936, Schilling moved to fascist Italy, where he conducted immunisation experiments on inmates of the psychiatric asylums of Volterra and San Niccolò di Siena; the Italian authorities were seeking ways to protect their troops against malaria outbreaks during the Italo-Ethiopian War. The Nazi government backed him with a grant for his Italian experimentation.

Schilling returned to Germany after meeting Leonardo Conti, the Nazis' health chief, in 1941, and by early 1942, he had a special malaria research station at Dachau, where he would remain in charge for the duration of the war. Schilling was sentenced to death by hanging on 13 December 1945.

Eduard Wirths (1909–45)
Eduard Wirths was the chief SS doctor at Auschwitz from September 1942 to January 1945 and had responsibility for everything undertaken by the nearly twenty SS doctors (including Josef Mengele, Horst Schumann and Carl Clauberg) who worked in the medical sections of Auschwitz. Wirths was appointed in the hope that he would stop the typhus epidemics that had plagued SS personnel at Auschwitz. In 1943, Wirths received a Christmas card from Langbein, a political prisoner who worked with him, which contained the message 'In the past year you have saved here the lives of 93,000 people.' It was signed 'One speaking for the prisoners of Auschwitz'. The figure of 93,000 was the difference in mortalities among prisoners from typhus in the year prior to Wirths' arrival.

Wirths was captured by the Allies and held in custody by British forces. Later, on 20 September 1945, he committed suicide by hanging.

Hermann Becker-Freyseng (1910–61)
Hermann Becker-Freyeseng was a consultant in aviation medicine with the Luftwaffe. His particular area of expertise was low-pressure chamber research. Fatalities in the various experiments undertaken by Becker-Freyseng were not unusual, in particular, the high altitude experiments performed on Dachau inmates. One of the most notorious was that detailed in a paper published by him and Konrad Schäfer entitled 'Thirst and Thirst Quenching in Emergency

Situations at Sea'. The researchers had requested from Himmler forty healthy camp inmates, mainly Jews, who were forced to drink salt water forced down their throats in tubes, or in some cases, had it injected into their veins. Half the subjects were then administered a drug called berkatit, a tomato-tasting compound to make the salt water more palatable, while all were subjected to an invasive liver biopsy without anaesthetic. All the subjects died, including those given the berkatit, which proved toxic, as the doctors suspected.

Becker-Freysing was found guilty of war crimes and crimes against humanity at the Doctors' Trial and was sentenced to twenty years in jail, commuted to ten. However, in 1946 Becker-Freyseng's name was one of a list of twenty who were to be brought to the United States to assist in the development of American space medicine, so he was duly put to work on projects related to the space race. Given responsibility for collecting and publishing the research undertaken by him and his colleagues, the resulting book, *German Aviation Medicine: World War II*, appeared just after Becker-Freyseng began his prison sentence.

Karl Franz Gebhardt (1897–1948)

Karl Franz Gebhardt served as Medical Superintendent of the Hohenlychen Sanatorium (in Lychen, north of Berlin, which became a military hospital for the Waffen-SS), Consulting Surgeon of the Waffen-SS, chief surgeon in the Staff of the Reich Physician SS and Police, and personal physician to Heinrich Himmler. He led surgical experiments performed on inmates at Ravensbrück and Auschwitz to champion the surgical management of badly contaminated traumatic wounds against the novel antibiotic treatments of battlefield injuries.

In order to absolve Gebhardt for his refusal to prescribe sulphonamide for the critically wounded Heydrich, Himmler suggested to Gebhardt that he should conduct experiments proving that sulphonamide was useless in the treatment of gangrene and sepsis; he carried out a series of experiments on Ravensbrück concentration camp prisoners, breaking their legs and infecting them with various organisms in order to prove the uselessness of the drugs in treating gas gangrene. He also attempted to transplant the limbs from camp victims to German soldiers wounded on the Eastern Front. Gebhardt was convicted of war crimes and crimes against humanity, and sentenced to death on 20 August 1947.

Karl August Genzken (1885–1957)

Karl August Genzken was complicit in a series of human experiments, notably on typhus, carried out on prisoners at Buchenwald and Natzweiler. The tests were conducted to gauge the efficacy of vaccines against typhus, smallpox, cholera, and other diseases. Genzken was also accused of involvement in experiments involving sulphanilamide, poison, and incendiary bombs. He was found guilty of war crimes, crimes against humanity, and membership of an illegal organisation; he was condemned to life imprisonment. His sentence was later reduced to twenty years and he was released in April 1954.

Nazi collaboration with Unit 731 and the Japanese biological warfare programme

It comes as no surprise to know that for the duration of the war the German and Japanese biological warfare programmes exchanged information, samples and equipment – usually conveyed by submarine. The last such submarine left Japan as late as May 1945; just before their August 1945 surrender, the Japanese destroyed many of the records relating to this cooperation and the biological warfare programme. In the 1930s, Hitler had ordered Otto Muntsch to examine Japan's use of chemical and biological weapons against China. The scientific cooperation was formalised in a series of agreements in 1938–39. Hojo Enryo, a Japanese army doctor and expert in biological weapons, 'frequently visited the Robert Koch Institute [in Berlin] as well as companies under German occupation to collect information about research on bacteriological warfare', and gave a lecture on this subject at the Berlin Military Academy of Medicine in October 1941. Gerhard Rose, 'the German expert on tropical diseases and epidemic typhus' and later a defendant at the Nuremberg Doctors' Trial, supplied samples of the yellow fever virus to Unit 731.

The Doctors' Trial (United States of America v. Karl Brandt, et al.)

This was the first of twelve trials for war crimes of high-ranking German officials and industry chiefs held in Nuremberg after the Second World War. Twenty of the twenty-three defendants were medical doctors accused of having been involved in Nazi human experimentation and mass murder under the guise of euthanasia. The indictment was filed on 25 October 1946; the trial lasted from 9 December until 20 August 1947. Of the twenty-three defendants, seven were acquitted and seven received death sentences; the remainder received prison sentences up to life imprisonment.

Operation Paperclip

Those we have just read about who got away with their crimes against humanity in order to assist the Americans in their biological weapons research did so under what became known as Operation Paperclip, the 'get out of jail' card to end all 'get out of jail' cards. Operation Paperclip was the secret United States intelligence programme, which clearly showed that even the most unspeakable crimes against humanity are excusable if that excuse enables the US to benefit militarily, scientifically and economically from the perpetrators of Nazi atrocities. More than 1,600 German scientists, engineers and technicians were taken to the US to carry out government research and work between 1945 and 1959. Conducted by the Joint Intelligence Objectives Agency (JIOA), it was largely executed by special agents of the US Army's Counterintelligence Corps (CIC). Many of these personnel were former members – former leaders, even – of the Nazi Party.

The aim of Operation Paperclip was quite simply to give the US a military advantage in the Cold War, as well as in the Space Race. Not to be outdone, though, in a comparable exercise, the Soviet Union relocated more than 2,200 German specialists – a total of more than 6,000 people including family members – with Operation Osoaviakhim during one night, on 22 October 1946.

This is how Paperclip was organised. Before the war ended, in February 1945, Supreme Headquarters Allied Expeditionary Force (SHAEF) set up T-Force, or Special Sections Subdivision, which was to grow to over 2,000 personnel by June. T-Force examined 5,000 possible German targets with a high priority on specialists in synthetic rubber and oil catalysts, new designs in armoured equipment, V-2 (rocket) weapons, jet and rocket-propelled aircraft, naval equipment, field radios, secret writing chemicals, aero medicine research, gliders, and 'scientific and industrial personalities'.

There emerged a rich fund of such 'personalities' so Special Sections Subdivision set up the Enemy Personnel Exploitation Section to manage and interrogate them. EPES established a detention centre, DUSTBIN, first in Paris and later in Kransberg Castle, outside Frankfurt. The US Joint Chiefs of Staff (JCS) established the first secret recruitment programme, Operation Overcast, on 20 July 1945, initially 'to assist in shortening the Japanese war and to aid our postwar military research'. In late summer 1945, the JCS established the JIOA, a subcommittee of the Joint Intelligence Community, to directly oversee Operation Overcast and later Operation Paperclip. In November 1945, Overcast was renamed Operation Paperclip by Ordnance Corps officers, who would attach a paperclip to the folders of the most 'troublesome cases' whom they wished to employ in America.

In a secret directive circulated on 3 September 1946, President Truman officially approved Operation Paperclip and expanded it to include 1,000 German scientists under 'temporary, limited military custody'. More than

1,600 Germans were secretly recruited to develop weapons 'at a feverish and paranoid pace that came to define the Cold War'. Albert Einstein, Eleanor Roosevelt and Rabbi Steven Wise all publicly opposed the programme while a Gallup poll revealed that most Americans at the time thought it a 'bad' idea. President Clinton adumbrated the issue when he signed the Nazi War Crimes Disclosure Act in 1998, which pushed through the declassification of American Intelligence records, including the FBI, Army Intelligence and CIA files of German agents, scientists and war criminals.

Back in 1943 things were looking grim for Germany: Barbarossa (June–December 1941) had failed badly, as had the push for the oilfields of the Caucusus (June 1942–February 1943); consequently, German resources were comprehensively depleted, and its military-industrial infrastructure became incapable of defending the Reich against the Red Army's inexorable westward advance. In early 1943, the German government began recalling scientists, engineers and technicians from combat duties to return to work in research and development. The recall included 4,000 rocket scientists posted to Peenemünde Island – the V-1 and V-2 rocket site – in the Baltic. Dieter K. Huzel, in *Peenemünde to Canaveral*, said of this exercise: 'Overnight, PhDs were liberated from KP [kitchen police or kitchen patrol] duty, masters of science were recalled from orderly service, mathematicians were hauled out of bakeries, and precision mechanics ceased to be truck drivers.'

The Nazis' recall required identifying and locating the scientists, engineers and technicians, then vetting their political and ideological reliability. Werner Osenberg, the engineer-scientist heading the Wehrforschungsgemeinschaft (Defence Research Association), recorded the names of the politically cleared men on the Osenberg List, thus officially reinstating them to scientific work. However, in March 1945, at Bonn University, a Polish laboratory technician found pieces of the Osenberg List stuffed down a toilet; the list found its way to MI6, who transmitted it to US Intelligence. Then US Army Major Robert B. Staver, chief of the Jet Propulsion Section of the Research and Intelligence Branch of the US Army Ordnance Corps, made good use of the Osenberg List to compile his list of German scientists to be captured and interrogated; Wernher von Braun, Germany's premier rocket scientist, was at the top of Major Staver's list. On 22 May, Staver transmitted to the US Pentagon headquarters Colonel Joel Holmes's telegram urging the evacuation of German scientists and their families as most 'important for [the] Pacific war' effort. By 1947, this operation had rounded up an estimated 1,800 technicians and scientists, along with 3,700 family members.

Paperclip 'captured' medical specialists, including those with experience of biological weapons, chemical weapons, and space medicine. One such

'Paperclip' was Walter Schreiber. Annie Jacobsen, in her *Operation Paperclip: The Secret Intelligence Program That Brought Nazi Scientists to America* (2014), tracks twenty-one of these Nazi scientists and technicians. Eight of her subjects had worked directly with Hitler, Himmler or Göring; fifteen were active Nazi Party members; ten served in paramilitary squads like the SA and SS; and six were tried at Nuremberg. In her review of Jacobsen's book, Wendy Lower concludes:

> Yet certain truths are obscured in Jacobsen's disturbing account. She writes that the Germans didn't use any chemical or biological weapons in World War II. Although they may not have deployed such weapons on the battlefield, the Germans did use carbon monoxide and hydrogen cyanide (Zyklon B, a pesticide) in mobile gas vans and gas chambers. In 1942–43, the Allies threatened retaliation if the Germans used chemical weapons. Apparently this warning applied only to Allied soldiers in combat and civilians in Allied cities, not to the Jews, Soviet PoWs and others who were murdered in Auschwitz, Birkenau and other Nazi extermination sites.
>
> Wendy Lower, *New York Times* 28 February 2014

Walter Schreiber (1893–1970)

Walter Schreiber was a medical officer with the German Army in the First World War and a brigadier general of the Wehrmacht Medical Service during the Second World War. He would later be a key witness against Hermann Göring during the Nuremberg trials. After the First World War, the United States, as we know, was assessing the potentiality of biological warfare agents in future military conflicts. As a professor of bacteriology and hygiene at the University of Berlin and an expert in epidemiology, Schreiber was invited to Walter Reed Army Medical Center (then Walter Reed General Hospital), in a scientific exchange between Germany and the United States. He reported on his work on sleeping sickness in Africa and exchanged strategies with US military opposite numbers on how to prevent biological warfare.

In his role in the German Army, and as representative of the Army Medical Inspectorate, Schreiber's brief was to prevent the spread of infectious disease and develop vaccines to guard against potential biological warfare agents. In 1942, he expressed his objections to the Reich's development of such weapons, stating during his witness testimony at the Nuremberg trials:

I personally made a report to Generaloberstabsarzt Handloser. ... It was an extremely serious matter for us physicians, for if there really should be a plague epidemic it was clear that it would not stop at the fronts, but would come over to us too. We had to bear a very grave responsibility.

Schreiber persisted with his objections to the experimentation being carried out at SS-controlled facilities. In October 1942, he reported what he heard at a conference where the results of human experiments at Dachau concentration camp were presented. In May 1943, he headed the third session of the advisory specialists of the Armed Forces, which led to a confrontation in which Schreiber spoke out against human experimentation in general, but especially with biological agents such as plague and typhus, testifying later at the Nuremberg trials that he 'pointed out that bacteria were an unreliable and dangerous weapon' but that he was 'confronted with a fait accompli', the decision had already been made: 'the Führer had given the Reichsmarschall [Hermann Göring] full powers, and so forth, for carrying out all the preparations.'

In September 1943, Schreiber took on the post of commander of Training Division C of the Military Medical Academy, under the authority of which he denied Kurt Blome, the head of the Posen Research Institute, permission to conduct his plague research in Sachsenburg. This was later overruled by Himmler. At a medical conference from 16 to 18 May 1944, Schreiber learned of research into gas gangrene experiments conducted by Dr Karl Gebhardt at Hohenlychen Sanatorium (Nuremberg document 619). In April 1945, he was stripped of his administrative duties except that of medical officer in charge of the military and civilian sector of Berlin.

On 30 April 1945, while caring for wounded in a makeshift hospital in the Reichstag Building in Berlin, Schreiber was taken prisoner by the Red Army and transported to the Soviet Union, where he spent time at Kransnogorsk PoW camp and Lubyanka prison. On 26 August 1946, the Soviets allowed Schreiber to appear as a witness at the Nuremberg trials, to testify against Göring and Kurt Blome, who, as we have seen, had been in charge of German offensive biological weapons development. Schreiber himself was not charged with any war crimes at the Nuremberg trials, although he was convicted *in absentia* by a Polish court of 'conducting gruesome medical experiments' at Auschwitz.

Operation Osoaviakhim

One of the key motivators for the US to press ahead with Operation Paperclip with such zeal and urgency was their awareness that the Soviets would be as anxious as they were to recruit Nazi specialists to help with and advance their own biological and chemical expertise and to accelerate their space programme. All of this took shape in Operation Osoaviakhim – the only difference was that the Americans recruited 'Paperclips' over several years while the Russians executed their transference of German scientific expertise in one night.

Operation Osoaviakhim (Операция Осоавиахим) happened on 22 October 1946, when MVD (previously NKVD) and Soviet Army units removed more than 2,200 German specialists – a total of more than 6,000 people including family members – from the Soviet occupation zone of Germany to work in the Soviet Union. A lot of related equipment was also relocated, the aim being to transplant research and production research centres such as the relocated V-2 rocket centre at Mittelwerk Nordhausen, from Germany to the Soviet Union, and collect as much material as possible from test centres like the Luftwaffe's central military aviation test centre at Erprobungsstelle Rechlin.

This is the experience of Fritz Karl Preikschat, a German engineer recruited to the Soviet Union via Operation Osoaviakhim and held in the Soviet Union for six years; presumably, it is fairly typical:

> They knew exactly where I lived, first of all: a few days before I was captured, a fellow came. They had a key – they had everything to the apartment, to the door. There was one interpreter who told me [in German]: 'Get up! You are being mobilized to work in Russia,' and there were about half a dozen soldiers with machine guns, who surrounded me. When I wanted to get to the toilet, they checked it out first to make sure there was no escape hatch. It was a very tight operation. They did that with every family. Many families came, while I was alone.
>
> Oral Interview with Fritz Karl Preikschat recorded by his son, Ekhard Preikschat, Bellevue, WA, USA, 21 April 1994

There was some opposition, for example, Carl Zeiss AG tried to prevent the removal of specialists and equipment of vital economic significance, unsuccessfully, as it turned out, with only 582 of 10,000 machines left in place at Zeiss. The operation took ninety-two trains to transport the specialists and their families – 10,000 to 15,000 people in all, along with their furniture and belongings. Those relocated were offered contracts; the specialists were told that they would be paid on the same terms as equivalent Soviet workers.

A major catalyst for Osoaviakhim was the Soviets' anxieties over the German economy and technological potential resurging, and a desire to cultivate this technological potential for the Soviet Union's benefit, especially where it might advance their nascent rocket programme.

Plan A – Jewish Holocaust revenge water poisoning

Plan A is a film released in September 2021 that recounts the true, but little-known, story of how, in 1945, a group of Jewish Holocaust survivors planned to poison the water system in five German cities, including Nuremburg, Frankfurt and Munich, killing 6 million Germans. The aim was to avenge the Holocaust: 'An eye for an eye. Six million for six million.' The film is based on the book *Nakam* (revenge) by chief historian of Yad Vashem (Israel's official memorial to the victims of the Holocaust), Dina Porat. The film directors interviewed four of the real-life conspirators, known as the *Nokmim* (Hebrew for The Avengers) – in total, fifty or so survivors, mainly former resistance fighters. Operation Paperclip apart, thousands of former Nazis escaped punishment although they were complicit in the Holocaust – these were *Schreibtischtäter*, 'desk murderers', and it was on these the *Nokmim* wanted to exact revenge.

Max, a Jewish Holocaust survivor, meets a radical group of Jewish resistance fighters, who, like him, lost all hope for their future after they were robbed of their existence and their entire families were killed by the Nazis. Max travels to Mandatory Palestine and meets future Israeli president Chaim Weizmann. On his return, though, Max is arrested by the British and the precious canisters of poison are thrown overboard. Plan B is then activated: this entailed poisoning German soldiers at an American detention camp in Nuremburg. The Holocaust survivors had members of their group working in the bakery that supplied bread to the camp, so they would be able to lace the loaves before they were delivered to the camp. Initially they ran into the problem of how to make sure that only the Germans and not the Americans would be killed, but then it was discovered that the prisoners ate dark bread while the guards preferred white. A bit hit-and-miss but, as we have seen, that is the nature of mass poisoning.

Chapter 9

The Biological Warfare Labs

The UK and the US and the Russians were active in biological warfare long before the start of the Second World War; the UK had their research and development at Porton Down while the US facility was at Fort Detrick, Maryland. The corresponding Soviet facility was called Biopreparat.

Porton Down

> Porton Down carries out research to ensure that the UK's military and wider public benefit from the latest technical and scientific developments. In the interests of national security, much of this work is secret. Inevitably, this has led to many myths and misconceptions springing up about Porton Down and the wider work carried out by the Defence Science and Technology Laboratory (Dstl).
> https://www.gov.uk/government/news/the-truth-about-porton-down

The site goes on to reassure us that:

> The UK's chemical and biological weapons programme was closed down in the 1950s. Since then Porton Down has been active in developing effective countermeasures to the constantly evolving threat posed by chemical and biological weapons. To help develop effective medical countermeasures and to test systems, we produce very small quantities of chemical and biological agents. They are stored securely and disposed of safely when they are no longer required.

Dstl have pioneered several products and procedures that are now used in the NHS. Dstl research, for example, provided the first evidence that giving specific blood products before casualties reach hospital could help save lives as it improves the ability to form blood clots. This is crucial in the prehospital management of trauma patients in the battlefield and in civilian life, not least in acts of terrorism.

Since 1916, over 20,000 volunteers have taken part in studies at Porton Down without whose participation they could not have developed the highly effective protective clothing and medical countermeasures that our Armed Forces rely on. Between 1953 and 1976, a number of secret aerial release trials were carried out to help the governments of the day understand how a biological attack might spread across the UK. Porton Down tells us that the unique information and data obtained has been and still is vital to the defence of the UK from this type of attack. Two separate and independent reviews of the trials have both concluded that the trials did not have any adverse health effects on the UK population.

In June 2019, Frank Gardner, BBC security correspondent, was allowed access to a level 4 laboratory at Porton Down; he tells us how there are four categories of laboratory, rated in ascending order of virulence or lethality, from non-hazardous to fatal pathogens. Inside the laboratories men and women, dressed in varying degrees of protective clothing, study a range of potential biological warfare agents. 'On the day we visited, we watched from the safety of behind a glass screen as they worked with *Yersinia pestis*, the bacteria that causes plague.'

Founded in 1916 as the War Department Experimental Station for testing chemical weapons during the First World War, Porton Down is the world's oldest biological-chemical warfare research facility. Its brief was to conduct research and development regarding chemical weapons agents used by the British Armed Forces in the First World War, such as chlorine, mustard gas and phosgene. The tight secrecy and security enveloping the facility has fuelled the growth of all manner of myths and rumours about its experiments, giving it an image as 'a sinister and nefarious establishment'. In 1919, the War Office's Holland Committee considered the future of chemical warfare and defence. The following year the Cabinet agreed to the Committee's recommendation that work should continue at Porton Down. From then on, a slow permanent building programme began, coupled with the gradual recruitment of civilian scientists. By 1922, there were 380 servicemen, 23 scientific and technical civil servants, and 25 'civilian subordinates'. By 1925, the civilian staff had doubled. In 1930, Britain ratified the 1925 Geneva Protocol, with reservations permitting the use of chemical warfare agents only in retaliation. By 1938, the deteriorating international situation was such that the Cabinet authorised offensive chemical warfare research and development and the production of war reserve stocks of chemical warfare agents by the chemical industry. This included conducting chemical warfare trials, known as the Rawalpindi experiments, on servicemen in the British Indian Army to test the effects of mustard gas. The experiments in Rawalpindi were part of a much larger project intended to test the effects of chemical weapons on humans. More than 20,000 British servicemen were subjected to chemical warfare trials between 1916 and 1989 at Porton Down.

According to documents held at the British National Archives in London, British Army scientists and doctors tested the effects of mustard gas on over 500 Indian soldiers over a ten-year period. Beginning in the early 1930s, scientists at Rawalpindi sent Indian soldiers, wearing shorts and cotton shirts, into gas chambers to experience the effects of mustard gas. The scientists hoped to determine the appropriate dosage to use on battlefields. Many of the subjects suffered severe burns from their exposure to the gas, some of which were so damaging that the subjects had to be hospitalised. According to the report, severely burned patients were often very miserable and depressed and in considerable discomfort. No long-term effects of exposure were documented or analysed.

During the Second World War, research focused on chemical weapons such as nitrogen mustard. As Allied armies moved across Germany, they discovered stockpiles of munitions that contained novel chemical warfare agents, including highly toxic organophosphorous nerve agents such as sarin, largely unknown to Britain and the Allies at the time.

The focus on biological weapons fell to the Biology Department, Porton (BDP), established in 1940 under Paul Fildes. Its work included anthrax and botulinum toxin, and in 1942, as we have seen, it carried out tests of an anthrax bioweapon at Gruinard Island. In 1946, it was renamed the Microbiological Research Department (MRD) and, in 1957, the Microbiological Research Establishment (MRE).

At the end of the Second World War, the Allies were surprised by the progress Germany had made in the field of organophosphorous nerve agents, such as tabun, sarin and soman. They were naturally eager to capitalise on this gift. Based on these nerve agents, VX nerve agent was developed at Porton Down in 1952.

So, in the late 1940s and early 1950s, the brief for research and development at Porton Down aimed at ensuring Britain had the means to arm itself with a modern nerve agent-based capability and to develop specific means of defence against these agents. On the offensive side, the decision was made to abandon the chemical warfare capability in favour of nuclear weapons. On the defensive side, work was done to develop the means of prophylaxis, therapy, rapid detection and identification, decontamination, and more effective protection of the body against nerve agents that exhibited effects through the skin, the eyes and respiratory tract.

To that end, tests were carried out on servicemen to determine the effects of nerve agents on human subjects, with one recorded death from a nerve gas experiment, namely Leading Aircraftman Ronald Maddison, aged 20, in 1953. Maddison was taking part in sarin nerve agent toxicity tests; sarin was dripped onto his arm and he died shortly afterwards. The ethics behind such experimentation have been constantly questioned.

In the 1950s, the station, now renamed the Chemical Defence Experimental Establishment (CDEE), was involved in the development of CS, a riot-control agent, and took an increasing role in trauma and wound ballistics work. Both assumed an importance in Porton Down's work during the Troubles in Northern Ireland from 1969.

Before that, on 1 August 1962, Geoffrey Bacon, a scientist at the Microbiological Research Establishment, died from an accidental infection of the plague bacterium *Yersinia pestis*. That same month, an autoclave exploded in a lab, shattering two windows.

In 1970, the establishment at Porton Down was renamed the Chemical Defence Establishment (CDE). Preoccupation with defence against nerve agents went on, but in the 1970s and 1980s, the Establishment was also studying chemical warfare by Iraq against Iran and against its own Kurdish population.

Until 2001, Porton Down was part of the UK government's Defence Evaluation and Research Agency (DERA) when it was split into QinetiQ, initially a fully government-owned company, and the Defence Science and Technology Laboratory (Dstl). In 2013, Dstl scientists tested samples from Syria for sarin, which is still manufactured there, to test soldiers' equipment.

The Dorset Biological Warfare Experiments

Gruinard was not the only open-air biological exercise using anthrax. The Dorset Biological Warfare Experiments were a series of exercises to simulate an anthrax attack conducted in 1953; the aim was to discover the extent to which a single ship or aircraft could dispense biological warfare agents over the United Kingdom.

In the early 1960s, Porton Down was asked to expand the scope of their tests to determine if using live bacteria instead of ZnCds (microscopic zinc cadmium sulphide) would significantly alter the results. Scientists from Porton Down chose South Dorset as the site for this next phase of testing, with *Bacillus subtilis* (also known as *Bacillus globigii* or *BG*) and *Escherichia coli* selected as the test agents. Early results clearly showed that one aircraft flying along the coast while spraying its agent could contaminate a target over 100 miles away, over an area of 10,000 square miles. This method of biological warfare attack and the test programme to study it was known as the Large Area Coverage (LAC) concept. The bacteria were sprayed across South Dorset without the knowledge or consent of the inhabitants.

It was later admitted that the bacteria could adversely affect some vulnerable people. Weymouth lay downwind of the spraying: when the trials became public knowledge in the late 1990s, Dorset County Council, Weymouth and Portland Borough Council and Purbeck District Council demanded a public inquiry to investigate the experiments. The government refused a public inquiry but instead commissioned Professor Brian Spratt to conduct an independent review of the possible adverse health effects. He concluded that individuals with certain chronic conditions may well have been affected.

In 1954, the British government sent biological warfare scientists to the Bahamas to release Venezuelan equine encephalitis viruses close to an uninhabited island.

Fort Detrick, Maryland, USA

As we have seen, Fort Detrick is a United States Army Futures Command installation located in Frederick, Maryland. It was the centre of the US biological weapons programme from 1943 to 1969. Since 1969, it has been home to most elements of the United States biological defence programme.

The Army's Chemical Warfare Service was given responsibility and oversight for the activities that one officer described as 'cloaked in the deepest wartime secrecy, matched only by … the Manhattan Project for developing the Atomic Bomb'. Three months after the start of construction, an additional $3 million was granted for five additional laboratories and a pilot plant. Lieutenant Colonel Bacon headed up 85 officers, 373 enlisted personnel, and 80 enlisted Women's Army Auxiliary Corps (WAAC) members under two WAAC officers. At its peak strength in 1945, Camp Detrick had 240 officers and 1,530 enlisted personnel including WAACs.

So sophisticated was the security at Camp Detrick that it was not until January 1946, four months after VJ Day, that the public learned of the wartime research in biological weapons. Two workers at the base died from exposure to anthrax in the 1950s. In 1964, another died from viral encephalitis.

Human experimentation and testing

A report from September 1994 revealed that between 1940 and 1974, hundreds of thousands of humans were subjected to tests and experiments involving hazardous substances. To quote from the study:

Many experiments that tested various biological agents on human subjects, referred to as Operation Whitecoat, were carried out at Fort Detrick, Maryland, in the 1950s. The human subjects originally consisted of volunteer enlisted men. However, after the enlisted men staged a sitdown strike to obtain more information about the dangers of the biological tests, Seventh-day Adventists (SDAs) who were conscientious objectors were recruited for the studies.

Staff Report prepared for the committee on veterans' affairs, 8 December 1994, John D. Rockefeller IV, West Virginia, Chairman at gulfweb.org

After the Second World War, Fort Detrick's mandate was to continue its mission of biomedical research and its role as the world's leading research campus for biological agents requiring specialty containment. When Fort Detrick began to concentrate more on the chemical defoliants, it conducted the first large-scale military defoliation effort at Fort Drum, New York, using the butyl esters of 2,4-D and 2,4,5-T, later designated Agent Purple.

Although many biological agents were standardised and many delivery systems developed, only a few biological weapons were standardised. The first was the M114 4 lb antipersonnel bomb, which held about 320 ml of *Brucella suis*. This was a small, 21-inch-long tube with a 1⅝-inch diameter, similar to a pipe bomb. One hundred and eight of the M114s were clustered in the M33 500 lb cluster bomb. The bombs were also tested at Dugway Proving Ground, Utah, throughout the 1950s, with various other fillings. The M115 500 lb antiplant bomb was standardised in 1953 for the dissemination of wheat stem rust. This filling consisted of dry particulate material adhered to a lightweight, dry carrier (i.e., feathers). Thus, the bomb was normally referred to as the feather bomb as weaponised at Fort Detrick.

In 1959, the yellow fever virus was standardised for use, with a mosquito as vector. The virus came from an individual in Trinidad who had been infected with the disease during an epidemic in 1954. Scientists inoculated rhesus monkeys with the serum to propagate the virus. In tests conducted in Savannah, Georgia, and at the Avon Park Bombing Range, Florida, uninfected mosquitoes were released by airplane or helicopter. Within a day, the mosquitoes had spread over several square miles and had bitten many people, demonstrating the feasibility of such an attack. Fort Detrick's laboratory was capable of producing half a million mosquitoes per month and had plans for a plant that could produce 130 million per month. Fort Detrick, however, was constrained by its production capability and required an expanded facility. Pine Bluff Arsenal was chosen to be the production site of the new agent.

During the Second World War, the Chemical Corps developed the 80 lb antiplant balloon bomb. Other later delivery systems included spray tanks, missiles, aerosol generators, drones, and marine mines. Of these, the submarine mine was one of the more covert forms of delivery. It was designed to be fired from a torpedo tube, to sink to the bottom for a specified period up to two hours, and then rise to the surface and expel about 42 litres of agent. After disseminating the agent, it scuttled itself.

On 25 November 1969, President Nixon outlawed offensive biological research in the United States. Since that time, any research done at Fort Detrick has been purely defensive, focusing on diagnostics, preventives and treatments for BW infections.

From the early 2010s, Fort Detrick's 1,200-acre campus has supported a multi-governmental community that conducts biomedical research and development, medical material management, global medical communications and the study of foreign plant pathogens. The lab is engaged in researching pathogens such as Ebola and smallpox. It is home to a myriad of agencies: the US Army Medical Research and Development Command (USAMRDC), with its bio-defence agency, the US Army Medical Research Institute of Infectious Diseases (USAMRIID). It also hosts the National Cancer Institute-Frederick (NCI-Frederick) and is home to the National Interagency Confederation for Biological Research (NICBR) and National Interagency Biodefense Campus (NIBC).

Bolivian haemorrhagic fever was one of three haemorrhagic fevers researched by the US as potential biological weapons before it suspended its biological weapons programme in 1969. Albert Nickel, a 53-year-old animal caretaker at Fort Detrick, died in 1964 from the disease after being bitten by an infected mouse. Bolivian haemorrhagic fever (BHF) is a haemorrhagic fever and zoonotic infectious disease originating in Bolivia after infection by *Machupo mammarenavirus*.

COVID-19 conspiracy

In 2020, a conspiracy theory regarding COVID-19 alleged that the SARS-CoV-2 virus was developed by the United States Army at Fort Detrick, presumably for bioterrorist or biological warfare purposes (Helen Davidson (20 January 2021), 'China revives conspiracy theory of US Army link to Covid', *The Guardian*).

This allegation has been promoted by Chinese government officials, most notably Ministry of Foreign Affairs spokesman Zhao Lijian, who has called for an inspection of the facility, although the allegation remains groundless

(Katerina Ang (28 May 2021), 'As US calls for focus on covid origins, China repeats speculation about US military base', *Washington Post*).

A petition organised by the Chinese public media *Global Times* urging the WHO to investigate Fort Detrick for COVID origins reportedly amassed 25 million signatures (Dan Levin (25 August 2021), 'Florida Sees Worst of Pandemic So Far', *New York Times*).

The demands to investigate the lab have been said to be intended to 'deflect' calls for further investigations in Wuhan (Bret Schafer, 'China Fires Back at Biden with Conspiracy Theories About Maryland Lab', *Foreign Policy*).

William C. Patrick III (1926–2010)

The brilliant William C. Patrick III was in charge of the American offensive biological warfare programme at Fort Detrick from 1951. After biological weapons development was ended, he continued to work at Fort Detrick on biowarfare defence projects until 1986.

His appointments from 1951 to 1966 at Fort Detrick speak for themselves: project engineer in the design and start-up operations in the virus production facility as well as the freeze-drying plant at Pine Bluff Arsenal, Arkansas; plant manager of the virus pilot plant at Fort Detrick; special envoy to Dugway Proving Ground Utah, during the field testing of several munitions systems; and chief of Agent Processing Branch, Pilot Plant Division, Biological Warfare Laboratories for several years. In 1965, he became chief of the Product Development Division of the former BWL. This division was responsible for initiating the weaponisation of an agent.

He told an astonishing but terrifying story to Michael Osterholm, related in his *Deadliest Enemy* (p. 131):

> Bill made a habit of carrying around a vial containing 7.5 grams of a harmless bacterial culture that looks just like anthrax under a microscope. In March 1999, testifying on Captol Hill before the House Permanent Select Committee on Intelligence, he pulled out his vial, explained what it was and declared, 'I've been through all the major airports and security systems of the State Department, the Pentagon, even the CIA, and nobody has stopped me.'

Osterholm reassures us the 7.5 grammes of a lethal agent would be more than enough to kill everyone in an average-sized office building. He goes on to remind us that no one ever predicted the world-changing cataclysmic events of 9/11 and that despite its horror:

at the end of the day on September 11 2001, the terrorist act was over and recovery could commence. With a bioterror event, the end of the day would be only the beginning and no one would even know it yet.

The half-life of such a disaster is equally devastating: if a large-sized shopping mall with up to 100,000 visitors a day were to be bioterrorised, after the panic, thousands of deaths and casualties and the collapse of local healthcare facilities, it would be years before the countless buildings and units could be used again, if ever. Decontamination would be impossible in the case of an agent such as anthrax, and your local shopping mall becomes a toxic, dilapidating monument to successful bioterrorism and an errant lack of preparedness or knowledge of where and how to begin safe restoration. Gruinard Island and Chernobyl spring to mind.

Building 470

Also called 'Anthrax Tower', 470 was a seven-story steel and brick building at Fort Detrick used in the small-scale production of biological warfare (BW) agents. In 1970, Building 470 was vacated and a deep clean decontamination began, finally completed in June 1971. Electric frying pans with a solid form of paraformaldehyde were placed throughout the building and then heated, releasing clouds of gas inside the sealed structure. Simulant bacteria, similar to anthrax, were left inside to serve as markers indicating whether or not the gas had worked. Thereafter, the army carried out extensive testing and found no evidence of any of the biological agents previously produced there. Samples from approximately 1,500 locations throughout the building tested negative for *B. anthracis*. The army declared the building safe for occupancy – although not for renovation – including by workers who had not been immunised against anthrax.

In 1958, a technician, struggling to prise open a jammed valve at the bottom of a fermentor, unintentionally released approximately 2,000 gallons of liquid *B. anthracis* culture. Because of the design of the building and the safety measures in place, it was possible to isolate the spill to one room. There was no contamination of Fort Detrick or the local community, and no one, including the technician, became ill. In fact, no one working in Building 470 ever died of anthrax, although three workers elsewhere in Fort Detrick had died of infection with agents that were being researched as biological weapons: one, a microbiologist in 1951, and another, an electrician in 1958, died of inhalational anthrax. The third worker died of Bolivian haemorrhagic fever.

Operation Whitecoat – Operation CD-22

As noted above, Operation Whitecoat was a biodefence medical research programme carried out by the United States Army at Fort Detrick from 1954 to 1973. Its method involved recruiting volunteer enlisted personnel who were nicknamed 'Whitecoats'. These volunteers, all conscientious objectors, including many members of the Seventh-day Adventist Church who traded off the draft for the trial, were expressly informed of the purpose and goals of each project before providing consent to participate. The stated purpose of the research was to defend troops and civilians against biological weapons; the assumption was that the Soviet Union was engaged in similar activities.

The programme ended in 1973 but human research for biodefence purposes continues at USAMRIID at Fort Detrick and at other government and civilian research institutes. However, these post-Whitecoat studies usually involve a person being inoculated with a known pathogen to determine how effective an investigational treatment will be.

Over the nineteen years of its existence more than 2,300 US Army soldiers, many of whom were trained medics, contributed to the Whitecoat experiments by allowing themselves to be infected with tularaemia or Q fever – considered the likely enemy choices for a biological attack. The goal was to determine dose response for these agents, so the volunteers were prescribed antibiotics to cure the infections. Some volunteers, under experimental protocol, were also given investigational vaccines for Q fever and tularaemia, as well as for yellow fever, Rift Valley fever, hepatitis A, *Yersinia pestis* (plague), Venezuelan equine encephalitis and other diseases. Some soldiers were granted two weeks' leave in exchange for being used as a guinea pig. Of the troops who were approached about participating, 20 per cent declined.

Other US biological tests

Project SHAD

SHAD was part of a larger programme by the US Department of Defense called Project 112 – a chemical and biological weapons research, development and testing project handled by the Deseret Test Center and United States Army Chemical Materials Agency from 1962 to 1973.

The aim of the Shipboard Hazard and Defense Project (SHAD) was to determine how well service members aboard military ships could detect and respond to chemical and biological attacks. Dee Dodson Morris of the Army Chemical Corps says:

The SHAD tests were intended to show how vulnerable Navy ships were to chemical or biological warfare agents. The objective was to learn how chemical or biological warfare agents would disperse throughout a ship, and to use that information to develop procedures to protect crew members and decontaminate ships.

One hundred and thirty-four tests were planned initially, but only forty-six were actually completed. Of the 5,500 or so veterans who took part, some were involved without their knowledge or consent. The Department of Defense was accused of continuing to withhold documents on Cold War chemical and biological weapons tests that used unsuspecting veterans as 'human samplers' after reporting to Congress it had released all medically relevant information.

Project 112
Project 112 was a biological and chemical weapon experimentation project conducted by the United States Department of Defense from 1962 to 1973. The main objective concerned the use of aerosols to disseminate biological and chemical agents that could produce 'controlled temporary incapacitation'. The test programme was to be conducted on a large scale at 'extracontinental test sites' in the Central and South Pacific and Alaska in conjunction with Britain, Canada and Australia.

At least fifty trials were conducted, of which around eighteen involved simulants of biological agents (such as BG), and at least fourteen involved chemical agents including sarin and VX, as well as tear gas and other simulants. Test sites included Porton Down, Ralston (Canada) and at least thirteen US warships.

VX, 'venomous agent X', is an extremely toxic synthetic chemical compound developed for military use in chemical warfare. It was first discovered at Porton Down during the early 1950s, based on research pioneered by Gerhard Schrader, a chemist working for IG Farben in Germany during the 1930s.

Project 112 included the following tests: selected protective devices in preventing penetration of a naval ship by a biological aerosol; the impact of meteorological conditions on weapon system performance over the open sea; the penetrability of jungle vegetation by biological agents; the penetration of an Arctic inversion by a biological aerosol cloud; the feasibility of an offshore release of *Aedes aegypti* mosquito as a vector for infectious diseases; the feasibility of a biological attack against an island complex; and the study of the decay rates of biowarfare agents under various conditions.

Tests used the following agents and simulants: *Francisella tularensis, Serratia marcescens, Escherichia coli, Bacillus globii,* staphylococcal enterotoxin Type B, and

Puccinia graminis var. tritici (stem rust of wheat). Agents and simulants were usually dispensed as aerosols using spraying devices or bomblets.

In May 1965, vulnerability tests in the US using the anthrax simulant *Bacillus globigii* were performed in the Washington, DC area by SOD (Special Operations Division) covert agents. One test was conducted at the Greyhound bus terminal and the other at the north terminal of the National Airport. In these tests, the bacteria were released from spray generators hidden in specially built briefcases. SOD also conducted a series of tests in the New York City subway system in June 1966 by dropping lightbulbs filled with *Bacillus subtilis var. niger*. In the latter tests, results indicated that a city-level epidemic would have occurred. Local police and transport authorities had no prior knowledge of these tests.

Operation Dew
Operation Dew refers to two separate field trials conducted by the United States in the 1950s off the south-east coast of the US, near Georgia, and North and South Carolina. The operation was designed to study the behaviour of aerosol-released biological agents and involved the release of 250 pounds of fluorescent particles from a minesweeper off the coast.

Operation Dew I comprised five separate trials to test the feasibility of maintaining a large aerosol cloud released offshore until it drifted over land, achieving a large area coverage. The tests released zinc cadmium sulphide along a 100 to 150-nautical-mile line approximately 5 to 10 nautical miles off the coast. They affected over 60,000 square miles of populated coastal region released from a navy minesweeper, the USS *Tercel*. Dew II involved the release of zinc cadmium sulphide and plant spores (*Lycopodium*) from an aircraft.

Operation Sea-Spray
Some biowarfare projects left much to be desired in terms of regulation or public safety. In September 1950, to simulate a biological warfare attack, the US Navy launched a project called Operation Sea-Spray in which balloons filled with *Serratia marcescens* – considered harmless at the time – were released and burst over urban areas of the San Francisco Bay area. Although the navy later claimed the bacteria were harmless, beginning on 29 September, eleven patients at a local hospital developed very rare, serious urinary tract infections. One of the afflicted patients, Edward J. Nevin, died. Cases of pneumonia in San Francisco also increased after the *S. marcescens* was released. Nevin's family sued the government for gross negligence, but a federal judge ruled in favour of the government in 1983 on the grounds that the government is immune, and that the chance that the sprayed bacteria caused Nevin's death was minute.

Serratia tests were continued until at least 1969. *Serratia marcescens* is a bacteria often found in damp areas such as bathrooms and is a relatively common hospital-acquired infection.

The bacterium was also combined with phenol and an anthrax simulant and sprayed across south Dorset in England by US and UK military scientists as part of the DICE trials, which ran from 1971 to 1975.

During the 1950s, the United States conducted a series of field tests using entomological weapons (EW):

Operation Big Itch
The aim of Operation Big Itch, in 1954, was to test munitions loaded with uninfected tropical rat fleas (*Xenopsylla cheopis*) as carried out at Dugway Proving Ground in Utah. The tests were designed to determine coverage patterns and survivability of the tropical rat flea for use in biological warfare as a disease vector. The fleas were loaded into two types of munitions and dropped from the air. When the cluster bombs reached 2,000 or 1,000 feet, the bomblets would fall by parachute, liberally spreading their vector. The E14 was designed to hold 100,000 fleas and the E23 could hold 200,000 fleas, but the E23 failed in over half of the preliminary Big Itch tests. One E23 malfunctioned during testing and the fleas were released into the aircraft, where they bit the pilot, bombardier and an observer. Consequently, the remaining Big Itch tests were conducted using only the smaller capacity E14. Guinea pigs were used as test subjects and placed around a 660-yard circular grid.

Big Itch was deemed a success: the tests showed that not only could the fleas survive the drop from an airplane but they also soon attached themselves to hosts. The weapon was able to cover a battalion-sized target area and disrupt operations for up to one day – the fleas were only active for about twenty-four hours.

Operation Big Buzz
In May 1955, over 300,000 uninfected mosquitoes (*Aedes aegypti*) were dropped over parts of the US state of Georgia to determine if the mosquitoes could survive to feed off humans. The operation was designed to determine the feasibility of producing, storing, loading into munitions, and dispersing the yellow fever mosquito from aircraft. The second goal was to establish whether the mosquitoes would survive their dispersion well enough to feed when on the ground. The mosquitoes were dropped from aircraft in E14 bombs 300 feet above the ground. In total, about 1 million female mosquitoes were bred for the testing; leftover mosquitoes were used in munitions loading and storage

tests. Mosquitoes were collected up to 2,000 feet from the release site. They were also able to suck blood meals from humans and guinea pigs.

Operation Drop Kick

Between April and November 1956, the US Army Chemical Corps carried out Operation Drop Kick to see if it was viable to use mosquitoes to carry an entomological warfare agent in different ways. The Corps released uninfected female mosquitoes into a residential area of Savannah, Georgia, and then estimated how many mosquitoes entered houses and bit people. Within a day, the mosquitoes had been busy and had bitten many a resident. In 1958, the Corps released 600,000 mosquitoes in Avon Park, Florida.

Operation May Day

Savannah got it again from April to November 1956. These tests were designed to reveal information about the dispersal of yellow fever mosquitoes in an urban area. The mosquitoes were released from ground level in Savannah and then recovered using traps baited with dry ice.

Recently discovered documents show that the US Army tested biological weapons in Okinawa in the early 1960s, when the prefecture was still under US rule. During these tests, rice blast fungus was released by the army using 'a midget duster to release inoculum alongside fields in Okinawa and Taiwan' in order to measure effective dosage requirements at different distances and the negative effects on crop production. Rice blast or *Pyricularia oryzae* produces a mycotoxin called tenuazonic acid, which has been implicated in human and animal disease.

Dugway Proving Ground, Maryland

Dugway Proving Ground (DPG) was established in 1942 to test biological and chemical weapons; it is about 85 miles south-west of Salt Lake City, Utah. It came about when the US Army Chemical Warfare Service (CWS) decided it needed a testing facility that was more remote than the US Army's Edgewood Arsenal in Maryland. During the Second World War, DPG tested toxic agents, flamethrowers, chemical spray systems, biological warfare weapons, firebombing tactics, antidotes for chemical agents, and protective clothing. The year 1943 saw the construction of the German Village and Japanese Village set-piece domestic 'hamlets' for practice in the firebombing of homes of the types found in urban areas of Nazi Germany and the Japanese Empire's home islands.

In October 1943, DPG established biological warfare facilities at UTTR's (Utah Test and Training Range) range telemetry and tracking radar installation, which is an isolated area within DPG known as the Granite Peak Installation. DPG was slowly phased out after the Second World War and became inactive in August 1946, only to be reactivated during the Korean War (1950–3) and in 1954 was confirmed as a permanent Department of the Army Installation. In October 1958, the United States Army Chemical Center, Maryland, moved the US Army Chemical, Biological, and Radiological Weapons School to Dugway Proving Grounds. In the late 1950s and early 1960s, Project Bellwether – a study of weaponised, mosquito-spread infections – was based at DPG.

The Dugway sheep incident
Much of the work at DPG was on aerial nerve agent testing. On the biological front, according to the *New Scientist*, Dugway was still producing anthrax spores as late as 2015 to be used to develop anthrax testing detection and countermeasures, more than four decades after the United States renounced biological weapons. There were at least 1,100 chemical tests at Dugway around the time of the Dugway sheep incident; this was when, in March 1968, 6,249 sheep died in Skull Valley, an area nearly 30 miles from Dugway's testing sites. When examined, the sheep were found to have been poisoned by an organophosphate chemical.

In total, almost 500,000 lb of nerve agent was dispersed during open-air tests. There were also tests involving other weapons of mass destruction, including 328 open-air tests of biological weapons, seventy-four dirty bomb tests, and eight furnace heatings of nuclear material under open-air conditions to simulate the dispersal of fallout in the case of meltdown of aeronautic nuclear reactors.

In May 2015, it was, as noted, revealed that a Dugway lab had inadvertently shipped live anthrax bacillus around the country at a time when Dugway was involved in developing a test to identify biological threats in the field. Shipped samples, of course, were supposed to be inert. In September 2018, the US Government Accountability Office (GAO) released findings of an investigation into the anthrax shipping lapses. The investigation explored whether 'systemic oversight changes regarding biosecurity have since been implemented across DOD facilities. The findings are mixed.' The US Army had sought thirty-five specific changes, but only eighteen of those changes have been made, as of the GAO report.

The Granite Peak Installation (GPI), Maryland

Also known as Granite Peak Range, this was a US biological weapons testing facility located in Dugway Proving Ground. One of the weapons tested here was a 91 lb bomb containing 'vegetable killer acid', VKA (2,4-Dichlorophenoxyacetic acid), now sold as an ingredient in household 'weed 'n' feed' products. Testing of other bioweapons proceeded from 1943 to 1945, including tests using anthrax. The M33 cluster bomb was used in a series of tests from August to October 1952 at GPI. The Army Chemical Corps exposed over 11,000 guinea pigs to *Brucella suis* via air-dropped M33s. The guinea pig trials prompted one Chemical Corps general to remark, 'Now we know what to do if we ever go to war against guinea pigs.'

Pine Bluff Arsenal (PBA), Arkansas
Predominantly a chemical warfare facility, in 1954, *Brucella suis* became the first agent weaponised by the United States at its Pine Bluff arsenal in Arkansas. Brucella species survive well in aerosols and resist drying. The programme focused on three agents of the Brucella group: Porcine brucellosis (agent US); Bovine brucellosis (agent AA); and Caprine brucellosis (agent AM). Biological weapons research was conducted at PBA from 1953 to 1969, but operations ceased when President Nixon banned biological weapons after the furore over Agent Orange. Between 1954 and 1967, at least seven different biological agents were produced at the facility. All biological agents were destroyed between 1971 and 1973.

When the United States Air Force (USAF) wanted a biological warfare capability, the Chemical Corps offered Agent US in the M114 bomblet, based on the 4 lb bursting bomblet developed for spreading anthrax during the Second World War. Though the capability was developed, operational testing indicated the weapon was less than what was required, so the USAF designated it as an interim capability until it could eventually be replaced by a more effective biological weapon.

The main drawback of using the M114 with Agent US was that it acted predominantly as an incapacitating agent, whereas the USAF administration wanted weapons that were deadly.

Fort Terry, Plum Island, Long Island

Fort Terry was originally a coastal fortification on Plum Island; its strategic position gave it a commanding view over the Atlantic entrance to the commercially vital Long Island Sound. In 1952, it became a military animal and biological warfare research facility, moving to civilian control in 1954 as the Plum Island Animal Disease Center. However, the biological warfare mission continued under civilian control until 1969, when the US ended offensive BW research.

Fort Terry was small and focused primarily on targeting enemy livestock. Anti-animal agents rinderpest and foot-and-mouth disease were the main areas of research; others included Rift Valley fever (RVF), African swine fever, and a host of exotic animal diseases including Blue tongue virus, Bovine influenza, Bovine virus diarrhoea (BVD), fowl plague, goat pneumonitis, mycobacteria, 'N' virus, Newcastle disease, sheep pox, Teschers disease, and vesicular stomatitis.

The Epidemic Intelligence Service (EIS)

The EIS is a programme of the US Centers for Disease Control and Prevention. It was set up in March 1951 on the recommendation of Dr Alexander Langmuir, chief of epidemiologic services, Communicable Disease Center at the US Public Health Service. Langmuir urged that it was of the utmost importance to plan appropriate defence measures against biological warfare germs, to develop new detection devices, and to train laboratory workers for rapid recognition of biological warfare germs. It arose from biological warfare concerns relating to the Korean War. Today's EIS is a two-year, hands-on post-doctoral training programme in epidemiology, focusing on fieldwork.

Chapter 10

The Soviet Biological Weapons Programme

Where and how did it all start? After taking power in 1917, the Bolshevik government was soon embroiled in conflict with anti-communist forces. Red and White Armies clashed and by the end of hostilities in 1921, 10 million people had perished. But most were not casualties of battles on the battlefields from Siberia to the Crimean peninsula. Most perished due to disease and famine, not least the typhus epidemic, which raged from 1918 to 1921. Red Army staff officers soon realised that disease was a formidable weapon and they determined to harness it as an unflinching, unquestioning ally. Enter biological weaponry and a Soviet scramble to weaponise nature. In 1928, typhus was enlisted.

Thoughout its history, the Soviet programme is known to have weaponised and stockpiled the following eleven bio-agents and to have researched many more: *Bacillus anthracis* (anthrax); *Yersinia pestis* (plague); *Francisella tularensis* (tularaemia); *Burkholderia mallei* (glanders); *Brucella sp.* (brucellosis); *Coxiella burnetii* (Q fever); *Venezuelan equine encephalitis virus* (VEE); Botulinum toxin; *Staphylococcal enterotoxin B;* smallpox; Marburg virus; Orthopoxvirus.

These programmes were conducted at dozens of secret sites, employing up to 65,000 people. Annual production capacity for weaponised smallpox, for example, was 90 to 100 tons. In the 1980s and 1990s, many of these agents were genetically altered to resist heat, cold and antibiotics. Defecting Soviet bioweaponeers such as Vladimir Pasechnik and Colonel Kanatjan Alibekov confirmed that the programme had been immense and was still ongoing. Indeed, Alibekov admitted that they had developed 2,000 strains of anthrax alone and made it as lethal as possible. In 1992, a Trilateral Agreement was signed with the United States and the United Kingdom, pledging to end biological weapons programmes and convert facilities to benevolent purposes, but compliance with the agreement – and the fate of the former Soviet bio-agents and facilities – is still largely unknown.

In 1925, Yakov Moiseevich Fishman was appointed the first head of the Red Army's Military-Chemical Directorate. In 1926, Fishman began research on *Bacillus anthracis.* In 1928, he prepared a key report on the Soviet Union's preparedness for biological warfare. It stressed that 'the bacterial option could be successfully used in war' and proposed a plan for the organisation of Soviet military bacteriology. Around the same time, Ivan Mikhailovich Velikanov, an expert on botulinum toxin and botulism, emerged as the lead scientist in the fledgeling Soviet biological weapons programme. In 1930, Velikanov was placed in command of a new facility, the Red Army's Vaccine-Sera Laboratory in Vlasikha, around 30 miles to the west of Moscow. Buildings at the site belonging to a smallpox institute were transferred to the military facility. Early programmes at the military lab focused on *Francisella tularensis*.

The Red Army opened the first laboratories for research on pathogenic microorganisms in 1928. Biowarfare facilities under the direct authority of the Soviet Ministry of Defence (MOD) included the Scientific Research Institute of Microbiology in Kirov (now Vyatka), the Center for Military-Technical Problems of Anti-Bacteriological Defense in Sverdlovsk (now Yekaterinburg), and the Center of Virology in Zagorsk (now Sergiyev Posad). There was another BW facility, the Scientific Research Institute of Military Medicine in Leningrad (now St Petersburg). Vozrozhdeniya Island, in the Aral Sea, was the main testing ground for biological agents developed at MOD facilities.

BW research was progressing in an institution controlled by the state security apparatus. In July 1931, the Joint State Political Directorate (OGPU), a predecessor of the NKVD, seized control of the Convent of the Intercession in Suzdal and then the following year created a special prison laboratory, or *sharashka*, where around nineteen leading plague and tularaemia specialists were coerced into working on the development of biological weapons. By 1936, scientists working on BW at both Vlasikha and Suzdal were transferred to Gorodomlya Island where they occupied an institute for the study of foot-and-mouth disease. German Intelligence reported that the institute was engaged in experiments focused on *Francisella tularensis* and *Yersinia pestis*.

Extensive as the Soviet BW programme was by the late 1930s, reportedly comparable in size to the one organised by the Japanese, it was disrupted by the frequent purges of the late 1930s. Many BW scientists and administrative staff faced charges of sabotage and espionage. Some were executed, while others were sent east to populate the gulags. This significantly hindered Soviet BW activities at that time.

In 1936, Ivan Velikanov led the Red Army's first expedition to conduct tests of biological weapons on Vozrozhdeniya Island. Around 100 personnel from Velikanov's Biotechnical Institute participated in the experiments. In July 1937, Velikanov was arrested by Soviet security and subsequently shot. Later that same summer, Leonid Moiseevich Khatanever, the new director of the Biotechnical Institute and an expert on *Francisella tularensis*, led a second expedition to Vozrozhdeniya. Two special ships and two aircraft were assigned to Khatanever for use in tests focused on the dissemination of tularaemia bacteria. Germany launched Operation Barbarossa, the fateful invasion of the Soviet Union, in June 1941 and following the capture of nearby Kalinin in October, the BW facility on Gorodomlya Island was evacuated and eventually relocated to Kirov.

In his account of the history of the Soviet BW programme, Alibek, who as Kanatzhan Baizakovich Alibekov had been a biological weapons scientist for Biopreparat, describes a quite separate branch of early BW research pursued in Leningrad. In 1928, the Revolutionary Military Council signed a decree regarding the weaponisation of typhus. The Leningrad Military Medical Academy began cultivating typhus in chicken embryos. He also alleges that human experimentation took place with typhus, glanders and melioidosis in the Solovetsky camp. This is all corroborated by a series of secret reports by the British Secret Intelligence Service (SIS) – or MI6. Fourteen highly detailed reports on the Soviet BW programme were issued in the period 1924–7. MI6 identifies scientists working on *Yersinia pestis* and other dangerous pathogens. The MI6 reports indicate that Petr Petrovich Maslakovets and Semen Ivanovich Zlatogorov (a world expert on plague) conducted some of their research at a so-called Plague Fort – Fort Alexander 1, at Kronstadt. Here they aimed to develop strains of plague that remained viable when loaded into artillery shells, aerial bombs and other means of dispersal. German Intelligence independently identified the secret BW programme allegedly managed by Zlatogorov and Maslakovets.

The programme in the Second World War

By 1939, the Soviet leadership is reported to have believed that the 'imperialistic and fascistic countries' had actively undertaken BW preparations and that the use of such weapons, in case of emergency, was a foregone conclusion. Stalin reacted, ordered an acceleration of BW preparations, and appointed Lavrentiy Pavlovich Beria, head of the NKVD, in overall command of the country's biological warfare programme. In May 1941, a number of measures codenamed Yurta were implemented to counter the perceived threat of biological sabotage by the German and Japanese intelligence services. As a result, there was a tightening-up of state control over personnel working on microbial pathogens and a focus on the gathering of intelligence from foreign embassies relating to the feasibility and use of biological weapons.

On 22 June 1941, Germany invaded the Soviet Union along a 2,900-kilometre front with such rapidity that, by September, the Red Army's BW facility – the Sanitary Technical Institute (STI) – on Gorodomlya Island, was under immediate threat. The facility was evacuated and the buildings partially destroyed. In the later summer of 1942, in the German offensive on Stalingrad, there was a second evacuation of STI, which was permanently relocated to Kirov, some 896 kilometres north-east of Moscow on the Vyatka River.

In his account of the Soviet BW programme, Alibek suggests that in the late summer of 1942 the Red Army engaged in the deliberate aerosol dissemination of *Francisella tularensis* against German troops near Stalingrad. However, a number of prominent scholars have disputed Alibek's version of events, not least Erhardt Geissler. In 1943, the Soviets are alleged to have deliberately released *Coxiella burnetti*, causing Q fever in Crimea.

Recently opened files confirm that Soviet Intelligence saboteurs operating in German-occupied Slavuta (in Ukraine) infected and killed 120 Germans (including civilians, government officials and soldiers) as well as troops with *Rickettsia prowazekii*, the organism responsible for typhus fever using infected lice as the vector.

In the Far East, the Soviet Union had been the subject of a BW attack in 1939 during the battles of Khalkin Gol (Nomonhan) by Japan's Unit 731 under Shirō Ishii. Further attacks were initiated against the Soviet Union by Unit 100 in the summer of 1942, and at a later unspecified date, again by Unit 731. On 9 August 1945, the Soviet Union invaded Japanese-controlled Manchuria. Two major Japanese offensive BW installations at Pingfang and Changchun were overrun by the Red Army. However, General Otozō Yamada, commander of the Kwantung Army, had already ordered their destruction and evacuation. The NKVD now switched its focus to apprehending any personnel associated with Units 100 and 731 and began a process of filtration of the 560,000–760,000 Japanese prisoners of war. In December 1949, the senior military figures identified by the Soviets as participating in the Japanese BW programme were put on trial in Khabarovsk. The defendants were found guilty and sentenced to terms ranging from two to twenty-five years in Soviet gulags. However, the officers, doctors and other personnel from Unit 731 were in fact transferred to the comparative comfort of the NKVD special prison camp No. 48 – a tsarist-era red-brick manor house located in Cherntsy (Ivanovo region). The leniency with which the Japanese BW specialists were treated – the longest sentence any served was seven years – has led a number of scholars to conclude that some sort of intelligence deal was struck between the Soviet authorities and the Unit 731 personnel held captive in the USSR.

The programme in the Cold War period

In the immediate post-war period, Lavrentiy Beria, the Soviet minister of internal affairs, maintained control of the Soviet BW programme and further developed its offensive capabilities. The key hub of the Soviet BW programme at this time was the Scientific-Research Institute of Epidemiology and Hygiene located in Kirov. It continued to utilise the biological weapons test site on Vozrozhdeniya Island in the Aral Sea. During the period 1947–9 a new military biological weapons facility, the USSR Ministry of Defence's Scientific-Research Institute of Hygiene, was established in Sverdlovsk. It occupied the site of the former Cherkassk-Sverdlovsk Infantry Academy on Ulitsa Zvezdnaya. The new facility became operational in July 1949. Its core staff were sourced from the Kirov BW facility. The first group to arrive from Kirov included the new director of the Institute of Hygiene, Major General Nikolai Fillipovich Kopylov. The Sverdlovsk facility launched a scientific programme in 1951 that focused on botulinum toxin.

In the early 1950s, the Soviet leadership became concerned that the USSR was vulnerable to attack by a new generation of virus-based biological weapons. At this time, the country only possessed a single facility focused on viruses, the Moscow-based D.I. Ivanovskii Institute of Virology. In 1952, as a response to this perceived area of weakness, the Soviet government issued a special decree for the creation of the Scientific-Research Sanitary Institute (NIIS) in Zagorsk. It later pursued major programmes focused on variola virus and viral haemorrhagic fevers.

PNIL – 'Aralsk-7'

In 1954, a biological weapons test site, officially referred to as 'Aralsk-7', was built on the islands of Vozrozhdeniya and Komsomolskiy. The MOD's Field Scientific Research Laboratory (PNIL) was stationed on Vozrozhdeniya Island to conduct the experiments. The settlement here had barracks, residential houses, a primary school, a nursery school, a cafeteria, warehouses and a power station. Personnel were subjected to regular immunisations and received hardship benefits. PNIL developed methods of biological defence and decontamination for Soviet troops. Samples of military hardware, equipment and protective clothing reportedly passed field tests at the island before being mass-produced. During the Soviet invasion of Afghanistan, military protective gear developed for Afghan conditions was tested at the PNIL.

The experiments were conducted on horses, monkeys, sheep and donkeys, and on laboratory animals such as white mice, guinea pigs and hamsters. In addition to common pathogenic strains, special strains developed for military purposes were tested at the island. Bacterial simulants were also used to study the dissemination of aerosol particles in the atmosphere.

Just four years after the creation of the Zagorsk facility, the CPSU and the USSR Council of Ministers in 1956 issued a decree 'for strengthening scientific-research work in the field of microbiology and virology'. This decree established a secret network of BW institutes within the USSR Ministry of Agriculture. Operating under the code name 'Ekologiya' (Ecology), the new network incorporated three virology facilities. These worked in close collaboration with Soviet military virologists and focused on both animal pathogens such as foot-and-mouth disease and exotic zoonotic infections.

In August 1958, a new Scientific-Research Technical Bureau (NITB) was created, the prime task of which was to establish covert dual-use BW facilities at a number of pharmaceutical and microbiological enterprises. Over the next decade or so, dual-use BW production plants were set up at Berdsk, Omutninsk, Penza and Kurgan. Historian Anthony Rimmington argues that this:

> was in fact a pivotal period in the Soviet programme, when BW production technology was being transferred from the military to facilities concealed within civil manufacturing plants. This was later to manifest itself as a key feature of the subsequent Biopreparat programme.

In addition to the centres developing antipersonnel BW agents, another group of facilities worked on microbial agents deleterious to livestock and plants. One such facility, the Scientific Research Agricultural Institute (NISKhI) in Gvardeyskiy, Kazakhstan, was established in 1958. Facilities involved in the development of anti-livestock and anti-crop agents included the Scientific Research Institute for Animal Protection in Vladimir and the centre in Sverdlovsk. Biological agents harmful to livestock and plants were tested at a special site near Novosibirsk. Munitions for the delivery of all types of biological agents were assembled at the Sverdlovsk facility.

Biopreparat

Inevitably, after the Second World War the Russians had soon realised that biological warfare capability had to be a three-horse race amongst the superpowers. They eventually responded with their own biological weapon installation – only on a bigger scale than Fort Detrick or Porton Down. The All-Union Science Production Association Biopreparat (Биопрепарат, literally 'biological preparation') was created in April 1974, and was the largest and most sophisticated offensive biological warfare programme ever seen. Biopreparat, known by its postal code PO Box A-1063, controlled the world's second-largest antibiotics industry and produced a number of biopharmaceutical and veterinary products, which were exported to many developing countries. Western sources believe that as many as 2,000 of Biopreparat's 9,000 scientific employees were experts on deadly pathogens. [Laurie Garrett, 'Inside Russia's Germ Warfare Labs', *Newsday*, 10 August 1997, Anthony Rimmington, 'From Military to Industrial Complex'.]

It was a vast network, masquerading as a civilian facility employing 30,000–40,000 personnel and incorporating five major military-focused research institutes, numerous design and instrument-making facilities, three pilot plants and five dual-use production plants; test sites conducted open-air testing of munitions with a live agent. The scope of the programme can really be assessed from facilities associated with just the civilian components: ten research and development institutes, fourteen production and mobilisation plants, and eight special weapons and facility design units. Production sites had the capacity to produce hundreds of tons of biological agent every year.

This army of scientists did some work devoted to enhancing traditional biological agents, but the Soviets were really passionate about discovering emerging pathogens and creating novel biological agents with a view to developing a new generation of biological weapons. Biopreparat also developed enhanced pathogens resistant to antibiotics and able to evade vaccine protection. Emerging infectious diseases studied as potential BW agents included Ebola and Marburg viruses. They eventually focused on the Marburg virus and developed formulations to weaponise it. Furthermore, the Soviets were attempting to develop so-called chimeras, biological agents that incorporated genetic components from different pathogens to create a novel organism with unique characteristics.

To summarise, the bacterial and viral pathogens researched and developed at Biopreparat with a view to their weaponisation included:

- *Bacillus anthracis* (the causative agent of anthrax).
- *Yersinia pestis* (the causative agent of plague). The network of anti-plague research institutes included the Mikrob Scientific Research Anti-Plague Institute in Saratov, the Rostov Anti-Plague Institute, the Volgograd Scientific Research Anti-Plague Institute, and the Irkutsk Anti-Plague Institute for Siberia and the Far East. These institutes were mainly responsible for civilian epidemiological investigations and did not have direct links with MOD or Biopreparat BW facilities but the anti-plague institutes developed vaccines and diagnostic materials for microbial pathogens modified by the military.
- *Francisella tularensis* (the causative agent of tularaemia).
- *Brucella sp.* (the causative agent of Brucellosis) – a highly contagious zoonosis caused by ingestion of unpasteurised milk or undercooked meat from infected animals, or close contact with their secretions.
- Smallpox virus.

- Venezuelan equine encephalitis virus.
- Marburg virus – causes Marburg virus disease in humans and other primates, a highly dangerous form of viral haemorrhagic fever.
- Bolivian haemorrhagic fever (BHF) is a haemorrhagic fever and zoonotic infectious disease originating in Bolivia after infection by *Machupo mammarenavirus*. The vector is the large vesper mouse (*Calomys callosus*), indigenous to northern Bolivia. Infected animals are asymptomatic and shed the virus in excreta, thereby infecting humans.
- Q Fever – Q fever is a disease caused by the bacterium *Coxiella burnetii*. This bacterium naturally infects some animals, such as goats, sheep and cattle. *C. burnetii* bacteria are found in the birth products (i.e. placenta, amniotic fluid), urine, faeces and milk of infected animals. People can be infected by breathing in dust that has been contaminated by infected animal faeces, urine, milk, and birth products.
- Botulinum toxin – one of the most poisonous biological substances known – is a neurotoxin produced by the bacterium *Clostridium botulinum*. Botulinum toxin is recognised as a very real potential agent for use in bioterrorism. It can be absorbed through the eyes, mucous membranes, respiratory tract, and through broken skin. The effects of botulinum toxin differ from other nerve agents in that botulism symptoms develop relatively slowly over several days, while nerve agent effects are generally much more rapid.

The VECTOR Institute

The State Research Center of Virology and Biotechnology VECTOR, also known as the Vector Institute, is a biological research centre in Koltsovo, Novosibirsk Oblast. It has research facilities and capabilities for all levels of Biological Hazard, CDC Levels 1–4. It is one of two official repositories for smallpox virus, the other being the CDC in Atlanta, Georgia, and was part of the system of laboratories known as the Biopreparat network of laboratories. It was established in 1974 and has, over time, made a significant Soviet contribution to smallpox research and COVD-19 research.

The facility is at the heart of Soviet biological warfare research, although exactly what is going on there remains uncertain. Here is what might be called a VECTOR mission statement:

- The mission of the Center is scientific and practical support for countering global infectious threats.
- Basic research of causative agents of especially dangerous and socially important viral infections, and their genetic variability and diversity, pathogenesis of viral infections.

- Ensuring constant readiness for implementing diagnostics of especially dangerous infectious agents.
- The development and introduction into healthy practice of diagnostic curative and preventive medicines.
- Post-graduate training, and scientific training of higher qualification in the field of virology, molecular biology and biotechnology through graduate school and higher education.

It includes a branch – the Institute of Medical Biotechnology – located in Berdsk, Novosibirsk Region.

Suspicions relating to the United States' compliance with the 1972 Biological Weapons Convention (BWC) led the USSR to augment their biowarfare programmes to an unprecedented level rivalling its prodigious investment in nuclear arms. In April 1974, a new agency, the All-Union Science Production Association Biopreparat, was created to spearhead the Soviet offensive BW programme. In the 1980s, the Soviet Ministry of Agriculture successfully developed variants of foot-and-mouth disease and rinderpest against cows, African swine fever for pigs, and psittacosis to kill chickens. These agents were prepared in order to be sprayed on enemy fields from airplanes over hundreds of miles. The secret programme was, ironically, code-named 'Ecology'. A facility to manufacture genetically engineered strains of smallpox on an industrial scale was launched in the Vector Institute in 1990.

In 1989, the defector Vladimir Pasechnik convinced the British that the Soviets had genetically engineered a strain of *Yersinia pestis* to resist antibiotics. This led to pressure on President Gorbachev by the British and Americans to open up for inspection several of his facilities, which took place in January 1991. Russia made smallpox available to Saddam Hussein in the early 1990s.

April 1992 saw President Yeltsin decree 'the termination of research on offensive biological weapons, the dismantlement of experimental technological lines for the production of biological agents and the closure of biological weapons testing facilities' (Leitenberg 2001), while in the September he agreed in a Joint Statement on Biological Weapons with the United States and the United Kingdom that the two Western nations would:

> have a blanket invitation to visit facilities of concern in Russia under ground rules that guarantee unprecedented access, including access to the entire facility, the ability to take samples, the right to interview the workers and scientists, and the right to record the visits on video and audio tape.

Yeltsin futher promised to end the Russian bioweapons programme and to convert its facilities for benevolent scientific and medical purposes. There is, however, precious little evidence of compliance with the agreement, as well as the fate of the former Soviet bio-agents and facilities. Leitenberg and Zilinskas (2012) state, 'In March 1992 ... Yeltsin acknowledged the existence of an illegal bioweapons programme in the former Soviet Union and ordered it to be dissolved. His decree was, however, not obeyed.' They conclude:

> In hindsight, we know that with the ultimate failure of the ... [negotiations] process and the continued Russian refusal to open the ... facilities to the present day, neither the Yeltsin or Putin administrations ever carried out 'a visible campaign to dismantle once and for all' the residual elements of the Soviet bioweapons program.

In the 1990s, specimens of deadly bacteria and viruses were stolen from western laboratories and delivered by Aeroflot aircraft to reinforce the Russian biological weapons programme. At least one of the pilots was a Russian Foreign Intelligence Service officer. At least two of the agents on the flight died, presumably from infection with the pathogens.

The Chimera Project attempted in the late 1980s and early 1990s to combine DNA from Venezuelan equine encephalitis and smallpox at Obolensk, and Ebola virus and smallpox at VECTOR. Journal articles by scientists suggest that in 1999 the experiments were still going on.

Kazakhstani BW facilities

In terms of BW capability within the former Soviet Union, Kazakhstani BW facilities were second only to those in Russia. Kazakhstani BW facilities slotted in to various parts of the Soviet BW structure and reported to different central authorities in Moscow. The four main facilities were the Vozrozhdeniya Island open-air test site in the Aral Sea, the Scientific Experimental and Production Base (SNOPB) in Stepnogorsk, the Scientific Research Agricultural Institute (NISKhI) in Gvardeyskiy, and the Anti-Plague Scientific Research Institute in Alma-Ata.

The Scientific Experimental and Production Base (SNOPB), Stepnogorsk

SNOPB was under the authority of the Biopreparat organisation. Known only by its post office box, No. 2076, this facility tested and certified methods of producing BW agents developed in the laboratories of Biopreparat and the MOD, and issued technical documentation and recommendations. From 1984 to 1987, specialists and equipment from Sverdlovsk were transferred to SNOPB. As well as anthrax, the Stepnogorsk facility produced staphylococcus toxin SNOPB and conducted development and experimental production of several civilian products, including vaccines, diagnostic tools, herbicides and medicines.

Here is an example of the facilities at SNOPB:

Buildings 241–244 and 251–271 were underground bunkers with reinforced-concrete walls two meters thick, reportedly capable of surviving a nuclear attack. From the outside they resembled small hills covered by soil and grass. Bunkers 241–244 contained weaponization lines where special machines filled the concentrated slurry of pathogenic microorganisms into bomblets and then sealed them. Weaponization could be completed by installing explosive bursters in the bomblets. The bomblets would then be installed in a large weapon, such as an aerial bomb or a missile warhead. Bunkers 251–271 contained refrigerated rooms for storing biological agents, capable of maintaining temperatures down to -40°C in a volume of 800 cubic meters. Buildings 251–271 were connected by a railway spur with loading equipment, and had a small helicopter landing site nearby.

> Gulbarshyn Bozheyeva, Former Soviet Biological Weapons Facilities in Kazakhstan (1999), Middlebury Institute of International Studies at Monerey

Scientific Research Agricultural Institute (NISKhI)

NISKhI belonged to a separate group of Soviet BW facilities that developed agents harmful to livestock and plants. You had to pass three security posts to get in. It occupied 19 hectares, included fifteen laboratories, a vivarium, greenhouses, agricultural technology, and a vaccine production facility, and employed more than 400 people. NISKhI was established in 1958 in Gvardeyskiy, outside the city of Otar, about 115 miles from Almaty. The institute could boast expertise in highly pathogenic and exotic diseases of livestock, fowl and crops caused by viruses and other agents, including rinderpest virus, Newcastle disease virus, African swine fever virus, sheep pox virus, goat pox virus, fowl pox virus, blue-tongue virus (catarrhal fever of sheep), herpes virus (Aujeszky's disease), and cereal rust fungi. In 1991, Moscow terminated all military research here and left the NISKhI without central administration or funding.

Anti-Plague Scientific Research Institute

The institute was established in 1949 in the suburbs of Almaty. It employed about 450 people and had four laboratories, including one devoted to genetic research, and a vaccine preparation plant with a capacity of 21 million vaccine doses per year. The institute developed diagnostic tests and vaccines for several infectious diseases, including anthrax, plague, tularaemia, brucellosis, cholera and listeria. In addition to serving civilian needs, the institute was involved in military-related research and development on defensive measures against BW agents. The institute, therefore, received Soviet intelligence on biological agents developed by Western militaries, including pathogenic strains modified for military purposes, and prepared vaccines and diagnostic preparations against them. In 1992, Moscow terminated funding for the institute's research and all military-related work ceased.

The poison laboratory of the Soviet secret services

The poison laboratory of the Soviet secret services, also known as Laboratory 1, Laboratory 12, and Kamera ('The Cell' in Russian), was a covert research-and-development facility of the Soviet secret police agencies. The laboratory manufactured and tested poisons whose primary use was in state-sponsored assassination. Of course, chemicals made up the chief vehicles but biological weapons were also implicated.

The year 1921 saw the first poison laboratory established within the Soviet secret services, under the name 'Special Office'. By 1939, Grigory Mairanovsky, head of NKVD Laboratory 12, and his colleagues tested a number of deadly poisons on prisoners from the Gulags, including mustard gas, ricin, digitoxin, curare, cyanide, and many others. The goal of the human experiments was to find a tasteless, odourless chemical that could not be detected post-mortem. Candidate poisons were given to the victims, with a meal or drink, as 'medication'. By 1991, several laboratories of the SVR, the Foreign Intelligence Service of the Russian Federation headquartered in Yasenevo near Moscow, were responsible for the 'creation of biological and toxin weapons for clandestine operations in the West'.

Curare

Curare is a common name for various plant extract alkaloid arrow poisons originating from indigenous peoples in Central and South America. Used as a paralysing agent for hunting and for therapeutic purposes, curare only becomes active by direct wound contamination by a poison dart or arrow or via injection. This causes weakness of the skeletal muscles and, when administered in a sufficient dose, eventual death by asphyxiation due to paralysis of the diaphragm. Curare is prepared by boiling the bark of one of the dozens of plant alkaloid sources, leaving a dark, heavy paste that can be applied to arrow or dart heads. Historically, curare has been used as an effective treatment for tetanus or strychnine poisoning and as a paralysing agent for surgical procedures.

Some notable poison biocrime victims

Isaiah Oggins (1898–1947) was an American-born communist and spy for the Soviet secret police. After working in Europe and the Far East, Oggins was arrested, served eight years in a Gulag, and was summarily executed on the orders of Stalin. In 1947, he was taken to the Kamera, where Grigory Mairanovsky's staff injected him with curare, which takes ten to fifteen minutes to kill.

That same year, **Archbishop Theodore Romzha** (1911–47), head of the Ukrainian Catholic Church, was killed by injection of curare provided by Mairanovsky and administered by a medical nurse who was a Ministry for State Security agent. Romzha actively resisted the incorporation of the Greek Catholic Church into Russian Orthodoxy. He had organised a celebration of the Feast of the Assumption to which more than 80,000 pilgrims flocked; but this was not tolerated by the Communist officials who now began plotting to eliminate Romzha. On 27 October 1947, on the way home, Bishop Romzha's horse-drawn carriage was rammed off the road by a Soviet military truck. The soldiers, in civilian clothing, beat the bishop and his companions. They were taken to Uzhhorod, where they were hospitalised. Romzha was making good progress when, late on the night of 31 October, the nuns who were nursing him were suddenly dismissed and a replacement was assigned to him by the regime. Soon after midnight, Romzha was found dead. The nurse had poisoned Romzha with that injection of curare. The Bishop's murder was personally ordered by Nikita Khrushchev.

On 8 August 1971, the KGB allegedly attempted to assassinate Nobel Prize laureate and dissident Alexander Solzhenitsyn (1918–2008) using ricin with an experimental gel-based delivery method. The attempt left him seriously ill but he survived.

Dissident Bulgarian author **Georgi Ivanov Markov** (1929–78) was assassinated in London in 1978 using a tiny pellet from an umbrella gun poisoned with ricin. Once the Bulgarian secret service had decided to kill Markov, KGB specialists gave the Bulgarians a choice between two KGB tools that could be put at their disposal for the job: either a poisonous topical gelatin to be smeared on Markov, or an instrument to administer a poison pellet, namely the umbrella. Subsequent investigations have concluded that a pellet fired from an umbrella is unlikely.

Georgi Markov originally worked as a novelist, screenwriter and playwright in Bulgaria, until his defection in 1978. Markov's membership in the Union of Bulgarian Writers was suspended and he was sentenced *in absentia* to six years and six months in prison for his defection. After relocating to London, he worked as a broadcaster and journalist for the BBC World Service, the US-funded Radio Free Europe and West Germany's Deutsche Welle. Markov used these platforms to wage a campaign of sardonic criticism against the Bulgarian regime, which, according to his wife at the time he died, eventually became 'vitriolic' and included 'really smearing mud on the people in the inner circles'.

> A month before he died he told his friends in West Germany that a stranger, a man, had phoned him in London three months previously. He had tersely informed Markov that unless he stopped writing for Radio Free Europe he would be executed. He would be eliminated in a refined way, something out of the ordinary, the man said. Markov's final script for Radio Free Europe, written in July 1978, was entitled 'The Mind under House Arrest'. In it, he reproached Bulgarian radio commentators for their cowardice in failing to voice their true thoughts.
>
> Dr Rufus Crompton, Senior Lecturer in Forensic Medicine, St George's Hospital Medical School, in 'Georgi Markov, Death in a pellet', at a meeting of the Medico-Legal Society, 13 March 1980

On 7 September 1978, Markov arrived at the south end of Waterloo Bridge having parked his car and waited to take a bus to the BBC at Bush House. While at the bus stop, he felt a slight sharp pain, like an insect bite or sting, on the back of his right thigh. He looked behind him and saw a man picking up an umbrella. The man hurriedly crossed to the other side of the street and got in a taxi, which then drove away. When he arrived at work at the BBC World Service offices, he noticed a small red pimple had formed at the site of the sting he had felt earlier and the pain continued. He told at least one of his colleagues at the BBC, Theo Lirkov, about this incident. That evening he developed a fever and was admitted to St James' Hospital in Balham, where he died four days later, on 11 September 1978, at the age of 49.

Dr Rufus Crompton performed an autopsy, noting a red mark on the back of Markov's leg. He cut a tissue sample from the area, with a matching sample from the other leg. These samples were sent for further analysis at Porton

Down. There, Dr David Gall, the research medical officer, found a tiny pellet in the tissue sample.

Porton Down did not detect any poison, although, after experimenting on a pig, they 'had strong circumstantial evidence for ricin'.

> So we are left with a clinical and a pathological picture which closely resembles the effects of ricin. The dose is right, because ricin kills in a dose of the order of 1 to 10 microgrammes per kilo, which would have fitted into that pellet, and the circumstances were right for ricin to have been used.

There was no known antidote to ricin at the time. Ten days before the murder, an attempt was made to kill another Bulgarian defector, **Vladimir Kostov**, in the same way as Markov, in a Paris Metro station. Kostov was a Bulgarian State radio and television correspondent in Paris who, in June 1978, had defected to Paris.

President of the Socialist Federal Republic of Yugoslavia **Josip Broz Tito** was a lucky man. In the late 1940s, the Laboratory concocted a powdered plague for use in a small container; Tito's intended assassin was vaccinated against plague but MGB agent Iosif Grigulevich, who had previously organised the assault on the villa of Leon Trotsky and now received the assignment to kill Tito, was recalled after the death of Joseph Stalin.

Some resistance groups were proficient with biological agents against the Germans during the Second World War. The Germans reported twenty-five such incidents in 1943, mostly incriminating the Polish and Soviet resistance. One involved the contamination of coffee with *Salmonella typhi* by a Czech saboteur; the investigation identified sixty examples of contamination. Polish resistance forces carried out thousands of such attacks, mainly targeting individuals, but most involved poisons and not pathogens. Although these attacks are known to have killed or harmed some Germans, the claimed results usually cannot be confirmed.

Chapter 11

The Cold War Years

> Any new war will be characterised by mass use of air power, various types of rocket, atomic, thermo-nuclear, chemical and biological weapons.
> Soviet Defence Minister Georgi Zhukov, while addressing the Communist Party Congress in Moscow, 1956

The Cold War period in Europe since 1945 has a number of key characteristics:

- Prodigious investments by the Soviet Union and the United States in biowar science and technology, which converted a *modus operandi* useful mainly in sporadic sabotage operations into one capable of inflicting mass casualties potentially equalling the lethality levels of thermonuclear weapons. This came mainly from increasingly successful methods of aerosol dissemination of biological agents.
- Other countries had BW programmes, but these were small compared with the USA and USSR. What information we have suggests that fewer than twenty countries had or attempted to organise programmes to develop BW capabilities including weapons utilising pathogens, toxins, or both, at any time between 1945 and 2015. The number active in any given year was small, probably no more than between five and eight.
- Biological arms control and disarmament was moving up national agendas and became a serious and urgent topic of discussion in the international community, resulting in the Biological Weapons Convention (BWC) prohibiting the possession of biological weapons.
- Secrecy: the Second World War saw the use of biological warfare and bioterrorism increasingly cloaked in secrecy, distorted in propaganda and a player in an intercontinental blame game between the former allies and the axis powers. This all intensified considerably during the Cold War.

Allegations were rife:

- The Eastern European press stated that Britain had used biological weapons in the Jebel Akhdar War in Oman in 1957. Declassified information by the British National Archives later revealed that the British government deliberately destroyed Aflaj irrigation systems and crops by air strikes in order to prevent locals in the interior of Oman from gathering crops and denying them access to water supplies. Wadi Beni Habib and the water channel at Semail were among the water supplies that were deliberately damaged.

- The Chinese alleged that the USA triggered a cholera epidemic in Hong Kong in 1961.
- In July 1964, the Soviet newspaper *Pravda* asserted that the US Military Commission in Columbia and Colombian troops had used biological agents against peasants in Colombia and Bolivia.
- In 1969, Egypt accused the 'imperialistic aggressors' of using biological weapons in the Middle East, specifically causing an epidemic of cholera in Iraq in 1966.

The growing Soviet threat was a source of great concern to the United States during the Cold War. The feeling was mutual. Soviet Defence Minister Georgi Zhukov, while addressing the Communist Party Congress in Moscow in 1956, delivered this bleak warning to the world: 'Any new war will be characterised by mass use of air power, various types of rocket, atomic, thermo-nuclear, chemical and biological weapons.'

The focus, indeed the race, between the main players was on perfecting delivery methods, vacuum drying, sizing the bacterium, developing strains resistant to antibiotics, blending bacteria with other diseases, diphtheria for example, and genetic engineering.

Project MKNAOMI

MKNAOMI was a joint US Department of Defense/CIA research programme that ran from the 1950s through the 1970s. It is generally considered to be a successor to the MKULTRA project, which had focused on human experimentation with LSD, mescaline and other mind-altering drugs. MKNAOMI, on the other hand, concentrated on biological projects including biological warfare agents – specifically, to store materials that could either incapacitate or kill a test subject and to develop devices for the dispersal of such materials.

The goal was to have a robust arsenal of lethal and incapacitating materials within the CIA's Technical Services Division (TSD) that would empower the TSD to serve as a repository for supplying biological and chemical materials.

At the same time, it was working to find countermeasures to chemical and biological weapons that might be used by the Russian KGB.

For nearly nine months, the congressional investigations of the Central Intelligence Agency were conducted *in camera*: a Senate committee relentlessly exposed evidence that middle-level CIA officials had deliberately ignored then President Richard Nixon's order to destroy all toxins and other biological weapons in 1970, and a House committee threatened to go to court if President Gerald Ford did not hand over top-secret CIA documents.

Former CIA Director Richard Helms reported that a KGB agent used poison darts and poison spray to assassinate two Ukrainian liberation leaders in West Germany. The CIA also wanted to find a substitute for the cyanide L-pill, the suicide capsule used in the Second World War. Cyanide takes up to fifteen minutes to work and causes an excruciatingly painful death by asphyxiation. William Colby, Director of Central Intelligence from 1973 to 1976, asserted, 'Agents didn't want to face that kind of fate.'

At the time, CIA scientists came up with an array of ingenious weaponry that would have passed muster with any James Bond. One such weapon was designed to use shellfish toxin and other poisons as ammunition. To illustrate his testimony, Colby handed a pistol to Committee Chairman Frank Church. Resembling a Colt .45 equipped with a fat telescopic sight, the gun fires a toxin-tipped dart, almost silently and accurately up to 250 feet. Moreover, the dart is so tiny – the width of a human hair and a quarter of an inch long – as to be almost undetectable, and the poison leaves no trace in a victim's body. According to Colby, U-2 Pilot Francis Gary Powers was issued with the shellfish toxin – secreted in the grooves of a tiny drill bit that was concealed in a silver dollar – when he was shot down over Russia in 1960, but chose not to use it. The agency has developed two other dart-launching pistols, as well as a fountain pen that can fire deadly darts and an automobile engine head bolt that releases a toxic substance when heated.

Charles Senseney, an engineer for the Defense Department, told the senators that he had devised dart launchers that were disguised as walking sticks and umbrellas. In addition, he developed a device that fitted into a fluorescent bulb and diffused a biological poison when the light was switched on. Senseney also participated in a joint test by the CIA and Defense Department of the New York City subway system's vulnerability to a poison gas attack in 1967. Without the knowledge of New York City officials, the scientists threw containers of a simulated poison on the tracks of two subway lines. Passing trains spread the harmless substance along more than 2 miles of track within minutes, leading the scientists to conclude that the system was defenceless against that kind of attack.

MKNAOMI provided surveillance, testing, upgrading and the evaluation of special materials and items to ensure that everything went smoothly during combat situations. In 1952, the US Army's Special Operations Command (SOC) was assigned to assist the CIA; both the CIA and SOC modified guns to fire special darts coated with biological agents and poisonous pills. The darts were to incapacitate guard dogs, allowing agents to infiltrate the area that the dogs were guarding. In addition, the SOC researched the potential to use biological agents against other animals and crops.

A 1967 CIA memo that was uncovered by the Church Committee contained evidence of at least three covert techniques for attacking and poisoning crops that had been tested under field conditions. On 25 November 1969, Richard Nixon banned any military use of biological weapons and Project MKNAOMI was terminated, by which time it had cost about $3 million. On 14 February 1970, a presidential order outlawed all stockpiles of bacteriological weapons and nonliving toxins. However, despite the presidential order, a CIA scientist was able to acquire an estimated 11 grams of deadly shellfish toxin and 8mg of cobra venom. The toxins were stored in a CIA laboratory, where they remained undetected for over five years.

The potato beetle war

This was a war against the humble potato beetle, a leading player in a campaign launched in Warsaw Pact countries during the Cold War to eradicate the Colorado potato beetle (*Leptinotarsa decemlineata*). At the same time it was a propaganda operation that alleged that the insect was covertly introduced into East Germany, Poland and Czechoslovakia by the United States in a manifestation of entomological warfare. Communist propaganda of the time had the world believe that the insect was being dropped from parachutes and balloons, with the intent of impoverishing the populations of these countries, causing famines, and expediting an economic crisis.

While many Cold War-era allegations can certainly be dismissed as propaganda, the idea of using the beetle for bellicose purposes did in fact have legs. During the First World War, the French drafted plans for using the potato beetle against the Germans and, in turn, during the Second World War, Germany worked on developing a beetle army of its own, while at the same time alleging that such a programme was also being carried out by the United States and the British.

After the Second World War, by 1950, nearly half of all potato fields in the German Democratic Republic were infested by the beetle: the pest came to be known as '*Amikäfer*', a neologism for '*Amerikanischer Käfer*' (the 'American beetle'). Propaganda posters were circulated that depicted the beetle strutting across Germany, with its yellow and black stripes replaced by red and white ones with white stars on a blue background on the thorax. Other posters depicted the beetle being dropped from American planes, with the caption '*Kampf für den Frieden*' ('The struggle for peace'). A letter was issued to 'the people of the world', stating: 'the beetles are smaller than the atomic bomb ... but they are also a weapon of the US imperialists in the fight against the peace-loving workers and peasants of East Germany.' Children's books on the beetle were published and '*Sondersuchtage*' ('Special Search Days') were organised in which everyone from young children to the elderly was expected to come out and harvest the pests for mass extermination.

In Poland, the war against the potato beetle (*stonka*) began in the second half of the 1940s when articles on the pestilence appeared in major newspapers and farmers' magazines such as *Przysposobienie Rolnicze i Wojskowe* ('*Agricultural and Military Almanac*'). The official organ of the ruling communist Polish United Workers' Party *Trybuna Ludu* ('*People's Tribune*') reported that after being dropped on the Baltic Sea by American planes, the beetle gained landfall and began to wage 'sabotage and diversionary actions aimed at socialist Poland'. As a result, the communist government declared a 'merciless war against the beetle'. A *Naczelny Nadzwyczajny Komisarz* ('General Special Commissar') was appointed to oversee the assault on the beetles, the country was divided into strategic sectors, and battle maps indicating hostile positions were drawn up. Simultaneously, instructions were issued to farmers describing simple and effective ways of eradicating the pest if pesticides were not available; for instance, drowning specimens in water with a small admixture of kerosene. Even Poland's socialist poets joined the struggle, exemplified by Maria Kownacka's poem *Alarm*, which instructs farmers to 'protect the potatoes!!!' and tells either the beetle or the imperialists that 'we will not let ourselves be starved!!!' (exclamation marks in original).

A Polish newsreel from 1950, *Walka z stonką* ('*The struggle against the beetle*'), claimed that 'the progressive opinion of the world has rightfully condemned the crimes of the American pilots who dropped tremendous amounts of the potato beetle on the fields of the German Democratic Republic ... from where the beetle invaded Polish territory.' The news report went on to describe the campaign launched by the Polish Ministry of Agriculture to eradicate the pest through the use of DDT (Azotox in its Soviet Bloc version), vigilance on Poland's Baltic coast, engagement of the Polish Air Force, and the general mobilisation of society, particularly the youth. The newsreel concluded: 'the American pest will be unsuccessful both in Poland and Germany. The warmongers' provocation will crash and burn. Everyone to war against the beetle!' In a 1951 book published by the Polish Ministry of Defence, Zofia Kowalska wrote that American planes dropped beetles, 'violating sovereign airspace', on the night of 24 May in East Germany, in the Zwickauer Land of Saxony. The propaganda campaign associated with the beetle ended by the early 1960s.

Potato beetle assaults notwithstanding, three years later, Major General Marshall Stubbs, the incoming chief chemical officer at Fort Detrick, soberly assessed the growing Soviet threat:

> Soviet chemical weapons are modern and effective and probably include all types of chemical munitions known to the West, in addition to several dissemination devices peculiar to the Russians. Their ground forces are equipped with a variety of protective chemical equipment and they are prepared to participate in large-scale gas warfare. They have a complete line of protective clothing which will provide protection in any gas situation and a large variety of decontaminating equipment.

As for the biological threat, he added:

> We can assume from available knowledge that they are equally capable in biological warfare. The mass of medical and technical reports published recently by their scientists indicates increased activity in this area. Soviet microbiologists and military authorities have conducted BW tests at an isolated location over a long period of time. It is also known that the Communists have conducted research and development leading to the large-scale production and storage of disease producing and toxic agents.

Development of rockets as delivery systems for biological agents reached its peak during the 1960s, including the M210 warhead for the Sergeant missile, which held 720 M143 bomblets. Each bomblet held about 212 ml of agent; if released at about 50,000 feet, the dispersion of the bomblets would cover about 60 square miles. In addition to the rocket programme, the Chemical Corps examined several drones for delivery of chemical and biological agents: the SD-2 Drone could carry over 200 lb of either nerve agent or biological agents. It had a range of about 100 nautical miles and could disperse agent over about 5 to 10 nautical miles. The SD-5 was an improvement that used a jet engine, giving it speeds of over Mach 0.75 and a range of over 650 nautical miles.

The Schu S4 strain of *F. tularensis* was standardised as 'Agent UL' for use in the M143 bursting spherical bomblet, with an anticipated fatality rate of 40 to

60 per cent. The rate of action was around three days, with a duration of action of one to three weeks (treated) and two to three months (untreated), with frequent relapses. UL was streptomycin resistant. The aerobiological stability of UL, though, was a major concern, being sensitive to sunlight, and losing virulence over time after release.

By the later 1960s, the US biological warfare programme was in decline. Funding for the programme gradually decreased throughout the 1960s, from $38 million in 1966 to $31 million in 1969. Despite budget and development constraints, the standardisation of dry *Pasteurella tularensis* was a significant improvement over the liquid suspension used by most agents. Dry agents were more adaptable to storage, shipping, and logistical considerations.

The Defense Department wanted to ramp up work on defoliation and antiplant activities in the light of ongoing events in Southeast Asia. In 1962, the Chemical Corps initiated a project for the production of wheat stem rust under Rocky Mountain Arsenal supervision. Other work included trying to find pathogens to destroy the opium poppy crop.

The army also conducted anti-animal testing at several stockyards. Antiplant testing using the wheat stem rust fungus was also conducted at Langdon, North Dakota, in 1960 and Yeehaw Junction, Florida, in 1968. By now, the army was well down the road to developing vaccines for most of the biological agents standardised or in development.

The CIA continued poisoning persons of interest: that they plotted to create exploding cigars for Fidel Castro in the 1960s is an example, and in the 1980s, as we shall see, South African government agents poisoned beer, whisky, cigarettes, chocolates, sugar and peppermints to murder anti-apartheid dissidents.

The Sverdlovsk incident, 1979

Accidents can happen wherever such volatile and contagious products are handled and stored. Sverdlovsk (now Ekatarinburg, Russia) came to the world's attention in April 1979 after an alarming outbreak of anthrax. Ironically, this powerful strain, Anthrax 836, was isolated after another accident. In 1953, a leak from the Kirov bacteriological facility leached anthrax into the city's sewer system. An unknown quantity of liquid anthrax had been accidently released by a broken reactor. The army desperately disinfected the sewer system but it was too late; infected rats were found and despite continual disinfection, anthrax remained present for years. In 1956, Vladimir Sizov, the man who identified the Kirov strain, discovered a very virulent variant in a captured rat;

he was ordered to cultivate this novel strain and it was eventually used in the weapons the USSR planned to install in S-18s pointing at Western cities.

The city of Sverdlovsk in the Ural Mountains had been a major production centre of the Soviet military since the Second World War. By the 1970s, 87 per cent of the city's industrial anthrax production was given over to military, with only 13 per cent for public consumption (not literally, of course). Tanks, ballistic missiles, rockets and other armaments all rolled off the numerous production lines. During the Cold War, Sverdlovsk became a Soviet 'closed city' to which travel was restricted for foreigners. The biological warfare facility in Sverdlovsk was built between 1947 to 1949 and was a spin-off of the Soviet Union's main military BW facility in Kirov. The new facility was known as the USSR Ministry of Defence's Scientific-Research Institute of Hygiene.

Research was undertaken at Sverdlovsk on bacterial pathogens, including *Bacillus anthracis*, augmented in 1951, with a programme that focused on botulinum toxin. In the 1970s, this was ended and all resources shifted to *B. anthracis*. In 1974, the facility was rebadged as the Scientific-Research Institute of Bacterial Vaccine Preparations.

The BW facility at Sverdlovsk was located right next to the Vtorchermet housing estate. A meat processing plant was located nearby, handy for supplying components of bacterial nutrient media. As well as the military institute, Compound 19, as it was known, boasted its own seventy-five-bed military hospital, a postal service, a range of shops, a kindergarten, schools, a social club, a sports stadium, parks and walkways, a civil registry office and its own special prosecutor's office. Sentries and construction workers at the site obviously required special security clearance.

In their authoritative account, Leitenberg, Zilinskas and Kuhn (2012) report that around 3 April 1979, a mass of *B. anthracis* spores were released from a four-storey building located in Compound 19. The building housed a production unit that produced dry *B. anthracis* spores for weapons use and was manned by forty staff. The spores created a plume, which the wind carried over parts of Sverdlovsk itself as well as over a number of rural villages. Russian sources reveal that the release occurred as a result of a defect in an air-handling system that carried exhaust from a spray dryer.

No one really knows precisely how many people died. Some (Meselson *et al.*) say at least sixty-eight people in Sverdlovsk itself as well as cases of animal anthrax in nearby villages (Rudnii *et al.*) while Leitenberg *et al.* quote a Russian source that indicates that, 'According to the official data, 95 people were infected, 68 (71.5 per cent) died [but] actually the number of the dead and infected was larger.' The leakage of anthrax hit the ceramics factory, south of Compound 19, the hardest. The factory, which employed 2,180, had a ventilation system that sucked air in from the outside, directing some to the workforce. At least eighteen workers at the factory died.

How did the Russians react? An emergency response plan was immediately mobilised, led by medical teams who checked for illness. Teracycline was administered to affected households, sick rooms were disinfected and potentially contaminated sheets and clothing were collected. Anyone with a fever was directed to polyclinics and those who were very ill were transferred to the local hospital. A Moscow-controlled Extraordinary Commission was eventually established to manage the response and on 22 April, firemen and factory workers began hosing down buildings with chlorine solution. There was also large-scale vaccination of the residents in the affected Chkalovskii district. In total, some 80 per cent of around 59,000 eligible individuals were injected with the Soviet STI anthrax vaccine manufactured by the Scientific-Research Institute of Vaccines and Sera based in Tbilisi, Georgia.

The first the West heard about it was through a story that appeared in January 1980 in an obscure Frankfurt-based magazine named *Possev* published by a group of Russian émigrés. It claimed that there had been an outbreak of anthrax in April 1979 in Sverdlovsk after an explosion at a military settlement south-west of the city. In 1986, Harvard University's Professor Matthew Meselson was granted approval by Soviet authorities for a four-day trip to Moscow, where he interviewed several senior Soviet health officials about the outbreak. His report concurred with the Soviet assessment that the outbreak was caused by a contaminated meat processing plant. This, and the revelation that all medical records of the victims were removed, was intended to hide serious violations of the Biological Weapons Convention that had come into effect in 1975 and was made plausible by a leaflet drop via letterboxes and media warning locals to refrain from buying meat from the unofficial market. Meselson concluded the Soviets' official explanation was completely 'plausible and consistent with what is known from medical literature and recorded human experiences with anthrax'.

The form of anthrax infection was pulmonary anthrax but Soviet scientists disguised it as gastrointestinal to confirm and conform to the 'meat' version. However, this version of events was torpedoed in October 1991 when the *Wall Street Journal* sent its Moscow Bureau chief, Peter Gumbel, to Sverdlovsk to investigate the outbreak. After interviewing numerous families, hospital workers and doctors, he found the Soviet version of events 'riddled with inconsistencies, half-truths and plain falsehoods'. This was followed by an admission in May 1992 by Boris Yeltsin, who had been Sverdlovsk's Communist Party chief at the time of the accident, that the KGB had revealed to him that 'our military development was the cause'. If the winds had been blowing towards the city at that time, it could have led to hundreds of thousands of people being exposed to the pathogen.

There were attempts by the Russians to clean up their act. In April 1992, Yeltsin issued a decree 'On ensuring the implementation of international pledges in the sphere of biological weapons', indicative of a desire, over time, to shift the Ministry of Defence's BW institutes from military jurisdiction to work for the civil economy. Sometime between 1992 and 1994, a representative from the US investment bank Paine Webber Incorporated held a meeting with members of Russia's Committee on Convention Problems of Chemical and Biological Weapons which was specifically focused on the potential for cooperation with Compound No. 19 (Ekaterinburg) relating to infectious diseases in animals and the production of veterinary vaccines. The project eventually failed because of the Russian military's desire to maintain the 'closed' status of its biological facilities.

Zilinskas and Mauger (2018) have provided the most up-to-date information on the current status of the Sverdlovsk military facility. Under the National System of Chemical and Biological Safety/Security of the Russian Federation, funding has been provided to the Sverdlovsk institute for the renovation of two facilities for the production of antibiotics for possible use in the civilian medical sector. Once all the renovations are complete, it is intended to be used to 'assess the effectiveness of means and methods of biological prospecting and the elimination of the consequences of emergency situations'. As of 2015, this major refurbishment project is still unfinished.

In August 2020, the US Commerce Department's Bureau of Industry and Security (BIS) imposed 'blacklist' restrictions on three Russian military biological institutes for their alleged involvement with the Russian biological weapons programme. One of these was the Sverdlovsk Institute (later operating as 48th Central Scientific Research Institute, Yekaterinburg). On 2 March 2021, additional US sanctions were imposed on the 48 Central Scientific Research Institute Yekaterinburg (aka 48th TsNII Yekaterinburg) along with its associated military BW institutes in Kirov and Sergiev Posad.

Sverdlosk was not the only biological incident to have been reported or discovered. In 1960, the wind shifted during a BW test on Konstantin Island, leading to widespread contamination and forcing an emergency evacuation. Thereafter, the island was never used again.

Aralsk-7 smallpox outbreak

In 1954, the existing biological weapons test site originally on Vozrozhdeniya Island in the Aral Sea was greatly expanded by the Soviet Ministry of Defence to include neighbouring Komsomolskiy Island, and named Aralsk-7. It only came to light in 2002: Aralsk-7 had previous form: in 1976, a mass death of fish occurred in the Aral Sea. In June 1986, outbreaks of plague were noted in the region and entire flocks of sheep shed their wool. In May 1988, over the course of only about an hour, approximately half a million saiga antelope dropped dead in the Turgay steppes north-east of the Aral Sea.

According to Soviet General Pyotr Burgasov (Peter Burgasov), field testing of 400 grams of smallpox at Aralsk-7 caused an outbreak on 30 July 1971. Burgasov, former Chief Sanitary Physician of the Soviet Army, former Soviet Vice-Minister of Health and a senior researcher within the Soviet BW programme, described the incident:

> On Vozrozhdeniya Island in the Aral Sea, the strongest recipes of smallpox were tested. Suddenly I was informed that there were mysterious cases of mortalities in Aralsk. A research ship [the *Lev Berg*] of the Aral fleet came to within 15 km of the island (it was forbidden to come any closer than 40 km). The lab technician of this ship took samples of plankton twice a day from the top deck. The smallpox formulation – 400 gr. of which was exploded on the island – 'got her' and she became infected. After returning home to Aralsk, she infected several people including children. All of them died. I suspected the reason for this and called the Chief of General Staff of Ministry of Defense and requested to forbid the stop of the Alma–Ata–Moscow train in Aralsk. As a result, the epidemic around the country was prevented. I called future Soviet General Secretary [Yuri] Andropov, who at that time was Chief of KGB, and informed him of the exclusive recipe of smallpox obtained on Vozrozhdeniya Island.
>
> Shoham D, Wolfson Z (2004), 'The Russian biological weapons program: vanished or disappeared?', Crit. Rev. Microbiol. 30 (4): 241–61

The incident led to ten people contracting smallpox; three unvaccinated individuals (a woman and two children) died from the haemorrhagic form of the disease. One crewmember of the *Lev Berg* contracted smallpox as the ship passed within 9 miles of the island. She fell ill on 6 August and eventually recovered by 15 August. On 27 August, this patient's 9-year-old brother developed a rash and fever; his pediatrician prescribed tetracycline and aspirin, and he recovered. During the next three weeks, eight more cases of fever and rash appeared in Aral. Five adults ranging in age from 23 to 60, and three children (4 and 9 months old, and a 5-year-old) were diagnosed with smallpox, both clinically and by laboratory testing. These children and the 23-year-old were previously unvaccinated. The two youngest children and the 23-year-old subsequently developed the haemorrhagic form of smallpox and died. The remaining individuals had previously been vaccinated, and all recovered after contracting an attenuated form of the disease.

The high ratio of haemorrhagic smallpox cases in this outbreak, combined with the rate of infectivity and the testimony of General Burgasov, has led to the belief that it was an enhanced weaponised strain of smallpox virus that was released from Aralsk-7.

Other events include:

- In 1988, a VECTOR doctor died two weeks after accidentally pricking himself through two layers of rubber gloves with a needle contaminated with the Marburg virus.
- The Soviet Union had an extensive biological weapons programme working to increase the usefulness of the Marburg virus. The development was led in the Vector Institute by a Dr Ustinov, who accidentally fell victim to the virus. The samples of Marburg harvested from Ustinov's organs were more powerful than the original strain. The new strain, called 'Variant U', had been successfully weaponised and approved by the Soviet Ministry of Defence in 1990.
- In 2004, a researcher at VECTOR died after accidentally pricking herself with a needle contaminated with the Ebola virus.
- The same year, there were two foot-and-mouth disease outbreaks at the US Biological Warfare facility on Plum Island.
- Between 2005 and 2015, US Army Dugway Proving Ground was erroneously shipping live anthrax A to labs: 'live anthrax samples had been sent from Dugway to 86 government and private labs and other facilities in the United States and seven other countries: Australia, Britain, Canada, Germany, Italy, Japan and South Korea.' (Deputy Secretary of Defense Bob Work, quoted in the *New York Times*, 23 July 2015)
- In 2012, the UK's Animal and Plant Health Agency sent out live samples of anthrax by mistake. Its Surrey lab was subject to a Crown Prohibition Notice (CPN), closing it until improvements were made.
- On 17 September 2019, there was a gas explosion at VECTOR. One worker suffered third-degree burns, and the blast blew out window panes. The lab contained highly contagious forms of bird flu and strains of hepatitis. The explosion happened in a decontamination room that was being renovated by a contractor.

The Korean War (1950–3)

As we have said, propaganda, fake news, disinformation, lies and deception were the hallmarks of biowarfare programmes in the Cold War period. The official mantra now was, at least from the US side, if it saves lives back home, it's justifiable. In an unstable and destabilising time when the crises just kept coming – the Berlin Blockade, the demise of Chiang Kai-shek in China, successful Soviet testing of the atomic bomb, the Korean War – anything was possible and total war looked probable: 'all military means were justified toward the end of saving Western civilisation' (Endicott, 1998). Biological weapons were now officially fair game from the opening shots of the Korean War, at the discretion of the president.

In the run-up to the Korean War, wheat rust was developed in 1950 as an agent to be used against the Soviet Union. The first production facility for bacterial agents was opened in the Pine Bluff Arsenal in Arkansas, and production of *Brucella suis* began in 1954, eventually reaching an output of 650 tons per month. During the 1950s and 1960s, the programme was further expanded; at its peak, it involved about 3,400 people and a number of agents: *Bacillus anthracis*, *Francisella tularensis*, *Brucella suis*, *Coxiella burnetti*, Venezuelan equine encephalitis (VEE) virus, yellow fever, botulin, staphylococcal enterotoxin, and the anti-crop agents *Pyricularia oryzae* and *Puccinia graminis*.

In addition, a defensive programme was launched in 1953 with the objective of developing countermeasures, including vaccines, antisera, and therapeutic agents, to protect troops from possible biological attacks.

One of the most contentious and seemingly intractable controversies of the time surrounds whether or not the US used lethal pathogens during the Korean War, as alleged in 1951 by China (Zhou Enlai), North Korea (Pak Hon-yong) and the Soviet Union. The USA continues to assert that these claims are based on fabricated evidence; at the time, the story was seized on by the world press and led to a highly publicised international investigation in 1952. Secretary of State Dean Acheson and other American and allied government officials denounced the allegations as a hoax. Today, scholars are still fiercely split about the truth of the claims.

What is known for certain, however, is that in June 1950, soon after the outbreak of the war, the US Defense Secretary George Marshall received the Report of the Committee on Chemical, Biological and Radiological Warfare and Recommendations, which advocated urgent development of a biological weapons programme. Fort Detrick was expanded, and a new one in Pine Bluff, Arkansas, was developed. In addition, it is a matter of record that the US Air

Force had operational plans in 1949 to use biological weapons should the crisis that was the Berlin Blockade lead to general war, while during the Korean War, biological weapons were an integral part of the plans of the Strategic Air Command for general war and of tactical plans for the US Air Force in Europe.

Here are just some of the many unexplained outbreaks of disease and the Chinese-North Korean preventative measures during the war:

- On 28 January 1952, the Chinese People's Volunteer Army headquarters received a report of a smallpox outbreak south-east of Incheon. From February to March 1952, more bulletins reported disease outbreaks in the area of Chorwon, Pyongyang, Kimhwa and Manchuria.
- Around the same time, the Chinese soon became concerned when thirteen Korean and sixteen Chinese soldiers contracted cholera and the plague, while another forty-four recently deceased tested positive for meningitis. It was not long before suspicions fell on the Americans. Korean Army entomological tests found fleas and spiders to be negative but the flies were positive for cholera – a disease absent from Korea for sixty years hitherto. The ticks found were unknown in Korea but were shown to be capable of carrying 'spring and summer recurrent fever' and encephalitis.
- On 11 February, North Korean soldiers reported three low-flying F-51 US planes dropping small grey cylinders and packets of yellow wrappers near their positions: the flies, fleas, spiders, mosquitoes and ants inside the 20cm cylinders were already dispersing when the soldiers arrived on the scene. Most of the insects tested negative but one flea was positive for plague bacillus. A few days before, the Chinese had captured Corporal James Chambers of the US 2nd Division of the 38th Regiment: he had been inoculated against plague. Documents taken from two PoW South Korean soldiers around the same time also revealed plague inoculation. Plague was unknown in Korea since 1912. At the end of February 1952, the army and civilian population were plague and cholera-free; one month later, the Chinese Army in Korea reported sixteen cases of plague in seven of its armies spread over a wide area. Three dead rats found were plague-infected. In addition, in Bal-Nam-Ri in Anju province, population 600, between 25 February and 11 March, fifty people contracted plague, of whom thirty-six died. In March, there were thirty-six cases of encephalitis and meningitis in the army, sixteen of whom died; near Pyongyang there were five cases of cholera, three of whom died. According to the official history of the Chinese Volunteer Army stationed in Korea, in total, 1952 saw 384 Chinese soldiers infected, with 126 fatalities. All the while, US air intrusions were increasing and more and more suspect

insects and other suspected vectors were turning up on the ground. Local epidemic disease prevention committees were set up in China to counter the extensive dropping of insects; resulting diseases identified included plague bacillis, cholera, meningitis, paratyphoid, Salmonella, relapsing fever, spirochaeta bacteria and *typhus rickettsia*.

- It became mandatory for all personnel passing through certain railway and highway junctions to show vaccine passports; otherwise, they would have to be vaccinated at the centres that were now set up. Fresh water sources were protected; tap water and sanitary management were escalated. Insects and rodents were to be collected and burnt. Glass covers were to be installed at counters in food shops. Strict quarantine was introduced for contagious patients and contaminated corpses were to be buried locally. Mountains of long-standing garbage were removed, 3 million tons in the north-east alone.
- By the end of March, the Central Epidemic Disease Prevention Committee had organised 129 epidemic prevention brigades comprising 20,000 healthcare professionals. It took only two weeks to inoculate 4,850,000 people with anti-plague vaccine.
- South of the Yalu River on the frontier between China and North Korea, communist soldiers reported US aircraft dropping unusual objects which included tree leaves, soya bean stalks and pods, feathers, cotton batten, cardboard boxes and bombs full of a myriad of live insects, rotting fish, rotten pork, frogs and rodents.
- Early March 1952 saw three children die suddenly in Fushun City. The autopsies revealed that the cerebral cortex nerves were affected – a possible sign of a form of encephalitis, a disease never before seen in this district.
- At the end of March in the industrial belt of the north-east, there were twenty-four sudden deaths, sixteen of which were diagnosed as acute toxic encephalitis or 'suspected as similar to encephalitis'. Infection was thought to be via the digestive system or the respiratory tract.
- Mysterious plague-carrying black bugs and bags full of fleas continued to be found while an unidentified pathogen was discovered in the first four months of 1953, causing 100 acute deaths. Respiratory anthrax and encephalitis infections continued apace.

On 22 February 1952, the North Korean Foreign Minister, Bak Hun Yong, made a 'serious protest' to the United Nations alleging that American planes had been dropping infected insects onto North Korea. He appealed to 'peace loving people all over the world' to put an end to the criminal acts of the US government. He added that in 1950, the US had spread cholera in the northern provinces of Korea, and the Americans were 'openly collaborating with the

Japanese bacteriological war criminals, the former jackals of the Japanese militarists whose crimes are attested to by irrefutable evidence. Among the Japanese war criminals sent to Korea were Shirō Ishii, Jiro Wakamatsu and Masajo Kitano.' Bak's accusations were flatly denied by the US government.

The Chinese sprang into epidemic prevention mode by sending the first of 3 million doses of plague vaccine to the front and began an impressive inoculation programme. This was followed by another 2½ million doses and 5 million of cholera vaccine. Special field hospitals were set up 'to receive, heal and isolate' the patients while mobile epidemic prevention teams were briefed to reinforce data collection, germ testing and epidemic prevention education amongst the troops and civilians and 'to pay special attention and not create panic or confusion'. All mightily impressive for the 1950s: if only other countries, not least Britain, had learnt something from this when COVID-19 struck seventy years later.

Things got increasingly fractious and complicated in February 1953 when China and North Korea produced two PoW US Marine Corps pilots to support their allegations. Colonel Frank Schwable was reported to have stated: 'The basic objective was at that time to get under field conditions various elements of bacteriological warfare and possibly expand field tests at a later date into an element of regular combat operations.' Schwable added that B-29s flew biological warfare missions to Korea from airfields in American-occupied Okinawa starting in November 1951. According to the US military, Schwable's statement was obtained following months of torture and abuse.

On release, the prisoners of war repudiated their confessions, which they claimed had been extracted by torture after the United States government threatened to charge the PoWs with treason for cooperating with their captors. The Communists also alleged that US Brigadier General Crawford Sams had carried out a secret mission behind their lines at Wonsan in March 1951, testing biological weapons. The US government said that he had actually been investigating a reported outbreak of bubonic plague in North Korea, but had determined it was haemorrhagic smallpox.

When he learnt about the outbreaks, Mao Zedong immediately requested Soviet assistance on disease prevention, while the Chinese People's Liberation Army General Logistics Department was mobilised for anti-bacteriological warfare. On the Korean battlefield, four anti-bacteriological warfare research centres were soon set up, while about 5.8 million doses of vaccine and 200,000 gas masks were delivered to the front. Within China, sixty-six quarantine stations were also established along the Chinese borders, while about 5 million Chinese in Manchuria were inoculated. The Chinese government also initiated the 'Patriotic Health and Epidemic Prevention Campaign' and urged every citizen to kill flies, mosquitoes and fleas. These disease prevention measures soon resulted in an improvement of health for Communist soldiers on the Korean battlefields.

Our wish is that the record of deceptions and plausible denials from the Korean War era ... will alert future generations to more seriously question special pleas about national security that are advanced in times of international tension.
Stephen Endicott, *The United States and Biological Warfare*, 1998

The Vietnam War (1960–75)

In Vietnam, the only agent considered to be of use was pneumonic plague – highly lethal, highly epidemic, restricted previously to a few river valleys. A report from the World Health Organization (WHO) alleges that the United States decided to conduct a biological war against Vietnam. Contagious diseases were spread in epidemic proportion within South Vietnam. WHO announced that by October 1966, 306 cases of plague including twenty-two fatalities had been reported in South Vietnam. In all, it was the suspected cause of 2,158 cases and 107 deaths. The report further stated that cases of plague had been reported from twenty-four out of forty-seven provinces in the South, and rodents had been found with plague in several ports and airports including Saigon, Nha Trang, Cam Rahn and Da Nang. In South Vietnam, cholera cases increased by 100 per cent, along with other intestinal diseases.

The WHO report was confirmed by an executive of the New England firm, Traveller's Research Corporation of Hartford, Connecticut. He said that the firm had contracted a project from the Defense Department to adapt bubonic plague for aerial dissemination in South Vietnam. The contract was a programme to produce large quantities of the bacilli that induce plague and tularaemia.

According to a North Vietnamese News Agency report of 17 October 1966, some larvae of killer insects had been let loose in September of that year on the Cham Thanh district of Tan province. All the rice, plants, fruit trees and orchards in a band of 2 kilometres were destroyed. Similar devastation had apparently occurred in mid-August in villages in the district of Nycay, Mekong Delta. Around the village of Huongny, 40 hectares of young plants were killed.

There are reports that the Viet Cong used sabotaged *Apis dorsata* nests against Americans during the Vietnam War. *Apis dorsata*, a giant honey bee of South and Southeast Asia, has a reputation for their aggressive defence strategies and vicious behaviour when disturbed, and are described by tropical entomologists as 'the most ferocious stinging insect on earth'. What was presumed to be a biological warfare agent turned out, in fact, to be the 'yellow rain' produced by *Apis dorsata* during mass defecation flights.

During the war, the Viet Cong dug a network of underground tunnels allowing them to pick their battles – sometimes hurling wasp and hornet nests into US positions to disrupt defences before launching an attack. Defending against these tunnel sorties was perilous in the extreme: sent down into a tunnel network to engage the enemy, many an American stumbled into booby traps. Feeling his way through a dank, dark passage in Cu Chi, a 'tunnel rat' might easily overlook a tripwire and bring down a load of scorpions on himself from a hidden cavity in the roof.

Vietnamese soldiers would relocate honey bee colonies to routes used by the Americans and then attach a small explosive charge. When a US patrol passed by, a patiently waiting Viet Cong triggered the blast and the angry insects drove the soldiers into disarray.

The US military responded by funding a research programme to come up with apparatus to spray the Vietnamese with the alarm pheromone of bees, thereby converting them into ferocious allies. But the 'weapon' was never deployed.

Viet Cong guerrillas used needle-sharp punji sticks dipped in faeces to cause severe infections after stabbing US soldiers.

Operation Ranch Hand

Operation Ranch Hand was a long-term US military Vietnam War operation lasting from 1962 until 1971. Taking inspiration from the British use of 2,4,5-T and 2,4-D (Agent Orange) during the Malayan Emergency in the 1950s, it was part of the herbicidal warfare programme called 'Operation Trail Dust'. Ranch Hand was, of course, more an example of chemical warfare but given its aims, extensive defoliation nature and the destruction of wide tracts of agriculture, it merits inclusion here. Ranch Hand involved spraying an estimated 20 million US gallons of defoliants and herbicides over rural South Vietnam in an attempt to deprive the Viet Cong of food and vegetation cover. Parts of Laos and Cambodia were also sprayed, but to a lesser extent. Nearly 20,000 sorties were flown between 1961 and 1971.

During the ten years of spraying, over 5 million acres of forest and 500,000 acres of crops were heavily damaged or destroyed. Around 20 per cent of the forests of South Vietnam were sprayed at least once, now updated to 24 per cent of Vietnam being defoliated. The spray planes were fitted with specially developed spray tanks with a capacity of 1,000 US gallons of herbicides. A plane sprayed a swathe of land that was 80 metres wide and 16 kilometres long in about four and a half minutes, at a rate of about 3 US gallons per acre.

The use of herbicides as a defoliant had long-term catastrophic effects on the people of Vietnam, on their land and on their ecology, as well as on those who fled in the ten-year mass exodus. According to the Vietnamese government, the US exposed approximately 4.8 million Vietnamese people to Agent Orange, and resulted in 400,000 deaths due to a range of cancers and other diseases, with 150,000 children born with severe birth defects. However, these figures have now been shown to be a massive underestimation such that current estimates for dioxin release, for example, are almost double those previously predicted.

The Red Cross of Vietnam estimates that up to 1 million people were disabled or had or have health problems as a result of exposure to Agent Orange. The United States government contends that these figures are unreliable. According to the Department of Veteran Affairs, 2.6 million US military personnel were exposed and hundreds of thousands of veterans are eligible for treatment for Agent Orange-related illnesses.

Cuba

False or unproven allegations also came out of Cuba, which accused the USA on several occasions of using BW agents. The latest was in 1997, when Cuba blamed the USA for spreading *Thrips palmi*, which provoked consultations in Geneva under the Biological and Toxin Weapons Convention. *Thrips palmi* is known commonly as the melon thrips and can cause damage to a wide range of vegetable crops.

Noam Chomsky claimed that evidence exists implicating the US in biological warfare in Cuba (in his *Rogue States: The Rule of Force in World Affairs* (2000)), but these claims are hotly disputed.

Allegations in 1962 held that CIA operatives had contaminated a shipment of sugar while it was in storage in Cuba. Indeed, during the tense missile crisis that year it seems that the US was ready to release pestiferous planthoppers to wreck the island's sugar cane crop and wipe out their export economy. Also in 1962, a Canadian agricultural technician assisting the Cuban government claimed he was paid $5,000 to infect Cuban turkeys with lethal Newcastle disease. Though the technician later claimed he had just trousered the money, many Cubans and some US citizens believed a clandestinely administered biological weapons agent was responsible for a subsequent outbreak of the disease in Cuban turkeys.

In 1971, the first serious outbreak of African Swine Fever in the Western Hemisphere occurred in Cuba. The Cuban government alleged that US covert biological warfare was responsible, which led to the pre-emptive slaughter of 500,000 pigs. The outbreak was labelled the 'most alarming event' of 1971 by the United Nations Food and Agriculture Organization.

The Cuban government blamed the US for a 1981 outbreak of dengue fever that made more than 300,000 people ill. Dengue, a vector-borne disease usually carried by mosquitoes, killed 158 people that year in Cuba, including 101 children under 15. Tensions between the two countries, coupled with confirmed US research into entomological warfare during the 1950s, made these charges seem plausible to many.

Southeast Asia allegations

In September 1981, the US Secretary of State accused the Soviet Union of supplying biological weapons, mainly fungal toxins (mycotoxins) to government forces, to kill dissident tribal people and enemy soldiers in Laos, Cambodia, and Afghanistan. Though the charges were denied by the Soviet government as well as by the other governments involved, the first major public pronouncement on the subject was made by former US Secretary Alexander Haig on 13 September 1981. He claimed that the US had obtained good evidence that in addition to a traditional lethal chemical agent, three potent mycotoxins had been used. The evidence came from the analysis of leaf and stem samples from Cambodia, which revealed the use of high levels of mycotoxins. The levels detected were up to twenty times greater than any natural outbreak. Reports of incidents in which fungal toxins were being used against Laotians and Cambodian villagers proliferated between 1979 and 1981. Researchers gave an alternative explanation for the so-called 'yellow rain' that had been witnessed. We have seen how they argued that mycotoxins are common in this region and that the coloured rain that refugees had spoken of could well be harmless showers of yellow faeces evacuated by swarming honeybees.

Two major reports on mycotoxin weapons were issued by the US State Department in 1982. The first report referred to 261 separate attacks in Laos in which 6,504 deaths are alleged to have occurred, and 124 attacks in Cambodia, causing the death of some 981 persons. The second report alleged the use of mycotoxins and provided the results of analyses on blood and urine samples obtained from the victims.

During the height of the Cold War, Austrian authorities arrested an East German spy, one Otto Wiltschko, who had posed as a beekeeper near an airfield at Freidstadt. The bees were intended to deter curious onlookers: one hive had a hidden radio transmitter while another hive concealed the receiver.

Afghanistan 1979–89

Ken Alibek, in his *Biohazard* (1998), asserts that the Soviet Union was using biological weapons against the Mujaheddin during the Soviet occupation of Afghanistan (1979–89). There was at least one attack with glanders between 1982 and 1984 using Ilyushin 28 planes based in southern Russia. He also asserts that 'anti-machinery' agents with corrosive properties were being developed at Sverdlovsk for use in Afghanistan. 'An excellent battlefield weapon. Sprayed from a single aeroplane over enemy lines, it could immobolize an entire division or incapacitate guerrilla forces hiding in rugged terrain and inaccessible to regular army troops' – as in Afghanistan.

Sergei Popov

> The idea was that a new weapon has to have new and unusual properties, difficult to recognize, difficult to treat. And finally, it has to be a more deadly weapon. Essentially I arranged the research towards more virulent agents causing more death and more pathological symptoms.
>
> Sergei Popov, 'NOVA interviews with biowarriors'

Sergei Popov (b. 1971) is a scientist and bioweaponeer who worked in the Soviet biological weapons programme. He defected to the West in 1992 and now lives and works in the United States. While in the Soviet Union Popov served as a division head at the State Research Center of Virology and Biotechnology (VECTOR) and at Obolensk, both branches of the Soviet bioweapons programme crucially dedicated to developing genetically enhanced products. His position led him to expand his researches into the fields of molecular biology and microbiology. The Siberian facility at VECTOR employed several thousand scientists, and among them many hundreds of PhD-level scientists.

Popov worked at VECTOR from 1976 to 1986 and at Obolensk from 1986 until 1992. His work included 'designer' bio-agents that would trigger the symptoms of lupus and rheumatoid arthritis, in which a victim's auto-immune system attacks its own body. His team inserted genes into viruses to make protein fragments of myelin (the sheathing around nerves). Victims that became infected would develop multiple sclerosis, a degenerative disease of the nervous system. By splicing myelin into *Legionella* (Legionnaires' disease), they also created an agent that caused brain damage, paralysis and death. The recombinant *Legionella* was very infectious and lethal, with only a few cells causing disease.

At Oblensk, Popov and his team spliced the diphtheria toxin gene into the plague bacterium, thus creating a highly virulent and deadly strain.

Popov has described Biopreparat's 'Project Bonfire', whose goal was to develop antibiotic-resistant microbial strains, and 'Project Factor', whose goal was to create microbial weapons with new biologic properties that would result in high virulence, improved stability, and new clinical syndromes.

In 1992, Popov defected to the United Kingdom and later travelled to the United States. He worked for Hadron Inc. in microbiology and pharmacology and at George Mason University, Fairfax, Virginia.

When asked what area he specialised in, Popov responded:

Initially I was involved in the production of synthetic genes. That means we created in tubes, in vitro, [gene] constructs that did not exist in nature. The hope was, making those constructs, it would be possible to provide bacterial agents and viruses with completely new properties which they did not have in natural conditions. So, for example, a virus could produce something absolutely difficult to imagine in natural circumstances, like peptides which destroy the immune system in a very special way.

... and that his most successful work was:

the finding that a bacteria called Legionella could be modified in such a way that it could induce severe nervous system disease. And the symptoms of nervous disorders [similar to those of multiple sclerosis] would appear several days after the bacterial disease was completely 'cured'. So there would be no bacterial agent, but symptoms – new and unusual symptoms – would appear several days later. Imagine a new weapon which is difficult to diagnose initially and then which is impossible to treat with conventional antibiotics. That would be [a good weapon] from the point of view of [masking] who originated the problem.

On Project Bonfire, he revealed:

Essentially Bonfire dealt with antibiotic-resistant strains of bacteria, and it was quite successful. It was found that it was possible to create, say, plague microbe resistant to almost 10 antibiotics. And a recombinant strain of anthrax had resistance to 10 different antibiotics. In addition, some research resulted in an anthrax strain which was resistant to existing vaccine, and that seems to me even more dangerous. So, essentially, it is impossible to treat that kind of strain.

He went on to describe the Hunter Program where whole genomes of different viruses were being combined together to produce completely new hybrid viruses. They [the Soviets] wanted to combine two microorganisms in one, say, a combination of encephalomyelitis virus and smallpox.

Chapter 12

The Later Twentieth and Early Twenty-First Centuries

Rhodesia's chemical and biological warfare programme (now Zimbabwe)

Rhodesia remains one of the few countries known to have actually used chemical and biological agents. Rhodesian CBW usage flourished towards the end of the country's long struggle against a growing African nationalist insurgency in the late 1970s. Among the biological agents, the Rhodesians worked on *Vibrio cholerae* and possibly *Bacillus anthracis*; they also investigated *Rickettsia prowazekii* (causative agent of epidemic typhus), and *Salmonella typhi* (causative agent of typhoid fever), and toxins – such as ricin and botulinum toxin.

The primary purpose was to kill guerrillas – be they recruits transiting to camps in Mozambique or guerrillas operating inside Rhodesia. The CBW effort attacked guerrillas on three fronts: first, through contaminated supplies either provided by contact men, recovered from hidden caches or stolen from rural stores, and to disrupt the relations between village supporters and the guerrillas; second, to contaminate water supplies along guerrilla infiltration routes into Rhodesia, forcing the guerrillas either to travel through arid regions, to carry more water, and so less ammunition, or travel through areas patrolled by the security forces; third, the Rhodesians sought to hit the guerrillas in their safe havens by poisoning food, beverages and medicines.

The Rhodesian Special Branch stockpiled contaminated goods in rural general stores knowing that guerrillas would probably raid these stores. During Rhodesian external operations, Rhodesian forces would add contaminated food and medical supplies to those discovered in those guerrilla camps overrun by Rhodesian troops. Similarly, guerrilla caches in the bush were replaced with contaminated supplies.

The Selous Scouts were also involved with the Rhodesian chemical and biological weapons programme. During 1976, members of the Selous Scouts polluted the Ruya River with *V. cholera* as well as contaminating the water supply of the town of Cochemane in Mozambique. There were deaths from cholera in both areas.

The Selous Scouts were a special forces unit of the Rhodesian Army that was chiefly responsible for infiltrating the black majority population and collecting intelligence on insurgents so that they could be attacked by regular elements of the security forces. The unit developed a reputation for brutality, and was responsible for attacking and killing civilians.

The unit was also involved with the Rhodesian chemical and biological weapons programme. By 1975, some of the prisoners who were held at the Selous Scouts' secret detention centre at Mount Darwin were being used by the Central Intelligence Organisation (CIO) for human testing of chemical and biological weapons. The bodies of these prisoners were dumped in mine shafts. According to former CIO Officer Henrik Ellert, an incident where Selous Scouts poisoned a well with unknown substances in an area of heavy rebel activity near Rhodesia's border with Mozambique killed 200 civilians.

The Rhodesian government has been accused of distributing *B. anthracis* in western Rhodesia, causing an anthrax outbreak in the country from 1978 to 1984, with 10,738 human cases and 200 fatalities. At times in the war, the Rhodesian CBW effort resulted in more insurgent deaths than those racked up by conventional Rhodesian military units. In total, the CBW programme resulted in at least 809 recorded deaths, but the true count almost certainly was well over 1,000.

Project Coast: the South African biological warfare programme

> Dastardly in its concept and execution, Project Coast was a reflection of the inherent evil of apartheid ... I pray that shedding light on the sordid past of apartheid's chemical and biological warfare programme will provide a salutary reminder to people that we must do all we can to uphold international law and leave no stone unturned in our efforts to prevent the deliberate use of disease as a weapon against people.
> Desmond Mpilo Tutu, Archbishop Emeritus, October 2002 – foreword to *Project Coast: Apartheid's Chemical and Biological Warfare Programme*, Chandré Gould and Peter Folb

The Project Coast programme started in 1980 and ended in 1993. It was a limited covert apartheid era programme in which *Bacillus anthracis*, *Vibrio cholerae* and *Clostridium* species were studied. Only small quantities of agents were ever produced and no large-scale weaponry. Anthrax was used for individual assassinations, and cholerae for contaminating water supplies during attacks against freedom fighters in Namibia and, perhaps, other countries. Project Coast succeeded a limited post-war CBW programme that mainly produced lethal agents CX powder and mustard gas, as well as tear gas for riot control purposes.

After 1975, the South African Defence Force (SADF) was tied up in conventional battles in Angola due to the South African Border War. The South Africans believed that its enemies had access to battlefield chemical and biological weapons, leading South Africa to initiate its own programme, initially as a defensive measure and to research vaccines. In time, this elided into studies on offensive uses of the new capability. Finally, in 1981, then president P.W. Botha ordered the SADF to develop the technology so that it could be used effectively against South Africa's enemies. Dr Wouter Basson, a cardiologist, was sent on a tour of other countries to report back on their various CBW capabilities. On his return, he recommended that South Africa's programme be expanded, and in 1983, Project Coast was formed, with Basson in charge. To conceal the programme, and to enable the procurement of CBW-related substances, Project Coast established four front companies: Delta G Scientific Company, Roodeplaat Research Laboratories (RRL), Protechnik and Infladel.

The purpose of Project Coast can be summarised as follows:

- To develop chemical warfare agents that could be used by security forces to control crowds.
- To do research into offensive and defensive chemical and biological warfare.
- To develop offensive chemical and biological weapons for operational use.
- To develop defensive training programmes for troops.
- To develop and manufacture protective clothing.

Much of the programme involved all the standard chemical weapon agents such as irritant riot control agents, lethal nerve agents and anticholinergic deliriants. The South African programme differed from the CBW programmes of many countries in that their major objective was to develop non-lethal agents to help suppress internal dissent leading to the investigation of unusual non-lethal agents, including illicit recreational drugs such as phencyclidine, MDMA, methaqualone and cocaine, as well as muscle relaxants and medicinal drugs such as diazepam, midazolam, ketamine, suxamethonium and tubocurarine, as potential incapacitating agents. Another unusual project attempted to develop a method of sterilising crowds using the male sterilant pyridine. A black mamba and its extracted venom formed part of the research, as did *E. coli* O157:H7 bacteria genetically modified to produce some of the toxins made by *Clostridium perfringens* bacteria. A list of purchases at Roodeplaat Research Laboratories and other documents include references to unusual items like the black mamba and biological agents such as anthrax, brucellosis, cholera and Salmonella among others.

Civil Co-operation Bureau worker Petrus Jacobus Botes, who claimed to have also directed bureau operations in Mozambique and Swaziland, asserted that he was ordered, in May 1989, to contaminate the water supply at Dobra, a refugee camp located in Namibia, with cholera and yellow fever organisms provided by a South African Army doctor. In late August 1989, he led an attempt to contaminate the water supply but it failed because of the high chlorine content in the treated water at the camp. Around the same time, South African government agents poisoned beer, whisky, cigarettes, chocolates, sugar and peppermints to murder anti-apartheid dissidents.

The Middle East

After the 1991 Gulf War, Iraq admitted to the United Nations inspection team to having produced 19,000 litres of concentrated botulinum toxin, of which approximately 10,000 litres were loaded into military weapons; the 19,000 litres have never been fully accounted for. This is approximately three times the amount needed to kill the entire current human population by inhalation, although in practice, it would be impossible to distribute it so efficiently, and, unless it is protected from oxygen, it deteriorates in storage.

An interesting variation on the typical biological weapon is the calmative or pacifying agent. The quest for non-lethal ways of pacifying or confusing an enemy began during the Second World War, with a very strange plan by the OSS (the forerunner of the CIA), whose agents tried to find out how they might chemically pacify Adolf Hitler. One plan – unsurprisingly never executed – was to surreptitiously inject his vegetables with female hormones.

North Korea

North Korea wasted no time developing its chemical industry and chemical weapon (CW) programme in 1954, at the end of the Korean War. However, it was only in the 1960s, when Kim Il-sung 'issued a "Declaration for Chemicalization" whose aim was to further develop an independent chemical industry capable of supporting various sectors of its economy, as well as support chemical weapons production' and established North Korea's Nuclear and Chemical Defense Bureau.

In October 2013, South Korea and the United States 'agreed to build a joint surveillance system to detect biochemical agents along the demilitarized zone' and to share information. As far as we know, stockpile is between 2,500 and 5,000 metric tons of chemical weapons. North Korea is one of the world's largest possessors of chemical weapons, ranking third after the United States and Russia. Chemical weapons apart, North Korea also almost certainly possesses some biological weapons, including anthrax, smallpox and cholera.

In 2015, Melissa Hanham of the James Martin Center for Nonproliferation Studies released an analysis of a photograph of North Korean supreme leader Kim Jong-un visiting the Pyongyang Bio-technical Institute, a factory supposedly for the production of *bacillus thuringiensis*. Other experts agreed that 'the photos most likely show an operational biological weapons facility'.

Human experimentation in North Korea

Human experimentation in North Korea has been reported by North Korean defectors and former prisoners. They have described suffocation of prisoners (entire families all in one go) in glass-walled gas chambers, testing deadly chemical weapons, and surgery without anesthesia. Given this, they vie with Nazi Germany and Imperial Japan for the title of the vilest perpetrators of repellent experimentation on living human beings in their notorious Kwalliso (penal labour colony) No. 22, or Hoeryong concentration camp.

One of the North Korean defectors is former prisoner Lee Soon-ok. In Lee's testimony to the US Senate and in her prison memoir *Eyes of the Tailless Animals* (1999), she recounted witnessing two instances of lethal human experimentation. The one that is relevant here was an experiment in which fifty healthy female prisoners were given poisoned cabbage leaves. All of the women were required to eat the cabbage, despite wails of distress from those who had already eaten. All fifty died after twenty minutes of vomiting blood and anal bleeding. Refusing to eat the cabbage would have meant reprisals against them and their families.

Water warfare in the twentieth and twenty-first centuries

RISE, Chicago, 1972
In 1972, a group named RISE (R for Reconstruction, the S for Society, and the E for Extermination; the I is a mystery) attemped to attack water treatment systems in the Chicago area. The group had decided to launch a new world society that was more in tune with (their) ecological values; the plan to

achieve this was by exterminating the already existing world population. The attempt failed when some of the group denounced the plans to the Chicago Police Department. Alarmingly, subsequent analysis, performed by the CDC, concluded that the group possessed viable cultures of *S. enterica serovar Typhi*, *Shigella sonnei*, *C. botulinum*, *Neisseria meningitidis* and *C. diphtheria*.

Group leader Allen A. Schwandner and Steve Pera (a biologist) were arrested and released on bail, during which time they fled to Cuba. Schwandner was arrested for counter-revolutionary activities against the Cuban regime, sentenced to six years, and died in prison. In 1974, Pera voluntarily returned to the United States, negotiated a plea agreement, and was sentenced to five years' imprisonment.

Serbian genocide
Accusations of well poisoning have also been brought against Serbs. There are accusations of well poisoning as a part of the 1995 Srebrenica massacre. General Philippe Morillon, Commander of the United Nations Protection Force (UNPROFOR), visited Srebrenica in March 1993. By then, the town was overcrowded and siege conditions prevailed. There was almost no running water as the advancing Serb forces had destroyed the town's water supplies; people relied on makeshift generators for electricity. Food, medicine and other essentials were extremely scarce. The conditions turned Srebrenica into a slow death camp.

Israel and Palestine
Accusations of well contamination by illegal Israeli settlers in the village of At-tuwani near Hebron emerged in 2004. Cases include that of putrifying chicken carcasses found in a well in 2004 after four Jewish settlers were seen in the village. Israeli police said they suspected militant Jews from a nearby wildcat settlement outpost called Havat Maon. 'No one has water,' said village elder Saber Ehrany, who accused settlers of trying to drive the villagers out. Police spokesman Doron Ben-Amo said it was 'unlikely' that the Palestinians would contaminate their own wells. In the years that followed various NGOs reported similar occurrences, accusing settlers of deliberately contaminating cisterns.

In December 2004, an international non-government organisation (NGO) established that settlers contaminated a cistern owned by a Palestinian family in At-Tuwani. On 9 December, a group of Israelis, apparently visitors to the nearby settlement of Ma'on, or settlement outpost Hill 833, walked through At-Tuwani and stopped next to a cistern in Humra Valley, opened the lid, and raised the bucket. Such activity raised suspicions in the village because of previous incidents when residents had found their cisterns poisoned with dead chickens or soiled nappies.

That same day, the family took a sample of the water from the cistern and handed it to the NGO for testing. Results showed the water had a pH of 2.4 (potable water has a pH of approximately 7) and many solubles. The NGO determined the water was 'contaminated' and not healthy for humans or animals. The family emptied the cistern, and resurfaced the interior with concrete. They were without use of the cistern for over a month. The NGO that did the testing agreed to fill the cistern with clean water once the work was complete.

Things got worse in 2016 when in his address to the European Parliament on 23 June 2016, in Brussels, Palestinian Authority president and PLO chairman Mahmoud Abbas made an unsubstantiated allegation 'accusing rabbis of poisoning Palestinian wells'. This was based on fake news saying Israeli rabbis were inciting the poisoning of water of Palestinians, led by a rabbi, Shlomo Mlmad, from the Council of Rabbis in the West Bank settlements. As it happened, no rabbi by that name was ever located, nor is such an organisation listed anywhere. Abbas said:

> Only a week ago, a number of rabbis in Israel announced, and made a clear announcement, demanding that their government poison the water to kill the Palestinians ... Isn't that clear incitement to commit mass killings against the Palestinian people?

The speech received a standing ovation and was described as 'echoing anti-Semitic claims'. Next day, on 26 June, Abbas admitted that 'his claims at the EU were baseless'.

In June 2016, *Al Jazeera* reported that:

> Yet again this year, thousands of Palestinians in the occupied West Bank are being deprived of their most basic need – access to water – as the Israeli national water company Mekorot restricted the water supply to villages and towns in northern West Bank. Since it occupied the West Bank in 1967, Israel has laid hands on Palestinian water resources through discriminatory water-sharing agreements that prevented Palestinians from maintaining or developing their water infrastructure. ... As a result, thousands of Palestinians are unable to access sufficient water supplies and became water-dependent on Israel. ... Israel has deliberately denied Palestinians control over their water resources and successfully set the ground for water domination, granting itself a further tool to exercise its hegemony over the occupied population and territory ... for instance, while people in the Palestinian community of al-Hadidiya in the

northern Jordan Valley have access to as little as 20 litres of water per person per day – settlers in the neighbouring [Israeli] settlement of Ro'i enjoy 460 litres of water per person for domestic use only, a swimming pool and flourishing agriculture.

Islamic State

ISIS knows all about the havoc that can be caused by poisoning wells; they also used the dams they captured to drown and then deprive thousands of downstream farmers of water. In August 2014, when ISIS rolled up at the Iraqi town of Snune, when they had efficiently completed their characteristic rape, murder and selling into slavery, they herded up all the livestock and stored grain and then poisoned every well in the town before burning the place to the ground.

In nearby Sheikh Romi village, ISIS polluted at least one well with oil and jammed up several more with jagged metal debris. In the villages to the south, the group clogged scores of wells with rocks and rubble, so reducing a lush agricultural district to a devasted and arid wasteland. Saddam Hussein targeted wells in Kurdistan, including a large one north of Halabja in Iraqi Kurdistan during his airborne chemical attack on the town in March 1988 (the Halabja massacre). Decades later, hydrologists are still trying to repair the damage. The assault was the largest chemical weapons attack directed against a civilian-populated area in history, killing between 3,200 and 5,000 people and incapacitating and injuring 7,000 to 10,000 more, most of them civilians. Preliminary results from surveys of the affected region showed an increased rate of cancer and birth defects in the following years. After Halabja was retaken from Iranian and Kurdish rebel forces, Iraqi troops in NBC suits came to Halabja to study the effectiveness of their weapons and attacks. The town, still littered with unburied dead, was then systematically razed by Iraqi forces using bulldozers and explosives. The Japanese government financed a $70 million project to provide access to safe drinking water in response to this.

The Smithsonian Institute reminds us:

From fatal disputes over access to well water in drought-ridden Somalia to fierce water-related skirmishes between herders in arid Mali, there have been myriad examples in the past few years alone. Relying on groundwater for drinking isn't solely a developing world challenge; though the figure has shrunk in recent decades, over a third of Americans still rely on groundwater for drinking, including more than 40 million who extract from private wells.

Chapter 13

Biological Weapons in the Arab World

The vast majority of episodes relating to chemical and biological warfare in the Middle East concern chemical warfare. Nevertheless, biological warfare does raise its ugly head.

The possession of biological weapons (and nuclear and chemical weapons) to deter enemies is a requirement of Islamic law. This is what Allah says in the *Quran*:

> And prepare against them whatever you are able of power and steeds of war by which you may terrify the enemy of Allah and your enemy.
>
> Al-Anfal, the Spoils of War, 60

In his interpretation of the verse, the luminary al-Alusi believes it to mean: 'Anything that can be used as a deterrence in war' (10/24 Dar al-Turath al-Arabi). Apart from being a principle of Islamic law that factors in punishments and disciplinary actions, deterrence is also a legitimate political principle sanctioned by states in their defence policies and established in military strategies.

However, this was qualified by Muhammad, who gave various injunctions to his forces and adopted practices towards the conduct of war that have implications for biological warfare. The most important of these were summarised by Muhammad's companion and first caliph, Abu Bakr, in the form of ten rules for the Muslim army:

> O people! I charge you with ten rules; learn them well! Stop, O people, that I may give you ten rules for your guidance in the battlefield. Do not commit treachery or deviate from the right path. You must not mutilate dead bodies. Neither kill a child, nor a woman, nor an aged man. Bring no harm to the trees, nor burn them with fire, especially those which are fruitful. Slay not any of the enemy's flock, save for your food. You are likely to pass by people who have devoted their lives to monastic services; leave them alone.
>
> Aboul-Enein, H. Yousuf and Zuhur, Sherifa,
> *Islamic Rulings on Warfare*, p. 22

Acquiring and possessing weapons of mass destruction (WMDs) is an integral element of legal and political requirements. There is, of course, a huge gulf between acquiring or successfully developing these weapons to deter potential aggressors and actually using them.

The Quran commands Muslims to fight against the enemy. However, there are restrictions to such combat. Burning or drowning the enemy is allowed only as a last resort if it is impossible to achieve victory by other means. The mutilation of corpses is prohibited. The Quran also discourages Muslim combatants from triumphalism, displaying pomp and unnecessary boasting when setting out for battle. According to Professor Sayyid Dāmād, author of *Islamic Views on Human Rights* (2003), no explicit injunctions against use of chemical or biological warfare were developed by medieval Islamic jurists as these threats were not existent then. However, Khalil al-Maliki's *The Quranic Concept of War* (1986) on jihad states that combatants are forbidden to employ weapons that cause unnecessary injury to the enemy, except under extreme circumstances. The book, as an example, forbids the use of poisonous spears, since it inflicts unnecessary pain.

Kazakhstan and Uzbekistan

The disintegration of the USSR gave birth to new Islamic states, which greatly facilitated the general proliferation of chemical and biological weapons. Inevitably, these countries formed international connections for the transfer of the relevant technology. The relatively young Islamic state of Kazakhstan, for example, has perfected cutting-edge technologies related to both chemical and biological weapons, hitherto possessed by the Soviet Union. Kazakhstan thus found itself in the position of being a potential key WMD manufacturer and supplier within the region.

Indeed, Kazakhstan inherited large and advanced chemical warfare facilities from the USSR and four major biological weapons plants: the Scientific Experimental and Production Base in Stepnogorsk (including a major Soviet anthrax plant), the Vozrozhdeniya Island open-air test site in the Aral Sea, the Scientific Research Agricultural Institute in Gvardeyskiy, and the Anti-Plague Scientific Research Institute in Alma-Ata.

In Uzbekistan, the Institute of Genetics, Tashkent, has been working on biological weapons to be used in agriculture.

Syria

Syria has never made a secret of its possession and deployment of chemical and biological weapons and boasts a consistent policy of systematic biological and chemical arms acquisition. One of Syria's goals is to attain strategic parity with Israel, which, in military contexts, means a programme of attaining biological and chemical weapons. Indeed, Syria has declared that it is arming itself with a technical response to surpass Israel's nuclear arms, code for biological weapons, which underlies the Syrian belief that even if chemical weapons are not enough to counteract Israel's nuclear deterrent, the addition of even more powerful biological weapons will certainly complete the job. In terms of storage, Syria has switched from above ground to underground storage and production, thus significantly limiting Israel's ability to detect and destroy such facilities.

Syria has been on the case since 1985, producing botulinum toxin and ricin toxin, as well as anthrax and cholera germs. Russian scientists in the pay of Syria are involved in the production of anthrax and its weaponisation in missile warheads.

Ricin and anthrax developments are particularly worrying: for ricin, the raw product castor beans are commonly grown in Syria; it has an optimal cost-effective ratio; and anthrax is an easily grown bacterium with long-term survivability for purposes of storage, eventual launching, and ability to endure in the environment. Cholera bacteria meanwhile are highly suitable for contaminating water and food systems through guerrilla warfare.

Egypt

> Briefly, we have the instruments of biological warfare in the refrigerator and we will not use them unless they [the Israelis] begin to use them.
> Egyptian President Anwar Sadat, 1972

The Egyptians probably initiated their programme in the 1960s. In the late 1990s, the US government was of the belief that the Egyptians retained a capability to employ BW but has not repeated that claim since then. As well as supplying Syria during joint plans for the 1973 Yom Kippur War, Egypt supplied chemical and biological weapons, and the know-how to manufacture them, to Iraq in the 1980s. It continues to maintain an active capability in biological arms, despite Egyptian protestations to the contrary and efforts to convince the world that it is a country anxious to eliminate such weapons.

Since the 1993 Chemical Weapons Convention, there was an unmistakeable inter-Arab movement, led by Egypt, to desist from joining the Convention, and to develop a chemical and a biological-attack option, as Egypt has done. When the Chemical Convention was signed in January 1993, President Mubarak was in Damascus with Assad, and both called on Arab states to refrain from joining the Convention.

Just before the 1990 Iraqi invasion of Kuwait, Egypt's defence and foreign ministers defended Iraqi acquisition of chemical and biological weapons, hopeful of reaping benefits from Egyptian-Iraqi cooperation. Anwar Sadat (in 1972) and Saddam Hussein (in 1990) were the only two Arab leaders who unequivocally declared that Egypt and Iraq possessed viable biological weapons. Egypt had initiated a combined chemical-biological weapons project in the 1960s code-named 'Izlis', centred at an Egyptian military-civilian facility at Abu-Za`abel Chemicals and Pesticides Company that includes a military installation called Industrial Plant Number 801. There is a second site at the El-Nasser Chemical Pharmaceuticals and Antibiotics Company.

At the beginning of 1970, some ten years after the start of the project, and after stocking chemical weapons used operationally in Yemen, Egypt also stockpiled quantities of viable biological weapons, as well as the means to launch them. It also appears that Sadat's statement, mentioned above, was timed to coincide with a decision to launch a surprise strike at Israel, and thereby strengthen Egypt's deterrent ability to preclude an Israeli non-conventional counterstrike of any sort.

The ancient Plagues of Egypt, which included pestilence and murrain (a plague, epidemic, or crop blight) as described above, have re-emerged in the twentieth century when Egyptian scientists imitated plague-producing agents as biological warfare agents. The production and storage of the plague bacterium and the Rift Valley fever virus are complex to say the least. To these we can add Egypt's development of botulinum toxin and a virus that causes encephalitis, as further biological warfare agents.

Libya

In the past, Libya has been active with an extensive biological-chemical weapons acquisition programme, though only ever partially productive. Immediately after the establishment of the Chemical Weapons Convention in April 1997, General Gadhafi met Mubarak to coordinate how the entire Arab world should proceed. There is also evidence of cooperation between Syria and Libya along the Libya-Syria-Iran-North Korea axis of missile and biological/chemical weapons development. Libya was a partner in North Korea's development of long-range missiles (along with Iran and Syria) – the Nodong (range 1,000–1,300 km) – which are ultimately intended to deliver carrying chemical and biological warheads. Other missiles in the Libyan ballistic programme included the TD-1 and TD-2 (2,000–3,500 km) plus the OTRAG (2,000 km). The Libyan programme received significant support from South Africa; Libya tried to conceal this within the 'Microbiological

Research Center' and the 'General Health Laboratories'. She developed three agents – anthrax, brucella and botulinum toxin, as biological warfare agents.

Iran

In the recent past, Iran has enjoyed the status as the most advanced Islamic country in the Middle East, both technologically and scientifically. Being a non-Arab Islamic state, it has a key role within the Islamic Bloc in general, particularly with regard to the proliferation of chemical and biological weapons. Iran most probably posed the greatest biochemical threat to the West. There has been evidence of aid from China, Russia, North Korea, Pakistan and South Africa for its chemical-biological programmes; at the same time, German companies were supplying assistance. All this despite Iran's own sophisticated biotechnological infrastructure and highly educated and experienced workforce in this field.

Its biological weapons corresponded with those produced by Syria: botulinum, ricin and anthrax, but its production capacity, especially of viruses, far exceeded that of Syria, with significance assistance from Russia, which, according to American Intelligence sources, imbued Iran's biological arsenal with a power almost equivalent to a nuclear effect. Iran also equipped itself with the means for guerrilla-warfare capabilities intended to deploy biological agents by spraying and by the fouling of water systems.

(I am indebted to Dany Shoham's 'The Chemical and Biological Threat of Islam.' (2000), https://www.semanticscholar.org/paper/The-Chemical-and-Biological-Threat-of-Islam-Shoham/afbfd17af17e15c26797c4ae612302e319220fd1 on which much of the above chapter is based.)

Iraq

The Iraqi BW programme was, as far as we know, started in 1974 at the Al-Hazen Ibn Al Haitham Institute (Al-Hazen Institute), sponsored by an Iraqi intelligence agency. There is an almost complete lack of information on the institute and its relationships between different organisations. The official line is that the Al-Hazen Institute is of no consequence and was a complete failure and was therefore totally liquidated, and had no relationship with or was in any way involved in the national BW programme. The agents studied were *Clostridium botulinum*, spores of bacillus, and influenza virus. According to Iraqi information supplied to the United Nations Special Commission (UNSCOM Chemical Destruction Group), the programme was rebooted in 1983.

Over the next three years, a bureaucratic structure was installed, and the new initiative was given the budget, personnel and management to create biological weapons capabilities. In 1986, a five-year plan for weapons development was adopted. One senior Iraqi military official told UN inspectors in 1998 that Iraq's leaders organised their BW programme to provide a strategic weapons capability until such time as they had developed nuclear weapons.

Where did a state like Iraq source its biological weapons from? Easy: the anthrax it used was bought direct, astonishingly enough, from the American Type Culture Collection in Rockville, Maryland, one of the world's biggest repositories of microorganisms. Iraqi scientists, like any other scientists, knew the best agents to buy from by scanning international biomedical medical journals. For as little as $35, they could obtain strains of tularaemia and Venzuelan equine encephalitis: no questions asked. Horrible to say, but six weeks after the copycat Aum Shinrikyo attack in Tokyo, Larry Harris, member of an Ohio white supremacist group, ordered three vials of plague from the American Type Culture Collection. He effortlessly swerved round the only security stipulation that orders had to be on a university letterhead; Harris simply cut and pasted his own. He was only thwarted by his ignorance of protocol, and impatience. When the plague had not arrived after two weeks he phoned the Collection to chase it up; any legitimate customer would have known that such an order would take a month or so to process; the Collection heard the alarm bells and turned him in.

Frighteningly, despite Congress passing a law in April 1996 requiring germ repositories and biotech firms to rigorously check the ID and professional credentials of prospective customers, biological weapons remained on the one-stop international marketplace.

On 27 December 1998, the Glasshouse nightclub in Pomona, Los Angeles, received a call saying that anthrax had been released in the club. Luckily, it was a hoax, but this was not revealed until after 750 clubbers were quarantined for four hours. Glasshouse was only one in a series of over a dozen anthrax hoaxes in the fortnight leading up to the 27th.

According to a UN assessment, the Iraqi BW programme could boast about 100 dedicated staff, including twenty-five key technical personnel now focusing particularly on *B. anthracis* and *Clostridium perfringens*, a pathogen usually associated with food poisoning but also implicated in wound gangrene. From time to time, their programme researched viral agents, including three apparently intended for use as incapacitants: camelpox virus, Enterovirus 70, and rotavirus. An anti-plant agent, wheat cover smut, was also explored. The greatest focus, however, was on toxin agents, including aflatoxin, botulinum toxin, and ricin.

Iraq also attempted to develop a number of biological munitions, including artillery rockets, aircraft bombs and missile warheads, typically chemical munitions modified to carry biological agents. The Iraqis also worked on aerial sprayers, including modification of existing drop tanks for use with their French-made Mirage F1 fighters and a helicopter system using an adapted agricultural sprayer. None of these systems was operational at the time of the Gulf War.

Muthana State Establishment, Iraq's primary chemical weapons research, development and production facility, was built in the early 1980s under the guise of a pesticide production plant badged the State Establishment for Pesticide Production, 'SEPP', and the Samarra Drying Industries Plant. Between 1981 and 1991, Muthana produced over 3,857 tons of chemical weapons agents, some of them used against Iranian forces and civilian Kurds. Muthana produced 60–80 tons of the nerve agent tabun annually between 1984 and 1986. Iraq first used this agent against Iran in 1984, making it the first nation to use nerve agents on the battlefield.

The research at Muthana State Establishment, or Project 922, near Samarra, was expanded in 1986 to include aflatoxin, trichothecene mycotoxins, and ricin. In 1990, the programme was further developed to include viruses and the genetic engineering of agents. It is estimated that about thirty agents were to some degree studied for possible military use. According to Iraqi sources, aflatoxin, botulin and anthrax organisms were placed in missiles and air-delivered bombs in preparation for the Gulf War, but were not used. After years of surveillance there are still many unanswered questions concerning the BW programme and what ongoing activity there is.

The Gulf War (1990–1)

By early 1991, when the Gulf War was underway, the Iraqis had allegedly produced and weaponized *B. anthracis*, *aflatoxin* and botulinum toxin. The Iraqis' strategy was to fill 200 R-400A aircraft bombs and twenty-five Al Hussein missile warheads with these agents but lack of supplies dictated otherwise. According to the Iraqis, they had filled 157 of the aircraft bombs (100 with *B. anthracis*, fifty with botulinum toxin and seven with *aflatoxin*) and twenty-five Al Hussein warheads (sixteen with botulinum toxin, five with *B. anthracis* and four with *aflatoxin*), but both UN and US investigators were unable to verify these numbers and the missile warheads were never tested. They were intended to be fitted with fuses that detonated on impact, meaning that the agent would be disseminated when the warhead hit the ground.

Iraq never employed its biological munitions; indeed, some senior Iraqi military officers were sceptical of their weapons' military effectiveness, hoping instead that the psychological effect of a *threatened* biological attack would have a strategic impact.

So it was that, on 2 August 1990, Saddam Hussein sent Iraqi troops into Kuwait – the pretext being to support Kuwaiti revolutionaries who had usurped the emirate. By 8 August, however, the pretence was dropped and Iraq announced that Kuwait had been annexed and was now a part of Iraq. In response, George Bush, reacting to a request from the Saudi government, sent US forces to Saudi Arabia in what became Operation Desert Shield. This focused world attention on, among other things, Iraq's chemical and biological weapons, weapons of mass destruction (WMD), and the United States' response. Four days after the Iraqi invasion, nearly 700,000 US troops and an international coalition of 100,000 military personnel were mobilised to the Gulf under Desert Shield, which included 53,000 UK Armed Forces personnel under Operation Granby. The air campaign, Operation Desert Storm, began on 17 January 1991. On 24 February, a ground war was conducted that lasted only four days. Thousands of Iraqi soldiers were killed in the hostilities, on the infamous Basra 'Death' Road, the main highway they used to enter and leave Kuwait. There were fewer than 300 deaths in the allied forces, but 300 nonetheless.

Iraq had not only used chemical weapons extensively in the previous few years, but also had publicly announced their intention to deploy biological and chemical weapons against the United States. William H. Webster, director of US Central Intelligence, estimated that Iraq had 1,000 tons of chemical weapons loaded in bombs, artillery rounds, rockets and missiles. Nevertheless, while the tubthumping got ever louder, much of Iraq's biological weapons programme remained illusive.

Iraq had that large biological agent production facility at al-Hakam turning out the agents that cause botulism, anthrax and other lethal diseases. From 1988, the plant had produced about 125,000 gallons of agent and by 1991, after insisting for years that the plant was used to produce animal feed, the Iraqis admitted in 1995 that the plant was a biological warfare production facility. The Iraqis also later admitted they had prepared about 200 biological missiles and bombs.

Throughout the Gulf War, the Iraqi Biological Research Centre for Military Defence, located at Salman Pak, studied the use of several bacteria (e.g. *B. anthracis, B. melitensis, C. botulinum* and *C. perfringens*), toxins (e.g. aflatoxin, trichothecene) and viruses (e.g. camelpox virus, influenza virus, rotavirus and West Nile virus) as bioweapons. This research culminated in the mass production of bioweapons either loaded into munitions (200 bombs and twenty-five ballistic missiles) or stored in spray tanks for later dissemination as aerosols. As a result, both troops on the battlefield and civilian populations in the region of conflict were threatened by the possible use of these weapons.

The United Nations Special Commission (UNSCOM), mandated to eliminate and prevent the revitalisation of the Iraqi BW programme, was expelled from Iraq, after seven years of work. This is when Operation Desert Fox – a major four-day bombing campaign on Iraqi targets from 16 to 19 December 1998 – began. During the operation, the United States and Britain bombarded and destroyed three locations associated with the BW programme.

Gulf War syndrome
All biological warfare operations have their dangers – not just for the enemy, obviously, but also for the forces dispensing them. We have seen countless examples of blowback, blue on blue or friendly fire down the ages, with devastating effects on one's own forces. That apart, the immunisation of your troops against the agents you are disseminating can be equally as lethal or debilitating.

Vaccines for anthrax and botulinum toxin were administered to US troops manoeuvring into the area. For nerve agent poisoning, troops had the MARK I nerve agent antidote kit. In the years after the war, however, vaccinated veterans have been afflicted by serious chronic health problems, commonly known as Gulf War Syndrome, attributed in part to the vaccinations that were intended to protect them. Since the terrorist attacks with anthrax in the United States in 2001 and the decision to vaccinate the US Armed Forces and American citizens against smallpox in 2003, the public health hazards of mass vaccinations against anthrax and smallpox have been widely discussed in medical journals, at medical conferences and in the popular media.

On 28 January 1991, Saddam Hussein menacingly told CNN News that his Scud missiles, which were already hitting Israel and Saudi Arabia, could be armed with chemical, biological or nuclear munitions.

After the war, allegations of chemical and biological exposures began to trickle in. Initially, the Department of Defense denied that any chemical or biological exposures had taken place. Veterans of the war said otherwise and by 1996, the media reported that almost 60,000 veterans of the Gulf War were victims of Gulf War Syndrome, claiming some sort of medical problems directly related to their activities in the war. Extensive research by the Department of Defense failed to find any one single cause for the problems. According to a report released by the Institute of Medicine (IOM) in 2013, about one-third

of Gulf War veterans suffer from chronic multisymptom illness (CMI) – a series of symptoms that cannot be medically explained.
Possible causes include:

- Chemical warfare agents, particularly nerve gas, or pyridostigmine bromide, which was given as a preventive measure to soldiers likely to be exposed to chemical warfare agents.
- Psychological factors, such as post-traumatic stress disorder. Veterans with Gulf War Syndrome symptoms have high rates of accompanying psychiatric disorders.
- Other chemical agents, such as smoke from oil well fires, pesticides, depleted uranium or exposure to solvents and corrosive liquids, used during repair and maintenance.

Source: The Johns Hopkins University, the Johns Hopkins Hospital, and the Johns Hopkins Health System.

When 37th Engineer Battalion on 4 March 1991 captured the Kamisiyah arsenal, north-west of Basra, the engineers blew up the Iraqi storage bunkers and the troops' chemical agent detectors were activated. Later the same year, a United Nations inspection team reportedly found the remains of chemical rockets and shells in one of the bunkers and found traces of sarin and mustard agent. In 1996, the Department of Defense acknowledged that one of the bunkers probably did contain sarin and mustard agent-filled munitions, and that up to 20,000 US soldiers may have been exposed to chemical agents as a result.

In 2016, Researchers from the University of Portsmouth tested victims of the syndrome to examine levels of residual depleted uranium in their bodies. They say their study 'conclusively proves' that none of them were exposed to any significant amounts. Researchers now believe the most likely culprit is exposure to the nerve agent sarin, which was released into the atmosphere when those Iraqi chemical weapons caches were bombed. They say steps meant to protect the soldiers could have compounded the problem – including anti-nerve agent medication and the extensive use of pesticides. Pesticides were sprayed on tents and other equipment such as uniforms, and were used on skin as an insect repellent during the war to prevent malaria exposure. 'The allies' own activities destroying an Iraqi nerve agent cache or spraying pesticides liberally on troops could be seen in hindsight as an inadvertent "own goal" and one to be avoided in future conflicts.'

The Royal British Legion said research suggested up to 33,000 UK Gulf War veterans could be living with the syndrome, with 1,300 claiming a war pension for conditions connected to their service. Andy Pike, head of policy and research at the charity, said:

> there has been little meaningful research published in the UK concerning effective treatment for those suffering from Gulf War illnesses. It is likely this lack of understanding has had a serious impact, leaving many veterans living with debilitating conditions 30 years after the end of combat operations.

In 2002, as the United States were poised to invade Iraq again, Saddam Hussein attempted to obtain antidotes for nerve gases in vast quantities, in an effort to protect his army from their own weapons.

Israel (again)

The fledgling state of Israel wasted no time in setting up their BW programme: it was initiated in the months before the establishment of the state in May 1948 and the subsequent outbreak of hostilities with neighbouring Arab countries. Biological agents were employed with limited success during 1948 against the British and invading Arab armies. As noted, Israel employed biological agents on several occasions during 1948 by contaminating water supplies. Some Israeli assets attempting to spread infectious agents were captured by the Egyptian Army in Gaza. Allegedly, the Israelis also tried to attack Syrian forces and there is evidence that they targeted Palestinian settlements too, apparently to prevent refugees from returning to their former homes.

Although we know Israel created a cutting-edge, world-class biological research establishment, it is not known what kinds of BW capabilities might come out of it.

We know too that Israel has conducted extensive research into biological weapons and defence and is ready to quickly produce biological weapons. Israel has at least one major research facility with sufficient security and capacity to produce both chemical and biological weapons. There are numerous reports that Israel has a biological weapons research facility at the Israel Institute for Biological Research at Nes Tona, about 12 miles south of Tel Aviv.

Reportedly, the facility has stockpiled anthrax and has provided toxins to Israeli Intelligence for use in covert operations and assassinations like the attempt on a Hamas leader in Jordan in 1997. It is located in a 14-acre compound. It has high walls and exceptionally high security, and is believed to have a staff of about 300, including 120 scientists.

Chapter 14

China

We have seen how China is embroiled in claims and counter-claims relating to the origin of the COVD-19 virus. Wuhan's Institute of Virology is at the centre of this ongoing dispute. Significantly, in 2015 a paper entitled 'The Unnatural Origin of SARS and New Species of Man-Made Viruses as Genetic Bioweapons' was written by eighteen Chinese military scientists and weapons experts. Their thesis was that a family of viruses called coronaviruses could be 'artificially manipulated into an emerging human disease virus, then weaponised and unleashed in a way never seen before'. Of course, the ongoing COVID-19 pandemic is a coronavirus that first emerged in Wuhan and was called SARS-CoV-2. The paper also highlighted how these engineered viruses will lead to a 'new era of genetic weapons' and imagined a bioweapon attack that could cause the 'enemy's medical system to collapse'.

In 1984, China became party to the Biological Weapons Convention (BWC) that 'effectively prohibits the development, production, acquisition, transfer, stockpiling, and use of biological and toxin weapons'. Publicly, China insists that it has observed its obligations under the BWC in 'good faith' and claims that it does not develop, produce, stockpile or possess biological weapons. China has denied ever having biological weapons or their delivery systems, assertions that have repeatedly been contested.

In 1993, US Intelligence assessed two civilian-run biological research centres that were previously known to have produced and stored biological weapons to be used by the Chinese military. In the same year, the US stated publicly for the first time, 'it is highly probable that China has not eliminated its BW program' since acceding to the BWC.

In 1994, Fu Genming, the then head of the People's Liberation Army's (PLA) Anti-Biological Warfare Unit, stated that the 'PLA does not have an offensive "biological warfare unit" or "bacteriological warfare unit". But it does have an anti-biological warfare unit.' Officially, this unit is known as the Military Medical Research Institute of the Beijing Military Region, or Institute of Military Medicine, and is tasked with studying infectious diseases.

Later, a 1999 US Intelligence report recorded that China may value 'possessing a small inventory of chemical and biological weapons, or the essential components of such weapons, as a deterrent against potential chemical and biological threats or attacks'. This, the Americans added, was especially likely since the Chinese allege that superpowers have attacked them using biological weapons in the past. An allegation that the US used BW agents – including smallpox, plague, typhus and anthrax – during the Korean War was reported to be accepted as uncontested fact within the People's Liberation Army (PLA).

Ken Alibek, the former First Deputy Director of the Soviet Biopreparat, has claimed that in the late 1980s in Xinjiang province – near China's nuclear testing site at Lop Nor – two epidemics of haemorrhagic fever 'were caused by an accident in a lab where Chinese scientists were weaponising viral diseases'.

In 1993, Beijing declared eight research facilities as having a 'national defensive biological warfare R&D programme'. These included vaccine-producing facilities, such as the Wuhan Institute of Biological Products that is used by Sinopharm, developer of their COVID-19 vaccine. A 2015 study has found twelve facilities affiliated with the governmental defence establishment and thirty facilities affiliated with the PLA to be involved in the research, development, production, testing or storage of biological weapons. The Wuhan Institute of Virology was conspicuous by its absence, although the US has recently determined it to have 'collaborated on publications and secret projects with China's military' and 'engaged in classified research, including laboratory animal experiments, on behalf of the Chinese military since at least 2017'. For more details, see my *The History of the World in 100 Pandemics, Plagues & Epidemics* (2021).

More recently, the emphasis on biotechnologies in China's 'Made in China 2025' initiative and its current five-year plan has been highlighted – the potential for military applications of this research is apparent when linked with other developments that are taking place in China. As the US has noted, China's National GeneBank DataBase (CNGBdb) is one of the world's largest repositories of genetic information. While this can be used towards peaceably developing more effective treatment plans against diseases and precision medicine, it can, of course, also be used to engineer precision bioweapons. Further, China's National Intelligence Law and its Military-Civil Fusion strategy will give its military access to all civilian research and infrastructure – 'Military-Civil Fusion' – theoretically turning all its work into weapons of war.

Down the years, China is thought to have researched all the usual potential BW agents – the causative agents of tularaemia, Q fever, plague, anthrax, Eastern equine encephalitis and psittacosis – and to possess the technology to mass-produce most traditional BW agents – including the causative agents of anthrax, tularaemia and botulism. There is also the possibility that China has weaponised ricin, botulinum toxins, and the causative agents of anthrax, cholera, plague and tularaemia. Highly virulent viruses such as SARS, influenza H5N1, Japanese encephalitis, and dengue have all been studied at the Wuhan Institute of Virology.

China also has an active interest in aerobiology, and aerosolisation experiments with microorganisms are thought to have been conducted.

Concerns over China's compliance with the BWC rumble on.

The official position of the US Department of State, as published in a 2021 report, is that China likely operated an offensive bioweapons programme before their 1984 signing of the BWC treaty, and continued to operate the programme afterwards. The report also expresses concern that China may have transferred controlled biological weapons-related items to nations of international concern, for example Iran.

Chapter 15

Bioterrorism in the Modern World

The very real possibility of the large-scale use of biological weapons by non-state-sponsored individuals or groups is a major concern and preoccupation for all governments today. However, it may come as some surprise, given the proliferation of biological and chemical weaponry in the preceding decades, that until 1997, as D.A. Henderson writes in the abstract to his paper 'John Bartlett and Bioterrorism':

> the subject of bioterrorism was not discussed within the medical community and deliberately ignored in national planning efforts. Biological weapons were regarded as 'morally repulsive'. This complacency stemmed from a 1972 Biological Weapons Convention where all countries agreed to cease offensive biological weapons research.
>
> *Clinical Infectious Diseases*, Volume 59, Issue suppl_2, September 2014, pp. S76–S79

Henderson points out how, by the 1990s, however, the Soviet Union was discovered to have an extensive bioweapons programme and Aum Shinrikyo – a fanatical Japanese religious cult – had launched a viable anthrax attack on Tokyo. Biological weapons such as smallpox and anthrax clearly had the potential to cause a national catastrophe. However, not much was done until John Bartlett in 1997 'led a symposium and programme to educate the medical community and the country of the need for definitive bioweapons programs. It was highly persuasive and received a final stimulus when the anthrax attack occurred in the United States in 2001.'

Since the turn of the twentieth century, the world has been subjected to a number of acts of bioterrorism. One example came courtesy of the Rajneesh cult, a religious group who, in 1984, deliberately contaminated salad bars with *Salmonella typhimurium* in multiple restaurants in The Dalles, Oregon. This assault resulted in 751 cases, forty-five of whom had to be hospitalised. Then there was the post-9/11 New York 'anthrax letters case'. Another religious cult, Aum Shinrikyo, launched its chemical gas attack with sarin down in the Tokyo metro in March 1995, but at the same time, it was developing a programme featuring rudimentary biological weapons containing *Clostridium botulinum* and *B. anthracis*. Who knows if they would ever have been viable?

In the Middle East over the last few decades, Al-Qaeda, Hezbollah, Hamas, Isis and Tanzim are among the organisations which are or have been of interest to the West. No one of course needs reminding about 9/11. Russia has its own issues with Chechnya. Al-Qaeda has been implicated in what was called 'multi-track biochemical microproliferation'.

It is vital to remember that, for the terrorist, the success of acts of bioterrorism is not simply measured by the number of physical casualties and infections – the psychological and social impacts are just as important because this is what amplifies the physical and ballistic impact. Fear, anxiety, economic disruption and social dislocation are what the bioterrorist craves in his targeting: he or she may kill and injure a handful of innocent people, but the universal dread, panic and anxiety that an incident causes, the economic burden and the social disarray are all worth their weight in gold. One distressing feature of bioterrorism is that it need not succeed in actually harming anyone or anything in order to have a dreadful impact.

Just as worrying, biological weapons boast a desirable cost to efficiency ratio that meets the needs of developing countries seeking non-conventional and less expensive munitions that are not too problematic to handle. The increasing attainability, diversity – toxins and pathogens – and versatility of biological weapons make them attractive to those rogue regimes and lawless organisations in search of an accessible weapon with massive and maximum impact.

The first conviction under the Biological Weapons Anti-Terrorism Act of 1989 was in 1995, when a US citizen was sentenced to thirty-three months in prison for possession of 0.7gm of ricin. The same year, a nonprofit organisation shipped plague bacteria, *Yersinia pestis*, to an alleged white supremacist.

Timeline of 'modern' bioterrorism and chemical terror

- 1920 Wall Street bombing.
- 1964–6 Dr Mitsuru Suzuki, physician Japan, *Shigella dysenteriae* and *Salmonella typhi*. Objective: revenge due to deep antagonism to what he perceived as a prevailing seniority system. Dissemination: sponge cake, other food sources. Official investigation started after anonymous tip to Ministry of Health and Welfare. He was charged, but was not convicted of any deaths; later implicated in 200–400 illnesses and four deaths.
- Salad bar Salmonella 1984.

- 1987–90 David J. Acer, Florida dentist. HIV. Infected six patients after he was diagnosed with HIV.
- 1989 Cyanide infused Chilian grapes.
- The 1989 Californian medfly attack.
- In 1994, a Japanese sect of the Aum Shinrikyo cult attempted an aerosolised release of anthrax from the tops of buildings in Tokyo.
- In 1995, two members of a Minnesota militia group were convicted of possession of ricin, which they had produced themselves for use in retaliation against local government officials.
- In 1996, Larry Wayne Harris, a white supremacist from Ohio, attempted to obtain bubonic plague cultures through the mail.
- 1996 Diane Thompson, clinical laboratory technician, Dallas, TX. *Shigella dysenteriae* Type 2. Removed *Shigella dysenteriae* Type 2 from hospital's collection and infected co-workers with contaminated pastries in the office breakroom. Infected twelve of her co-workers, she was arrested, convicted, and sentenced to twenty years in prison.
- 1998 Richard J. Schmidt, a gastroenterologist in Louisiana. HIV. Convicted of attempted second degree murder for infecting nurse Janice Allen with HIV by injecting her with blood from an AIDS patient.
- 1999 Brian T. Stewart, a phlebotomist. HIV. Sentenced to life in prison for deliberately infecting his 11-month-old baby with HIV-infected blood to avoid child support payments.
- In 2001, anthrax was delivered by mail to US media and government offices. There were five deaths.
- In December 2002, six terrorist suspects were arrested in Manchester; they were using their apartment as a 'ricin laboratory'. Among them was a 27-year-old chemist who was producing the toxin. Later, on 5 January 2003, British police raided two residences around London and found traces of ricin, which led to an investigation of a possible Chechen separatist plan to attack the Russian embassy with the toxin; several arrests were made.
- 2003 Thomas C. Butler, United States professor. *Yersinia pestis*. Thirty vials of *Y. pestis* missing from lab (never recovered); Butler served nineteen months in jail.
- On 3 February 2004, three US Senate office buildings were closed after ricin was found in a mailroom that served Senate Majority Leader Bill Frist's office.

To emphasise the importance of clinicians being prepared for such attacks, Maynard and Tetley published 'Bio-terrorism: the lung under attack' in March 2004 in *Thorax*.

See also, Rathish B. et al. Comprehensive Review of Bioterrorism. [Updated 5 April 2022]. StatPearls Publishing; 2022 Jan-. Available from: https://www.ncbi.nlm.nih.gov/books/NBK570614/

Salad bar Salmonella

> The first significant biological attack on a US community was not carried out by foreign terrorists smuggled into New York, but by legal residents of a US community. The next time it happens it could be with more lethal agents. ... We in public health are really not ready to deal with that.
>
> Michael Skeels, Director of the Oregon State Public Health Laboratory

Salad bars in The Dalles, Oregon, were the unlikely settings for two successive waves of illness in 1984 when 751 diners succumbed to salmonellosis caused by *Salmonella typhimurium*; forty-five victims were hospitalised. No one died. Four salad bars were identified in the first wave and ten restaurants in the second wave as the origins of infection. The cause of the contaminations remained a mystery at the time and was only revealed by accident in 1986. Several thousand of Rajneesh's followers had moved onto the 'Big Muddy Ranch' in rural Wasco County in 1981, which they later incorporated as a city called Rajneeshpuram. As it happened, a group of prominent followers of Rajneesh (later known as Osho) led by Ma Anand Sheela planned to incapacitate the voters of the city so that their own candidates would win the 1984 Wasco County elections. Having previously gained political control of Antelope (renamed Rajneesh), Oregon, Rajneesh's followers sought election to two of the three seats on the Wasco County Circuit Court, as well as the sheriff's office, that were up for election in November 1984. This was after being denied building permits to develop Rajneeshpuram. Fearing they would not gain enough votes, some Rajneeshpuram officials deliberately contaminated the bars with Salmonella cultures; at least eight terrorists helped spread the bacteria. The protagonists of the attack included Sheela Silverman (Ma Anand Sheela above), Rajneesh's second in command, and Diane Yvonne Onang (Ma Anand Puja), a nurse and secretary-treasurer of the Rajneesh Medical Corporation. They purchased Salmonella bacteria from a medical supply company in Seattle, Washington, while staff cultured it in labs in the commune. The group also tried to introduce the agent into The Dalles' water system. Its relative success is demonstrated by the fact that two visiting Wasco County commissioners were infected when they drank glasses of water containing Salmonella bacteria during a visit to

Rajneeshpuram in August 1984. Both men fell ill and one was hospitalised. Afterward, members of Sheela's team spread Salmonella on produce in supermarkets and on doorknobs and toilet handles in the county courthouse, but these attempts were ineffective. In September and October 1984, they contaminated the salad bars.

The salad bar method of delivery involved one terrorist concealing a plastic bag containing a light-brown liquid laced with the Salmonella bacteria (referred to by the perpetrators as 'salsa'), and either spreading it over the food at a salad bar, or pouring it into salad dressing. By 24 September 1984, more than 150 people were violently ill. By the end of September, there were 751 cases of acute gastroenteritis; lab tests found that all of the victims were infected with *Salmonella enterica Typhimurium*. Symptoms included diarrhoea, fever, chills, nausea, vomiting, headaches, abdominal pain and bloody stools. Victims ranged in age from an infant, born two days after his mother's infection and initially given a 5 per cent chance of survival, to an 87-year-old.

Local residents turned out in droves on election day to prevent the cult from winning any of the polls, thus rendering the plot a resounding failure. Only 239 of the commune's 7,000 residents voted anyway; most were not US citizens and had no vote. The economic, psychological and social impacts were substantial: the outbreak cost local restaurants hundreds of thousands of dollars when health officials shut down the salad bars of the affected establishments. All but one of the restaurants affected went out of business. Some residents feared further attacks and stayed at home. One resident said: 'People were so horrified and scared. People wouldn't go out, they wouldn't go out alone. People were becoming prisoners.'

This episode, the first and the single largest bioterrorist attack in United States history, demonstrates how difficult it is to detect a biological attack when agents and methods are indistinguishable from accidental food poisoning episodes that happen all the time.

Rajneesh later shifted the blame onto a number of his followers at a press conference in September 1985; he stated that Sheela and nineteen other commune leaders, including Puja, had left Rajneeshpuram for Europe. He said that he had received information from commune residents that Sheela and her team had committed a number of serious crimes. Calling them a 'gang of fascists', he said they had tried to poison his doctor and Rajneesh's female companion, as well as the Jefferson County district attorney and the water system in The Dalles. He said that he believed they had poisoned a county commissioner and Judge William Hulse, and that they may well have been responsible for the salmonellosis outbreak. He invited state and federal law enforcement officials to the Ranch to investigate and urged state and federal authorities to investigate. Search warrants were issued in Rajneeshpuram. A sample of bacteria matching the contaminant that had caused the poisonings was found in a Rajneeshpuram medical laboratory.

And it was not just salmonellosis that the investigations turned up: they also uncovered experimentation at Rajneeshpuram with poisons, chemicals and bacteria. Michael Skeels, director of the Oregon State Public Health Laboratory at the time, described the scene at the Rajneesh laboratory as 'a bacteriological freezer-dryer for large-scale production' of microbes. A copy of *The Anarchist Cookbook* was found, and literature on the manufacture and usage of explosives and military biowarfare. Investigators believed that the commune had previously carried out similar attacks in Salem, Portland, and other cities in Oregon. In court, the terrorists boasted that they had attacked a nursing home and a salad bar at the Mid-Columbia Medical Center, but nothing was ever proven. As a result of the investigation, it was discovered that there had been an aborted plot by Rajneeshees to murder Charles Turner, a former United States Attorney for Oregon.

Sheela and Puja were convicted of attempted murder and received sentences ranging from three to twenty years, to be served concurrently. Sheela was handed down twenty years for the attempted murder of Rajneesh's physician, twenty years for first-degree assault in the poisoning of Judge Hulse, ten years for second-degree assault in the poisoning of Commissioner Matthews, four and a half years for her role in the attack, four and a half years for the wiretapping conspiracy, and five years' probation for immigration fraud; Puja received fifteen, seven and a half, and four and a half years, respectively, for her role in the first four of these crimes, as well as three years' probation for the wiretapping conspiracy. Both Sheela and Puja were released on parole early for good behaviour, after serving twenty-nine months of their sentences in a minimum-security federal prison. Sheela's green card was revoked; she relocated to Switzerland, where she remarried and went on to run two nursing homes. Rajneesh was never prosecuted for crimes related to the Salmonella attack.

Investigators requested that details of the incident not be published in the *Journal of the American Medical Association* (*JAMA*) for twelve years, for fear of copycat crimes; *JAMA* complied. A detailed account of the incident and investigation was eventually published in *JAMA* in 1997. A 1999 empirical analysis in *Emerging Infectious Diseases*, published by the CDC, described six motivational factors associated with bioterrorism, including charismatic leadership, no outside constituency, apocalyptic ideology, loner or splinter group, sense of paranoia and grandiosity, and defensive aggression. According to the article, the 'Rajneesh Cult' satisfied all motivational factors except for an 'apocalyptic ideology'.

The 1989 Californian medfly attack

> State officials have probably noticed an increase as well as an unusual distribution of Medfly infestation in Los Angeles County since March, 1989
>
> Letter of responsibility

In 1989, an inexplicable sudden invasion of Mediterranean fruit flies (*Ceratitis capitata*, 'medflies') descended on California and began ferociously devastating crops. The medfly is one of agriculture's most destructive pests, a voracious eater that is attracted to more than 250 different types of fruits and vegetables. In tiny, nearly invisible holes drilled into the fruit's skin, the female medfly lays up to 1,000 eggs in her average forty-day life span. Those eggs turn to larvae, which then dine on – and destroy – the fruit's pulp. Scientists were perplexed, stating that the whole thing and the sudden appearance of the insects 'defies logic'; some speculated that 'biological terrorists' must be responsible while investigations suggested that an outside hand played a role in the infestation.

That outside hand may well have been a shadowy group or individual going by the name of 'The Breeders'. It was they who claimed responsibility for the bioterrorist attack, as financial retaliation for the environmental damage caused by the state's Malathion aerial spraying; the group's members have never been identified. It was December 1989 when Los Angeles Mayor Tom Bradley heard about a two-page letter addressed to him which was sent to the *Los Angeles Times* and *Fresno Bee* from an 'ecoterrorist organization' calling itself 'The Breeders'. They threatened to expand its medfly infestation and promised to make the aerial spraying programme politically and financially unviable through the coordinated release of thousands of medflies. The claim was taken seriously although initially, the letter was dismissed as 'some crank trying to get a lot of publicity'; however, there was evidence linking the group to the infestation. The dense medfly population coupled with the low number of medfly larvae found in the infested areas left entomologists baffled as to how the infestation could be completely natural.

Three months after the attack, in March 1990, California ended its decade-long Malathion programme and looked for alternative strategies in their battle against destructive insects, not least the introduction of millions of radiation-sterilised medflies to interrupt the reproductive cycle and control the population. Malathion is a widely used pesticide in agriculture, residential landscaping, public recreation areas, and public health pest control programmes such as mosquito eradication. In the US, it is the most commonly used organophosphate insecticide. California is the world's fifth largest supplier of food and agriculture commodities. Between 1975 and 1993, California spent in excess of $170 million on medfly eradication programmes to contain twelve different infestations. A major 1981 medfly infestation cost California $40 million on its own; 1989's attack cost $60 million in eradication efforts.

The United States Department of Agriculture made efforts to contact The Breeders through a classified advertisement placed in the *Los Angeles Times*. The ad read: 'Breeders, if you're for real send one of your little friends. We want to talk. Call John at USDA.'

In the year following the attack, 61,731 passengers and 2,430 cargo shipments were searched entering through airports, but no larvae were ever discovered.

The anthrax letters – Amerithrax

One New York City day in the autumn of 2001 was no one's red letter day – for that was when a salvo of letters containing anthrax spores were sent by mail to two US senators' offices on Capitol Hill and news media agencies along the east coast. Before 2001, the last case of inhalation anthrax reported in the United States was in 1976. Officials recovered four letters, postmarked 18 September 2001 and 9 October 2001. The powder form allowed the anthrax to float in the air and for it to be inhaled. It naturally contaminated the postal facilities they were processed through as well as the buildings where they were opened.

The attack led to twenty-two people being seriously incapacitated, five of whom died of anthrax poisoning or of complications resulting from it, and probably thousands were contaminated and prescribed antibiotics over a long period. In all, forty-three people tested positive for exposure to anthrax, and 10,000 more were considered at risk of possible exposure.

The United States Army Medical Research Institute of Infectious Diseases (USAMRIID) was the principal consultant to the FBI on scientific aspects of the anthrax attacks. In July 2008, a top US biodefence researcher at USAMRIID committed suicide just as the FBI was about to prefer charges relating to the incidents. The scientist, Bruce Edwards Ivins, with eighteen years' service at USAMRIID, had been told about the impending prosecution. The FBI's identification of Ivins as the anthrax attacker remains controversial. Although the anthrax preparations used in the attacks were of different grades, all of the material derived from the same bacterial strain. Known as the Ames strain, it was first researched at USAMRIID. The Ames strain was subsequently distributed to at least fifteen bioresearch labs within the US and six locations overseas.

Although the fatalities and clinical cases were mercifully small, the attack certainly achieved its disproportionate aim of generating psychological and political terror, igniting anxiety, panic and fear in many, coming as it did so soon after the world-changing Twin Tower and Pentagon events of 9/11. The disproportionate attributable costs related to the investigation, clean-up and installation of detection equipment, scanning mail and other measures to prevent further attacks were substantial and ran to billions of dollars: the US Postal Service was paralysed, the Hart Senate Office building over the road from the Hill where the first package landed was closed for months. Furthermore, the quality of life of those afflicted survivors has been significantly affected. And who knows if the terrorists had more anthrax stock just waiting to go in the mail? The letters that went with the white powder strongly condemned the US and Israel, and celebrated Allah's magnificence.

The particular strain used was traced to the US Army's laboratory at Fort Detrick, but the perpetrators of the attacks remain undetected. This episode shows that, despite all the security in the world, bioterrorism remains a threat and demonstrates the importance of a level of preparedness of clinical microbiologists and other scientists and public health officials to identify agents of BW.

The first case of anthrax was diagnosed on 4 October 2001. Over the next two months, there were eleven confirmed cases of inhalation anthrax – the most serious form of the disease – and eleven confirmed cases of cutaneous anthrax. Of the eleven cases of inhalation anthrax, seven were postal workers who handled the letters or worked in a postal facility where the letters were processed. Two cases were from the AMI Publishing Company, where a photo editor received a contaminated letter. The last two cases were a 94-year-old Connecticut woman and a New York City hospital employee. Investigators conjectured that the Connecticut woman's mail may have been cross-contaminated in a mail facility but no anthrax spores were discovered in her home. The exposure source of the New York City hospital remains unknown. Both mysteries have worrying implications for any future attack.

The FBI conducted a rigorous seven-year investigation. Some years after the attacks, advances in genetic testing enabled the FBI to conduct more complex and robust testing of the spores used in the attack. After analysis, it was determined they came from a strain called the Ames strain and from a single spore batch known as RMR-1029, from a specific research lab. The attack and the subsequent investigation came to be known as Amerithrax. The FBI officially concluded the Amerithrax investigation on 19 February 2010.

A few days after the New York attack the Postal Department in India received seventeen 'suspicious' letters thought to be infected with anthrax spores. None of the white powdered letters tested positive and the attack was dismissed as a copycat hoax – but it does underline how such hoaxes can amplify terror.

Aum Shinrikyo essentially involves sarin and is therefore more chemical terrorism than bioterrorism. However, the organisation did experiment with anthrax and so merits inclusion here.

Japan: Aum Shinrikyo

> After 25 years, most people think that Aum is part of history. It's not.
> Ayuko Watanabe, Japan's Public Security Intelligence Agency

It all started in Shoko Asahara's one-bedroom flat in Tokyo's Shibuya ward in 1984, starting off as a yoga and meditation class known as Oumu Shinsen no Kai (オウム神仙の会, 'Aum Immortal Mountain Wizard Association') and steadily blossoming in the following years into a terror organisation. It attracted a considerable number of disaffected graduates from Japan's elite universities, thus leading to it being dubbed a 'religion for the elite'.

Aum Shinrikyo, the name means 'supreme truth', originated as a spiritual group blending founder Shoko Asahara's (b. Chizuo Matsumoto) idiosyncratic interpretations of elements of early Indian Buddhism and Tibetan Buddhism, as well as Hinduism, taking Shiva as the main image of worship and incorporating millennialist ideas from Christianity, Yoga and the writings of Nostradamus. Asahara declared himself to be both Christ and the first 'enlightened one' since Buddha, as well as identifying himself as the 'Lamb of God'.

Some scholars refer to Aum as an offshoot of Japanese Buddhism, and this was how the movement generally defined and saw itself. The group gained official status as a religious organisation in Japan in 1989. Asahara attracted a sizeable global following, speaking at universities and authoring books. At its peak, Aum could claim tens of thousands of members worldwide.

Aum was convinced the world was about to implode into the Third World War, instigated by the United States, after which only its elite members would survive. Asahara predicted that this nuclear Armageddon would occur in 1997. In his lectures, Shoko Asahara referred to the United States as 'The Beast' as in the Book of Revelation, predicting it would eventually attack Japan. Arthur

Goldwag, author of a book on conspiracies and secret societies, characterises Asahara as one who 'saw dark conspiracies everywhere promulgated by Jews, Freemasons, the Dutch, the British royal family, and rival Japanese religions'. In time, Aum became increasingly violent, kidnapping, injuring and killing opponents, and using lethal chemical and biological agents.

In the beginning, though, it was all very innocent and seemingly as far away from a doomsday cult as you could get. Aum's public relations activities included publishing comics and animated cartoons associating its religious ideas with popular anime and manga themes, including space missions, powerful weapons, world conspiracies, and a quest for ultimate truth. Aum published several magazines including *Vajrayana Sacca* and the pleasant enough sounding *Enjoy Happiness* – more missionary than Armageddon. There was a definite hint of more serious things to come when Isaac Asimov's science fiction *Foundation Trilogy* was referenced 'depicting as it does an elite group of spiritually evolved scientists forced to go underground during an age of barbarism so as to prepare themselves for the moment … when they will emerge to rebuild civilization'.

On the face of it, Asahara and his leading disciples continued their humble lifestyles, the only worrying sign being the armoured Mercedes-Benz gifted by a wealthy follower. Advertising and recruitment campaigns, dubbed the 'Aum Salvation plan', soon led to Aum becoming one of the fastest-growing religious groups in Japan's history. Initiation rituals, say the authors of the book (David E. Kaplan and Andrew Marshall) *The Cult at the End of the World: The Terrifying Story of the Aum Doomsday Cult, from the Subways of Tokyo to the Nuclear Arsenals of Russia* (1996), often involved the use of hallucinogens, such as LSD. Increasingly ascetic practices passed off as 'yoga' ranged from renunciants being hung upside down to being given shock therapy.

Things started to go wrong, badly wrong, in the late 1980s:

- Accusations of deception of recruits, holding cult members against their will, extorting money donations from members and murdering a cult member who tried to leave in February 1989.
- In October 1989, the group's negotiations with Tsutsumi Sakamoto, an anti-cult lawyer threatening a lawsuit against them, failed; the suit could potentially have bankrupted the group. In the same month, Sakamoto recorded an interview on the Japanese TV station TBS, which then had the interview secretly shown to the group without notifying Sakamoto, intentionally breaking protection of sources. The group then pressured TBS to cancel the broadcast. The following month, Sakamoto, his wife and his child went missing from their Yokohama home. The police were unable to

resolve the case at the time despite some of his colleagues publicly voicing their suspicions surrounding the group. It was not until after the 1995 Tokyo subway attack that they were found to have been murdered and their bodies dumped by Aum members.
- Kaplan and Marshall allege that Aum 'commonly took patients into its hospitals and then forced them to pay exorbitant medical bills'.
- The cult planned assassinations of several individuals critical of the cult, such as the heads of Buddhist sects Soka Gakkai and The Institute for Research in Human Happiness. After cartoonist Yoshinori Kobayashi satirised the cult, he was added to Aum's assassination list. An attempt was made on his life in 1993.
- In July 1993, cult members sprayed copious amounts of liquid containing *Bacillus anthracis* spores from a cooling tower on the roof of Aum Shinrikyo's Tokyo headquarters. However, their plan to cause an anthrax epidemic failed. The attack resulted in a large number of complaints about bad smells but no infections.
- Towards the end of 1993, the cult was covertly manufacturing sarin and, later, VX gas. Aum tested its sarin on sheep at Banjawarn Station, a remote pastoral property in Western Australia, killing twenty-nine sheep. Both sarin and VX were then used in several assassinations (and assassination attempts) in 1994–5.
- On 21 June 1995, Asahara admitted that in January 1994 he ordered the killing of a sect member, Kotaro Ochida, a pharmacist at an Aum hospital. Ochida, who tried to escape, was held down and strangled by another Aum member who was allegedly told that he too would be killed if he did not strangle Ochida.
- On the night of 27 June 1994, the cult carried out a chemical weapons attack against civilians when they released sarin in Matsumoto, Nagano. (See below.)
- In December 1994, Masami Tsuchiya of Aum synthesised 100 to 200 grams of VX, which was used in an attack on three people. Two people were injured and a 28-year-old man was killed – the first fully documented victim of VX. The victim, whom Shoko Asahara suspected was a spy, was attacked early in the morning of 12 December 1994, on the street in Osaka by Tomomitsu Niimi and another Aum member, who sprinkled the nerve agent on his neck. He chased them for about 100 yards (91 m) before collapsing, dying ten days later without coming out of a deep coma. Doctors in the hospital suspected at the time he had been poisoned with an organophosphate pesticide. But the cause of death was established only after cult members arrested for the subway attack in Tokyo confessed to the murder. Ethyl methylphosphonate,

methylphosphonic acid, and diisopropyl-2-(methylthio) ethylamine were later found in the body of the victim.
- In February 1995, several cult members kidnapped Kiyoshi Kariya, a 69-year-old brother of a member who had escaped, on a Tokyo street and took him to a compound in Kamikuishiki near Mount Fuji, where he was murdered. His corpse was destroyed in a microwave-powered incinerator and the remnants disposed of in Lake Kawaguchi. Before Kariya was abducted, he had been receiving threatening phone calls demanding to know the whereabouts of his sister; prudently, he had left a note saying, 'If I disappear, I was abducted by Aum Shinrikyo.'
- According to the testimony of Kenichi Hirose at the Tokyo District Court in 2000, Asahara aimed for Oum to be self-sufficient in copies of the Soviet Union's AK-74 rifle; one rifle was smuggled into Japan, to be studied so that Aum could reverse-engineer and mass-produce the AK-74. On 6 April 1995, police seized AK-74 components and blueprints from a vehicle used by an Aum member.

Police initiated an operation to simultaneously raid cult facilities across Japan in March 1995. Prosecutors alleged Asahara was tipped off about this and that he ordered the Tokyo subway attack to divert police.

The Matsumoto sarin attack

Ten years after its yoga class-bedsit foundation, things had clearly changed, markedly: on the night of 27 June 1994, acolytes of what had transmogrified into a paranoid Japanese doomsday religious cult released sarin nerve agent in a residential area of Matsumoto, Japan, which killed seven and injured 500. The agent was aerosolised sarin released from a converted refrigerator truck in the Kaichi Heights area.

Aum Shinrikyo had two objectives: to attack three judges who were expected to rule against the cult in a lawsuit in a real estate dispute, and to run a practice, testing the efficacy of its sarin – which the cult was manufacturing at one of its facilities – as a weapon of mass murder. The residents of Matsumoto had also angered Aum founder Shoko Asahara by vigorously opposing his plan to set up an office and factory in the south of the city. Opponents of the plan garnered 140,000 signatures on an anti-Aum petition, 70 per cent of Matsumoto's population at the time.

Aum decided to target a three-storey apartment building where the city's judges resided. At 10:40 pm, members used that converted refrigerator truck to release a cloud of sarin, which floated near the home of the judges. The truck's cargo space held 'a heating contraption that had been specifically designed to turn' 12 litres of liquid sarin into an aerosol, and fans to diffuse the aerosol throughout the neighbourhood.

Things took off at 11:30 pm when Matsumoto police received an urgent report from paramedics that multiple casualties were being transported to hospital. The patients were suffering from darkened vision, eye pain, headaches, nausea, diarrhoea, myosis (excessive constriction of the pupil) and numbness in their hands. Some victims described having seen a fog with a pungent and irritating smell floating by. In total, 274 people were treated. Five dead residents were discovered in their apartments, and two died in hospital immediately after admission. An eighth victim, Sumiko Kono, remained in a coma for fourteen years and died in 2008.

The day after the attack, dead fish were found floating in a pond near the scene. The bodies of dogs, birds and a large number of caterpillars were found in the area. Grass and trees had withered. Nearly all of the casualties were discovered within a radius of 150 metres from the centre, near the pond. People close to open windows or in air-conditioned rooms were exposed to the aerosol.

To make matters worse, after the incident, police misguidedly focused their investigation on Yoshiyuki Kōno, whose wife was a victim comatised by the aerosol. Kōno had stored a large amount of pesticide in his home and although it was later proved that sarin cannot be manufactured from pesticides, Keiichi Tsuneishi, a Japanese historian, claimed the nerve agent is synthesisable from organophosphorus pesticides. Kōno was now known in the media as 'the Poison Gas Man'. He subsequently received hate mail, death threats and intense legal pressure. After the truth was out, every major Japanese newspaper apologised to Kōno, including those that had not named him as a suspect. After the Tokyo attack, when the blame was shifted to Aum, Matsumoto's police chief, on behalf of the police department and media, publicly apologised to Kōno. Kōno's wife later awoke from her coma, but recovered neither speech nor body movement and died in 2008.

The defining agent involved in the Tokyo subway attack was sarin; however, as we shall see, drone technology was being deployed around the same time to unleash botulism and Ebola.

Tokyo subway sarin

A second attack, on 20 March 1995, spread sarin through a crowded Tokyo subway from five leaking bags filled with a binary chemical weapon, most closely chemically similar to sarin. The first the passengers knew of this was when they noticed a strong chemical smell similar to paint thinner before feeling stinging fumes in their eyes. This callous attack on five trains was responsible for killing thirteen commuters, seriously injuring fifty-four and affecting 980 more, although some estimates claim as many as 6,000 people were affected by the sarin. Exact numbers are difficult to come by since many victims were fearful and reluctant to come forward. The toxin felled victims in seconds, leaving them choking and vomiting, some blinded and paralysed. Some dead.

After the attacks, it was reported that the cult had adapted a Russian Mil Mi-17 military helicopter from which to spray toxins, a drone for unmanned chemical and biological attacks, and their own strains of botulism. They had also allegedly attempted to obtain the Ebola virus from Zaire. At the cult's headquarters in Kamikuishiki, police found explosives and chemical weapons. Terrifyingly, there were stockpiles of chemicals that could be used for producing enough sarin to kill 4 million people. Police also found laboratories set up to manufacture drugs such as LSD, methamphetamine, and a crude form of truth serum, a safe containing millions of US dollars in cash and gold, and cells, many of which were still occupied by prisoners. During the raids, Aum insisted that the chemicals were for fertilisers.

On 30 March 1995, Takaji Kunimatsu, chief of the National Police Agency, was shot four times near his house in Tokyo, leaving him seriously wounded. While many suspected Aum involvement, the *Sankei Shimbun* reported that dissident Hiroshi Nakamura was suspected of the crime, but nobody has ever been charged.

The next month, Hideo Murai, the head of Aum's Ministry of Science, was stabbed to death outside the cult's Tokyo headquarters in a crowd of about 100 reporters, on camera. The assailant, a Korean member of Yamaguchi-gumi, was arrested and eventually convicted of the murder. Yamaguchi-gumi is one of the largest criminal organisations in the world. According to the National Police Agency, it had 8,200 active members at the end of 2020; the Yamaguchi-gumi are also among the world's wealthiest gangsters, bringing in billions of dollars a year from extortion, gambling, the sex industry, arms trafficking, drug trafficking, real estate and construction kickback schemes. They are also involved in stock market manipulation and internet pornography. This all goes to show the murky environment in which Aum operated and the threat they posed not only to law and order but also to lawlessness and disorder itself.

On the evening of 5 May, a burning paper bag was discovered in a toilet in Tokyo's Shinjuku station. It was revealed to be a hydrogen cyanide device which, had it not been extinguished in time, some say would have released enough gas into the ventilation system to potentially kill 10,000 commuters.

On 4 July, several undetonated cyanide devices were found at other locations in the Tokyo subway.

During this time, numerous cult members were arrested for various offences, but arrests of the most senior members on the charge of the subway gassing remained elusive. In June, an individual with no actual connections to Aum hijacked All Nippon Airways Flight 857, a Boeing 747 bound for Hakodate from Tokyo. The hijacker claimed to be an Aum member in possession of sarin and plastic explosives, but these claims, thankfully, were false.

Asahara was finally found skulking within a wall of one of the cult buildings known as 'The 6th Satian' in the Kamikuishiki complex on 16 May and was arrested. That same day, the cult posted a parcel bomb to the office of Yukio Aoshima, the governor of Tokyo, blowing off the fingers of his secretary's hand. Asahara was initially charged with twenty-three counts of murder and sixteen other offences. This 'trial of the century' ruled that Asahara was guilty of masterminding the attack and sentenced him to death. The indictment was appealed unsuccessfully and a number of senior members accused of participation, such as Masami Tsuchiya, also received death sentences. On 6 July 2018, Asahara and six other Aum Shinrikyo members were executed by hanging.

That was not the end of it, though: at 12:10 am, on New Year's Day 2019, at least nine people were injured (one seriously) when a car was deliberately driven into crowds celebrating the new year on narrow Takeshita Street in Tokyo. Local police reported the arrest of Kazuhiro Kusakabe, the suspected driver, who allegedly admitted to intentionally ramming his vehicle into crowds as a terrorist attack in 'retaliation for an execution'.

The terrorist group disbanded but has since reformed, in January 2000, under the name Aleph, a reference to the first letter of the Hebrew alphabet. It is proscribed in many countries but remains legal in Japan. A June 2005 report by the National Police Agency tells us that Aleph had approximately 1,650 members, of whom 650 lived communally in compounds. The group operated twenty-six facilities in seventeen prefectures, and about 120 residential facilities.

The economic, healthcare and social costs of the attacks were prodigious. They resulted in twenty-one deaths and thousands of hospitalisations and outpatient consultations, a particularly heinous case of scapegoating and vitriolic showcase trial by media.

The global smallpox threat

The World Health Organization declared the disease eradicated in 1979, but some pus samples still remain in laboratories in the Centers for Disease

Control and Prevention in Atlanta, USA, and in the State Research Center of Virology and Biotechnology VECTOR in Koltsovo, Novosibirsk Oblast, Russia. Both are under WHO supervision. The US smallpox stockpile, which includes samples from Britain, Japan and the Netherlands, is stored in liquid nitrogen.

The Guardian reported in 2014: 'A government scientist cleaning out an old storage room at a research centre near Washington made a startling discovery last week – decades-old vials of smallpox packed away and forgotten in a cardboard box.' The virus samples were found in a cold room connecting two laboratories at the National Institutes of Health in Bethesda, Maryland, that has been home to the Food and Drug Administration since 1972. The implications for possible bioterrorism if similar vials exist unrecorded are horrendous.

The Guardian went on to explain: 'The six glass vials of freeze-dried virus were intact and sealed with melted glass, and the virus might have been dead, said officials at the Centers for Disease Control and Prevention.' Smallpox can be lethal even after it is freeze-dried, but the virus usually has to be kept cold to remain alive and lethal. Initially, a CDC official said he believed the vials were stored for many years at room temperature, which would suggest the samples were dead. But FDA officials maintained later that the smallpox was in cold storage for decades.

The Guardian added: 'vials of smallpox were found at the bottom of a freezer in an "Eastern European" country in the 1990s, according to Dr David Heymann, a former World Health Organization official ... [and] professor at the London School of Hygiene and Tropical Medicine.' And then there's the terrifying threat from so-called 'smallpox martyrs'... Simply recruit a suicide volunteer, infect him or her in Baghdad or Homs; have them go through the virus's two-week incubation period until the coughing starts. Then buy him a ticket to London, Paris or Berlin, or any big city. All he has to do is watch the in-flight movie and emit the occasional cough or sneeze.

Should we be worried?

There are a number of forms of terrorism closely linked to bioterrorism; they are:

Ecotage

Closely linked to bioterrorism is ecotage. Ecotage is sabotage carried out for ecological reasons and motives. Here is a time line of some recent ecotage events:

- *c.*1969–85 – ecological activist James F. Phillips, operating covertly under the code name 'The Fox', carried out a series of ecotage actions and subversive campaigns against corporations that were polluting the Fox River in Illinois.
- 1998 – arson of buildings at Vail Mountain in the United States by the Earth Liberation Front (ELF).
- 11 March 1999 – genetically engineered potatoes were uprooted at a Crop and Food research centre in New Zealand.
- 25 December 1999 – in Monmouth, Oregon, fire destroyed the HQ of the Boise Cascade logging company, costing over $1 million ($1.6 million in 2020 dollars). ELF claim responsibility.
- 2001 – members of the ELF were prosecuted for setting off a firebomb that caused $7 million in damage ($11 million in 2020 dollars) at the University of Washington's Center for Urban Horticulture.
- 1 August 2003 – a 206-unit condominium being built in San Diego, California, was burnt down, causing damage in excess of $20 million ($31 million in 2020 dollars). A 12-foot banner at the scene read: 'If you build it, we will burn it.' It was signed: 'The E.L.F.s are mad.'
- 22 August 2003 – arsonists connected with the Earth Liberation Front attacked several car dealerships in east Los Angeles, burning down a warehouse and vandalising over 100 vehicles, most of them SUVs or Hummers (notorious fuel guzzlers) and causing over $1 million in damage ($1.4 million in 2020 dollars).

In 2001, the FBI named the ELF as 'one of the most active extremist elements in the United States', and a 'terrorist threat'.

Ecoterrorism

Ecoterrorism is defined as an act of violence committed in support of environmental causes, against people or property.

The FBI defines ecoterrorism as 'the use or threatened use of violence of a criminal nature against the people guilty of destroying the environment or their property by an environmentally-oriented, subnational group for environmental-political reasons, or aimed at an audience beyond the target, often of a symbolic nature'. The FBI credited ecoterrorists with US $200 million in property damage between 2003 and 2008. A majority of states in the US have introduced laws aimed at penalising ecoterrorism.

An early example comes with the the War of Desmoiselles, or War of the Maidens. This was a series of peasant revolts in Ariège (in Occitanie, south-western France) in response to the new forest codes implemented by the French government in 1827. In 1829, groups of peasant men dressed in women's clothes (to hide their identities) terrorised forest guards and charcoal-makers whom they felt had wrongfully taken their lands to exploit it – this being their main source of income and way of life for generations. The revolts persisted until May 1832. Colonial Algeria typifies the attitude of colonialists in relation to land use. The French confiscated a lot of locally owned land because they believed that the nomads were not using it properly, resulting in a series of battles.

Agroterrorism
Defined as a malicious attempt to disrupt or destroy the agricultural industry and/or food supply system of a population through 'the malicious use of plant or animal pathogens to cause devastating disease in the agricultural sectors'. It is closely related to biological and entomological terrorism.

Chapter 16

The Biowarfare and Bioterror Future

As of now, biowarfare and bioterrorism have claimed few lives when compared with the more 'conventional' forms of warfare and terrorism using bullets and bombs, and, since 9/11, commercial passenger aeroplanes ('We have some planes'). The possibility that the use of infectious agents will cause terror, social, economic, public health and political dislocation, and will result in any number of casualties, remains very real, but at the same time the threat and possible fallout should be kept in proportion and neither overestimated nor sensationalised by the ill informed.

The bad news
- Groups like Aum Shinrikyo have attempted to perfect the complex methods of aerosol dispersal of biological agents. Al-Qaida sought to acquire biological weapons and while many Al-Qaida assets in Afghanistan may have been erased in the past decade, the organisation has been replaced by the Taliban and ISIS, who glory in equally destructive and nefarious tactics inspired by evil ideologies, and can exert increasing expertise.
- Through advances in technological innovation and sophistication of equipment, and the dissemination of technical, ballistic and biochemical knowledge through the Internet and the dark web across the world, the necessary equipment and materials have become cheaper, smaller, and easier to operate, and methods have become easier to carry out.
- In earlier times, what was achieved in an expensive, obtrusive laboratory – openly or surreptitiously – is now feasible by a skilled individual operating in a garage or bedroom, and will be difficult to prevent or detect. Laboratories may have cameras and colleagues looking over your shoulder, as well as established preventive measures in place to protect workers and the environment against inadvertent releases. None of this exists in a private garage or apartment.
- The work done by scientific and medical researchers is fully transparent and accountable (we think) within private companies, public institutions and by various states, and is undertaken and ostensibly applied for beneficial purposes. In the future, it may result in biofuel-producing bacteria, lighting

from luminescent microorganisms, or even biological computers, but there is another side to the coin: by its very binary nature, life sciences technology and advanced technological capabilities executed as a common good could facilitate the development of a biological weapon, including mechanisms for effective dissemination by actors who have no interest in the common good.
- Terrorists in the more unstable parts of the world could conceivably forcibly access the expertise and/or agents generated by a state-directed BW programmes. Civil war, revolution and general lawlessness in countries possessing an active BW programme pose a significant bioterrorist proliferation risk.

The better news
- Incubation periods for the guilty agents vary but they will usually allow for diagnosis and reaction before symptomatic cases flood in and potentially overwhelm health services – the longer the incubation period, the more this applies.
- Unless a multiresistant, highly virulent 'superbug' is disseminated, effective antibiotics are available to combat many bacterial agents.
- Considerable skills, training and expertise remain a requisite for even DIY research and development noted above. The likelihood of lone-wolf individuals successfully producing and disseminating DIY bioscience remains real, but small.
- Technological advances such as networked video cameras and software designed to expose and extrapolate significant intelligence and surveillance information have become powerful tools in counterterrorism, and have sharpened the effectiveness of antiterrorism countermeasures in order to disable or prevent attacks. Technological and surveillance advances have led to an increase in our forensic ability to investigate an incident (or a potential incident) and track down the cause and origins.

Predict, plan, prepare

In 2015, Bill Gates delivered a TED Talk in which he made this prediction:

> If anything kills over 10 million people in the next few decades it's most likely to be a highly infectious virus rather than a war – not missiles but microbes ... we've invested a huge amount in nuclear deterrents but we've actually invested very little in a system to stop an epidemic. We're not ready for the next epidemic.

The Soviets may have got it right when they gave the name Biopreparat (biological preparation) to the sprawling facility that is the engine room of their bioweapons programme. Whether this was sheer serendipity or whether it was meant to convey preparedness to counter hostile biological attack or to launch a biological attack, only time will tell. Nevertheless, either way, all countries need to be prepared for either, or both.

When we received the terrible news, six years after Gates's prediction, towards the end of 2020 that global COVID-19 deaths had exceeded 5 million from 250 million cases, who can say that Gates had got it wrong? He was, of course, alluding to a future natural pandemic involving yet another crowd disease but, as we shall see, his words apply as much to biological warfare and bioterrorism as they do to natural contagion. Back in those oblivious pre-COVID days, barely a few thousand people watched Gates online; today, as we begin to endure the fourth year of the very world he predicted, his talk has been viewed more than 50 million times. Nothing like a rampant global pandemic to focus attention.

Later, in February 2021, with the benefit of COVID-19 experience, Gates was able to qualify and refocus his prediction. In an interview on Derek Muller's YouTube channel Veritasium, Gates pinpointed two real and prominent threats facing today's world: climate change and bioterrorism.

> One is climate change. Every year there would be a death toll even greater than the one we would have in this [COVID-19] pandemic. Also, related to pandemics is something people don't like to talk about much, which is bioterrorism, that somebody who wants to cause damage could engineer a virus. So that means the chance of running into this is more than just the naturally caused epidemics like the current one.

What does the future hold for biowarfare and bioterrorism, and for us, either as active, aggressive agents in, or as unfortunate targets of? We cannot possibly know; all we can do is speculate and hope, just as the ancient Greeks did some 3,000 years ago when the mythical Pandora's box was incautiously thrown open, and to mix that highly symbolic myth with a metaphor: the genie was out of the bottle. However, despite the doomy prognostications of apocalyptic disaster, all was not quite lost to the whole gamut of evil in Cassandra's dystopian future-world for, according to Hesiod in his eighth-century BC *Works and Days* (90), in the bottom of that unpropitious box floundered something called Hope. There is hope that we can avert the cataclysm, but it certainly will not happen if we fail to activate and facilitate it: we need to plan and we need to start planning now – both for the next COVID-19 and for the real possibility of biowar or acts of bioterrorism and biocrime. Our inclination to stand idly by as climate change inexorably remodels our world needs to stop and we need to be alert to avert or at least mitigate a potential global biological disaster.

As this book illustrates, despite its 111,000 or so words spanning milennia, outbreaks of biological warfare and acts of bioterrorism have so far been, thankfully, rare. While one death or casualty is of course one too many, the only significant deployment of a biological agent resulting in substantial loss of life was by Japan against the Chinese in the 1940s. Despite frighteningly massive strides in BW science and technology, the only subsequent uses have resulted in mercifully few casualties.

Some scientists and historians argue that it is inevitable that biowarfare will proliferate due to continuing industrial-scale advances in the biological sciences at the laboratory level, the globalisation of biological skills and technology, and the growing accessibility of viable technology. They argue that this will inevitably result in more and more lethal use of biological weapons. Increasing religious radicalisation and maybe growing impatience with capitalism, inexorable climate change and increasing poverty combined with inflammatory ideologies cannot be helping. Capabilities once restricted to the Soviet Union/Russia and the United States might be increasingly accessible even to 'nonstate actors' and lone-wolf bedsit activists in the future.

There is another side to this coin, however. Others remain unconvinced of this one-way road to doom, arguing that biological weapons are harder to develop and employ than many concede. However, if compelling proof were needed that the richer countries of the world, those with most to lose, were actively pursuing the research and development of biological weaponry incorporating the very latest artificial intelligence then go no further than 'the super soldier'.

ISIS today

Throughout 2022, US Central Command (CENTCOM) and partner forces conducted hundreds of operations against the Islamic State in Iraq and Syria (ISIS). These operations degraded ISIS and removed a cadre of senior leaders from the battlefield, to include the emir of ISIS and dozens of regional leaders as well as hundreds of fighters. All these operations were part of the mission to degrade the terror group's ability to direct and inspire destabilising attacks in the region and globally, to include against the US homeland.

The Biowarfare and Bioterror Future   251

During calendar year 2022, CENTCOM conducted 313 total operations against ISIS in Iraq and Syria.
Source: CENTCOM Press release Dec. 29, 2022

Meet the super soldier

A December 2020 report in *The Times* apprised us that 'Beijing [is] making genetically enhanced troops, says US'. China's apparent success in creating the super soldier, 'a genetically perfected warrior aided by advanced bionic technologies', is causing some alarm here in the West. Writing in the *Wall Street Journal*, John Ratcliffe, director of US National Intelligence, reveals that 'China has even conducted human testing on members of the People's Liberation Army in the hope of developing soldiers with biologically enhanced capabilities.' In other words, advanced medical technologies that can manipulate genes to enhance human performance – a technique known as CRISPR. CRISPR stands for Clustered Regularly Interspaced Short Palindromic Repeats, which are the hallmark of a bacterial defence system that forms the basis for CRISPR-Cas9 genome editing technology.

The China Aerospace Science and Industry Corporation has delivered the first carbon fibre exoskeletons; they reduced strains on the body in high exertion environments, weigh 9 pounds and can save 5–10 per cent of a soldier's energy expended walking, climbing and carrying equipment. *Jane's Defence Weekly* anticipates they will be deployed on border patrols in the Himalayas. It seems that the Chinese soldier's long march will get even longer. Beijing called the article a 'miscellany of lies'.

Not to be outdone, the Pentagon is researching the viability of developing helmets that stimulate the brain to acquire new skills more quickly and to relay a soldier's thoughts. If the helmet makes the soldier a better and more deadly soldier, a super special force, then all well and good, so long as he/she/it is on our side. However, I'm less enthusiastic about tuning in to a soldier's thoughts ...

In February 2020, the BBC revealed in an article called 'The Myth and Reality of the Super Soldier' [https://www.bbc.co.uk/news/world-55905354] that:

The French armed forces have been given the go-ahead to start research on developing 'enhanced soldiers'. A report laid out conditions under which work on implants and other technologies designed to improve battlefield performance should be carried out in the future. The report stresses that other nations are exploring such possibilities, and that France must keep up. ... 'Human beings have long sought ways to increase their physical or cognitive abilities in order to fight wars,' it warned. 'Possible advances could ultimately lead to capacity enhancements being introduced into soldiers' bodies.'

The report mentioned research on implants that could 'improve cerebral capacity' or help soldiers tell enemy from ally. These could also allow commanders to locate them or read their vital signs from a distance'.

What the experts say:

Next-Generation Biowarfare: Small in Scale, Sensational in Nature

The character of biological warfare is currently undergoing a substantial change. This change derives from two parallel developments: one in society, the other in science. First, biological security threats are moving from the realm of weapons of mass destruction to the domain of information warfare, where small-scale, targeted attacks may still have a massive psychological impact. The COVID-19 pandemic has shown us how effectively fears of infection can close down societies, sow mistrust among allies, and create political turmoil. Future biological wars may use the same dynamics to inflict shock and confusion upon the enemy by the mere threat of mass casualties, thereby circumventing several previous limitations of biological warfare. Second, rapid developments in the field of synthetic biology may broaden the repertoire of bioweapons, enabling tactical versatility and more precise attacks. Preparedness to defend against biological attacks must keep pace with these developments, taking into account not only defense against disinformation but also the need to rapidly mobilise resources at the front line of molecular biology. Better preparedness calls for closer collaboration between frontline civilian scientists and national security establishments to build rapidly scalable networks of expertise and infrastructure for medical intelligence. From Weapons of Mass Destruction to Weapons of Mass Disruption.

'Next-Generation Biowarfare: Small in Scale, Sensational in Nature?',
David Gisselsson, published online 22 April 2022

The future of biological warfare

The realisation that a handful of envelopes containing *B. anthracis* in 2001 was sufficient to cause widespread panic, and precipitated the first evacuation of the houses of the US government since the war of 1812, provided a clear demonstration of the power of cheap biological weapons. In an age of terrorism, biological weapons are perfectly suited for asymmetric warfare where the relatively low costs of producing such weapons combined with their potential for amplification through communicability have a disproportionately strong effect on targeted populations. Consequently, biological weapons are likely to remain very attractive to terrorists and fringe groups like millennial sects. Thus the near horizon is likely to witness continued concern about low-intensity use of biological weapons fashioned around known pathogenic microbes such as *Salmonella* spp. and *B. anthracis*, which have already been used in terrorism.

'The future of biological warfare', Arturo Casadevall, *Microb Biotechnol*, Volume 5(5), September 2012

Facing the future of bioterrorism

Greater access to cheap but powerful biotechnology tools – and a reduced need for expertise in operating those tools – is also making it easier for malicious actors to utilise that technology for ill. Terrorist groups could use synthetic biology to craft bioweapons, using data to manufacture dangerous pathogens or modifying easily accessible pathogens to make them more virulent. At present, there are still some barriers to entry that prevent such actors from operating with free reign, as widespread access to certain pathogens, tools and data is still limited. But these barriers will only continue to recede over the next decade.

'Facing the future of bioterrorism', Barry Pavel, Atlantic Council, 7 September 2021

The history of biological warfare

Human experimentation, modern nightmares and lone madmen in the twentieth century.

During the past century, more than 500 million people died of infectious diseases. Several tens of thousands of these deaths were due to the deliberate release of pathogens or toxins, mostly by the Japanese during their attacks on China during the Second World War. Two international treaties outlawed biological weapons in 1925 and 1972, but they have largely failed to stop countries from conducting offensive weapons research and large-scale production of biological weapons. And as our knowledge of the biology of disease-causing agents – viruses, bacteria and toxins – increases, it is legitimate to fear that modified pathogens could constitute devastating agents for biological warfare.

'The history of biological warfare', Friedrich Frischknecht, EMBO Rep., June 2003, 4(Suppl 1): S47–S52

Epilogue

The Illegal 2022 Russian Invasion of Ukraine

In February 2022, Russian forces, as widely predicted, crossed their border with Ukraine and began what is an illegal occupation of Ukrainian sovereign territory. It took less than a month for the invaders to launch a concerted but groundless 2022–3 disinformation campaign with support from China, claiming that public health facilities in Ukraine are 'secret US-funded biolabs' purportedly developing biological weapons. The claim was substantiated by China's Ministry of Foreign Affairs and Chinese state media. It was also promoted by QAnon and gained zealous support among far-right groups in the US.

Chatham House commented:

> Certainly the use of disinformation around chemical and biological weapons appears to be part of a wider information strategy to discredit Ukraine and justify the Russian invasion by alleging a perceived existential threat, particularly for a domestic Russian audience.
>
> Chatham House, March 2022

11 March saw Russia call a meeting of the UN to discuss the allegations, which Reuters described as an attempt to re-assert the unproven allegations without evidence. The UN responded that there was no evidence of a Ukraine biological weapons programme, while the United States and its allies, raising the stakes, accused Russia of spreading the claim as a false flag prelude to Russia potentially launching biological or chemical attacks.

In July 2022, things entered fantasy world when two Russian State Duma members claimed that a biolabs commission investigation found that Ukraine had administered drugs to its soldiers that 'completely neutralize the last traces of human consciousness and turn them into the most cruel and deadly monsters', and that this was evidence that 'this system for the control and creation of a cruel murder machine was implemented under the management of the United States'.

Monkeypox

On 21 August 2022, Foreign Policy.com ran an article entitled 'Kremlin Claims Monkeypox Could Be a Secret US Bioweapon', in which Ivana Stradner reports that the recent monkeypox outbreak 'was engineered by US military biological laboratories'. As it happened, the 2021 Munich Security Conference, a panel of experts – including officials from the United States and China – discussed a hypothetical monkeypox outbreak to understand how to reduce high-consequence biological threats. The panel's hypothetical outbreak, which projected a massive 271 million fatalities, was set for May 2022. The real outbreak, it turns out, began in May as well. The head of Russia's defence ministry's radiation, chemical, and biological defence troops, Igor Kirillov, implied that monkeypox could have originated in a US-funded Nigerian biolab.

This, of course, meshes quite nicely with previous attempts by Russia to disseminate false bioweapons narratives. In the Cold War, the KGB launched Operation Denver, a worldwide disinformation campaign pointing the finger at the US government for synthesising HIV. Specifically, the KGB successfully spread the narrative that the CIA was using AIDS to target and kill Black Americans and Africans. Another KGB disinformation campaign successfully spread the narrative that the United States, in league with South Africa and Israel, had developed 'ethnic weapons' engineered to kill only Arabs and Africans. Before monkeypox, 'Russian Ambassador to the United Nations Vassily Nebenzia accused Ukraine and the United States of a plot to use migratory birds and bats to spread pathogens. Nebenzia also recycled the KGB's "ethnic weapons" canard, accusing the US Defense Department of collecting Russian genetic information to develop "bioagents capable of selectively targeting different ethnic populations".'

Appendix

Arms Treaties

Arms treaties are important. They set standards of international behavior regarding the acquisition of and use of weapons of mass destruction. But they are almost invariably ignored when countries believe their natural security is at stake.

Ken Alibek, *Biohazard*

In 1921, three years after the First World War, the Allies wanted to reaffirm the Treaty of Versailles, and in 1922, the United States introduced the Treaty Relating to the Use of Submarines and Noxious Gases in Warfare at the Washington Naval Conference. Four of the war victors, the United States, the United Kingdom, the Kingdom of Italy and the Empire of Japan, gave consent to ratification, but it failed to enter into force as the French Third Republic objected to the submarine provisions of the treaty. At the 1925 Geneva Conference for the Supervision of the International Traffic in Arms, the French suggested a protocol for non-use of poisonous gases. The Second Polish Republic suggested the addition of bacteriological weapons. It was signed on 17 June.

The Geneva Protocol of 1925

In 1924, a subcommittee of the Temporary Mixed Commission of the League of Nations, the Temporary Mixed Commission on Armaments was set up as a committee of eminent figures formed by the League of Nations to consider the problem of international disarmament in its widest aspects and to suggest potential initiatives, plans and solutions. The 'Protocol for the Prohibition of the Use in War of Asphyxiating, Poisonous or Other Gases and of Bacteriological Methods of Warfare', the Geneva Protocol, was signed on 17 June 1925. It came into force on 8 February 1928.

The Protocol is a treaty prohibiting the use of chemical and biological weapons in international armed conflicts. It prohibits the use of 'asphyxiating, poisonous or other gases, and of all analogous liquids, materials or devices' and 'bacteriological methods of warfare'. It is silent about production, storage or transfer. Later treaties did cover these aspects – the 1972 Biological Weapons Convention (BWC) and the 1993 Chemical Weapons Convention (CWC).

The Geneva Protocol 1925 is currently signed by sixty-five of 121 states. The WHO identified the threat of biological and chemical warfare officially in the midst of the Vietnam War and Cold War, after UN resolution 2162B (XXI) was adopted in 1967, condemning all actions contrary to the Geneva Protocol. This was updated in 2004 into WHO guidance 'Public health response to biological and chemical weapons' and is mainly concerned with the effects of pathogens on human beings.

Wednesday, 24 October 1945 saw the official founding of the United Nations: negotiations to prohibit biological weapons then became part of the agenda of the international community. By 1960, the United States, and other countries, possessed a large collection of bioweapons, including many types of bacteria, fungi and toxins. During the late 1960s, there was growing concern around the world about the use of biological weapons and the ineffectiveness of the Geneva Protocol. In 1968, the UK submitted a proposal to the Committee on Disarmament of the United Nations, intended to prohibit the development, production and stockpiling of biological agents. This proposal also outlined the need for inspections for alleged violators. Several months later, the Warsaw Pact nations submitted a similar proposal.

In 1969, President Nixon ended and dismantled the US bioweapons programme. This 'Statement on Chemical and Biological Defense Policies and Programs' was a speech delivered on 25 November that year, in which Nixon announced the end of the US offensive biological weapons programme and reaffirmed a no-first-use policy for chemical weapons. The statement excluded toxins, herbicides and riot-control agents as they were not chemical and biological weapons, though herbicides and toxins were both later banned. It also called for destruction of the US arsenal. The United States also undertook never to use any biological or toxic weapons under any circumstances. Proponents argued that a biological attack would likely inflict a great toll on civilian populations while remaining largely militarily ineffective. 'The United States shall renounce the use of lethal biological agents and weapons, and all other methods of biological warfare. The United States will confine its biological research to defensive measures such as immunization and safety measures.' (Statement issued by President Nixon, 25 November 1969, *Foreign Relations, 1969–1976*, Vol. E-2, Documents on Arms Control, 1969–1972.)

Under pressure from the WHO, the new Convention on the Prohibition of the Development, Production and Stockpiling of Bacteriological (Biological) and Toxin Weapons and on their Destruction (better known as BWC) was signed in 1972 by the US, UK and Soviet governments, as well as by more than 100 other nations. The treaty's preamble states that the use of biological weapons would be 'repugnant to the conscience of mankind'. Coming into force in March 1975, and having been continuously reviewed since, it prohibits:

(i) the possession of biological agents except for 'prophylactic, protective, or other peaceful purposes';
(ii) the development of technologies intended for the dispersal of biological agents for offensive military purposes;
(iii) [and] mandates the destruction of existing stocks.

It was the first multilateral disarmament treaty to ban the production of an entire category of weapons of mass destruction.

Although the treaty does not define or specify what constitutes a biological weapon, it soon became clear that the agreement proscribes the possession of any weapon that incorporates any pathogenic microorganism or poison of biological origin, including those developed using science that did not exist at the time the treaty was negotiated.

The Soviet Union had no intention ever to respect the treaty. Its efforts to develop biological weapons accelerated after the BWC entered into force. Because the BWC lacks verification procedures, the treaty's signatories tried to negotiate a protocol to provide them during the 1990s. The attempt failed. While the United States is often blamed, Russia and the members of the Non-Aligned Movement also undermined the negotiations. US opposition reflected widely held views in Washington that the proposed agreement was fatally flawed, unlikely as it was to uncover treaty violations or otherwise enhance confidence in treaty compliance.

Review conferences, held every five years since the treaty entered into force, provide an opportunity for the international community to reaffirm its continued importance. At those meetings, the parties have also concurred that the agreement comprehensively applies to new scientific developments.

At the Fifth BWC Review Conference in 2001, the United States charged four BWC States Parties – Iran, Iraq, Libya and North Korea – and one signatory, Syria, with operating covert biological weapons programmes. Moreover, a 2019 report from the US Department of State concluded that North Korea 'has an offensive biological weapons program and is in violation of its obligations under Articles I and II of the BWC' and that Iran 'has not abandoned its ... development of biological agents and toxins for offensive purposes'.

As of September 2021, 183 states have become party to the treaty. Four additional states have signed but not ratified the treaty, and another ten states have neither signed nor acceded to the treaty.

The USA Patriot Act

Commonly known as the Patriot Act, the formal name of the statute is the Uniting and Strengthening America by Providing Appropriate Tools Required to Intercept and Obstruct Terrorism (USA PATRIOT) Act of 2001. The Patriot Act was enacted following the September 11 attacks and the 2001 anthrax attacks, with the stated goal of dramatically tightening US national security, particularly as it related to foreign terrorism.

Title VIII Sec. 817 amends the biological weapons statute to define the use of a biological agent, toxin or delivery system as a weapon, other than when it is used for 'prophylactic, protective, bona fide research, or other peaceful purposes'. Penalties for anyone who cannot prove reasonably that they are using a biological agent, toxin or delivery system for these purposes are ten years' imprisonment, a fine, or both.

Sources and Bibliography

Introduction
Abdulkadir, Gunduz, 2011, 'The Honey, The Poison, The Weapon', *Wilderness and Environmental Medicine*, 22, 182–184
Alibek, K., 1999, *Biohazard*, New York
Ansari, I, 2020, 'Deliberate release: Plague – A review', *J Biosaf Biosecur* 2(1): 10–22
Arnon, S.S., 2001, 'Botulinum toxin as a biological weapon: medical and public health management'. *JAMA*, 2001; 285 (8):1059–1070
Barnaby, Wendy, 1999, *The Plague Makers: The Secret World of Biological Warfare*, Frog Ltd, 1999
Barras V., 2014, 'History of biological warfare and bioterrorism', *Clin Microbiol Infect*, 20(6): 497–502
Brainard, J., 2016, 'Contextual Factors Among Indiscriminate or Large Attacks on Food or Water Supplies', 1946–2015, *Health Security*, 14(1): 19–28
Carus, W.S., 2015, 'The history of biological weapons use: what we know and what we don't', *Health Security*, 13(4): 219–255
Chrystal, Paul, 2021, *A History of the World in 100 Pandemics, Plagues and Epidemics*, Barnsley
Cole, Leonard A., 1996, *The Eleventh Plague: The Politics of Biological and Chemical Warfare*, Basingstoke
Councell, Clara E., 1941, 'War and Infectious Disease', *Public Health Reports (1896–1970)*, 56, No. 12 (1941): 547–73
Cox, Rory, 2018, 'The Ethics of War up to Thomas Aquinas' in (eds. Lazar & Frowe) *The Oxford Handbook of Ethics of War*, Oxford
Croddy, Eric, 2005, *Weapons of Mass Destruction: An Encyclopedia of Worldwide Policy, Technology, and History*, ABC-CLIO
Dembek, Zygmunt (ed.), 2007, *Medical Aspects of Biological Warfare*, Washington, DC: Borden Institute
Demircan A., 2009, 'Mad honey sex: therapeutic misadventures from an ancient biological weapon', *Annals of Emergency Medicine*, 54 (6): 824–9
Dennis D.T., 2001, 'Tularemia as a biological weapon: medical and public health management', *JAMA*, 285 (21): 2763–73
Eckart, Wolfgang Uwe, (2006), *Man, Medicine, and the State: The Human Body as an Object of Government Sponsored Medical Research in the 20th Century*, Franz Steiner Verlag
Eitzen, Edward M., 1997, *Medical Aspects of Chemical and Biological Warfare* (PDF), United States Government Printing Office
Eneh, O.C., 2012, 'Biological weapons – agents for life and environmental destruction', *Res J Environ Toxicol*, 2012; 6, 65–87
Friedlander, A.M., 1997, 'Anthrax', in Sidell, F.R., ed., *Medical Aspects of Chemical and Biological Warfare*, Falls Church, VA: Office of the Surgeon General (Army); 467–478
Frischknecht, F. 2003, 'The history of biological warfare human experimentation, modern nightmares and lone madmen in the twentieth century', *EMBO Rep*. 2003; 4, available at: http://www.ncbi.nlm.nih.gov/pmc/articles/PMC1326439

Harris, Robert & Paxman, Jeremy, 2002, *A Higher Form of Killing: The Secret History of Chemical and Biological Warfare*, London
Henderson, D.A., 'Smallpox as a biological weapon: medical and public health management', *JAMA*, 1999, Vol. 281, 2127–37
Inglesby, T.V., 1999, 'Anthrax as a biological weapon: medical and public health management', *JAMA*, 281, 1735–45
Inglesby, T.V., 2000, 'Plague as a biological weapon: medical and public health management', Working Group on Civilian Biodefense, *JAMA*, 283(17):2281–2290
Kirby, Reid, 'Using the flea as weapon' (web version via findarticles.com), *Army Chemical Review*, July 2005, accessed 11 November 2021
Lee, M.R., 2009, 'The history of ergot of rye (Claviceps purpurea) I: from antiquity to 1900', *J. Royal College Physicians of Edinburgh*, 39: 179–184
Lockwood, J.A., 2009, *Six-legged Soldiers: Insects as Weapons of War, Terror, and Torture*, Oxford
Mangold, Tom, 1999, *Plague Wars: a true story of biological warfare*, London
Maves, R.C., 2020, 'Zoonotic Infections and Biowarfare Agents in Critical Care: Anthrax, Plague, and Tularemia', in Hidalgo, J., (ed.) *Highly Infectious Diseases in Critical Care*, Heidelberg
Maynard, R.M. & Tetley, T.D., 'Bioterrorism: the lung under attack', *Thorax*, 2004; 59: 188–189
Mayor, Adrienne, 2014, 'Animals in Warfare', in Campbell, Gordon Lindsay (ed.), *The Oxford Handbook of Animals in Classical Thought and Life*, Oxford, 292–293
Orent, Wendy, 2004, *Plague, The Mysterious Past and Terrifying Future of the World's Most Dangerous Disease*, New York
Patrick, William C., 1994, 'Biological Warfare: An Overview', in *Director's Series on Proliferation*, Livermore, California: Lawrence Livermore National Laboratory
Pita, René, 2010, 'Anthrax as a Biological Weapon: From World War I to the Amerithrax Investigation', *International Journal of Intelligence and Counter Intelligence*, 23:1, 61–103
Pohanka, M., 2020, 'Bacillus anthracis as a biological warfare agent: infection, diagnosis and countermeasures', *Bratisl Lek Listy*, 121(3):175–181
Poupart, J.A., 1992, 'History of biological warfare: catapults to capsomeres', *Ann NY Acad Sci.* 666: 9–20
Riedel, S., 2005, 'Anthrax: a continuing concern in the era of bioterrorism', *Proc (Bayl Univ Med Cent)*. 18(3):234–43
Robertson, A.G., 1995, 'From asps to allegations: biological warfare in history', *Mil Med*, 1995; 160: 369–373
Sidell, Frederick, *Jane's Chem-Bio Handbook*, 2005, Second Edition, Jane's Information Group
Sotos, J.G., 2001, 'Botulinum toxin in biowarfare', *JAMA*, 285(21):2716
Tansey, T., 2014, 'Typhus and tyranny', *Nature*, 511(7509), 291
Van Huis, A., 2021, 'Cultural aspects of ants, bees and wasps, and their products in sub-Saharan Africa', *Int J Trop Insect Sci* 41, 2223–2235
Van Zandt, Kristopher E., 2013, 'Glanders: an overview of infection in humans', *Orphanet Journal of Rare Diseases*, 8: 131
Whitby, Simon M., 2002, *Biological Warfare Against Crops*, Basingstoke

1. Sumerians, Hittites, Assyrians and Scythians

Anglim, Simon, 2003, *Fighting Techniques of the Ancient World (3000 BC to 500 AD): Equipment, Combat Skills, and Tactics*, Dunne Books
Bradford, Alfred S., 2001, *With Arrow, Sword, and Spear: A History of Warfare in the Ancient World*, Praeger Publishing

Drews, Robert, 1995, *The End of the Bronze Age: changes in warfare and the catastrophe c.1200 BC*, Princeton University Press
Ellis, John, 2004, *Cavalry: The History of Mounted Warfare*, Barnsley
Keegan, John, *A History of Warfare*, London, 1993
Kelhoffer, J.A., 2005, 'John the Baptist's "Wild Honey" and "Honey" in Antiquity', *Greek, Roman, and Byzantine Studies* 45: 59–73
Kern, Paul Bentley, 1999, *Ancient Siege Warfare*, Indiana University Press, 1999
Khamsi, Roxanne, 2007, 'Were "cursed" rams the first biological weapons?', *New Scientist*, 26 November 2007
Kuznetsov, P.F., 2006, 'The emergence of Bronze Age chariots in eastern Europe', *Antiquity*, 80 (309): 638–45
Littauer, M.A., 1979, 'Wheeled vehicles and ridden animals in the ancient Near East', Leiden
Lorenzi, Rossella, 2007, 'Killer Donkeys were First Bioweapon', *Discovery News*, 3 December 2007
Martín-Serradilla, J.I., 2008, 'Was the "Hittite plague" an epidemic of tularemia?', *Med Hypotheses* 71(1):154–5
Mayor, Adrienne, 2009, *Greek Fire, Poison Arrows and Scorpion Bombs: Biological & Chemical Warfare in the Ancient World*, New York
Sidnell, P., 2006, *Warhorse: Cavalry in Ancient Warfare*, London
Trevisanato, S.I., 2004, 'Did an epidemic of tularemia in Ancient Egypt affect the course of world history?', *Med Hypotheses* 63(5): 905–10
Trevisanato, S.I., 2007, 'The "Hittite plague", an epidemic of tularemia and the first record of biological warfare', *Med Hypotheses*, 69(6): 1371–4

2. Ancient Greeks: Myth and History

Camp, J.M., 1977, 'The Water Supply of Ancient Athens from 3000 to 86 BC', Ph.D dissertation, Princeton University
Cartledge, Paul, 2020, *Thebes: The Forgotten City of Ancient Greece*, London
Gaebel, Robert E. (2004), *Cavalry Operations in the Ancient Greek World*, Norman, OK
Gantz, Timothy, 1993, *Early Greek Myth: A Guide to Literary and Artistic Sources*, Baltimore, MD
Gregory, Raymond, 2010, *The Greco-Roman Roots of the Western Just War Tradition*, London
Grmek, Mirko, D., 1983, *Diseases in the Ancient Greek World*, Baltimore
Harden, A., 2013, *Animals in the Classical World: Ethical Perspectives from Greek and Roman Texts*, Springer
Kousoulis, A.A., 2012, 'The plague of Thebes, a historical epidemic in Sophocles' Oedipus Rex', *Emerg Infect Dis*. 18(1):153–7
Neville, James W., 1977, 'Herodotus on the Trojan War', *Greece & Rome* 24, 1: 3–12.
O'Driscoll, Cian, 2015, 'Rewriting the Just War Tradition: Just War in Classical Greek Political Thought and Practice', *International Studies Quarterly*
Papagrigorakis, M.J., 2013, 'The Plague of Athens: an ancient act of bioterrorism?', *Biosecur Bioterror*. 11(3):228–9
Powell, Corrin, 2013, 'A Philological, Epidemiological, and Clinical Analysis of the Plague of Athens' (2013), Senior Honors Projects, 22, http://collected.jcu.edu/honorspapers/22
Ross, Ronald, 1906, 'Malaria in Greece', *Jnl Trop.Med*. 9, 341–7
Scott, J.A., 1924, 'The Use of Poisoned Arrows in the Odyssey', *Classical Journal* 240–1
Smith, Christine A., 'Plague in the Ancient World: A Study from Thucydides to Justinian', *The Loyola University History Department Student Historical Journal* 28, 1996–1997
Sutherland, Caroline, 2001, 'Archery in the Homeric Epics', *Classics Ireland* 8 111-20

3. Biological Warfare in the Bible

Cunningham, Andrew, 2000, *The Four Horsemen of the Apocalypse: Religion, War, Famine and Death in Reformation Europe*, Cambridge

Ehrenkranz, N. Joel, 2008, 'Origin of the Old Testament Plagues: Explications and Implications', *Yale J Biol Med*. 81(1): 31–42

Freemon, Frank R., 2005, 'Bubonic plague in the Book of Samuel', *J R Soc Med*, 2005 Sep, 98(9): 436

Jones, Lori & Nevell, Richard, 2016, 'Plagued by Doubt and Viral Misinformation: The Need for Evidence-based Use of Historical Disease Images', in *The Lancet*: Infectious Diseases[1], volume 16, issue 10, 235–240

Marr, J.S., 1996, 'An epidemiologic analysis of the ten plagues of Egypt', Caduceus (Springfield, Ill.), 12: 7–24

Neufeld, Edward, 1980, 'Insects as Warfare Agents in the Ancient Near East (Ex. 23:28; Deut. 7:20; Josh. 24:12; Isa. 7:18-20)', *Orientalia*, NOVA SERIES, 49, No. 1, 30–57

Sabbatani, S., 2010, 'The plague of the Philistines and other pestilences in the Ancient World: exploring relations between the religious-literary tradition, artistic evidence and scientific proof', *Infez Med*, 18:199–207

Trevisanato, S.I., 2005, *The Plagues of Egypt: Archaeology, History, and Science Look at the Bible*, Georgia Press

Trevisanato, S.I., 2005, 'Ancient Egyptian doctors and the nature of the biblical plagues', *Medical Hypotheses*, 65: 811–813

4. Rome and her Enemies

Chadwick, Nora, 1958, 'Scela Mum Meic Datho: The Story of Mac Datho's Pig', *Scottish Gaelic Studies*, 8: 130–45

Dawson, A. 'Hannibal and Chemical Warfare', *The Classical Journal*, 63, No. 3 (1967): 117–25

Fears, J.R., 2004, 'The plague under Marcus Aurelius and the decline and fall of the Roman Empire', *Infect Dis Clin North Am*, 2004, 18(1): 65–77

Green, M., 1992, *Animals in Celtic Life and Myth*, London

Mayor, Adrienne, 2009, *Poison King: The Life and Legend of Mithridates the Great, Rome's Deadliest Foe*, Princeton

Meyer, Kuno, ed., 1894, 'The Story of Mac Dáthó's Pig and Hound', Hibernica Minora, Anecdota Oxoniensia: Mediaeval and Modern Series 4: Part 8, Oxford: pp. 51–64

Sabbatani, S., 2009, 'The antonine plague and the decline of the Roman Empire', *Infez Med*, 17(4): 261–275

Scheidel, Walter, 2009, 'Disease and Death in the Ancient City of Rome', Princeton/Stanford Working Papers in Classics

5. The Middle Ages

Derbes, V.J., 1966, 'De Mussis and the great plague of 1348. A forgotten episode of bacteriological warfare', *JAMA*, 196:59–62

Jones, David E., 2007, *Poison Arrows: North American Indian Hunting and Warfare*, University of Texas Press

Voigtländer, N., 2012, 'Persecution Perpetuated: The Medieval Origins of Anti-Semitic Violence in Nazi Germany', *The Quarterly Journal of Economics*, 127(3): 1339–1392

Wheelis, M., 'Biological warfare at the 1346 Siege of Caffa', *Emerg Infect Dis*. 2002, 8 (9): 971–975

6. The Seventeenth to Nineteenth Centuries

Carus, W.S., 2016, 'Biological warfare in the 17th century', *Emerg Infect Dis*, 2016

Conway, Stephen, 1986, 'To Subdue America: British Army Officers and the Conduct of the Revolutionary War', *The William and Mary Quarterly*, 43, No. 3, 78

Dixon, David, 2005, *Never Come to Peace Again: Pontiac's Uprising and the Fate of the British Empire in North America*, Norman, OK

Dowd, Gregory Evans, 2002, *War under Heaven: Pontiac, the Indian Nations, & the British Empire*, Baltimore

Fenn, Elizabeth A., 2002, 'Biological Warfare in Eighteenth-Century North America: Beyond Jeffery Amherst', *Journal of American History*, 86, No. 4: 133–4

Finzsch, Norbert, 2008, 'Extirpate or remove that vermine: genocide, biological warfare and settler imperialism in the eighteenth and nineteenth centuries', *Journal of Genocide Research*, 10 (2): 215–232

Jacobs, Wilbur R., 1972, *'Pontiac's War – A Conspiracy?': Dispossessing the American Indian: Indians and Whites on the Colonial Frontier*, New York

Knollenberg, Bernhard, 1954, 'General Amherst and Germ Warfare', *Mississippi Valley Historical Review*, 41 (3): 489–494

Mayor, Adrienne, 1995, 'The Nessus Shirt in the New World: Smallpox Blankets in History and Legend', *The Journal of American Folklore*, 108 (427) 54–77

Mear, C., 'The origin of the smallpox in Sydney in 1789', *Journal of the Royal Australian Historical Society*, 94 (1): 1–22

Ranlet, Philip, 2000, 'The British, the Indians, and Smallpox: What Actually Happened at Fort Pitt in 1763?', *Pennsylvania History: A Journal of Mid-Atlantic Studies*, 67 (3), 427–441

Thalassinou, E., 2015, 'Biological warfare plan in the 17th century – the Siege of Candia, 1648–1669', *Emerg Infect Dis.*, 21(12): 2148–2153

Ua hÉaluighthe, Diarmuid, 1952, 'St Gobnet of Ballyvourney', *Journal of the Cork Historical and Archaeological Society*, 57: 43–61

Warren, Christopher, 2013, 'Smallpox at Sydney Cove – Who, When, Why', *Journal of Australian Studies*, 38: 68–86

Wheelis M., 1999, 'Biological and toxin weapons: research, development and use from the Middle Ages to 1945', in Geissler E. (ed.), SIPRI Chemical & Biological Warfare Studies, Oxford, 8–34

7. The First World War

Anderson, Ross, 2001, 'The Battle of Tanga, 2–5 November 1914', *War in History*, 8, No. 3: 294–322

Anderson, Ross, 2002, *The Battle of Tanga 1914*, Stroud

Avery, D., 1999, 'Canadian biological and toxin warfare research, development and planning, 1925–1945', in *Biological and toxin weapons: research, development, and use from the Middle Ages to 1945*, Oxford

Bausum, Ann, 2014, 'Sergeant Stubby: How a Stray Dog and His Best Friend Helped Win World War I and Stole the Heart of a Nation' (print), Washington, D.C: National Geographic

Carter, G.B., 1999, 'British biological warfare and biological defence, 1925–1945', in *Biological and toxin weapons: research, development, and use from the Middle Ages to 1945*, Oxford

Cummins, Bryan, 2003, *Colonel Richardson's Airedales: The Making of the British War Dog School, 1900–1918*, Alberta

Kramer, Alan, 2007, *Dynamic of destruction: Culture and mass killing in the First World War*, Oxford

8. The Second World War

Allen, Arthur, 2015, *The Fantastic Laboratory of Dr Weigl: How Two Brave Scientists Battled Typhus and Sabotaged the Nazis*, London

Bernstein, B.J., 1988, 'America's biological warfare program in the Second World War', *J Strateg Stud.*, 11(3): 292–317

Clarke, Carter W., 1933, 'Signal Corps Pigeons', *The Military Engineer*, 25, 133–38

Corera, Gordon, 2019, *The Secret Pigeon Service: Operation Columba, Resistance and the Struggle to Liberate Europe*, New York

Couffer, Jack, 1992, *Bat Bomb: World War II's Other Secret Weapon*, University of Texas Press

Croddy, E., 2001, 'Tularemia, Biological Warfare, and the Battle for Stalingrad (1942-1943)', *Military Medicine*, 166 (10): 837–838

Garrett, Benjamin C., 1996, 'The Colorado Potato Beetle Goes to War', *Chemical Weapons Convention Bulletin*, 33

Glines, V., 2005, 'Top Secret World War II Bat and Bird Bomber Program', *Aviation History*, 15, 5, 38–44

Grunden, Walter E., 2005, *Secret Weapons and World War II*, University of Kansas

Itoh, Mayumi, 2010, *Japanese Wartime Zoo Policy: The Silent Victims of World War II*, Palgrave Macmillan

Jones, R.V., 1978, *Most Secret War: British Scientific Intelligence 1939–1945*, London (published in the US as *The Wizard War: British Scientific Intelligence 1939–1945*)

Snowden, F.M., 2012, 'Mosquito wars: malaria and bioterrorism in Italy, 1943–1945', *Skinmed*, 10(6): 388-9

Tatu, L., 2021, 'Botulinum Toxin in WW2 German and Allied Armies: Failures and Myths of Weaponization', *Eur Neurol* 84: 53–60

Japan and Unit 731

Barenblatt, D., 2004, *A Plague upon humanity: The hidden history of Japan's biological warfare program*, New York

Felton, Mark, 2012, *The Devil's Doctors: Japanese Human Experiments on Allied Prisoners of War*, Barnsley

Gold, Hal, 1996, *Unit 731 Testimony*, Charles E. Tuttle Co

Guillemin, Jeanne, *Hidden Atrocities: Japanese Germ Warfare and American Obstruction of Justice at the Tokyo Trial*, New York

Harris, S.H., 1992, 'Japanese biological warfare research on humans: a case study of microbiology and ethics', *Ann N Y Acad Sci.* 666: 21–52

Harris, S.H., 1994, *Factories of death: Japanese biological warfare 1932–45 and the American cover-up*, London

Williams, Peter, 1989, *Unit 731: Japan's Secret Biological Warfare in World War II*, Free Press

Nazi human experimentation

Annas, George J., 1990, *The Nazi Doctors and the Nuremberg Code: Human Rights in Human Experimentation*, Oxford

Baumslag, Naomi, 2011, *Murderous Medicine: Nazi Doctors, Human Experimentation, and Typhus*, Westport, CT

Berger, Robert L., 1990, 'Nazi Science – The Dachau Hypothermia Experiments', *N Engl J Med* 322:1435–1440

Bogod, David, 2004, 'The Nazi Hypothermia Experiments: Forbidden Data?', *Anaesthesia*, 59 (12): 1155–1156

Cina, Stephen J., 2010, *When Doctors Kill*, Heidelberg

Freyhofer, Horst H., 2004, *The Nuremberg Medical Trial: The Holocaust and the Origin of the Nuremberg Medical Code*, Peter Lang

Geissler, E., 1999, 'Biological warfare activities in Germany, 1923–45', in *Biological and toxin weapons: research, development, and use from the Middle Ages to 1945*, Oxford

Hanauske-Abel, H., 1996, 'Not a slippery slope or sudden subversion: German medicine and National Socialism in 1933', *British Medical Journal*, 313 (7070): 1453–1463

Hulverscheidt, Marion, 2006, 'German Malariology Experiments with Humans, Supported by the DFG Until 1945', *Beiträge zur Geschichte der Deutschen Forschungsgemeinschaft*, Vol. 2., ed. Wolfgang Uwe Eckhart, Stuttgart

Jacobsen, Annie, 2014, *Operation Paperclip: The Secret Intelligence Program that Brought Nazi Scientists to America*, New York

Kalechofsky, Roberta, 'Human Experimentation: Before the Nazi Era and After', archived from the original in November 2021

Lichtblau, Eric, 2014, *The Nazis Next Door: How America Became a Safe Haven for Hitler's Men*, Mariner Books

Lifton-Robert, Robert J., 2000, *The Nazi Doctors: Medical Killing and the Psychology of Genocide*, London

López-Muñoz, F., 2009, 'The pharmaceutical industry and the German National Socialist Regime: I.G. Farben and pharmacological research', *Journal of Clinical Pharmacy and Therapeutics*, 34 (1): 67–77

McCoy, Alfred, 2007, 'Science in Dachau's Shadow: Hebb, Beecher, and the Development of CIA Psychological Torture and Modern Medical Ethics', *Journal of the History of the Behavioral Sciences*, 43 (4)

Mellanby, Kenneth, 1947, 'Medical Experiments on Human Beings in Concentration Camps in Nazi Germany', *British Medical Journal*, 1 (4490): 148–150

Moreno, Jonathan D., 2001, *Undue Risk: Secret State Experiments on Humans*, London

Pellegrino, E., 1997, 'The Nazi Doctors and Nuremberg: Some Moral Lessons Revisited', *Annals of Internal Medicine*, 127 (4): 307–308

Seidelman, W., 1996, 'Nuremberg lamentation: for the forgotten victims of medical science', *British Medical Journal*, 313 (7070): 1463–1467

Simpson, Christopher, 1988, *Blowback: America's Recruitment of Nazis and Its Effects on the Cold War*, New York

Spitz, Vivien, *Doctors from Hell: The Horrific Account of Nazi Experiments on Humans*, Boulder, CO

Szybalski, Waclaw, 'The genius of Rudolf Stefan Weigl (1883–1957), a Lvovian microbe hunter and breeder', in memoriam, McArdle Laboratory for Cancer Research, University of Wisconsin, Madison WI

Weindling, P.J., 2005, *Nazi Medicine and the Nuremberg Trials: From Medical War Crimes to Informed Consent*, Basingstoke

Weyers, Wolfgang, 2003, *The Abuse of Man: An illustrated history of dubious medical experimentation*, Ardor Scribendi

9. The Biological Warfare Labs
Porton Down

Carter, G.B., 1992, *Porton Down: A Brief History*, Stationary Office Books

Carter, G.B., 2000, *Chemical and Biological Defence at Porton Down 1916–2000*, Stationery Office Books

Evans, Robert, 2019, *Gassed: British Chemical Warfare Experiments at Porton Down*, Lume Books

Hammond, P.M & Carter, G.B., 2001, *From Biological Warfare to Healthcare: Porton Down, 1940–2000*, Basingstoke

Ministry of Defence, 1992, *Porton Down: 75 Years of Chemical and Biological Research*, London

Schmidt, Ulf, 2015, *Secret Science: A Century of Poison Warfare and Human Experiments*, Oxford

Fort Detrick
Covert, N.M., 'Cutting edge: a history of Fort Detrick', 4th edn. http://www.medcom. amedd.army.mil/detrick/
Lebeda, F.J., 2018, 'Yesterday and today: the impact of research conducted at camp Detrick on Botulinum Toxin', *Mil Med.*, 183(5–6): 85–95

10. The Soviet Biological Weapons Programme
Alibek, Ken, 1999, *Biohazard: The Chilling True Story of the Largest Covert Biological Weapons Program in the World – Told from Inside by the Man Who Ran It*, New York
Birstein, Vadim J., 2004, *The Perversion of Knowledge: The True Story of Soviet Science*, Westview Press
Bozheyeva, G.Y., 1999, 'Former Soviet Biological Weapons Facilities in Kazakhstan: Past, Present and Future', Monterey, Calif: Monterey Institute of International Studies, Center for Nonproliferation Studies, Occasional Paper 1
Bozheyeva, G., 2000, 'The Pavlodar Chemical Weapons Plant in Kazakhstan: History and Legacy', *The Nonproliferation Review*, Vol. 7, 136–145
Broad, W.J., 2002, 'Traces of Terror: The Bioterror Threat; Report Provides New Details of Soviet Smallpox Accident', *New York Times*, 15 June 2002
Fedorov, L.A., 2013, 'Soviet Biological Weapons: History, Ecology, Politics', URSS
Guillemin, Jeanne, 2001, *Anthrax: The Investigation of a Deadly Outbreak*, University of California Press
Kouzminov, Alexander, 2006, *Biological Espionage: Special Operations of the Soviet and Russian Foreign Intelligence Services in the West*, Greenhill Books
Leitenberg, Milton, 2012, *The Soviet Biological Weapons Program: a history*, Cambridge MA
Meselson, M., 1994, 'The Sverdlovsk anthrax outbreak of 1979', *Science*, 266 (5188): 1202–1208
Noah, D.L., 1994, 'The Sverdlovsk anthrax outbreak of 1979', *Science*, 1994; 266: 1202–1208
Rimmington, Anthony, 2018, *Stalin's Secret Weapon: The Origins of Soviet Biological Warfare*, Oxford
Rimmington, Anthony, 2021, *The Soviet Union's Invisible Weapons of Mass Destruction: Biopreparat's Covert Biological Warfare Programme*, Heidelberg
Rózsa, L., 2006, 'Biological Weapons in Non-Soviet Warsaw Pact Countries', in Wheelis, M. (ed.), *Deadly Cultures: Biological Weapons since 1945*, Cambridge MA
Shoham, D., 2004, 'The Russian Biological Weapons Program: Vanished or Disappeared?', *Critical Reviews in Microbiology*, 30 (4): 241–261
Vaksberg, Arkadiï, 2011, *Toxic Politics: The Secret History of the Kremlin's Poison Laboratory – from the Special Cabinet to the Death of Litvinenko*, Santa Barbara, CA
Zilinskas, Raymond A., 2018, *Biosecurity in Putin's Russia*, Lynne Rienner Publishers, Inc

11. The Cold War Years
Chrystal, P., 2018, *The Cold War: British Army of the Rhine*, Barnsley
Croddy, Eric, 2002, 'The Post-World War II Era and the Korean War', *Chemical and Biological Warfare: A Comprehensive Survey for the Concerned Citizen*, Heidelberg
Crompton, Rufus, 'Georgi Markov – Death in a Pellet', a report to the Medico-Legal Society (PDF)
Endicott, Stephen, 1998, *The United States and Biological Warfare: Secrets from the Early Cold War and Korea*, Bloomington
Hornblum, Allen M., 2013, *Against Their Will: The Secret History of Medical Experimentation on Children in Cold War America*, New York
Maddrell, Paul, 2006, *Spying on Science: Western Intelligence in Divided Germany 1945–1961*, Oxford

Korea

Chen, Shiwei, 2009, 'History of Three Mobilizations: A Reexamination of the Chinese Biological Warfare Allegations against the United States in the Korean War', *Journal of American-East Asian Relations*, 16.3 213–247

Cowdrey, Albert E., 1984, 'Germ Warfare and Public Health in the Korean Conflict', *Journal of the History of Medicine and Allied Sciences*, 39

Ellis, John, 1992, 'Biological Warfare Allegations: The Korean War Case', *Annals of the New York Academy of Sciences*, 666

Endicott, Stephen, 1979, 'Germ Warfare and "Plausible Denial": The Korean War, 1952–1953', *Modern China*, 5.1, 79–104

12. The Later Twentieth and Early Twenty-first Centuries

Rhodesia; Project Coast, South Africa

Cross, G., 2017, *Dirty War: Rhodesia and Chemical Biological Warfare, 1975–1980*, Helion & Company

Gould, Chandré, 2006, 'South Africa's Chemical and Biological Warfare programme 1981–1995', PhD thesis, Rhodes University

Gould, Chandré, 2002, *Project Coast: Apartheid's Chemical and Biological Warfare Programme*, United Nations Publications

Martinez, Ian, 'The History of the Use of Bacteriological and Chemical Agents during Zimbabwe's Liberation War of 1965–80 by Rhodesian Forces', *Third World Quarterly*, 23 (6): 1159–1179

Melson, C.D., 2005, 'Top Secret War: Rhodesian Special Operations', *Small Wars and Insurgencies* (No. 1 ed.), 16: 57–82

Purkitt, Helen E., 2001, 'The Rollback of South Africa's Chemical and Biological Warfare Program', Air University, Counterproliferation Center, Maxwell Airforce Base, Alabama

Purkitt, Helen E., 2005, *South Africa's Weapons of Mass Destruction*, Bloomington

Singh, J.A., 2008,' Project Coast: eugenics in apartheid South Africa', *Endeavour*, 32(1): 5–9

Stiff, P., 1982, *Selous Scouts: Top Secret War*, Alberton, South Africa

Purkitt, Helen, E., 2001, 'The Rollback of South Africa's Chemical and Biological Warfare Program', Air University, Counterproliferation Center, Maxwell Airforce Base, Alabama

13. Biological Weapons in the Arab World

Aboul-Enein, 'Islamic Rulings on Warfare, Strategic Studies Institute', US Army War College, Darby PA

Cordesman, A.H., 1991, *Weapons of Mass Destruction in the Middle East*, Brassey's Ltd.

Shoham, Dany 2000, 'The Chemical and Biological Threat of Islam', https://www.semanticscholar.org/paper/The-Chemical-and-Biological-Threat-of-Islam-Shoham/afbfd17af17e15c26797c4ae612302e319220fd1

14. Bioterrorism in the Modern World

Atlas, R.M, 2001, 'Bioterrorism before and after September 11', *Crit Rev Microbiol*, 27(4): 355–79

Berger, T., 'Toxins as biological weapons for terror-characteristics, challenges and medical countermeasures: a mini-review', *Disaster Mil Med.*, 2016; 2:7

Bower, W.A., 2015, 'Clinical Framework and Medical Countermeasure Use During an Anthrax Mass-Casualty Incident', MMWR Recomm Rep, 2015, 4; 64(4):1–22

Carus, W. Seth, 2002, Working Paper: 'Bioterrorism and Biocrimes. The Illicit Use of Biological Agents Since 1900', Feb 2001 revision

Chrystal, Paul, 2021, *The History of the World in 100 Pandemics, Plagues and Epidemics*, Barnsley
Cleri, D.J., 2003, 'Smallpox, bioterrorism, and the neurologist', *Arch Neurol*, 60(4): 489–494
Erenler, A.K., 2018, 'How Prepared Are We for Possible Bioterrorist Attacks: An Approach from Emergency Medicine Perspective', *Scientific World Journal*, 8
Gage, Beverly, 2009, *The Day Wall Street Exploded: A Story of America in Its First Age of Terror*, New York
Haberman, Clyde, 'Retro Report: The Battle Over the Medfly', *New York Times*, 14 March 2014
Henderson, D.A., 1999, 'The looming threat of bioterrorism', *Science*, 1999, 283, 1279–82
Henderson, D.A., 2014, 'John Bartlett and Bioterrorism', *Clinical Infectious Diseases*, Vol. 59, 2014, S76–S79
Jernigan, J.A, 2001, 'Bioterrorism-related inhalational anthrax: the first 10 cases reported in the United States', *Emerging Infectious Diseases*, 7(6), 933-944
Khan, A.S., 2000, 'Biological and chemical terrorism: strategic plan for preparedness and response', MMWR Recomm Rep., 2000; 49(RR-4):1–14
Koblentz, G.D., 2012, 'From biodefence to biosecurity: the Obama administration's strategy for countering biological threats', *Int Aff.* 88(1): 131–48
Kournikakis, B., 2011, 'Anthrax letters in an open office environment: effects of selected CDC response guidelines on personal exposure and building contamination', *J Occup Environ Hyg.*, 8:113–22
McCann, Joseph T., 2006, *Terrorism on American Soil: A Concise History of Plots and Perpetrators from the Famous to the Forgotten*, Sentient Publications
Melnick, Alan L., 2008, *Biological, Chemical, and Radiological Terrorism: Emergency Preparedness and Response for the Primary Care Physician*, Heidelberg
Nelson, C.A., 2021, 'Antimicrobial Treatment and Prophylaxis of Plague: Recommendations for Naturally Acquired Infections and Bioterrorism Response', MMWR Recomm Rep., 70(3): 1–27
Nestle, Marion, 2003, *Safe Food: Bacteria, Biotechnology, and Bioterrorism*, University of California Press
O'Brien, C., 2021, 'The electrochemical detection of bioterrorism agents: a review of the detection, diagnostics, and implementation of sensors in biosafety programs for Class A bioweapons', *Microsyst Nanoeng*, 7, 16
Oliveira, M., 2020, 'Biowarfare, bioterrorism and biocrime: A historical overview on microbial harmful applications', *Forensic Sci Int*, 314
Ralston, M.S.A., 'Neuroterrorism Preparedness for the Neurohospitalist', *The Neurohospitalist*, 2019; 9(3): 151–159
Sanders, Richard, 2002, 'The History of Bioterrorism in America, Race and History', http://raceandhistory.com, Sunday, 24 November 2002
Seto, Yasuo, 2001, 'The Sarin Gas Attack in Japan and the Related Forensic Investigation', Organisation for the Prohibition of Chemical Weapons, 1 June 2001
Sheer, Jennifer L.O., 2011, 'Breeders: A Case Study', *Encyclopedia of Bioterrorism Defense*, 15
Takahashi, H., 2004, 'Bacillus anthracis incident, Kameido, Tokyo, 1993', *Emerg Infect Dis.* 10(1): 117–20
Thompson, Christopher M., 2006, 'The Bioterrorism Threat By Non-State Actors' (PDF), United States Navy
Wright, S., 2006, 'Terrorists and biological weapons: Forging the linkage in the Clinton Administration', *Politics Life Sci.*, 25(1–2): 57–115
Zink, T.K., 2011, 'Anthrax attacks: lessons learned on the 10th anniversary of the anthrax attacks', *Disaster Med Public Health Prep.* 5(3): 173–4

Aum Shinrikyo

Danzig, Richard, 2000, 'Aum Shinrikyo Insights into How Terrorists Develop Biological and Chemical Weapons' (PDF), Center for a New American Security

Kaplan, David E., 1996, *The Cult at the End of the World: The Terrifying Story of the Aum Doomsday Cult, from the Subways of Tokyo to the Nuclear Arsenals of Russia*, New York

Lifton, Robert Jay, 2000, *Destroying the World to Save It: Aum Shinrikyo, Apocalyptic Violence, and the New Global Terrorism*, New York

Metraux, Daniel A., 1995, 'Religious Terrorism in Japan: The Fatal Appeal of Aum Shinrikyo', *Asian Survey*, 35 (12): 1153

Olson, Kyle B.,1999, 'Aum Shinrikyo: Once and Future Threat?', *Emerg Infect Dis*, 5 (4): 513–6

Reader, Ian, 2000, *Religious Violence in Contemporary Japan: The Case of Aum Shinrikyo, 2000*, Curzon Press

Epilogue

'Ukraine war: Fact-checking Russia's biological weapons claims', *BBC News*, 15 March 2022

Wong, Edward (2022-03-11), 'US Fights Bioweapons Disinformation Pushed by Russia and China', *New York Times*

'In Ukraine, US-military-linked labs could provide fodder for Russian disinformation', *Bulletin of the Atomic Scientists, 2022-03-09*

Landay, Jonathan; (2022-03-11), 'UN says no evidence to back Russian claim of Ukraine biological weapons program', *Reuters*

'China Pushes Conspiracy Theory About US Labs in Ukraine', Bloomberg, 8 March 2022

Index

48th Central Scientific Research Institute, Yekaterinburg, *see* Sverdlovsk
1922 Treaty Relating to the Use of Submarines and Noxious Gases in Warfare, 256
1925 Geneva Conference for the Supervision of the International Traffic in Arms, 256
1925 Geneva Protocol for the Pacific Settlement of International Disputes, 152
1972 Biological Weapons Convention (BWC), 176, 183
1989 Biological Weapons Anti-Terrorism Act, 229
1993 Chemical Weapons Convention (CWC), 216, 257
2001 USA Patriot Act, 259
2002 International Symposium on the Crimes of Bacteriological Warfare, Changde, China, 124

Accidents, 154–5, 157, 159, 162–3, 165, 189–94, 196, 226, 244
Achilles, 9
Aelian, 24
Aeneas Tacticus, 23–4
Afghanistan, 203
African swine fever, 176, 202
Agamemnon, 9–10
Agent Orange, 200–201
Agricultural ruination, 5, 30, 111, 113–15, 117, 126–7, 131–2, 173, 176, 186, 199, 200–201, 234–5
Agroterrorism, 246
AIDS/HIV, 255
Airborne dissemination of disease/chemicals, 99, 136, 154–5, 161–2, 183, 199, 227, 240–1
Akhenaten, 3
Aleph, 243
Alexander the Great, 22, 25
Alibek, Ken (Kanatjan Alibekov), 168, 170–1, 203, 226, 256
All-Union Science Production Association Biopreparat (Биопрепарат), *see* Biopreparat

Al-Qaeda, 229, 247
American mainland, biological attacks on, 123–4
American Type Culture Collection, Rockville, Maryland, 219
Amerithrax, *see* Anthrax Letters, the
Anatolia, 4
Animals, infected as vectors, 88–9, 111, 126
Annales Xantenses, 5
Anthrax, xx–xxi, 54, 88, 90, 92–6, 99, 110–11, 116–18, 122, 126–7, 132–4, 154–5, 158–9, 165, 168, 174, 178, 189–90, 194, 204–208, 216, 218–19, 239
Anthrax Letters, the, 235–6
Anthrax simulant (*Bacillus globigii*), 109, 110, 154, 162
Anti-crop bombs, 110
Antidotes, 53–4
Anti-Plague Scientific Research Institute, Almaty, 179
Anti-plant balloon bomb, 157
Antonine Plague, 56–8
Apache ant torture, 84
Apollo, 9–10, 12, 16, 20–1, 51
Apollodorus, 8, 12
Appian, 51, 54, 56
Aquillius, Manlius, 52
Aralsk-7 smallpox outbreak, 192–3
Ark of the Covenant as plague vector, 34
Armies as disease spreaders, 4
Army Epidemic Prevention Research Laboratory, Japan, *see* Unit 731
Arrowheads, poisoned, 1, 7, 25, 56, 75, 179–80, 185, 215
Assassin bugs, 86–7
Artemis and Niobe, 17
Arzawans, 3
Ashurbanipal, 7
Asian Holocaust, the, 127
Assyria, 4–7
Athens, Plague of, 19ff
Aum Shinrikyo attack, Tokyo, 219, 228–9, 237–40, 247
Auschwitz, 139, 148

Australian Aborigines, smallpox atrocities against, 77–8
Autariatae, 51
Avian flu, 194

Babylon, 45
Banting, Sir Frederick Grant, 96–7
Baoshan raid, the, 121–2
Barracks as reservoirs of infection spread, 2
Becker-Freyseng, Hermann, 142–3
Bees, 55–6, 59–60, 66–7, 70, 94, 113–14, 199–200, 202–203
Bees, Battle of, or The Battle of Tanga, 1914, 94
Bible, The, 27ff
Biocrime, 180–1, 249–50
Biological agents, xix, 152
Biological bombs, 89, 90–1, 99, 101, 118, 132
Bio(logical) – warfare, xix, 3, 6, 10–11, 28–39, 74–5, 98, 128, 161, 176–7, 183, 195, 249–50
Biological warfare, opposition to, 49, 52, 79, 98, 147, 228
Biological Warfare Committee (US), 109
Biological weapons, xviii–xvixv, 79, 87, 99, 106–108, 136, 152, 188, 198
Biological Weapons Convention 1975, The, 191, 225
Biopreparat, 151, 168ff, 204, 249
Biosecurity, 165, 249–50
Bioterrorism, xx, 6, 28–39, 55, 95, 106–107, 112–13, 157–9, 175, 183, 229–31, 249–50
  motivational factors for, 233–4
  psychological, political, social and economic impact of, 232, 236, 252
B. abortus, 26
B. pseudomallei, see Melioidosis
B. subtilis (also known as *B. globigii* or *BG*), 154–5
B. subtilis var. niger, 162
B. suis, 110, 146, 156, 166
Blackburn, Dr Luke Pryor and yellow fever, 82
Blome, Kurt, 136, 139–41, 148
Blood coagulation experiments and Polygal, 139, 151
Blood transfusion experiments, 117–18
Blowback, 114, 118, 120, 222
'Blue on blue', 54, 118, 120, 201, 222–4
Boils, plague of, 30–1
Bolivian haemorrhagic fever, 157, 159, 175
Bond, James 007, 185
Botulinum toxin, 99, 109, 111, 118, 133, 172, 175, 209, 216–18, 241–2
Breeders, The, 234–5

British Germ Defence Unit, 92
Brucellosis, 26, 99, 109, 110, 174, 195
  Porcine brucellosis (agent US); Bovine brucellosis (agent AA); Caprine brucellosis (agent AM), 166
Buchenwald, 137–8
Bug Pit of Bukhara, The, 85–6
Building 470, Fort Detrick, 159
Burkholderia mallei, see glanders

Cabbage, poisoned torture, 210
Calmative/pacifying agents, 209
Cambodia, 202
Camp Detrick, *see* Fort Detrick
Canadian biological warfare programme, the, 134
Candia, Siege of, 68–9
Castro, Fidel, 189
CDC, Atlanta, Georgia, 175
Chemical Defence Experimental Establishment (CDEE), Porton Down, the, 154
Chemical warfare/experimentation, xx, 70, 102, 110, 118–19, 152, 154, 188, 208, 209–10, 214, 220
Chernobyl, 159
Chimeras, 174, 177
China, 157–8, 196–7, 225–7, 251
  and COVID-19, 225–6
  and 'The Unnatural Origin of SARS and New Species of Man-Made Viruses as Genetic Bioweapons' (2015), 225
  and the illegal Russian invasion of Ukraine, 254
Chiron, 12
Chloropicrin, 100
Cholera, 64, 72, 89, 91, 108, 114, 116–18, 122, 129, 184, 196, 197–9, 207–208, 216
Chrysame of Thessally and the mad bull, 13–14
CIA/CIA's Technical Services Division (TSD), 184–6, 209, 255
Cicero, 49
Claviceps purpurea (ergot fungus), 5
Clearchus of Hereclea, 23
Clostridium perfringens (food poisoning/gangrene), 7, 101, 137, 208–209, 219
Clostridium tetani (tetanus), 1, 7, 101, 137
Colorado potato beetle, 115, 186–7
Columbia, 184
Comfort women, 127
Commodus, 56
Corpses, rotting, xiii, xv–xvi, xviii, 6, 17, 22, 52, 60, 62, 65, 70–1, 90, 113, 197, 211, 215
COVID-19, 175, 215, 249, 252

Index

COVID-19 conspiracy, 157–8
Crimes against humanity, 102–105, 144–5
CRISPR (Clustered Regularly Interspaced Short Palindromic Repeats), 251–2
Crop spraying with bacteria, 98, 111
Crouch, Archie, 119–20
CS gas, 154
Cuba, 201
Curare, 92, 179–80
Cushing, Frank Hamilton, 85
CX powder and gas, 208
Cyanide L-pill, 175
Cyprian, Plague of, 57

Dachau, 135–8, 148
Dark Harvest Commando, 112–13
Darkness, plague of, 32
Darts, poisoned, 185
David, King, 38
Death of the firstborn children, plague of Egypt, 32–3
Decapitation, 103
Decontamination, 159, 173, 188, 194
Defence Science and Technology Laboratory (Dstl), 151, 154
Defoliants, 110, 131, 156, 189, 200–201
Deianeira, 15
Dengue fever, 202
Deuteronomy, Book of, 28, 36, 40, 46
DICE Trials, 163
D.I. Ivanovskii Institute of Virology, Moscow, 172
Dilger, Anton Casimir, 89
Dio Cassius, 54, 56
Dio Chrysostom, 8
Diodorus Siculus, 12, 25, 52
Diphtheria, 184, 204
Disease, affliction by, 46, 52
Disease mortality in war, xvii, 200–201
Displacement, population, 201
Divine retribution, xvii, 1, 4, 20, 27, 36–8, 41–2, 46–7, 50, 51, 57–8
Doctors' Trial, the, 135, 144
Dog slobber, 70
Domitian, 56
Dorset Biological Warfare Experiments, 154–5, 163
Dracunculiasis, 38
Drone technology, 241–2
Drugs, medicinal, 208–209
Drugs, recreational, 208–209, 242
Dugway Proving Ground, Utah, 134, 156, 158, 163–6, 194
Dugway sheep incident, the, 165
Dysentry, 108, 116

Earth Liberation Front (ELF), 245
Ebola, xxi, 157, 174, 194, 241–2
Economic ruin, 4–5, 36–7
Ecotage, 244–5
Ecoterrorism, 245–6
Edessa, Siege, of, 58
Eggs, as a biological weapon, 110–11
Egypt, 1, 4, 216
'Ekologiya' (Ecology), 173
Encephalitis, 197
Enslavement, 40
Entomological Division of the SS Institute for Practical Research in Military Science, 136
Entomology, 24–5, 113–14, 163, 202
Epidemic Intelligence Service (EIS), the, 167
Epidemic jaundice experiments, 137
Epidemic prevention measures, China, 197–8
Epidemic Prevention Research Laboratory, Tokyo, 102, 116
Epidemic Prevention and Water Purification Department of the North China Army of the Imperial Japanese Army, Beijing, 129
Epidemic Prevention and Water Supply Units, 105
Ergotism, 5–6
Eshnunna Code, Babylon, 1
'Essential Oils for Biological Warfare Preparedness', 54
Ethics of biowarfare, 154
Ethnic cleansing/genocide, 40, 73, 79, 82–4, 211, 255
Exodus, Book of, 27–8
Ezekiel, Book of, 47–8

Faeces, death by, 25, 65, 200
Fake news/disinformation, 212, 254, 255
Famine, 35–9, 40–1, 46, 47
Fildes, Sir Paul Gordon, 133, 153
Florus, 52
Flu, *see* influenza
Fomite transmission, 2, 35, 68–9, 70–2, 80–1
Food contamination, 63, 90, 100, 117, 127, 132, 138, 150, 182, 189, 206, 209
Foot and mouth disease, 98, 136, 141, 167, 173, 176, 194–5
Fort Detrick, Maryland, 109–10, 133, 151, 155f, 159, 160
Fort Terry, Plum Island, Long Island, 166–7, 194
Four Horsemen of the Apocalypse, 40–1
France, 251–2
Francisella tularensis released against German troops, 171
Frontinus, 51

Frostbite research, 104, 116, 123
Fu-go fire balloons, 123–4

Gas gangrene experiments, 148
Gates, Bill, 248–9
Gebhardt, Karl Franz, 143, 148
Geneva Convention 1925, 108
Genocide, 40, 211
Genzken, Karl August, 143–4
German Military Bacteriological Institute, Berlin, 98
German Village and Japanese Village set-piece domestic 'hamlets' for practice in the firebombing of homes, 164
Germany and biological weapons in WWI, 88, 98
Germ warfare, *see* biowarfare
Germany's biological warfare programme, 1939, 108, 144
Glanders, 88, 90–2, 122, 126–7, 203
Glasshouse, Los Angeles, 219
Gobnait, Saint, 59–60
'God' as bioterrorist and warmonger, xvii, 1, 4, 20, 27, 36–9, 51
'God' and pestilence, xvii, 1, 4, 20, 27, 35–9, 42, 51, 57–8
Granite Peak Installation (GPI), Maryland, 165–6
grayanotoxin poisoning (mad honey), 53
Gruinard Island, 111–13, 133, 153, 159
Gulf War (1990–91), The, 209, 220–1
Gulf War Syndrome, 222–4

Hailstones, plague of, 31
Halabja massacre, 213
Hamas, 229
Hansen's Disease, 46
Harmatelian-envenomated arrows, 25
Harris, Sheldon, 130–1
Health Control Station of the Hungarian Royal Defence Forces, 101
Hellebore, 18
Hepatitis A, 160
Heracles, 13–15
Herodotus, 7, 8, 18–19, 20
Hesiod, 249–50
Hezbollah, 229
High altitude experimentation, 96, 138
Hille Feyken, 15–16
Himilco, 50–2
Hippocrates, xviii, 26, 51
Hitler, Adolf, 209
Hittites, xx, 2–3
Honey, mad, *see* grayanotoxin
Human subject experimentation (non-consensual), 108

Germany (*Blitzableiter* (Lightning Rod)), 134f, 137, 148
Japan, 102–106, 116–17, 123, 127, 130
North Korea, 210
USA, 161
Human subject experimentation (voluntary), 106, 137, 156, 160
Humoral theory, xviii
Hunter Program, the, 205
Hydrogen cyanide, Shinjuku station, Tokyo, 242–3

Iliad, The, 8–10, 12
Immersion hypothermia project, the, 136–7
Immunisation, 222
India, 22
Indigenous populations, infecting with diseases, 70–4, 76, 79–0, 81–4, 97
Inebriation, 4, 11, 50–1, 62, 65
Infection control, 2
Influenza, 1, 51, 97, 217
Insects, 24–5, 30, 35, 41, 55, 57, 66, 84, 85, 113–21, 128, 136, 163, 196, 199
Iran, 217–18, 227
Iraq, 176, 184, 209, 213, 218
Iraqi Biological Research Centre for Military Defence, 221
Ishii, Surgeon General Shirō, 102, 116–19, 125
Islamic State (ISIS), 213, 247, 250–1
Israel, 211–12, 215–16
biological weapons programme, 224
Israel Institute for Biological Research, Nes Tona, 224
Italy, biological weapons programme, 101

Japan, 213
Japan, biological weapons programme, 116ff
Jebel Akhdar War, Oman, 1957, 183–4
Jews and others, persecution of, 147
Jews, scapegoating of, 63, 238
Julius Caesar, 55
Justinian, Plague of, 57–8, 63

Karlštejn Castle, 65
Kazakhstani BW facilities, 177, 215
KGB, 185, 191–192, 255
Khabarovsk war crime trials, the, 131–2
Kirrha, Siege of, 17–18
Korean War, The, 195f
Kostov, Vladimir, 182
Kuwait, 221
Kwantung Army Military Horse Epidemic Prevention Workshop (or Kwantung Army Warhorse Disease Prevention Shop or Manchuria Unit 100), 105, 126

Index 275

Kwantung Army Technical Testing Department (later Manchuria Unit 516), 105

Laboratory 1, Laboratory 12, Kamera, *see* Poison laboratory of the Soviet secret services, 179
Lagash and Umma, 7
Laos, 202
Large Area Coverage (LAC) concept, 155
Legionella (Legionnaires' disease), 204
Leprosy, *see* Hansen's Disease
Leviticus, Book of, 46
Libya, 217–18
Livestock, infection of, 88–9, 92–3
Livy, 50–2
Locusts, plague of, 31–2, 42–3
Lucius Licinius Lucullus, 55
Lupus, 203–204

M33 cluster bomb, 156, 166
M114 4 lb antipersonnel bomb, which held *Brucella suis*, 156
M143, 188–9
M210 warhead, 188
Maddison, Leading Aircraftman Ronald, 154
Maggot bomb, *see* Yagi bomb
Maharbal, 50–1
Malaria experimentation, 23, 52, 77–8, 130
  German, 135–6
Malathion, 234–5
Malayan Emergency, The, 200
Mandrake, 50–1, 55
Marburg virus, 174–5, 194
Mari Tablets, 2
Markov, Georgi Ivanov, 180–2
Matsumoto sarin attack, 239–40
Medfly attack, California 1989, 239
Melioidosis, 92, 99
Mengele, Josef, 102
Merck, George W., 109
MI6, 146, 170
Microbiological Research Establishment (MRE), Porton Down, 153
Microbiology, 87
Middle East, 214f
Ministry of Defence, MOD, Moscow, 169, 192
Miriam, 46
Mithridates, 53f
Mithridatium, 54
Monkeypox, 255
Mosquitos as vector, 156, 161, 163–4, 202
Multiple sclerosis (MS), 203–204
Mustard agent, 223
Mycotoxins, 202

Nagel, Hans-Christoph, 136
Naphtha, 57
Napoleon Bonaparte and his use of malaria, 78
National Consortium for the Study of Terrorism and Responses to Terrorism, xvii, xxiii
Native American Indians, smallpox atrocities against, 71–7
Nazi biological warfare programme, the, 134, 144
Nazi concentration camps, 147
Nazi scientists and engineers, 146–7, 148–9
Nazi War Crimes Disclosure Act, 1998, 146
Nazi-Japanese biological warfare collaboration, 144
Nebuchadnezzar II, 1, 39
Needle sticking, 56, 194
Nessus, 13–16
Newcastle disease, 201
Nineveh, 1
Ningbo, 119–20
NKVD, 149, 170, 171
North Korea, 209–10, 217–18
Numbers, Book of, 46–7
Nuremberg trials, 147

Odysseus, 11, 12
Odyssey, The, 11
Oedipus, 25–6
Oggins, Isaiah, 180
Olympia Oil and Cake Company, Tinsley, Sheffield, 132
Operation Alberich, 93–4
Operation Big Buzz, 163–4
Operation Big Itch, 163
Operation Denver, 255
Operation Desert Fox, 222
Operation Desert Shield, 221
Operation Dew, 162
Operation Drop Kick, 164
Operation Granby, 221
Operation May Day, 164
Operation Osoaviakhim (Операция Осоавиахим), 145, 148–9
Operation Overcast, 145
Operation Paperclip, 138, 144–7, 150
Operation Ranch Hand, 200
Operation Seaspray, 162
Operation Trail Dust, 200
Operation Vegetarian, 132–3
Operation Whitecoat, 156, 160
Opium poppy crop, 189
Orion, 12
Osenberg List, the, 146
Ovid, 7, 8, 12–13, 15

Owen, Wilfred, 88
Oxygen deprivation experiments, 139

Palestine, 211–12
Pandemic, 51
Paratyphoid, 116–17
Pasteur Institute, Paris, 99–101
Pasteur, Louis, xviii
Pathogens, xix
Patrick III, William C., 158–9
Pausanias, 12–13
Pestilence, 1, 21, 28–39, 46–7, 52, 60
Pestilentia manu facta, 56
Pheretima, 18–19
Philoctetes, 16
Phosphorous bomb experiments, 138
Pine Bluff Arsenal, Arkansas, 156, 158, 166, 195
Pingfang, *see* Unit 731
Plague, 6, 68, 70, 95–6, 98–9, 111, 116
    In *The Aeneid*, 50
    In *The Bible*, 28–43, 45–7, 54, 217
    In Egypt, 217
    In Germany, 108, 148
    In *The Iliad*, 10
    In Japan, 103, 105, 117–19, 127, 129–30
    In Korea, 196
    In the Middle Ages, 62–4
    In the Roman Republic and Empire, 52, 54, 56–8
    In the UK, 152, 154
    In the US, 160, 229
    In the USSR, 170, 174, 176, 182, 204–205
    In Vietnam, 199
    Of Thebes, 25–6
Plan A – Jewish Holocaust revenge water poisoning, 150
Planthoppers pestiferous, 201
Pleuropneumonitis, 106
Pliny the Elder, 13, 54
PNIL – 'Aralsk-7', 172–3
Poison gas, 69–70, 96, 153
Poison laboratory of the Soviet secret services, 179
Poisoning/drugging, 50–1, 53–6, 64–5, 127, 138, 182, 185, 210, 232
Polish biological sabotage operations, 101
Polyaenus, 13–14, 18, 22–3, 50
Popov, Sergei, 203
Porton Down, 98, 111–12, 132–3, 151–3, 161, 182
Post-traumatic stress disorder (PTSD), 223
Pot bombs, 57
Pregnancy experiments, 123
Project 112, 131, 161
Project Bonfire, 204–205

Project Coast: the South African biological warfare programme, 207–208
Project Factor, 204
Project MKNAOMI, 184
Project MKULTRA, 184
Project SHAD, 160–1
Psittacosis, 109–11, 176
Public health surveillance, 1
Public safety, 21, 23, 68, 100, 134, 159, 162
Pyridine, 208–209

QAnon, 254
Q Fever (*Coxiella burnetii*), 160, 171, 175
QinetiQ, Porton Down, 154
Quarantine, 2, 68–9, 83, 112, 120, 197, 219
Quran, The, and war, 214

Rabies, 1, 70
Racism, *see* xenophobia/racism
Rajneesh cult, 228, 231
Rape, 40, 103, 127
    experiments, 123
Rascher, Sigmund, 137–8
Rat fleas (*Xenopsylla cheopis*), 163
Ravensbruck, 135, 137
Rawalpindi experiments, the, 152–3
Red Army's Vaccine-Sera Laboratory, Vlasikha, the, 169
Redrust fungus, 126–7
Report of the Committee on Chemical, Biological and Radiological Warfare and Recommendations, 195
Reval, Sweden, 70
Revelation, Book of, 40–3, 238
Revelation 8: the Seven Trumpets, 42f
Revelation 16: the Seven Bowls, 43–5
Rheumatoid arthritis, 203–204
Rhodesia (Zimbabwe), BW programme 206
Rice blast fungus, 131, 164
Ricin, 91, 96, 180, 216, 229
Rift Valley Fever, 160, 167, 217
Rinderpest, 99, 111, 176
RISE, Chicago, 210–11
Rodents, 41, 85, 98, 120, 130, 163, 189–90
Romzha, Archbishop Theodore, 180
Rose, Gerhart, 136, 144
Russia, illegal invasion of Ukraine, 254
Rye ergot, 5

Sachsenhausen, 137
Saipan, attack on, 123
Salad bar, Oregon attack, 228–33
Salmonella enterica serovar Typhi, 21, 111
Salmonella paratyphi, 101
Salmonella typhimurium, 228, 231–3

Samson, 48
Sanitary Technical Institute (STI) – Gorodomlya Island, USSR, 170–1
Sargon II and Sennacherib, 4–5
Sarin, 153–4, 161, 223, 228–9, 239–40, 242
Scapegoating, 63
Scaphism, 24–5, 84
Schilling, Claus, 136, 142
Schreiber, Walter, 147
Schreibtischtäter, 'desk murderers', 150
Schwable, Colonel Frank, 198
Scientific Experimental and Production Base (SNOPB), Stepnogorsk, 177–8
Scientific Research Agricultural Institute (NISKhI), Gvardeyskiy, Kazakhstan, 172, 178
Scientific-Research Institute of Bacterial Vaccine Preparations, Sverdlovsk, 190
Scientific-Research Institute of Epidemiology and Hygiene, Kirov, 172
Scientific-Research Institute of Vaccines and Sera, Tbilisi, Georgia, 191
Scientific-Research Sanitary Institute (NIIS), Zagorsk, 172
Scientific-Research Technical Bureau (NITB), 173
Scorpions, 34, 38, 57, 200
Scythian archers, 7
Second Sino-Japanese War, the, 101, 128, 140
Selous Scouts, Rhodesia, 206–207
Seneca the Elder, 56
Serbia, 211
Serratia marcescens, 162–3
Shigella dysenteriae, 101
Siemienowicz, Kazimirz, 69–70
Simyra, 3–4
Singapore biological weapons base, 130
Smallpox, 70–4, 76, 79–80, 82–4, 118, 157, 175, 176, 196, 222, 228, 243–4
Smallpox: Soviet development as a biological weapon, 106–107, 174, 176, 192–3, 196
Snakes, 38, 43, 54
Social distancing, 2
SOD (the Special Operations Division), USA, 162
Solomon, 39
Solzhenitsyn, Alexander, 180
Soman, 153
Sophocles, *Oedipus Rex*, 25
South African biological warfare programme, 207–208, 217–18
Soviet biological weapon programme, 106–107, 202–203
Sparta, 21
Srebrenica, 211

St Anthony's Fire (ergotism), 5
staphylococcus toxin, 178
Starvation, 117, 130, 132, 211
State Research Center of Virology and Biotechnology (VECTOR), *see* VECTOR Institute
State Research Institute, Insel Riems, 136
Stele of the Vultures, 7
STIs, injections of, 118, 123
Storms, 31, 51
Strabo, 54
Strughold, Hubertus, 138
Strychnine, 14
Submarine mine, 157
Suffield Experimental Station, Alberta, 96
Sugar cane, Cuba, 201
Sulphonamide experiments, 137
'Super Soldier', the 251–2
Surface infection, 2, 35, 232
Sverdlovsk, 203
Sverdlovsk incident, the, 189–90
Syphilis as a weapon, 64–5
experiments, 123
Syria, biological and chemical arms programmes, 215–16

Tabun, 153, 220
Taliban, the, 247
Tetrahedron, 54
Thrips palmi, 201
Thucydides, 8, 19–20
Tiglath Pileser I, 1
Tito, Josip Broz, 182
Tokyo subway sarin attack, 241–2
'Tony's Lab', Washington DC, 89
(Medical) Torture, 24–5, 54, 84–7, 116–18, 135, 137–8, 210
Toxicology, 53–4
Trade as a spreader of disease, 4, 50
Traub, Erich, 136, 141–2
Trillat, André, 99
Trojan War, 8–10
Tuberculosis, 6, 62
Tularaemia, *F. tularensis* (rabbit fever), 3, 4, 99, 105–106, 118, 160, 174, 188–9
Tumours and haemorrhoids, 34–5
Turkeys, infected, 201
Typhoid fever, 100
Typhus, 108, 114, 117, 129, 136, 168, 170–1

Ugarit, 4
UK Animal and Plant Health Agency, Caernarfon, 194
Ukraine, illegal invasion of by Russia, 254
Unit 100, Japan, 126–7, 171

Unit 731, Japan, 102–105, 116–17, 125–6, 132, 171
Unit 864, Japan, 129–30
Unit 1855, Japan, 129
Unit Ei 1644, Japan, 128
US Army Chemical, Biological, and Radiological Weapons School, 165
US Army Chemical Corps, 91, 164, 166
US Army Chemical Warfare Service (CWS), 164
United States Army Medical Research Institute of Infectious Diseases (USAMRIID), 160, 235
US Biological Weapons Programme, 108–109, 155f
US Central Command (CENTCOM), 250–1
USSR Ministry of Defence's Scientific-Research Institute of Hygiene, Sverdlovsk, 172, 190
Uzbekistan, 215

Vaccinations, 80, 83, 93, 191, 199, 222
Vaccinations, withheld, 79–80, 83
Vaccines, 195, 197–9
VECTOR Institute, Koltsovo, Novosibirsk Oblast, 175, 194, 203–204
Vectors, xix, 3, 34–5, 88–9, 115, 156, 163, 175
'Vegetable killer acid', VKA (2,4-Dichlorophenoxyacetic acid), 166
Venezuelan equine encephalitis virus, 111, 155, 160, 175
Vietnam War, 199f
Vigo Ordnance Plant, Indiana, 109
Vipers, 25
Virgil, 8, 49–50
Vivisection, human, 103–104, 117, 125
 on pregnant women, 123, 138
Von Rosen, Baron Otto Karl, 92
VX nerve agent, 153, 161, 239

War crimes, Japanese, suppression of in the West, 126, 130–1
War crimes trials, Japan, 125–7, 131
War Research Service (WRS), 109
Water deprivation, 22, 24, 62, 103, 117, 212–13
Water sources poisoning, 17–18, 21, 22–4, 29–30, 52, 60, 128, 150, 183–4, 206–207, 209, 210–11, 213, 231
Weapons of Mass Destruction (WMDs), xix, 108, 165, 215, 221, 252
Weapons of Mass Disruption, 252
Weber, Bruno, 139
Wehrforschungsgemeinschaft (Defence Research Association), 146
Weigl, Rudolf Stefan Jan, 114–15
Well poisoning, 5–7, 61–3, 90, 93–4, 113, 117, 128, 211–12
Wheat stem rust, 189, 195
Wild animals, 55–6
Wirths, Eduard, 142
Wine poisoning, 50–1, 55, 64
Wuhan Institute of Biological Products, China, 226
Wuhan Institute of Virology, China, 226

Xenophobia/racism, 63–4
Xenophon and the honey trap, 24, 53

Yagi bomb, 122
Yamaguchi-gumi, 242
Yellow fever, 81–2, 108, 156, 160, 164

Zhongma Fortress – Zhong Ma Prison Camp or Unit Tōgō, Japan, covert biological warfare research, 101–102
Zimbabwe, *see* Rhodesia
ZnCds (microscopic zinc cadmium sulphide), 154–5, 162
Zoonotic infection/experiments, 3, 10, 26, 126, 157
Zyklon-B, 108, 147